MUSASHI #9

volume 1

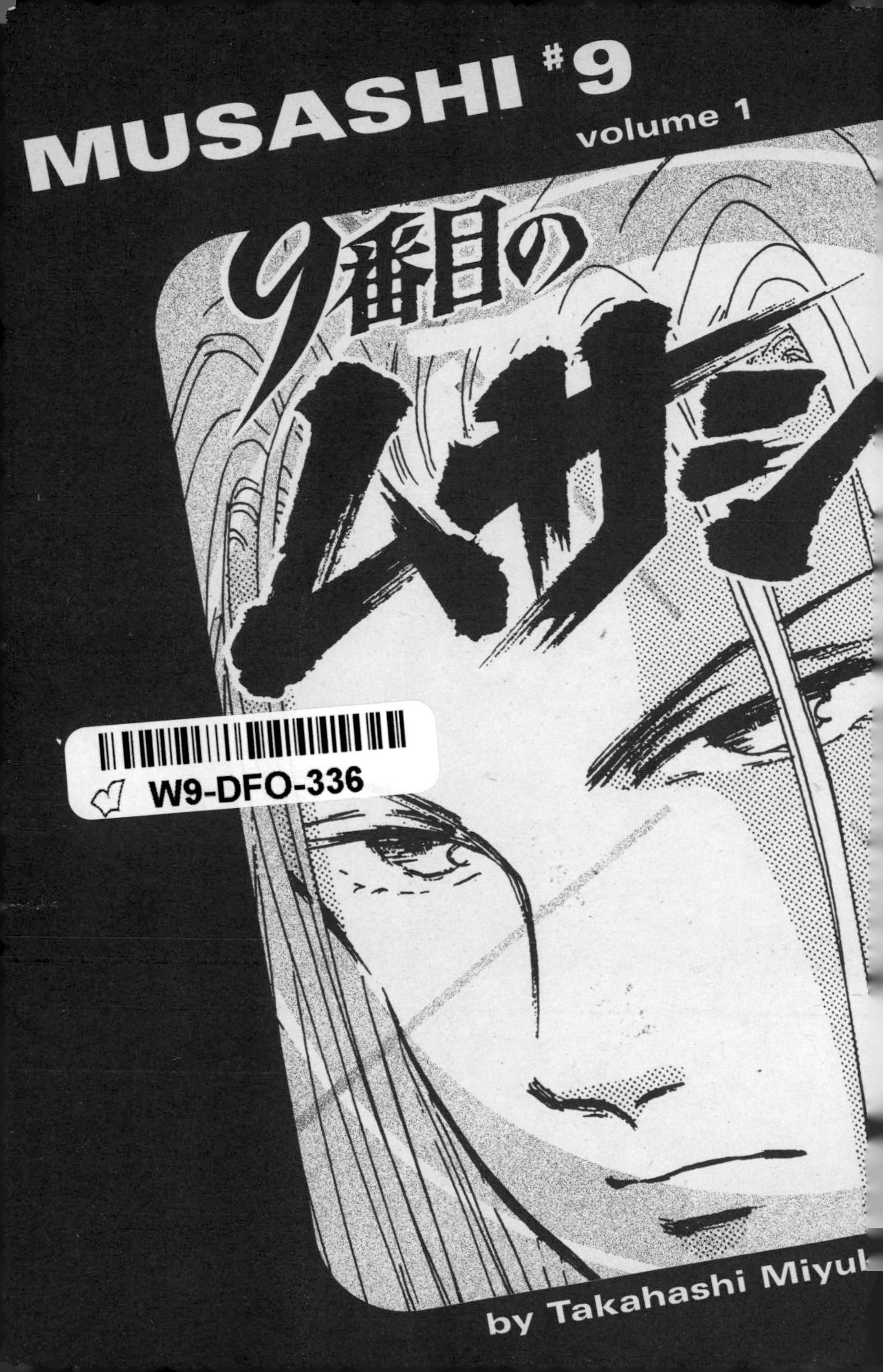
9番目のムサシ

by Takahashi Miyuk

contents

MUSASHI #9

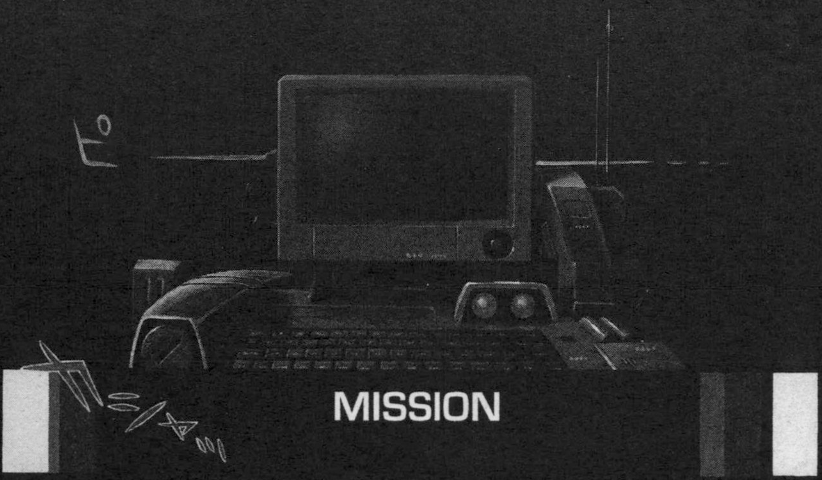

MISSION

MISSION DIRECTIVE: BLUE BOOK

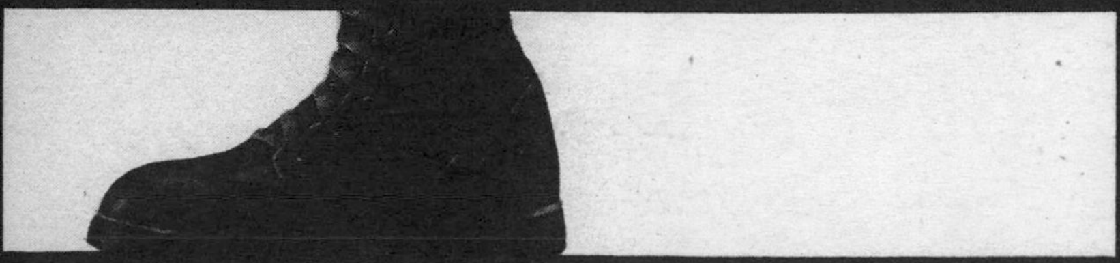

OP NUMBER: 9

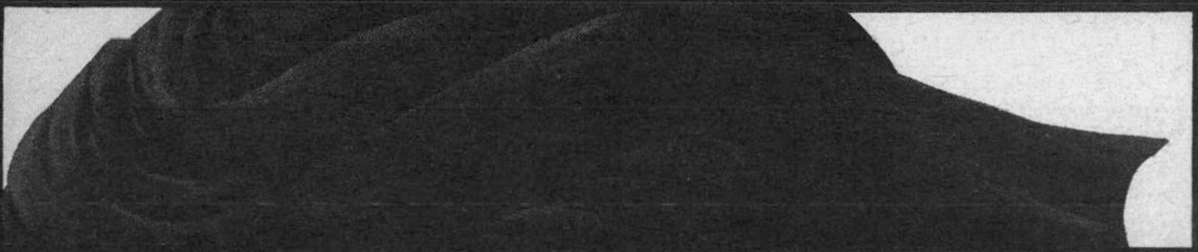

OP CODE: MUSASHI

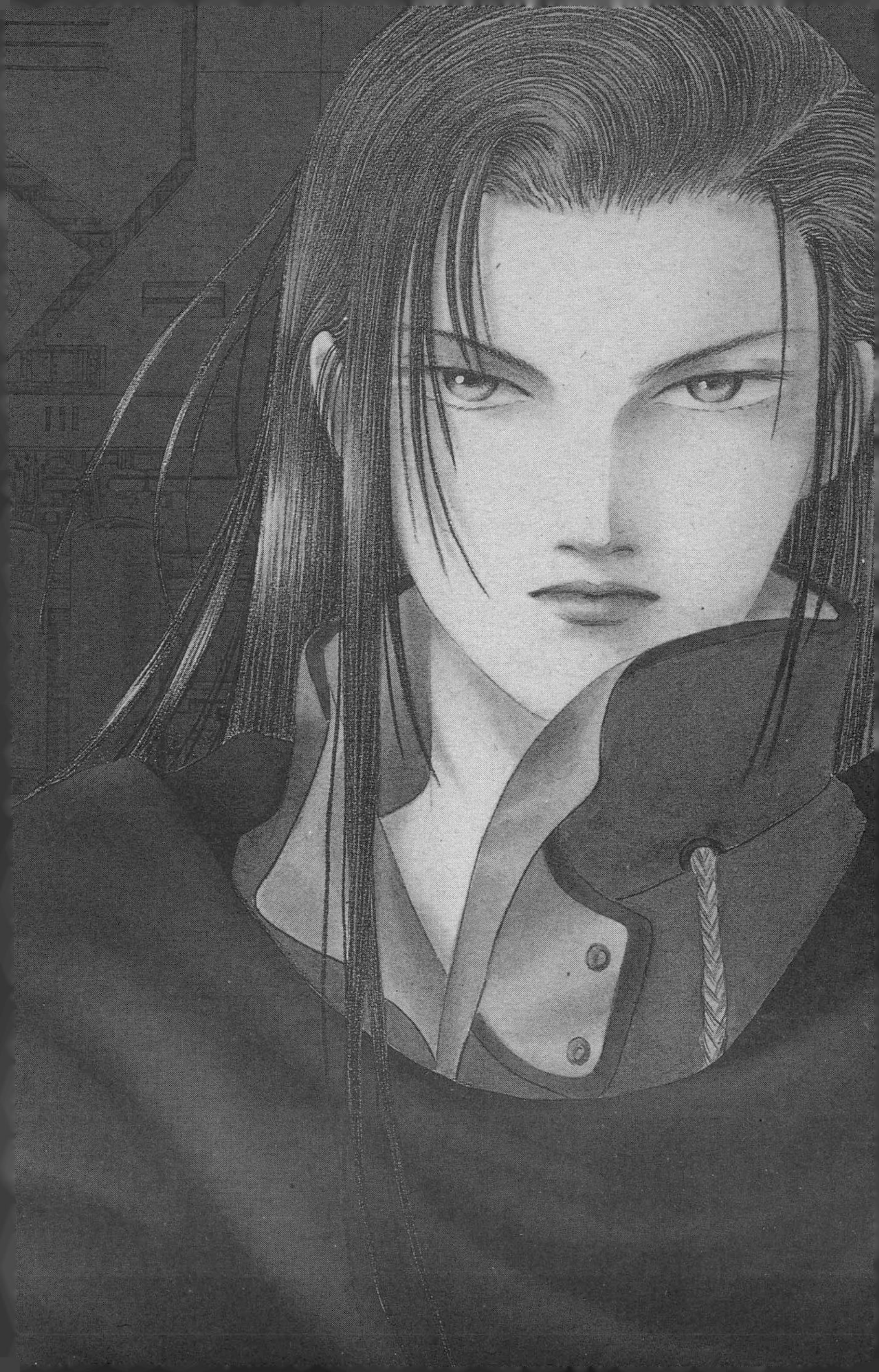

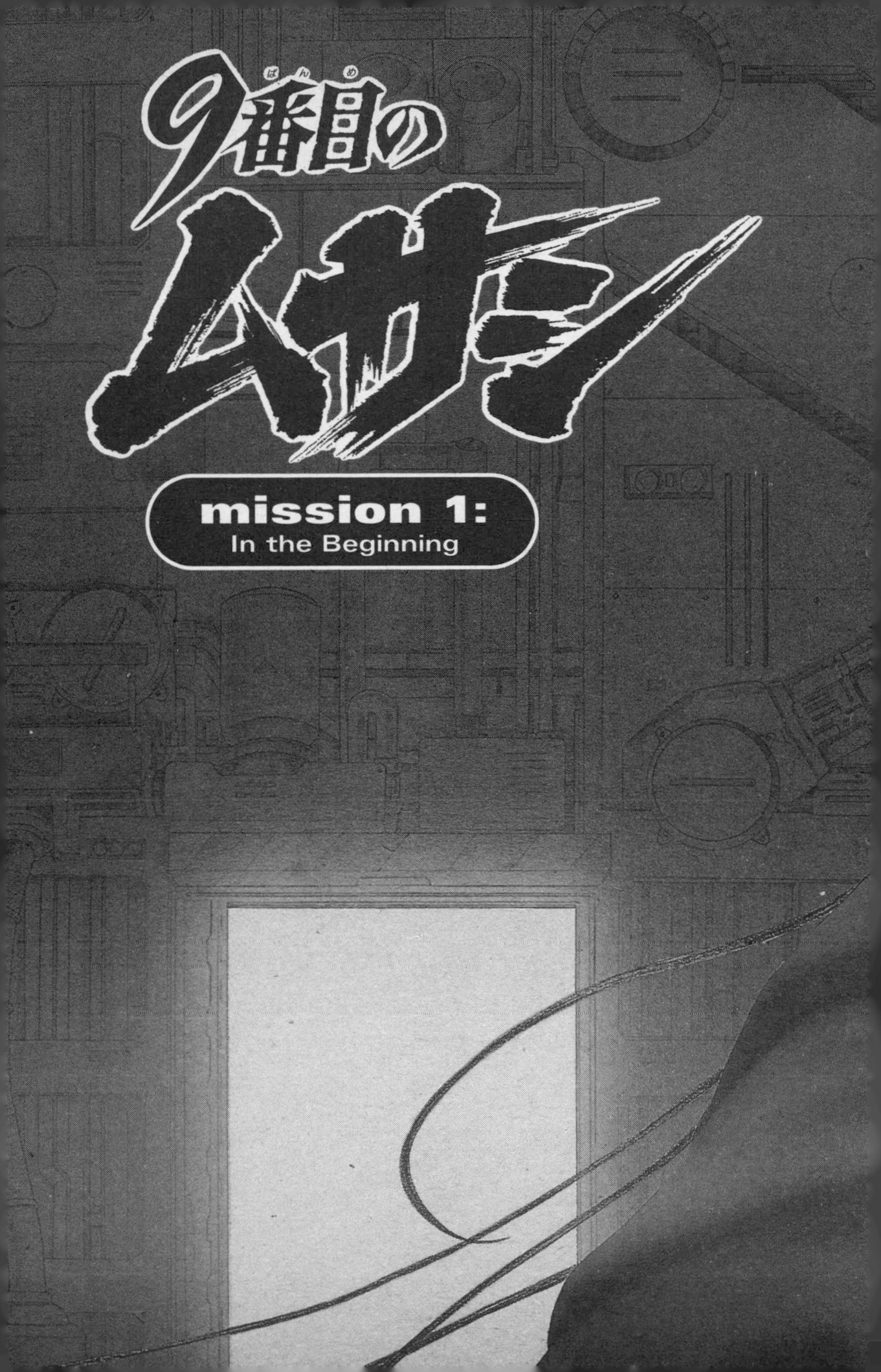
9番目のムサシ
mission 1:
In the Beginning

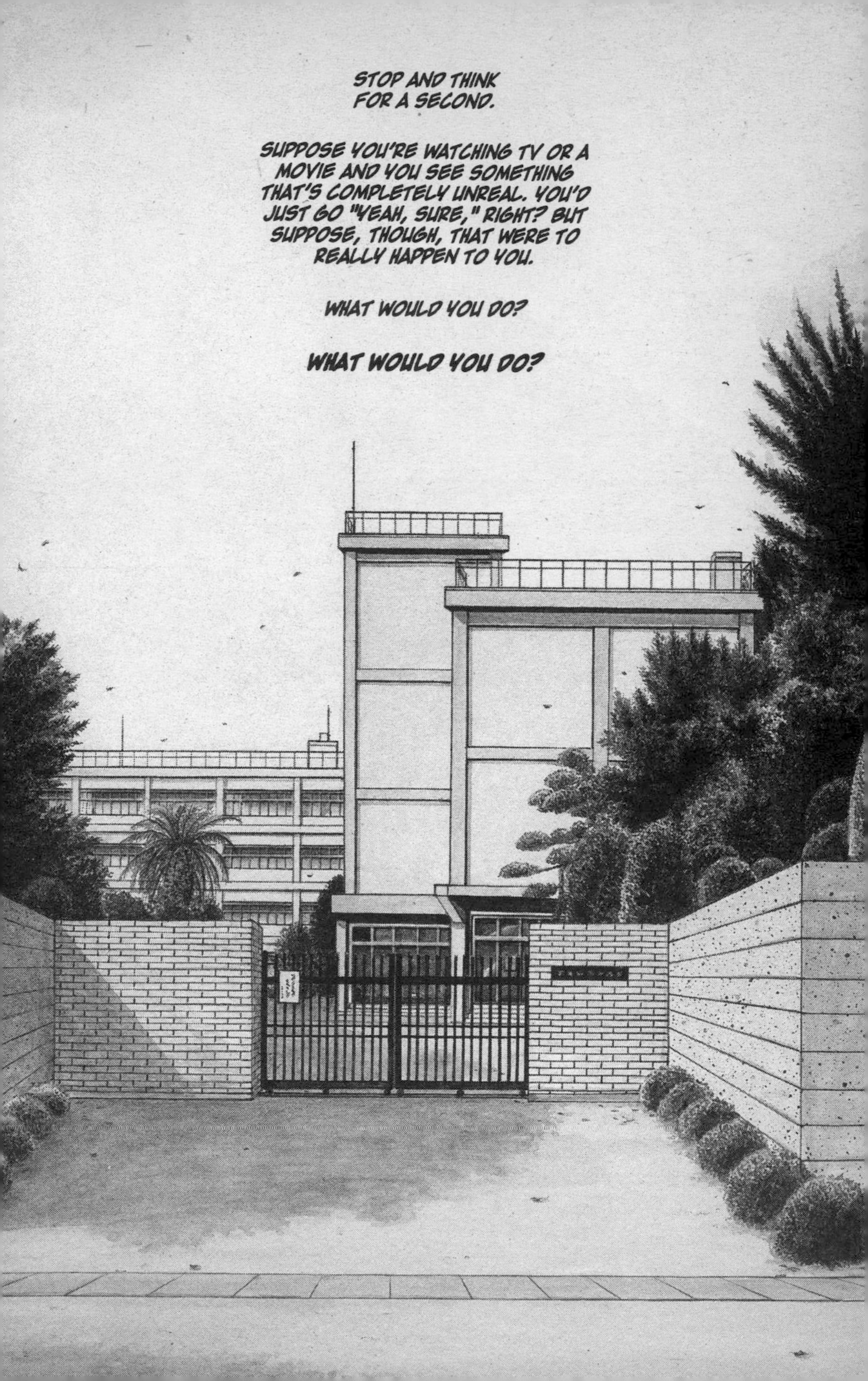
STOP AND THINK FOR A SECOND.
SUPPOSE YOU'RE WATCHING TV OR A MOVIE AND YOU SEE SOMETHING THAT'S COMPLETELY UNREAL. YOU'D JUST GO "YEAH, SURE," RIGHT? BUT SUPPOSE, THOUGH, THAT WERE TO REALLY HAPPEN TO YOU.
WHAT WOULD YOU DO?
WHAT WOULD YOU DO?

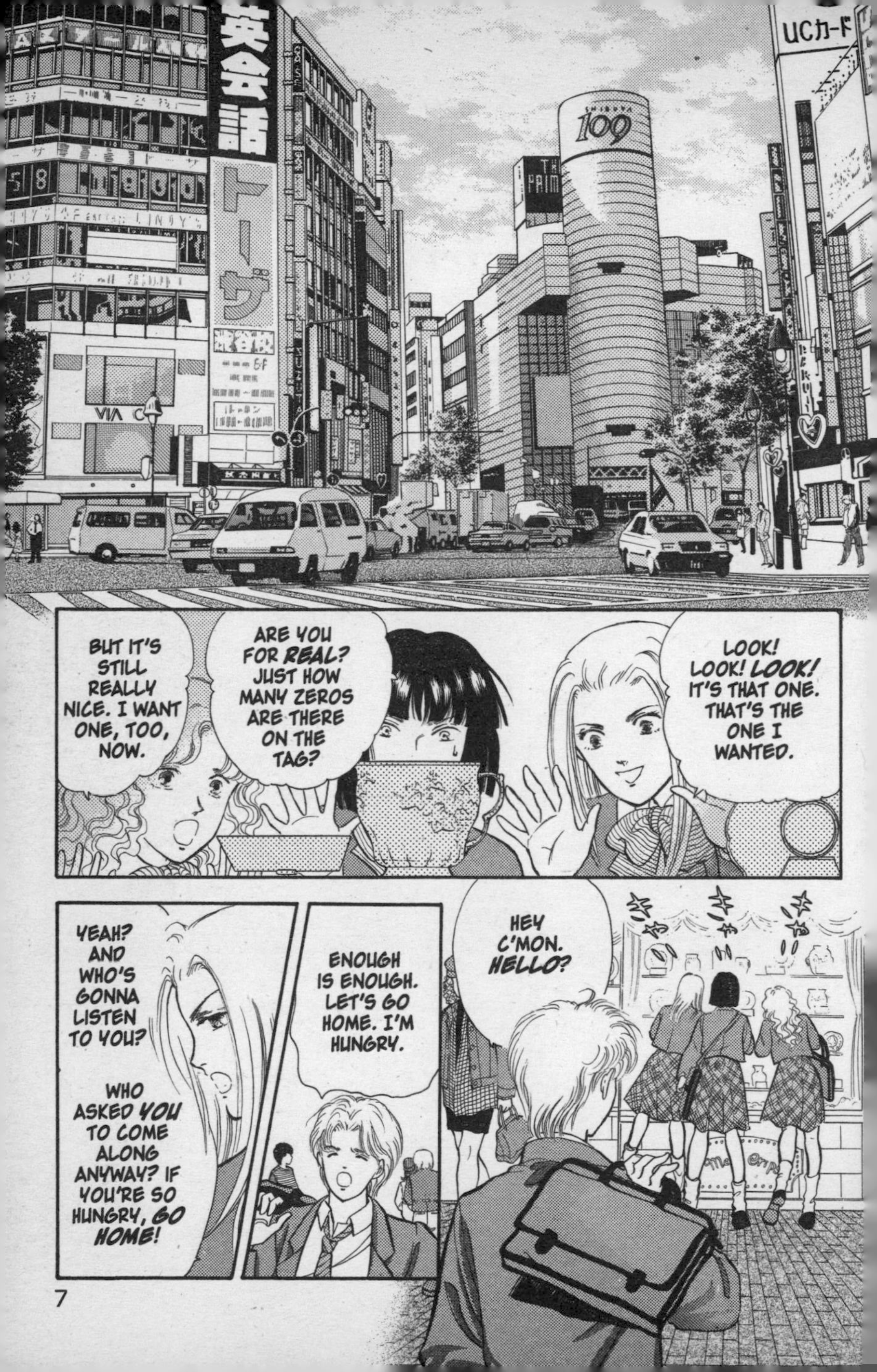
英会話
UCカード
SHIBUYA 109
LOOK! LOOK! *LOOK!* IT'S THAT ONE. THAT'S THE ONE I WANTED.
ARE YOU FOR *REAL?* JUST HOW MANY ZEROS ARE THERE ON THE TAG?
BUT IT'S STILL REALLY NICE. I WANT ONE, TOO, NOW.
HEY C'MON. *HELLO?*
ENOUGH IS ENOUGH. LET'S GO HOME. I'M HUNGRY.
YEAH? AND WHO'S GONNA LISTEN TO YOU?
WHO ASKED *YOU* TO COME ALONG ANYWAY? IF YOU'RE SO HUNGRY, *GO HOME!*

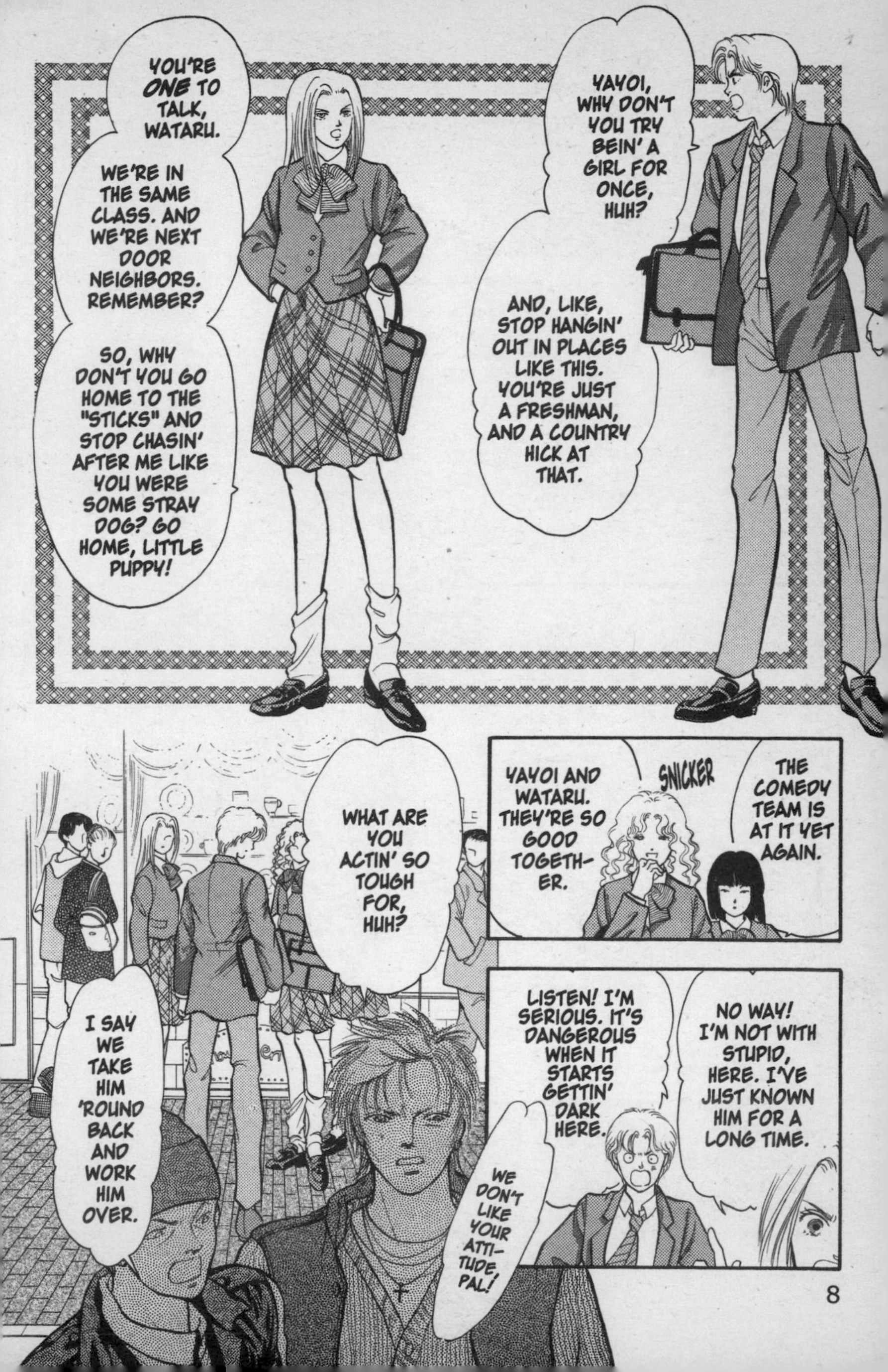
YAYOI, WHY DON'T YOU TRY BEIN' A GIRL FOR ONCE, HUH?
AND, LIKE, STOP HANGIN' OUT IN PLACES LIKE THIS. YOU'RE JUST A FRESHMAN, AND A COUNTRY HICK AT THAT.
YOU'RE *ONE* TO TALK, WATARU.
WE'RE IN THE SAME CLASS. AND WE'RE NEXT DOOR NEIGHBORS. REMEMBER?
SO, WHY DON'T YOU GO HOME TO THE "STICKS" AND STOP CHASIN' AFTER ME LIKE YOU WERE SOME STRAY DOG? GO HOME, LITTLE PUPPY!
THE COMEDY TEAM IS AT IT YET AGAIN.
SNICKER
YAYOI AND WATARU. THEY'RE SO GOOD TOGETH-ER.
NO WAY! I'M NOT WITH STUPID, HERE. I'VE JUST KNOWN HIM FOR A LONG TIME.
LISTEN! I'M SERIOUS. IT'S DANGEROUS WHEN IT STARTS GETTIN' DARK HERE.
WHAT ARE YOU ACTIN' SO TOUGH FOR, HUH?
WE DON'T LIKE YOUR ATTI-TUDE, PAL!
I SAY WE TAKE HIM 'ROUND BACK AND WORK HIM OVER.

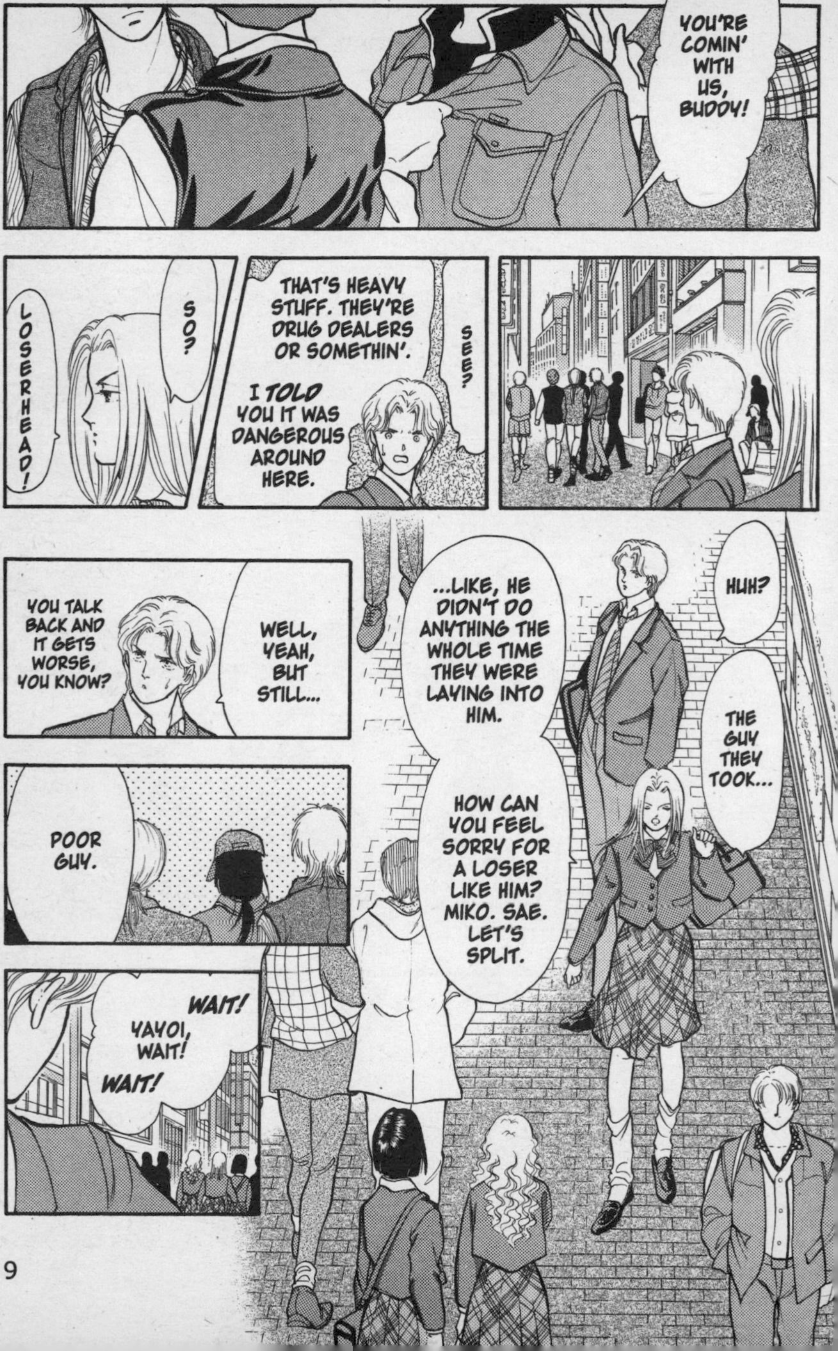
YOU'RE COMIN' WITH US, BUDDY!
SEE?
THAT'S HEAVY STUFF. THEY'RE DRUG DEALERS OR SOMETHIN'.
I *TOLD* YOU IT WAS DANGEROUS AROUND HERE.
SO?
LOSERHEAD!
HUH?
THE GUY THEY TOOK...
...LIKE, HE DIDN'T DO ANYTHING THE WHOLE TIME THEY WERE LAYING INTO HIM.
HOW CAN YOU FEEL SORRY FOR A LOSER LIKE HIM? MIKO. SAE. LET'S SPLIT.
WELL, YEAH, BUT STILL...
YOU TALK BACK AND IT GETS WORSE, YOU KNOW?
POOR GUY.
WAIT!
YAYOI, WAIT!
WAIT!

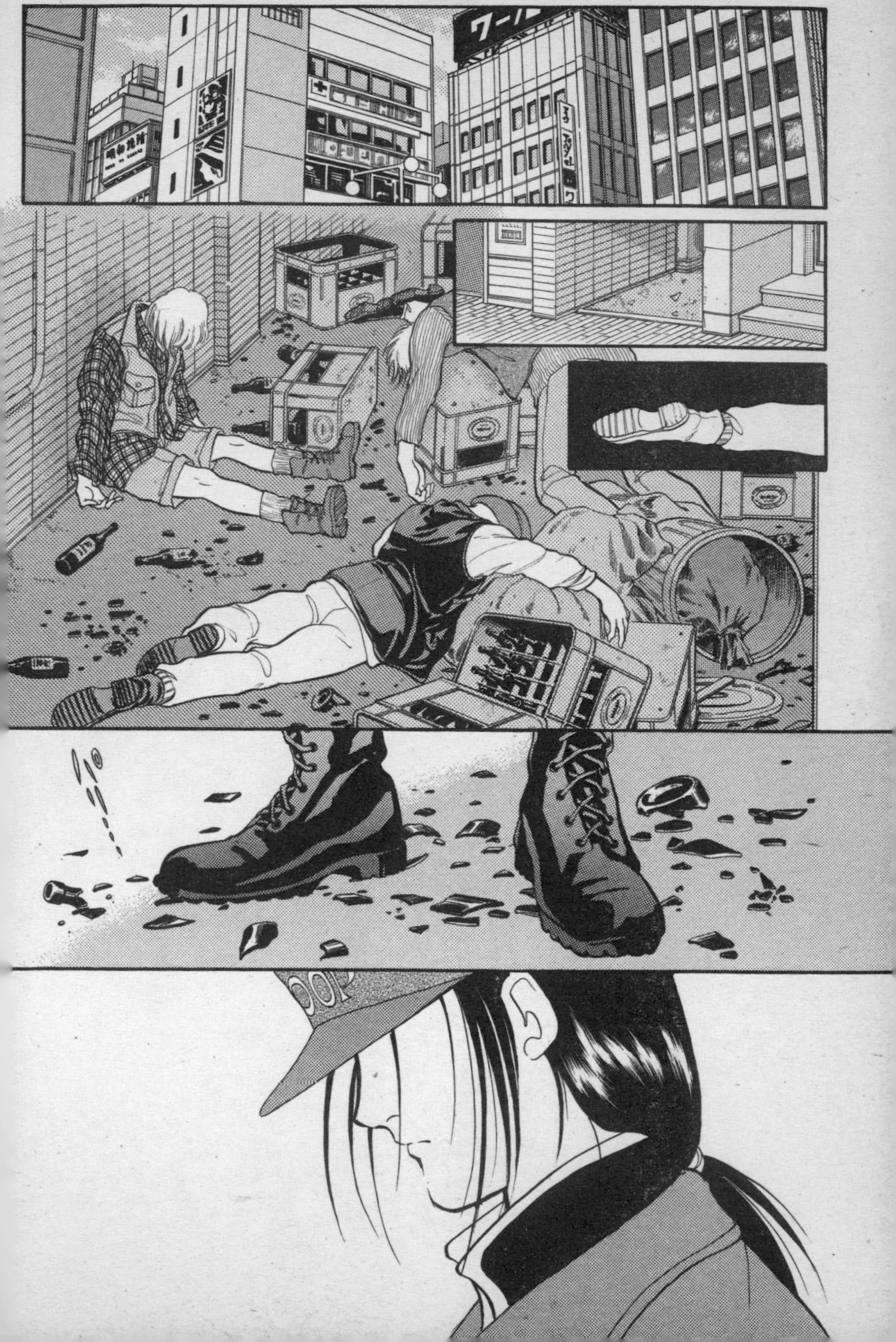

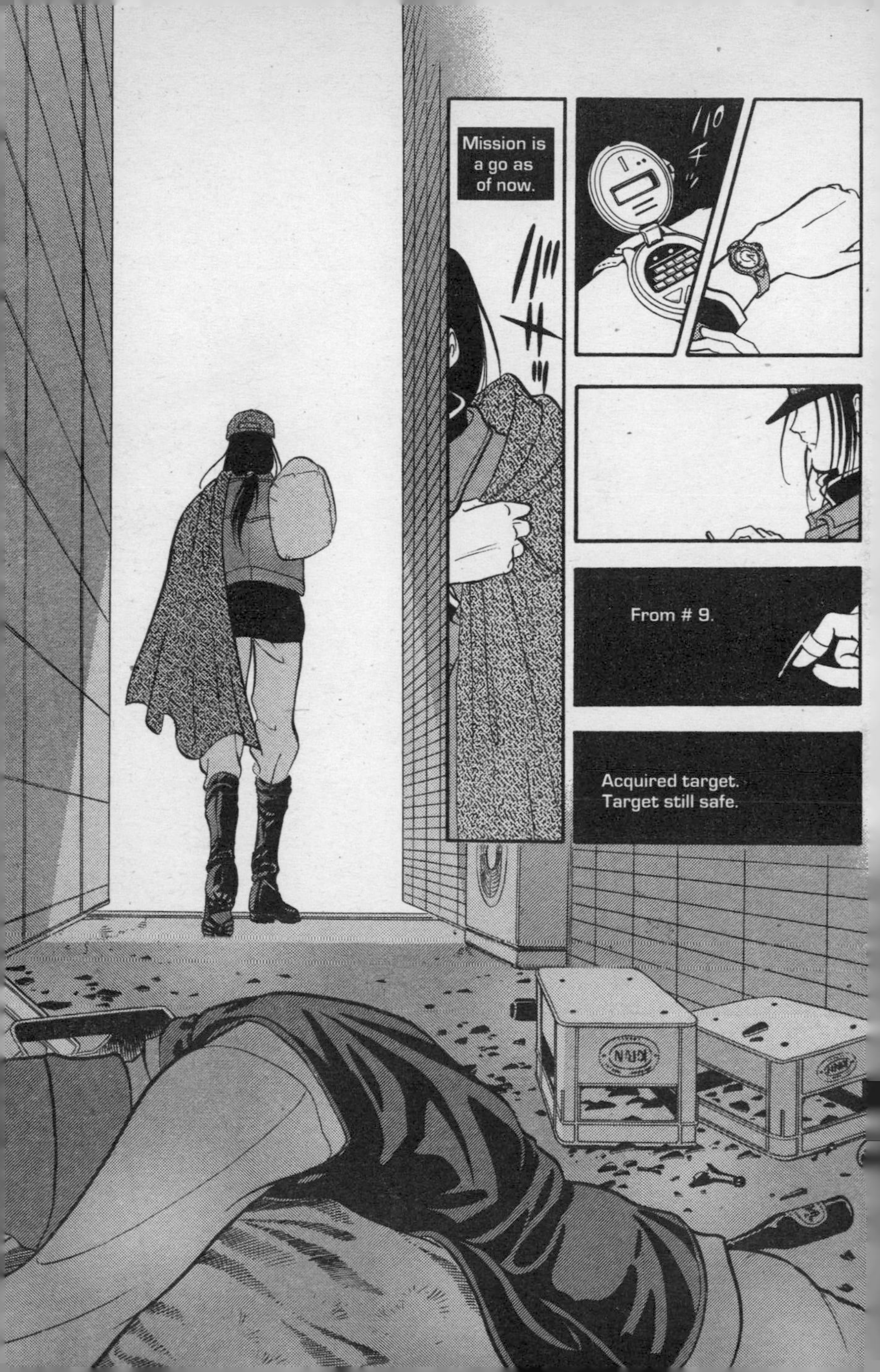
From # 9.
Acquired target.
Target still safe.
Mission is a go as of now.

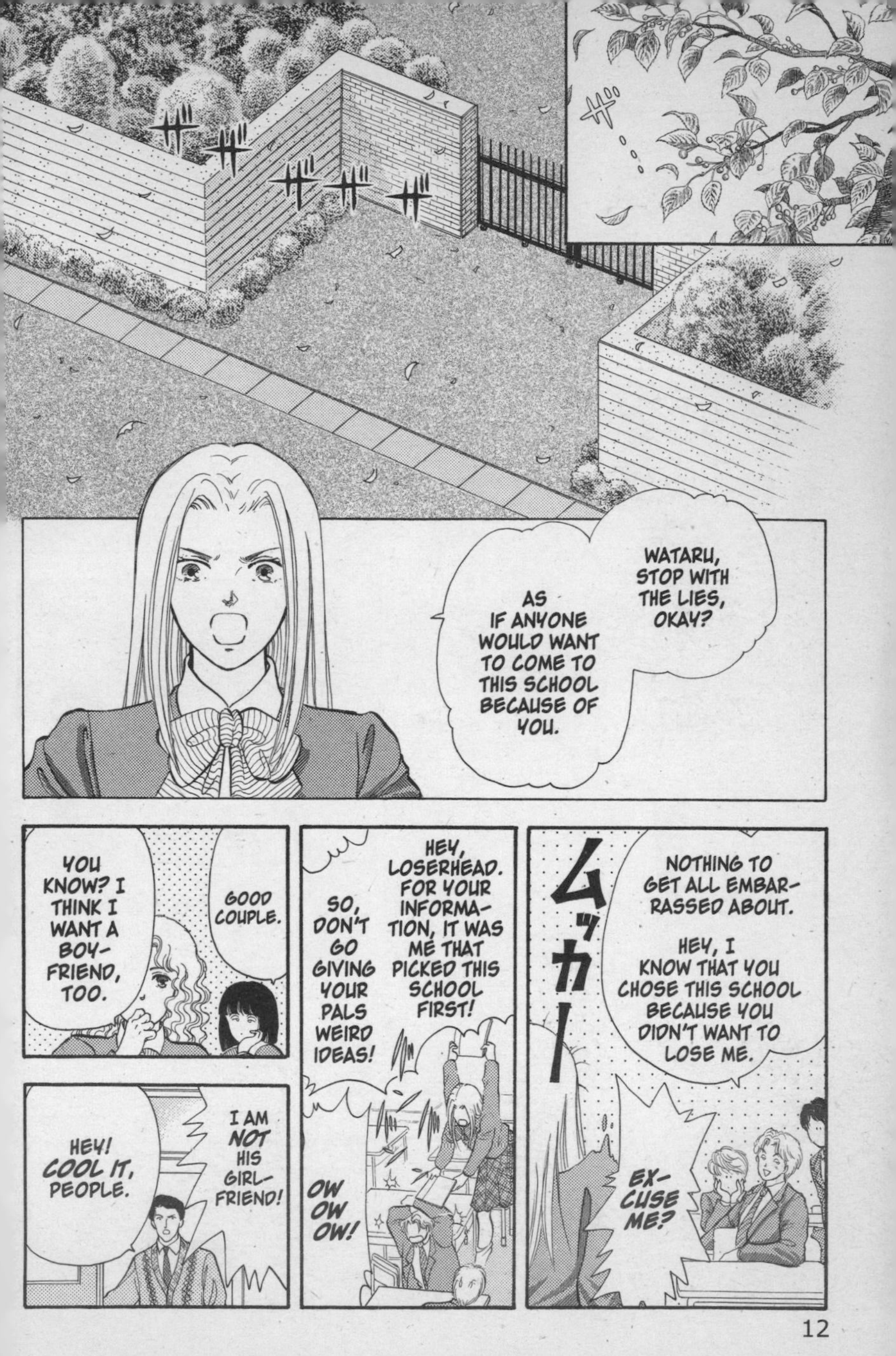
WATARU, STOP WITH THE LIES, OKAY?
AS IF ANYONE WOULD WANT TO COME TO THIS SCHOOL BECAUSE OF YOU.
NOTHING TO GET ALL EMBARRASSED ABOUT.
HEY, I KNOW THAT YOU CHOSE THIS SCHOOL BECAUSE YOU DIDN'T WANT TO LOSE ME.
ムッカー
EX-CUSE ME?
HEY, LOSERHEAD. FOR YOUR INFORMATION, IT WAS ME THAT PICKED THIS SCHOOL FIRST!
SO, DON'T GO GIVING YOUR PALS WEIRD IDEAS!
OW OW OW!
GOOD COUPLE.
YOU KNOW? I THINK I WANT A BOY-FRIEND, TOO.
I AM NOT HIS GIRL-FRIEND!
HEY! COOL IT, PEOPLE.

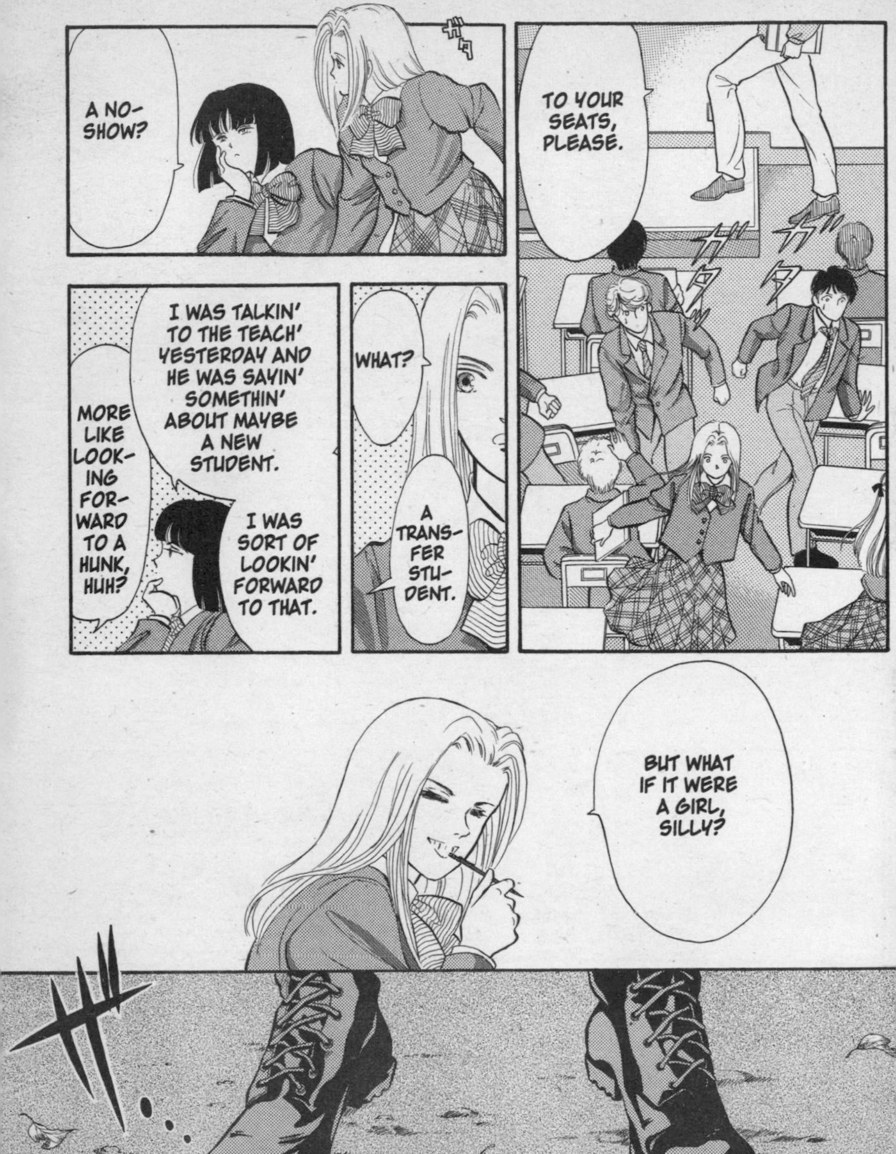
TO YOUR SEATS, PLEASE.
A NO-SHOW?
WHAT?
A TRANSFER STUDENT.
I WAS TALKIN' TO THE TEACH' YESTERDAY AND HE WAS SAYIN' SOMETHIN' ABOUT MAYBE A NEW STUDENT.
I WAS SORT OF LOOKIN' FORWARD TO THAT.
MORE LIKE LOOKING FORWARD TO A HUNK, HUH?
BUT WHAT IF IT WERE A GIRL, SILLY?

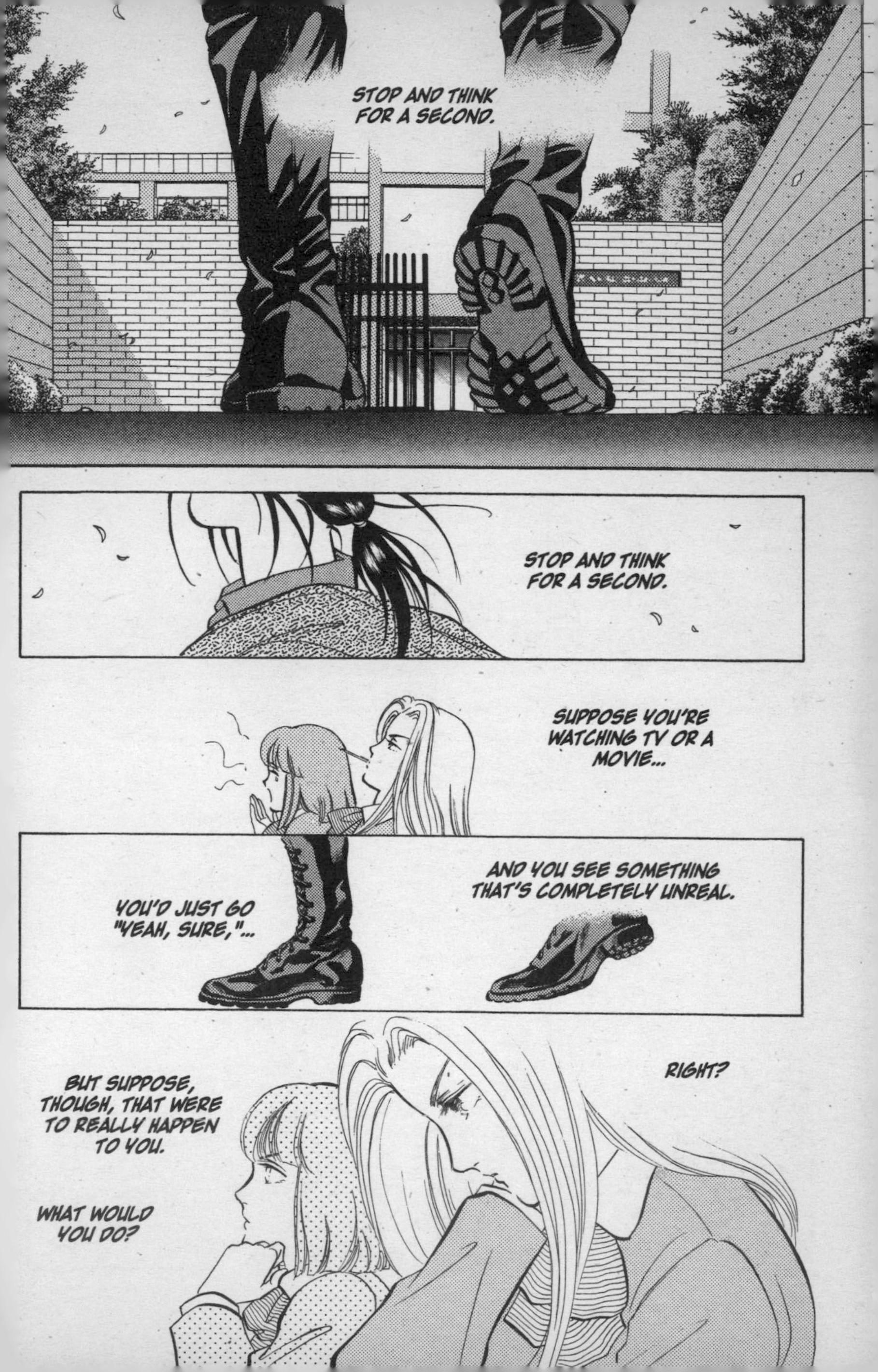

STOP AND THINK FOR A SECOND.
STOP AND THINK FOR A SECOND.
SUPPOSE YOU'RE WATCHING TV OR A MOVIE...
AND YOU SEE SOMETHING THAT'S COMPLETELY UNREAL.
YOU'D JUST GO "YEAH, SURE,"...
RIGHT?
BUT SUPPOSE, THOUGH, THAT WERE TO REALLY HAPPEN TO YOU.
WHAT WOULD YOU DO?

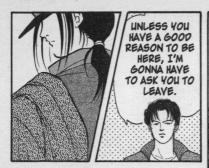

WHAT WOULD YOU DO?
STOP. WHERE DO YOU THINK YOU'RE GOING?
UNLESS YOU HAVE A GOOD REASON TO BE HERE, I'M GONNA HAVE TO ASK YOU TO LEAVE.
HUH?
RECORD OF TRANSFER
OH. I GUESS YOU'RE TRANS-FERRING HERE.
THE SECRETARY'S OFFICE IS ON THE RIGHT. AND GO DOWN TO THE END.
AND DO SOME-THING ABOUT YOUR OUTFIT.
THEY PROBABLY COULDN'T DO YOUR UNIFORM IN TIME, BUT THE CAPE AND CAP HAVE TO GO.

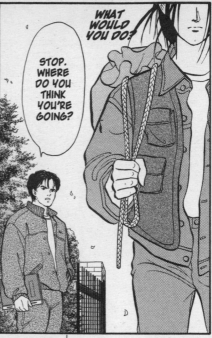

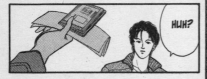

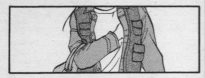

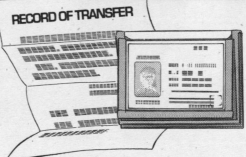

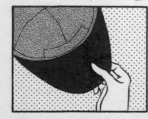

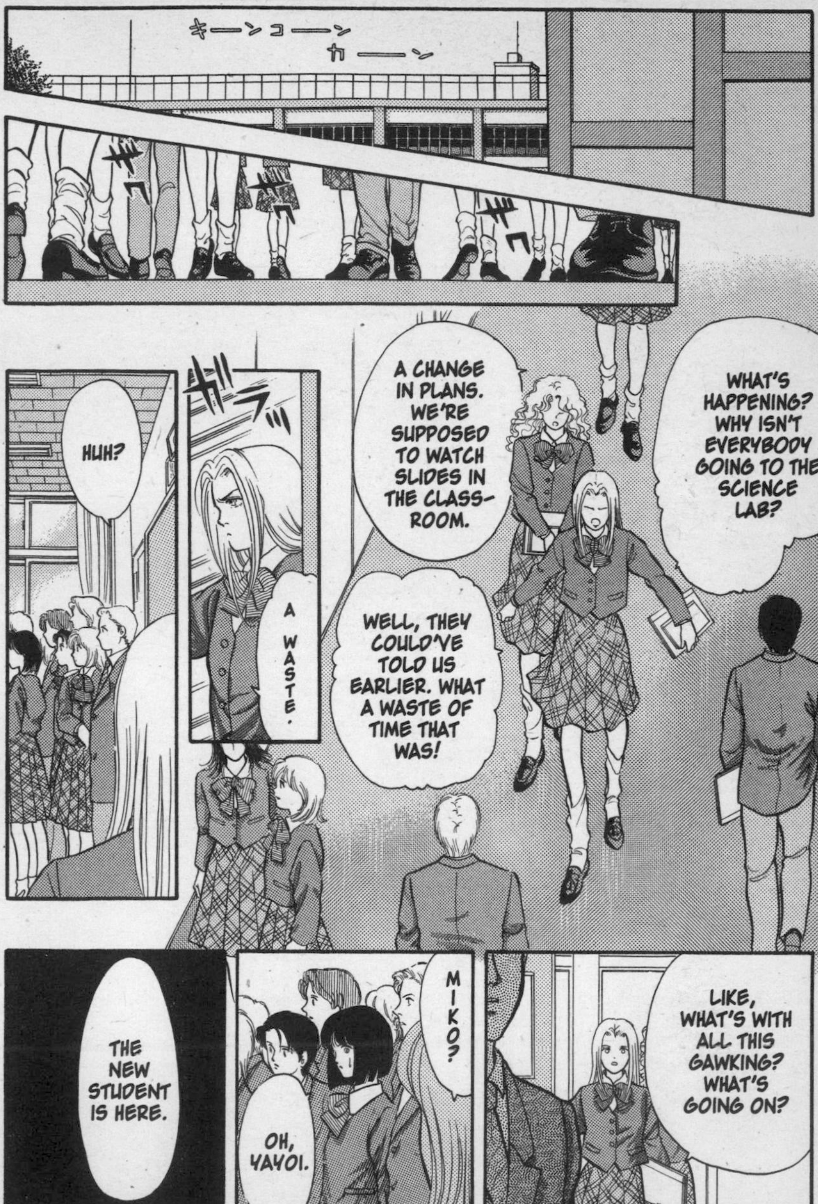
キーンコーン
カーン
WHAT'S HAPPENING? WHY ISN'T EVERYBODY GOING TO THE SCIENCE LAB?
A CHANGE IN PLANS. WE'RE SUPPOSED TO WATCH SLIDES IN THE CLASS-ROOM.
WELL, THEY COULD'VE TOLD US EARLIER. WHAT A WASTE OF TIME THAT WAS!
ガラッ
A WASTE.
HUH?
LIKE, WHAT'S WITH ALL THIS GAWKING? WHAT'S GOING ON?
MIKO?
OH, YAYOI.
THE NEW STUDENT IS HERE.

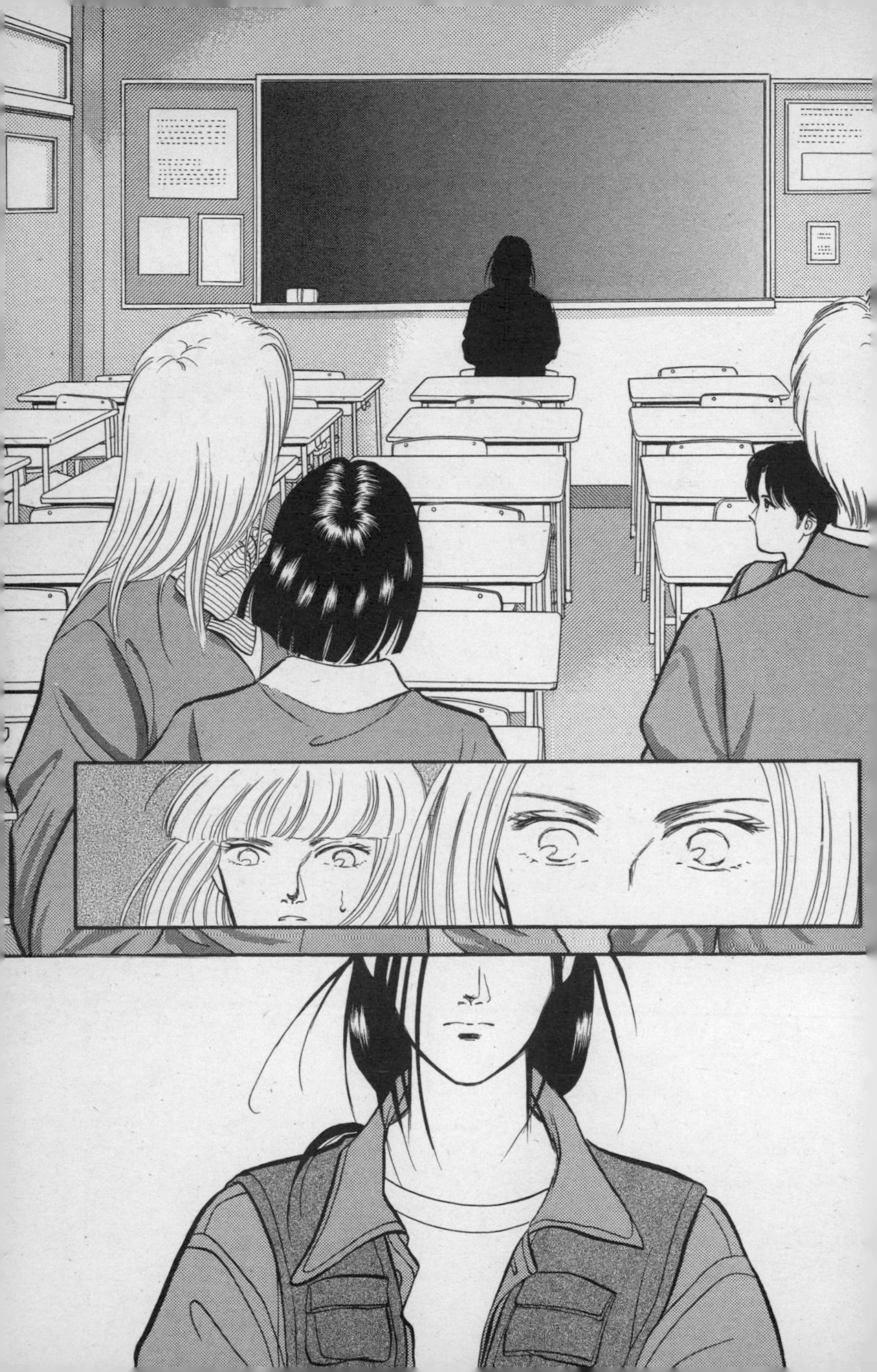

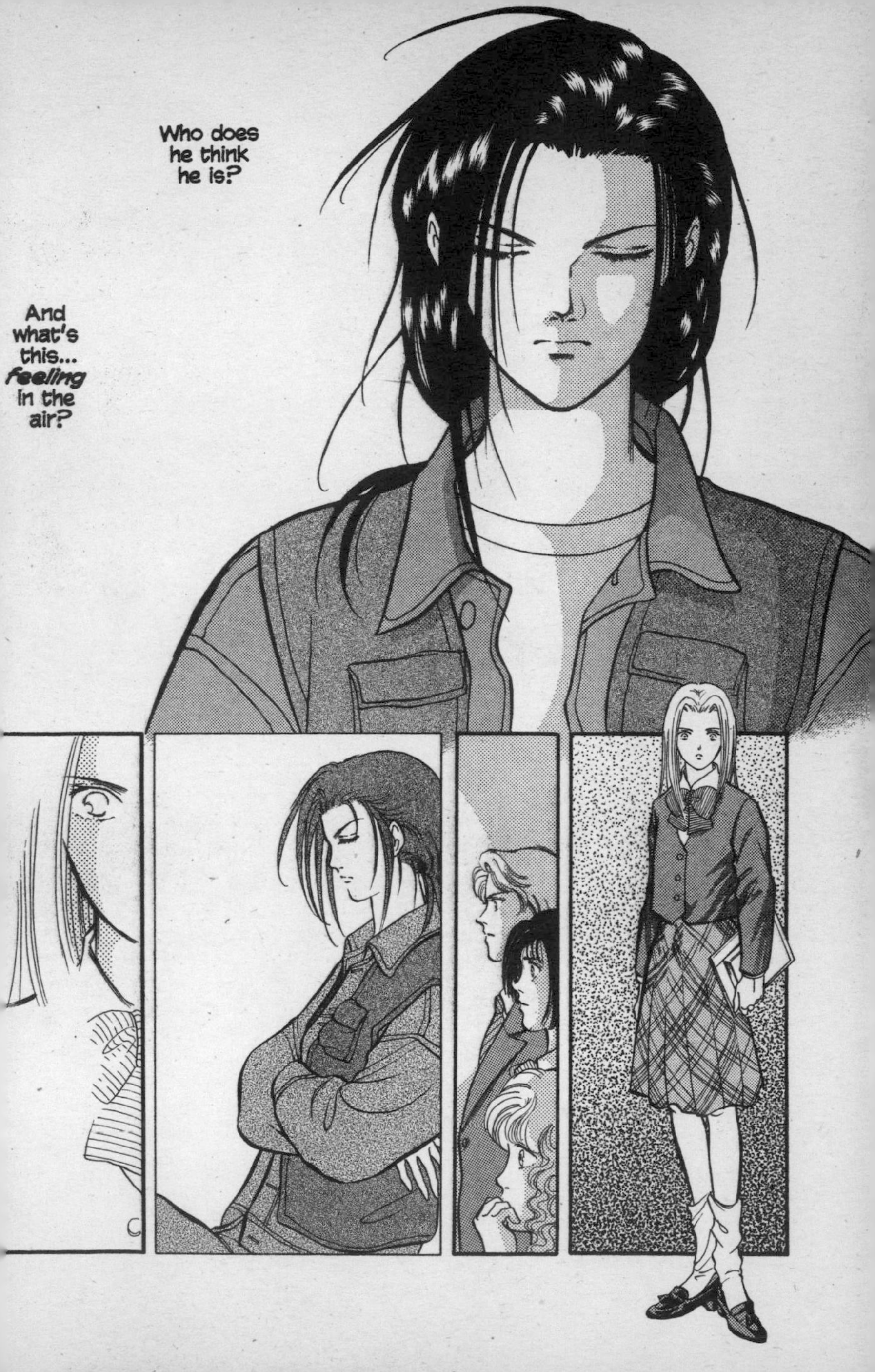
Who does he think he is?
And what's this... *feeling* in the air?

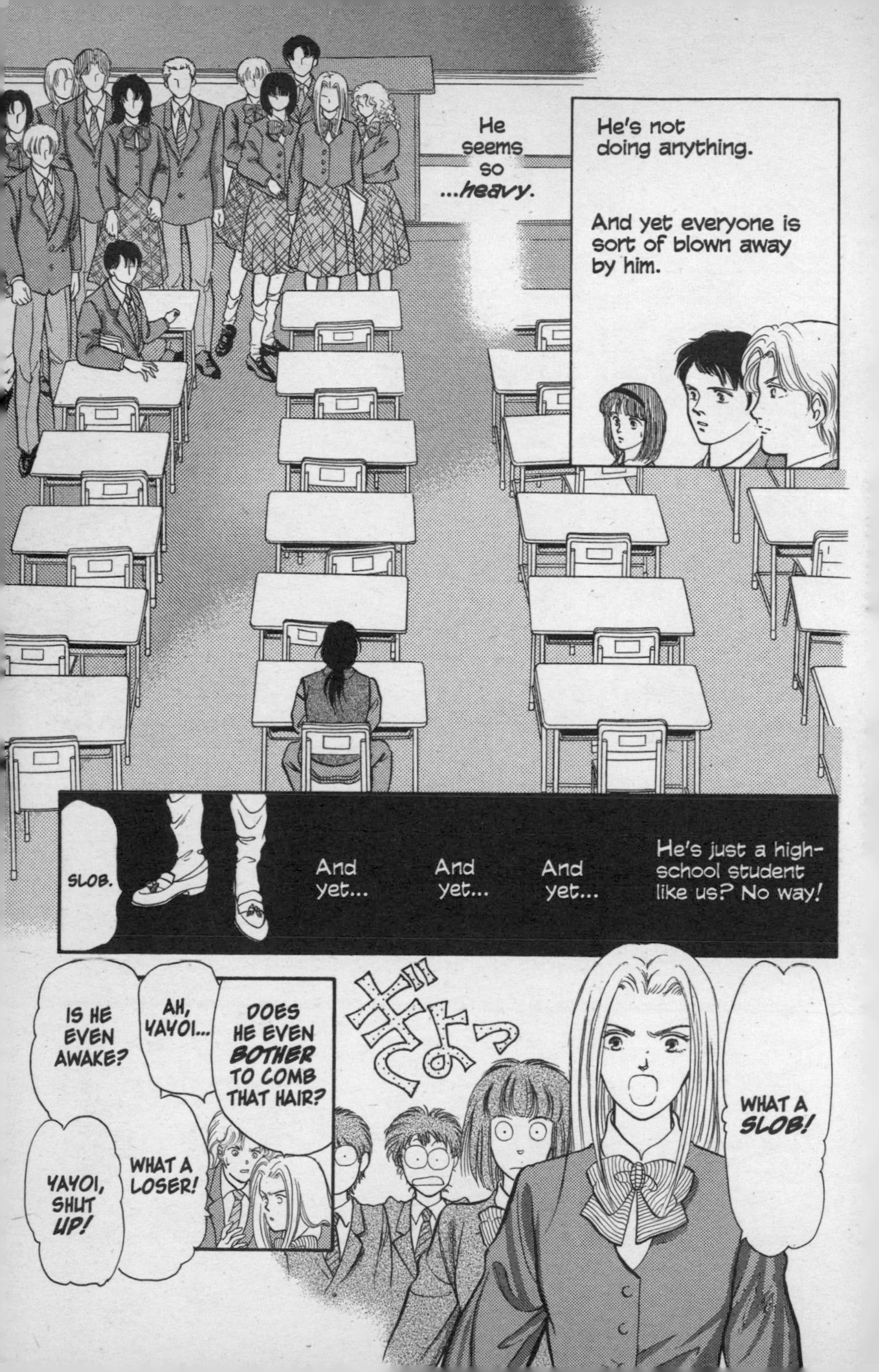
He's not doing anything.
And yet everyone is sort of blown away by him.
He seems so ...heavy.
He's just a high-school student like us? No way!
And yet...
And yet...
And yet...
SLOB.
WHAT A SLOB!
ぎょっ
DOES HE EVEN BOTHER TO COMB THAT HAIR?
AH, YAYOI...
IS HE EVEN AWAKE?
WHAT A LOSER!
YAYOI, SHUT UP!

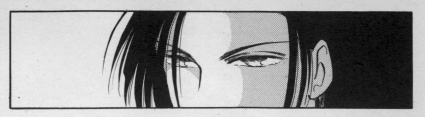

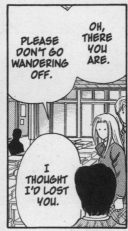

HEY, PEOPLE...
WAUGH!
WHY THE SURPRISE? AND WHY ARE YOU ALL STANDING...?
OH, THERE YOU ARE.
PLEASE DON'T GO WANDERING OFF.
I THOUGHT I'D LOST YOU.
IT LOOKS LIKE YOU'VE ALREADY SETTLED INTO A DESK.
CLASS, THIS IS SHINOZUKA KOU.
KOU WILL BE JOINING US AS OF TODAY.
I'M SURE YOU'LL ALL MAKE YOUR NEW CLASSMATE FEEL WELCOME.
Shinozuka Kou? Well, at least his *name* is normal.
INCIDENTALLY, SCIENCE CLASS IS GOING TO BE MOVED TO THE LAB.
GIMME A BREAK!
TALK ABOUT VACILLATING.
I'LL BET YOU CAN'T SPELL THAT.

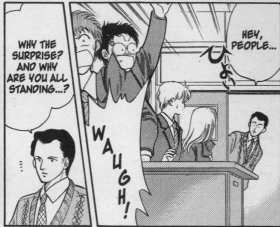

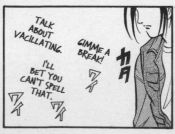

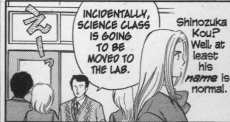

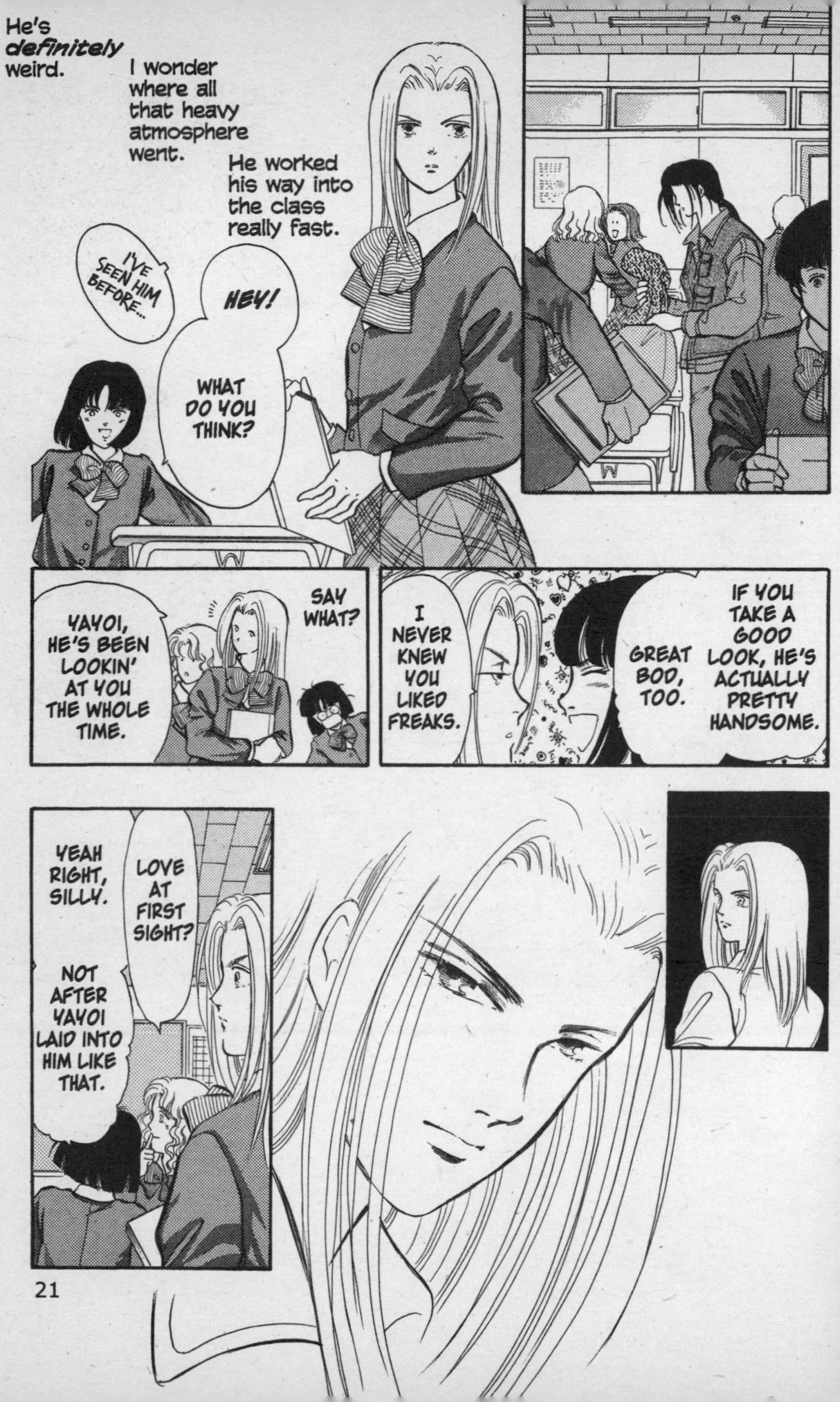
He's *definitely* weird.
I wonder where all that heavy atmosphere went.
He worked his way into the class really fast.
HEY!
WHAT DO YOU THINK?
I'VE SEEN HIM BEFORE...
IF YOU TAKE A GOOD LOOK, HE'S ACTUALLY PRETTY HANDSOME.
GREAT BOD, TOO.
I NEVER KNEW YOU LIKED FREAKS.
SAY WHAT?
YAYOI, HE'S BEEN LOOKIN' AT YOU THE WHOLE TIME.
LOVE AT FIRST SIGHT?
YEAH RIGHT, SILLY.
NOT AFTER YAYOI LAID INTO HIM LIKE THAT.

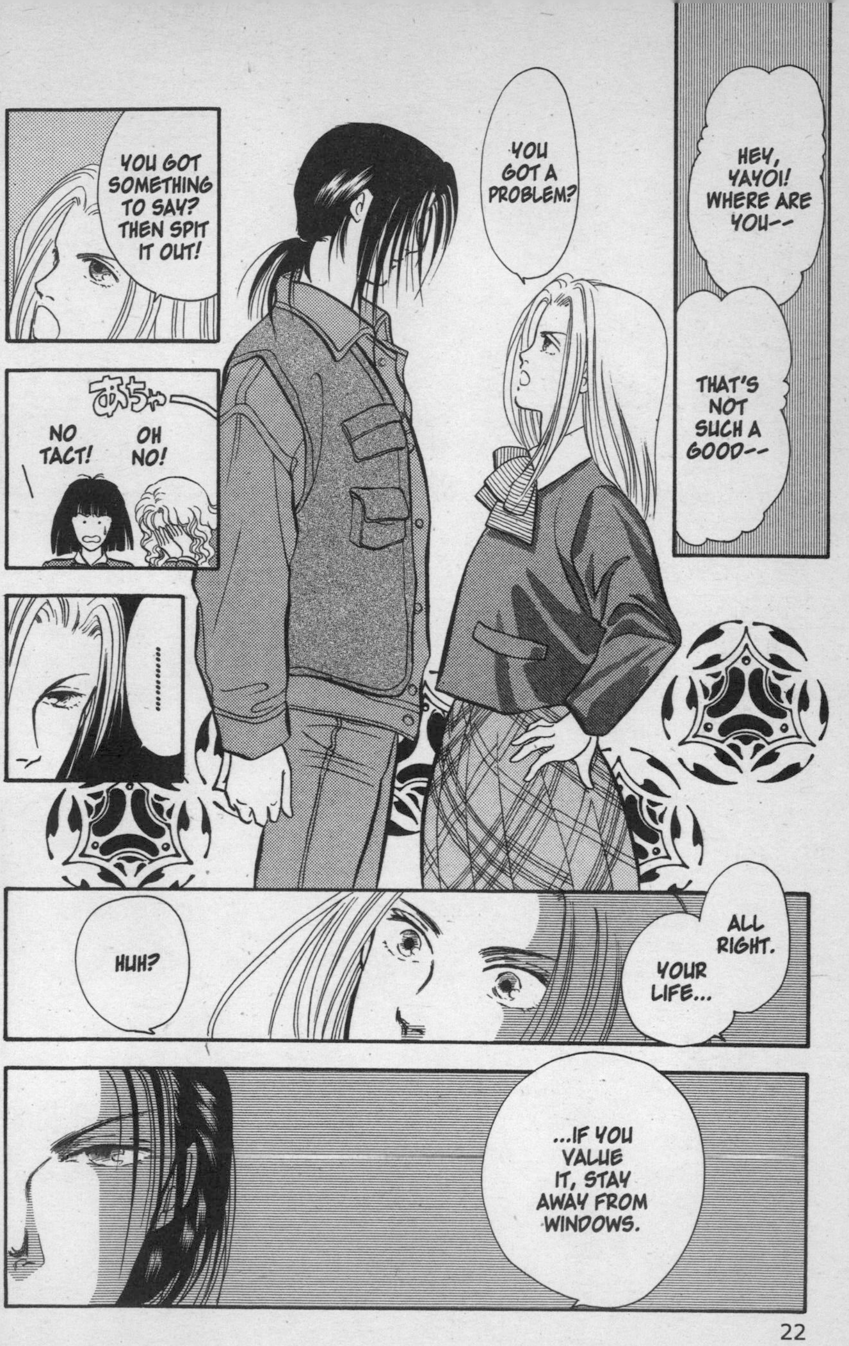
HEY, YAYOI! WHERE ARE YOU--
THAT'S NOT SUCH A GOOD--
YOU GOT A PROBLEM?
YOU GOT SOMETHING TO SAY? THEN SPIT IT OUT!
あちゃ
OH NO!
NO TACT!
....
ALL RIGHT.
YOUR LIFE...
HUH?
...IF YOU VALUE IT, STAY AWAY FROM WINDOWS.

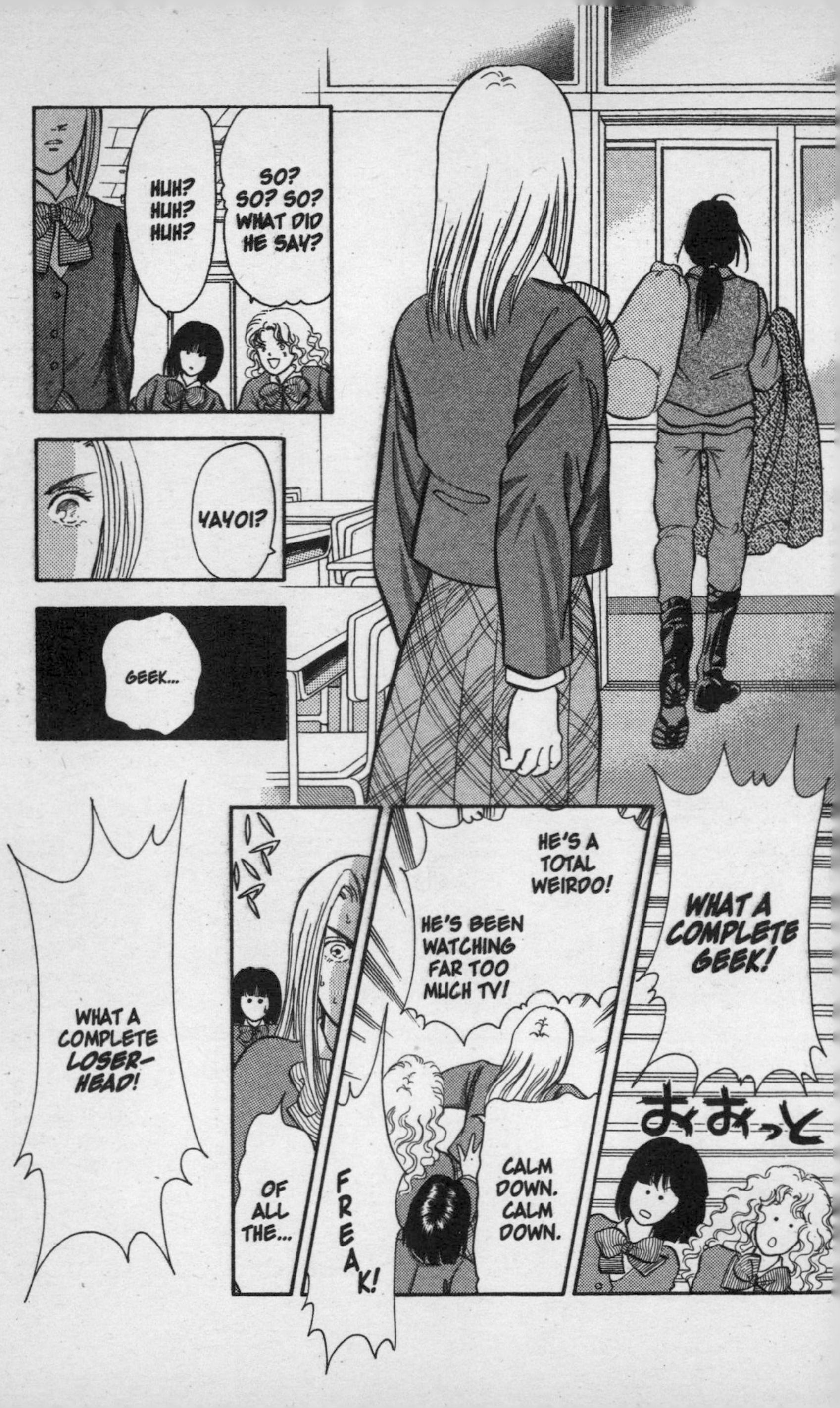
SO? SO? SO? WHAT DID HE SAY?
HUH? HUH? HUH?
YAYOI?
GEEK...
WHAT A COMPLETE GEEK!
おおっと
HE'S A TOTAL WEIRDO!
HE'S BEEN WATCHING FAR TOO MUCH TV!
CALM DOWN. CALM DOWN.
FREAK!
OF ALL THE...
WHAT A COMPLETE LOSER-HEAD!

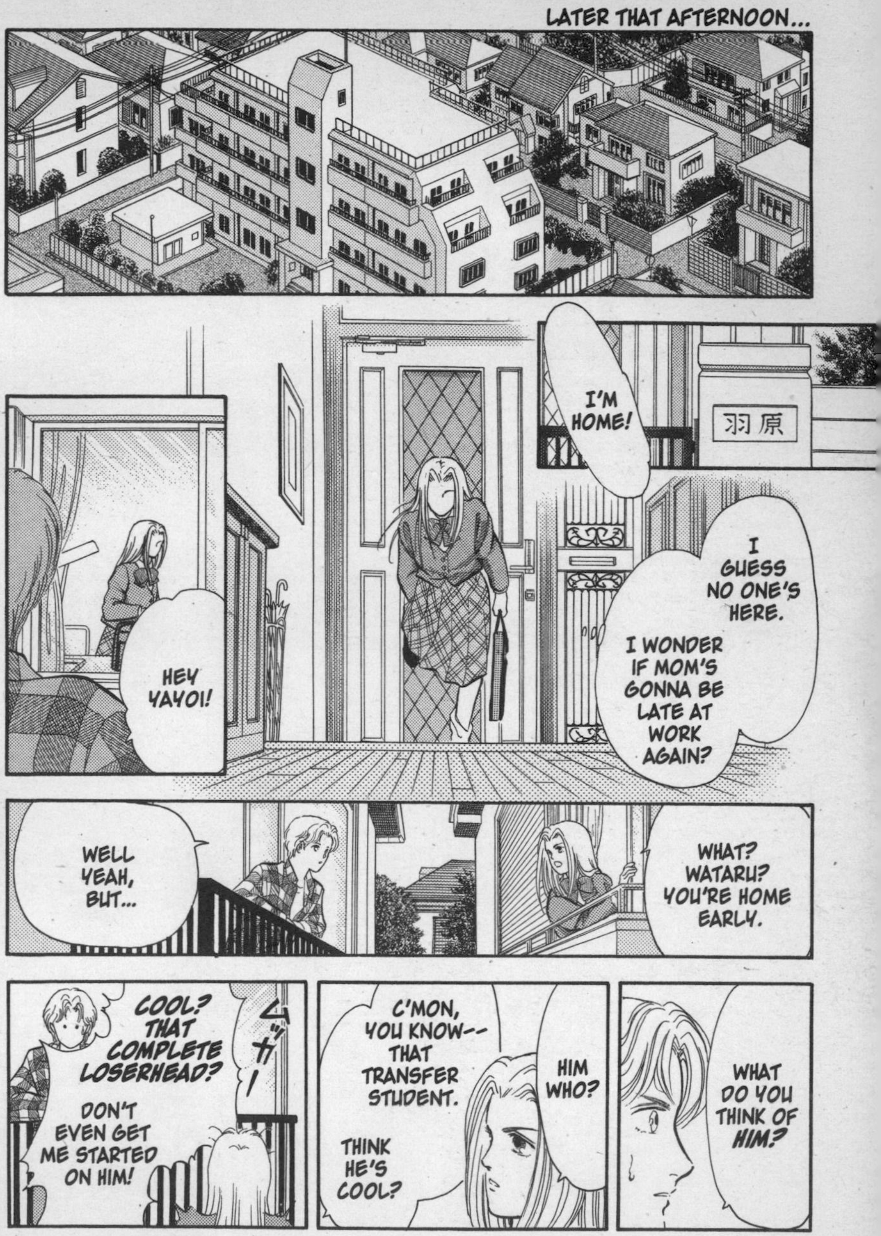
LATER THAT AFTERNOON...
I'M HOME!
羽原
I GUESS NO ONE'S HERE.
I WONDER IF MOM'S GONNA BE LATE AT WORK AGAIN?
HEY YAYOI!
WHAT? WATARU? YOU'RE HOME EARLY.
WELL YEAH, BUT...
WHAT DO YOU THINK OF *HIM?*
HIM WHO?
C'MON, YOU KNOW--THAT TRANSFER STUDENT.
THINK HE'S COOL?
ムッカー!
COOL? THAT COMPLETE LOSERHEAD?
DON'T EVEN GET ME STARTED ON HIM!

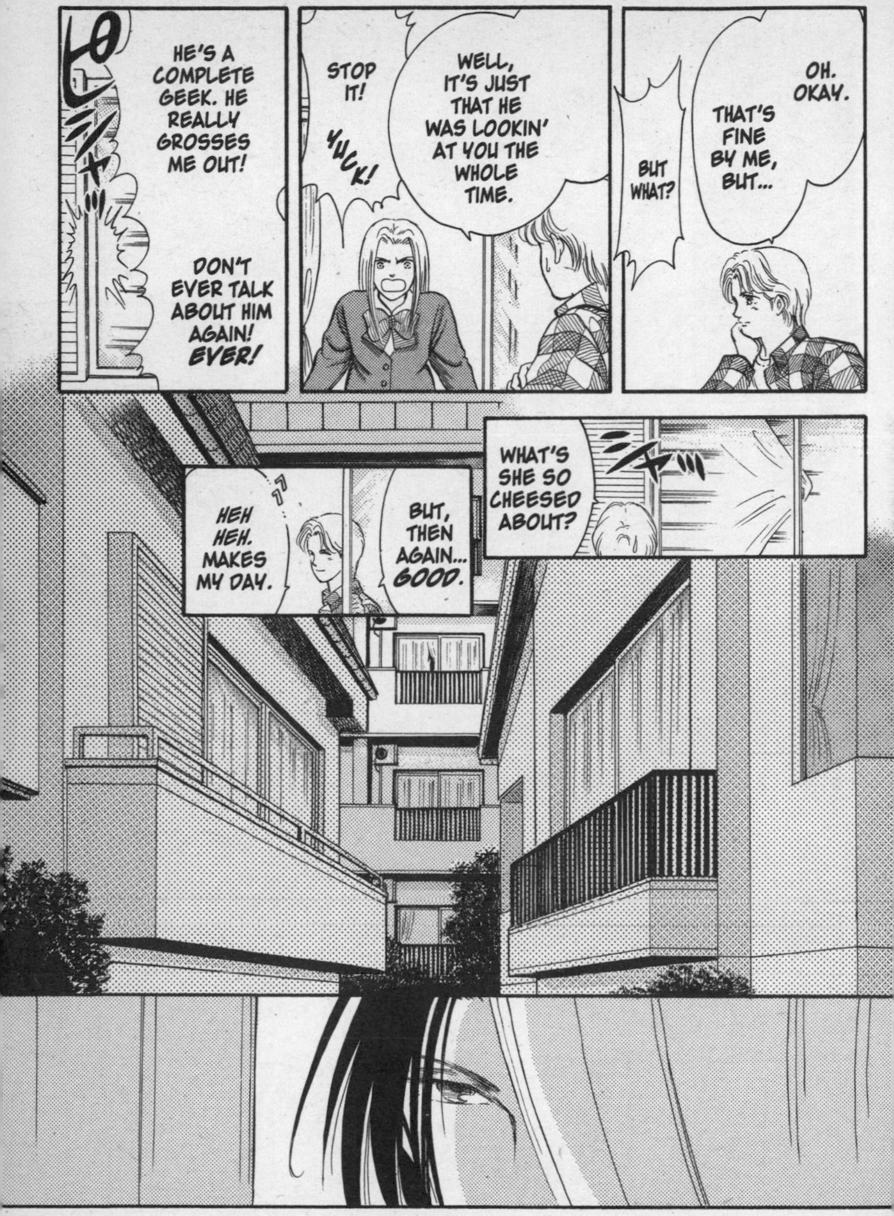
OH. OKAY.
THAT'S FINE BY ME, BUT...
BUT WHAT?
WELL, IT'S JUST THAT HE WAS LOOKIN' AT YOU THE WHOLE TIME.
STOP IT!
YUCK!
HE'S A COMPLETE GEEK. HE REALLY GROSSES ME OUT!
DON'T EVER TALK ABOUT HIM AGAIN! EVER!
WHAT'S SHE SO CHEESED ABOUT?
BUT, THEN AGAIN... GOOD.
HEH HEH. MAKES MY DAY.

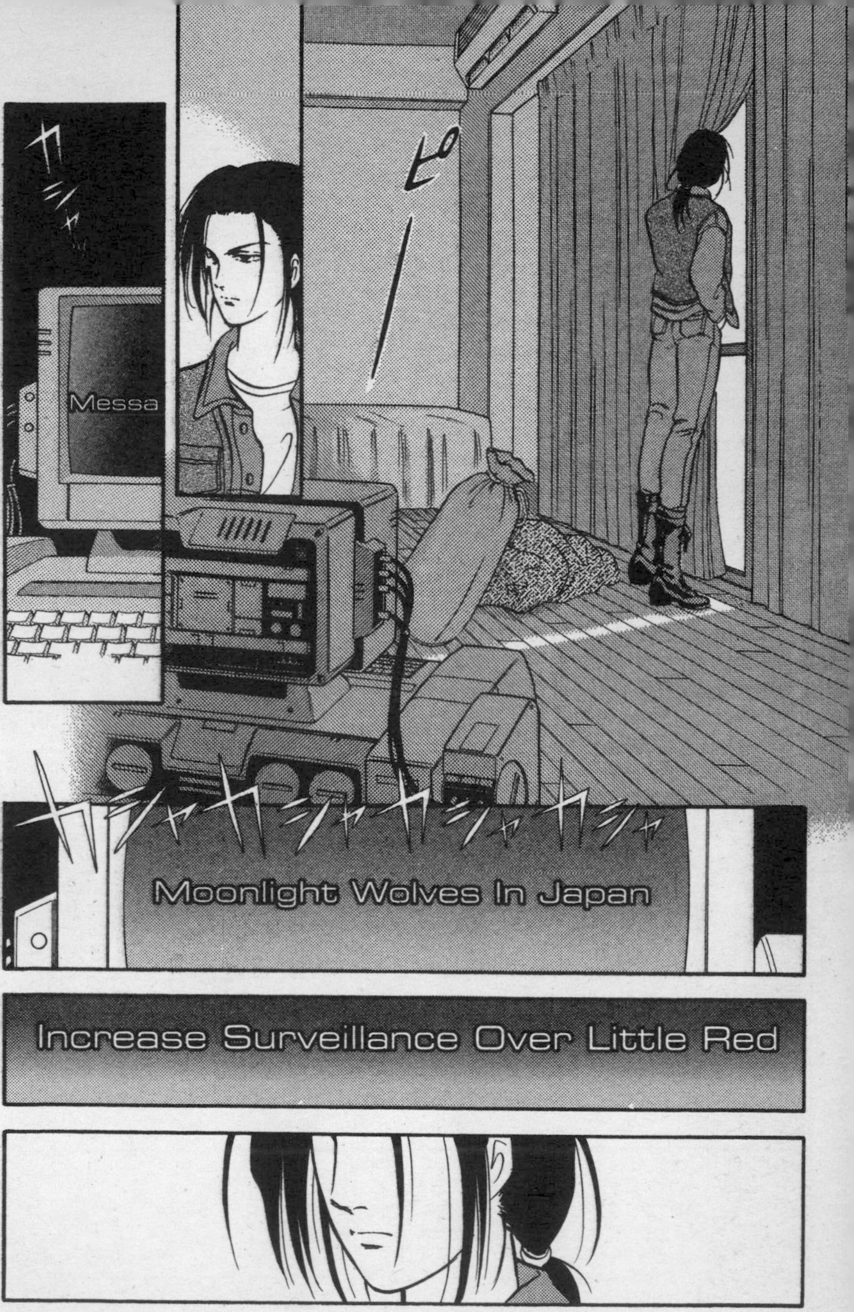

ピ
Messa
カシャカシャカシャカシャ
Moonlight Wolves In Japan
Increase Surveillance Over Little Red

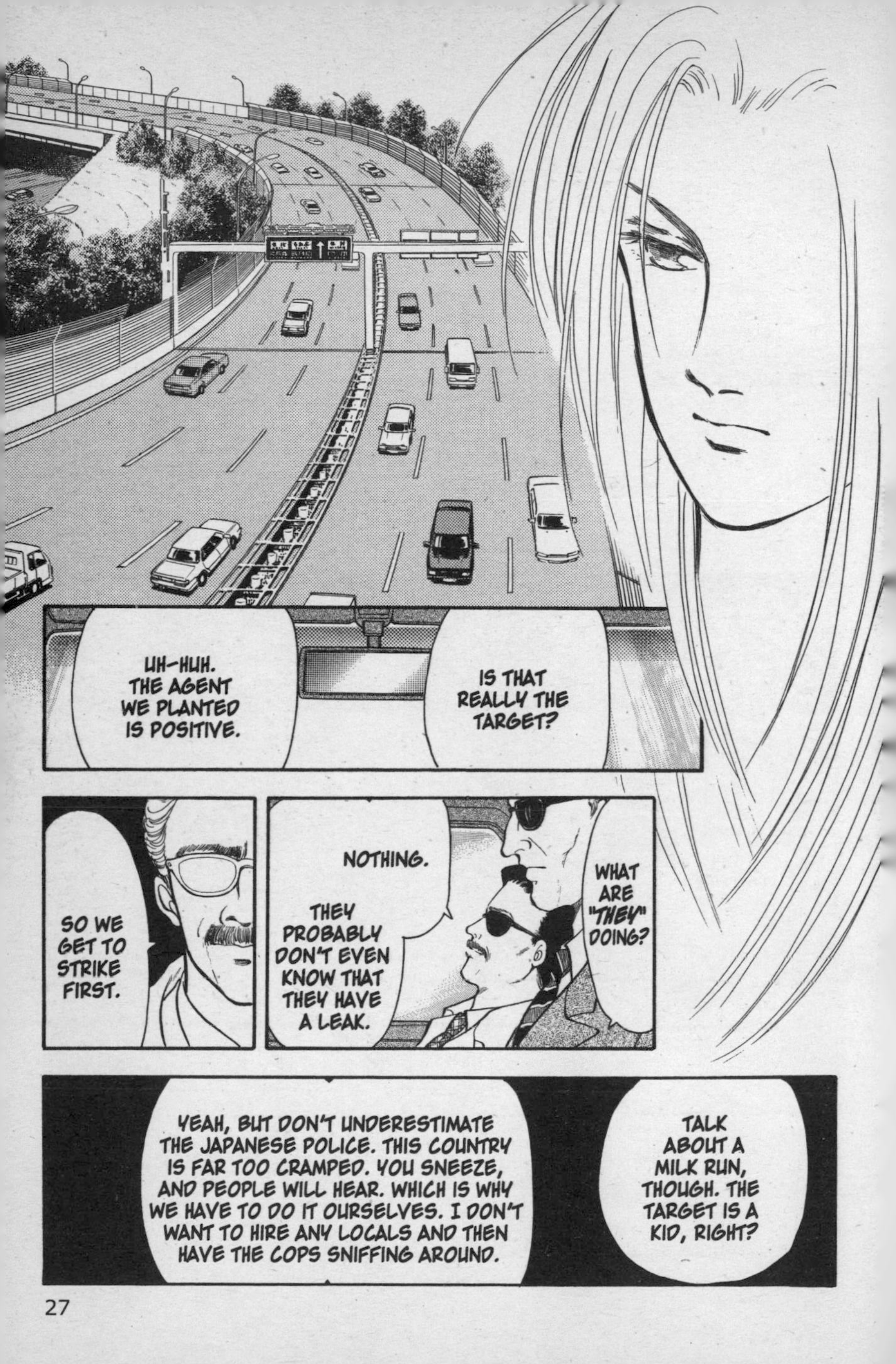
IS THAT REALLY THE TARGET?
UH-HUH. THE AGENT WE PLANTED IS POSITIVE.
WHAT ARE "THEY" DOING?
NOTHING.
THEY PROBABLY DON'T EVEN KNOW THAT THEY HAVE A LEAK.
SO WE GET TO STRIKE FIRST.
TALK ABOUT A MILK RUN, THOUGH. THE TARGET IS A KID, RIGHT?
YEAH, BUT DON'T UNDERESTIMATE THE JAPANESE POLICE. THIS COUNTRY IS FAR TOO CRAMPED. YOU SNEEZE, AND PEOPLE WILL HEAR. WHICH IS WHY WE HAVE TO DO IT OURSELVES. I DON'T WANT TO HIRE ANY LOCALS AND THEN HAVE THE COPS SNIFFING AROUND.

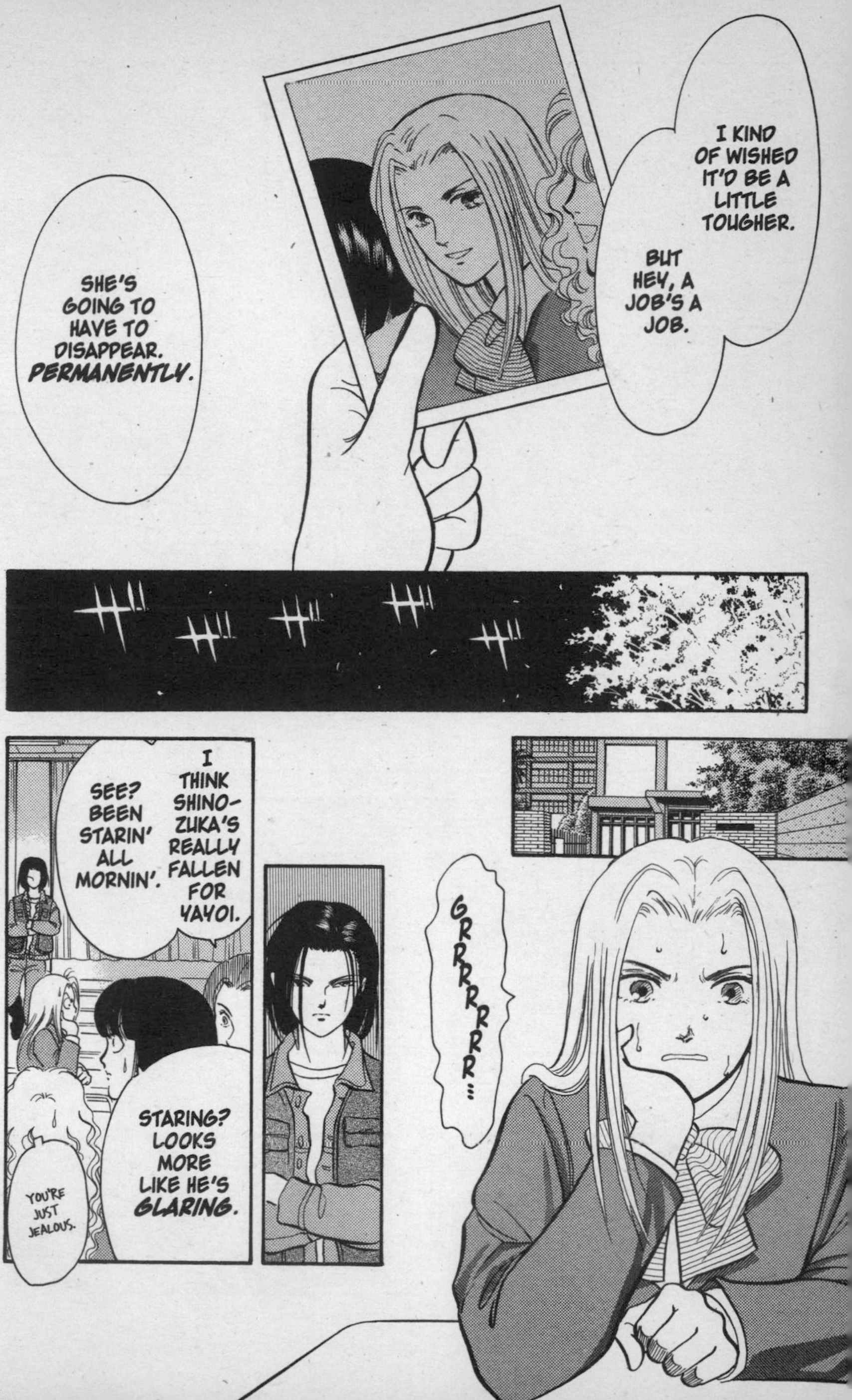
I KIND OF WISHED IT'D BE A LITTLE TOUGHER.
BUT HEY, A JOB'S A JOB.
SHE'S GOING TO HAVE TO DISAPPEAR. PERMANENTLY.
GRRRRRRR...
I THINK SHINOZUKA'S REALLY FALLEN FOR YAYOI.
SEE? BEEN STARIN' ALL MORNIN'.
STARING? LOOKS MORE LIKE HE'S GLARING.
YOU'RE JUST JEALOUS.

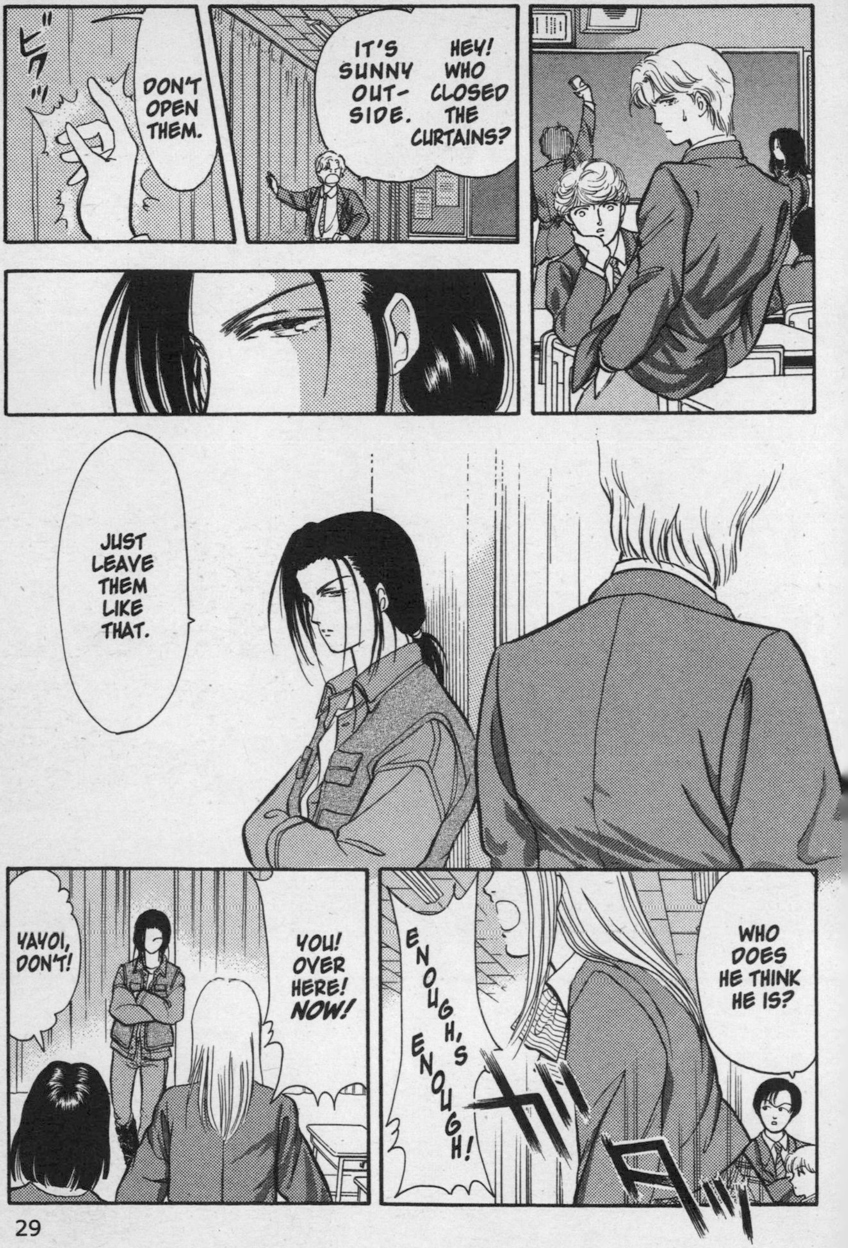
HEY! WHO CLOSED THE CURTAINS?
IT'S SUNNY OUT-SIDE.
ビクッ
DON'T OPEN THEM.
JUST LEAVE THEM LIKE THAT.
WHO DOES HE THINK HE IS?
ENOUGH'S ENOUGH!
YOU! OVER HERE! NOW!
YAYOI, DON'T!

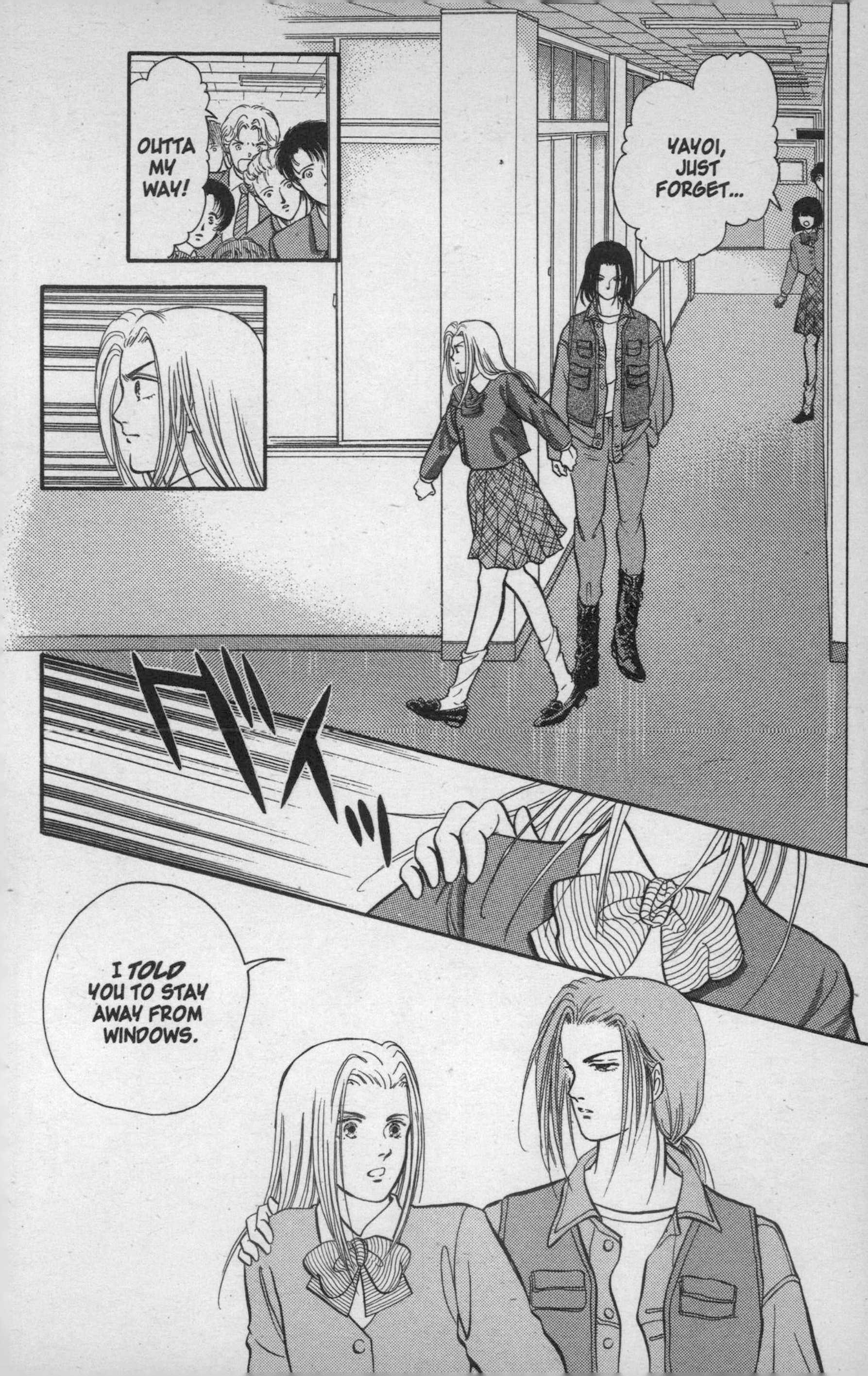
YAYOI, JUST FORGET...
OUTTA MY WAY!
I TOLD YOU TO STAY AWAY FROM WINDOWS.

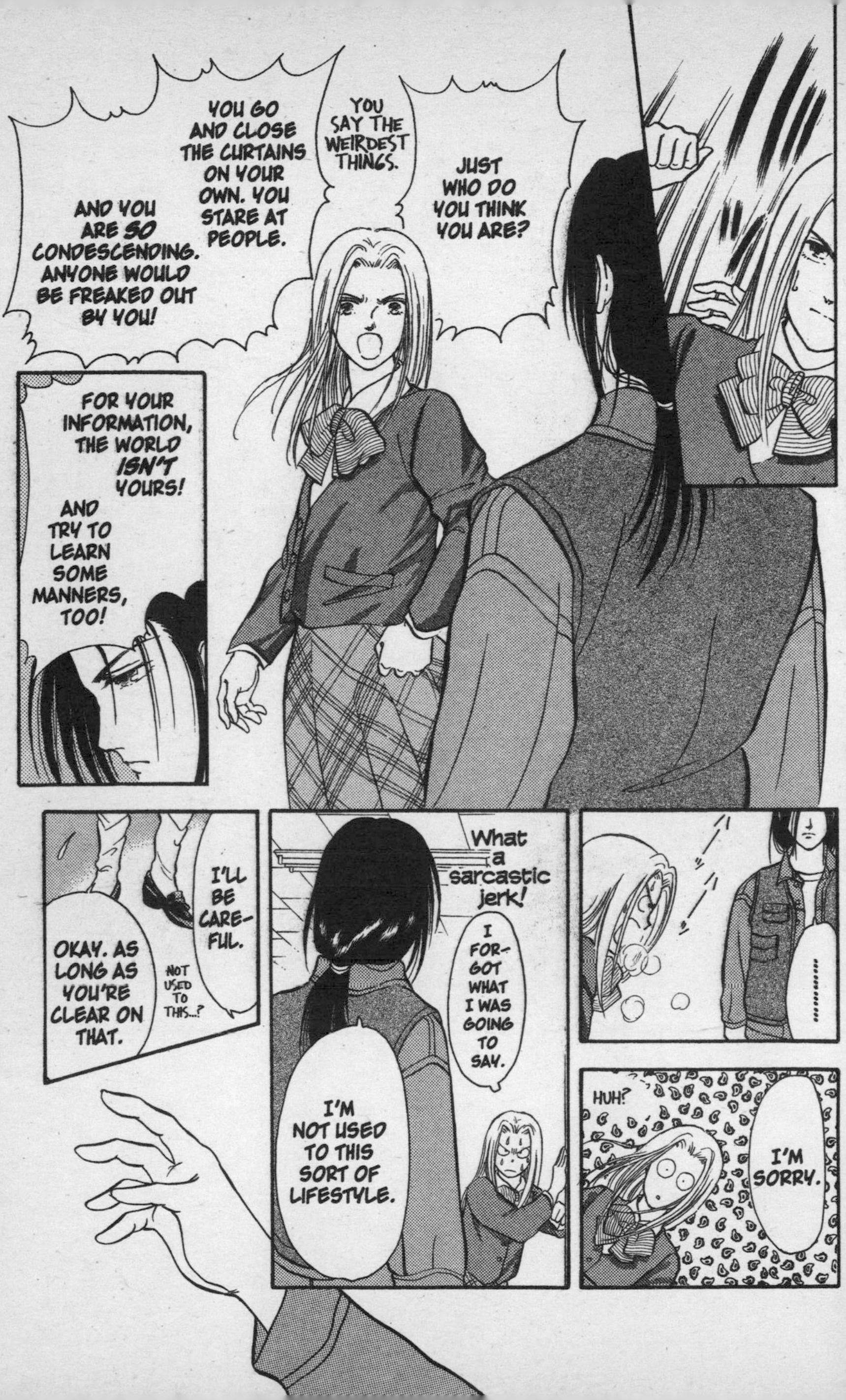
JUST WHO DO YOU THINK YOU ARE?
YOU SAY THE WEIRDEST THINGS.
YOU GO AND CLOSE THE CURTAINS ON YOUR OWN. YOU STARE AT PEOPLE.
AND YOU ARE SO CONDESCENDING. ANYONE WOULD BE FREAKED OUT BY YOU!
FOR YOUR INFORMATION, THE WORLD ISN'T YOURS!
AND TRY TO LEARN SOME MANNERS, TOO!
....
I'M SORRY.
HUH?
What a sarcastic jerk!
I FORGOT WHAT I WAS GOING TO SAY.
I'M NOT USED TO THIS SORT OF LIFESTYLE.
I'LL BE CAREFUL.
NOT USED TO THIS...?
OKAY. AS LONG AS YOU'RE CLEAR ON THAT.

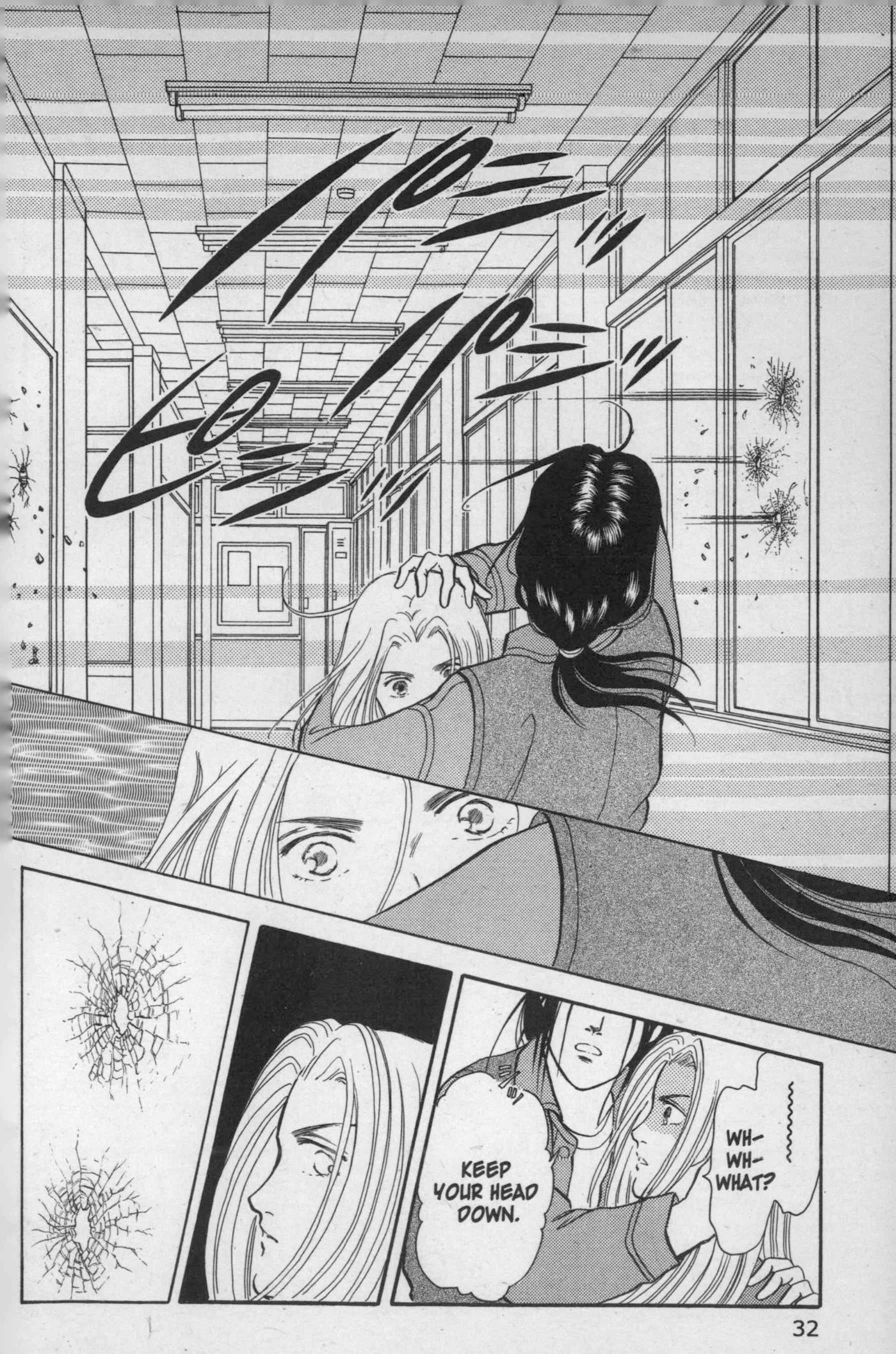
WH- WH- WHAT?
KEEP YOUR HEAD DOWN.

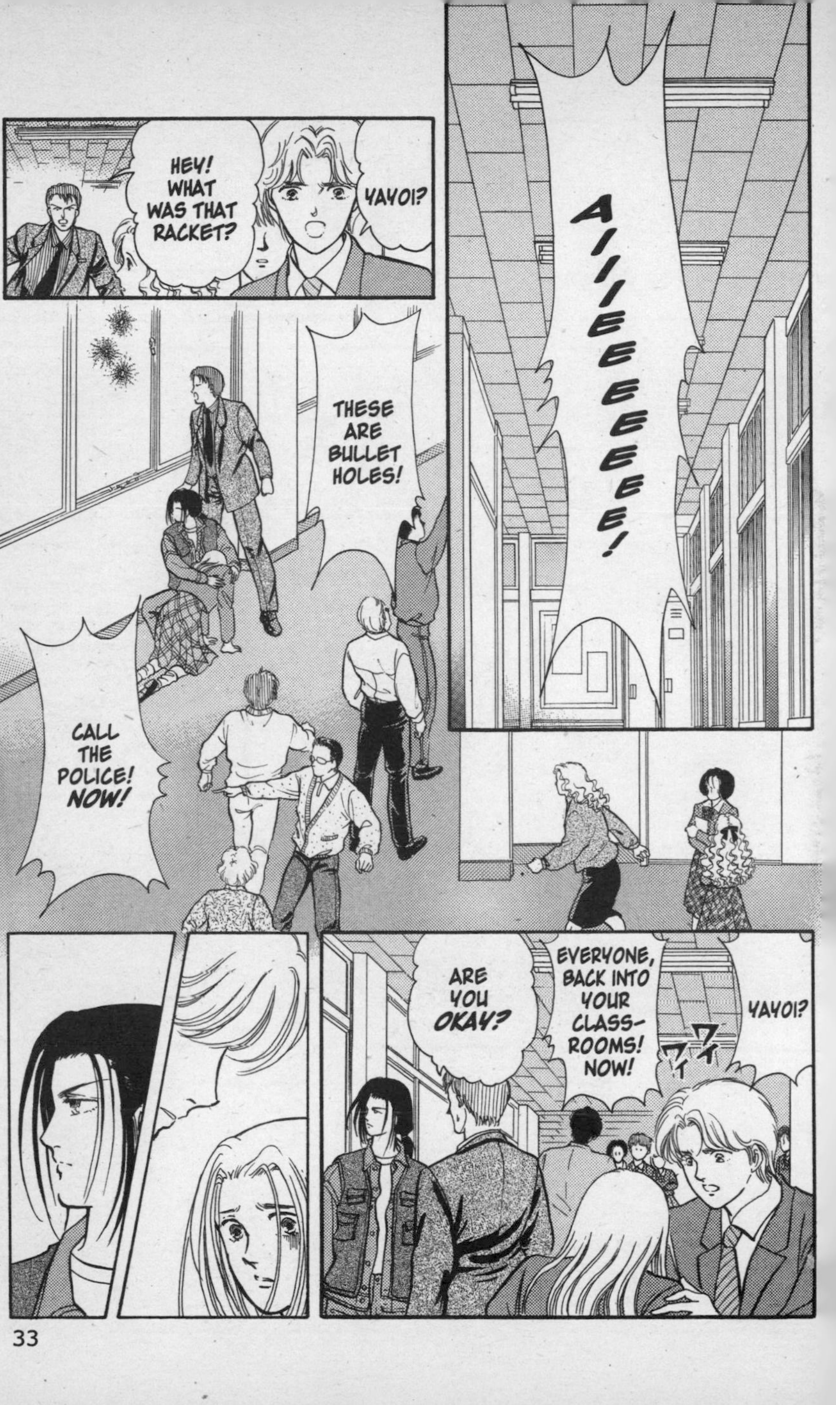
AIIIEEEEEEE!
YAYOI?
HEY! WHAT WAS THAT RACKET?
THESE ARE BULLET HOLES!
CALL THE POLICE! NOW!
YAYOI?
ワイワイ
EVERYONE, BACK INTO YOUR CLASS-ROOMS! NOW!
ARE YOU OKAY?

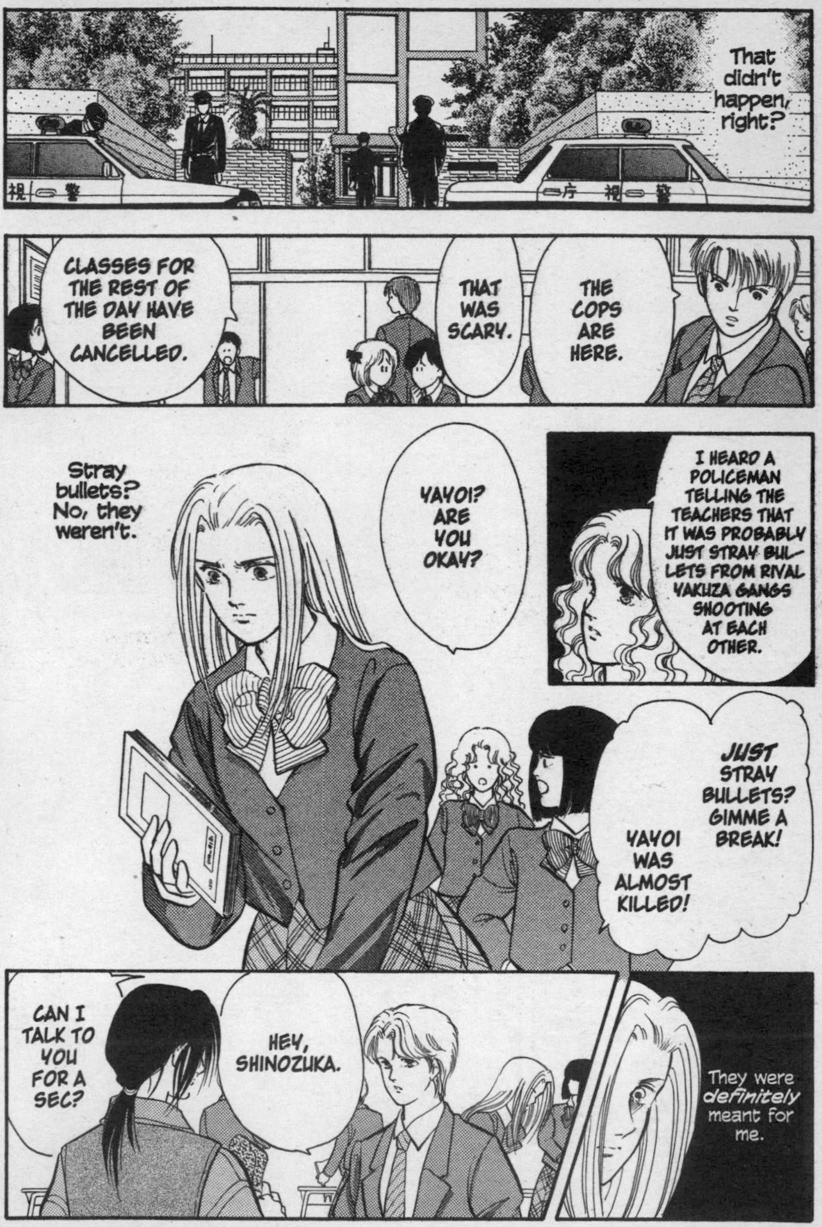
That didn't happen, right?
THE COPS ARE HERE.
THAT WAS SCARY.
CLASSES FOR THE REST OF THE DAY HAVE BEEN CANCELLED.
YAYOI? ARE YOU OKAY?
I HEARD A POLICEMAN TELLING THE TEACHERS THAT IT WAS PROBABLY JUST STRAY BULLETS FROM RIVAL YAKUZA GANGS SHOOTING AT EACH OTHER.
JUST STRAY BULLETS? GIMME A BREAK!
YAYOI WAS ALMOST KILLED!
Stray bullets? No, they weren't.
They were *definitely* meant for me.
HEY, SHINOZUKA.
CAN I TALK TO YOU FOR A SEC?

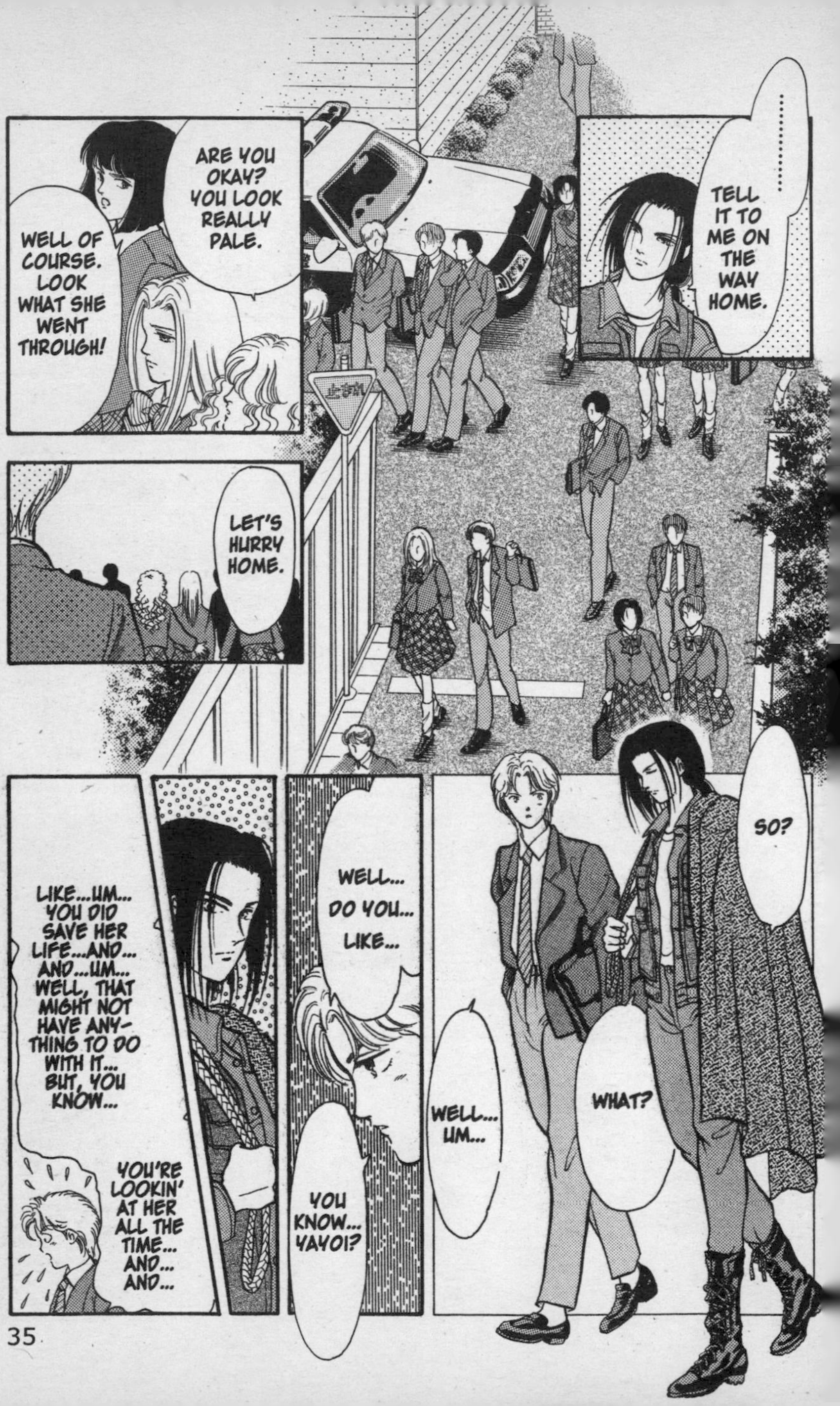
......
TELL IT TO ME ON THE WAY HOME.
ARE YOU OKAY? YOU LOOK REALLY PALE.
WELL OF COURSE. LOOK WHAT SHE WENT THROUGH!
LET'S HURRY HOME.
SO?
WHAT?
WELL... UM...
WELL... DO YOU... LIKE...
YOU KNOW... YAYOI?
LIKE...UM... YOU DID SAVE HER LIFE...AND... AND...UM... WELL, THAT MIGHT NOT HAVE ANY-THING TO DO WITH IT... BUT, YOU KNOW...
YOU'RE LOOKIN' AT HER ALL THE TIME... AND... AND...

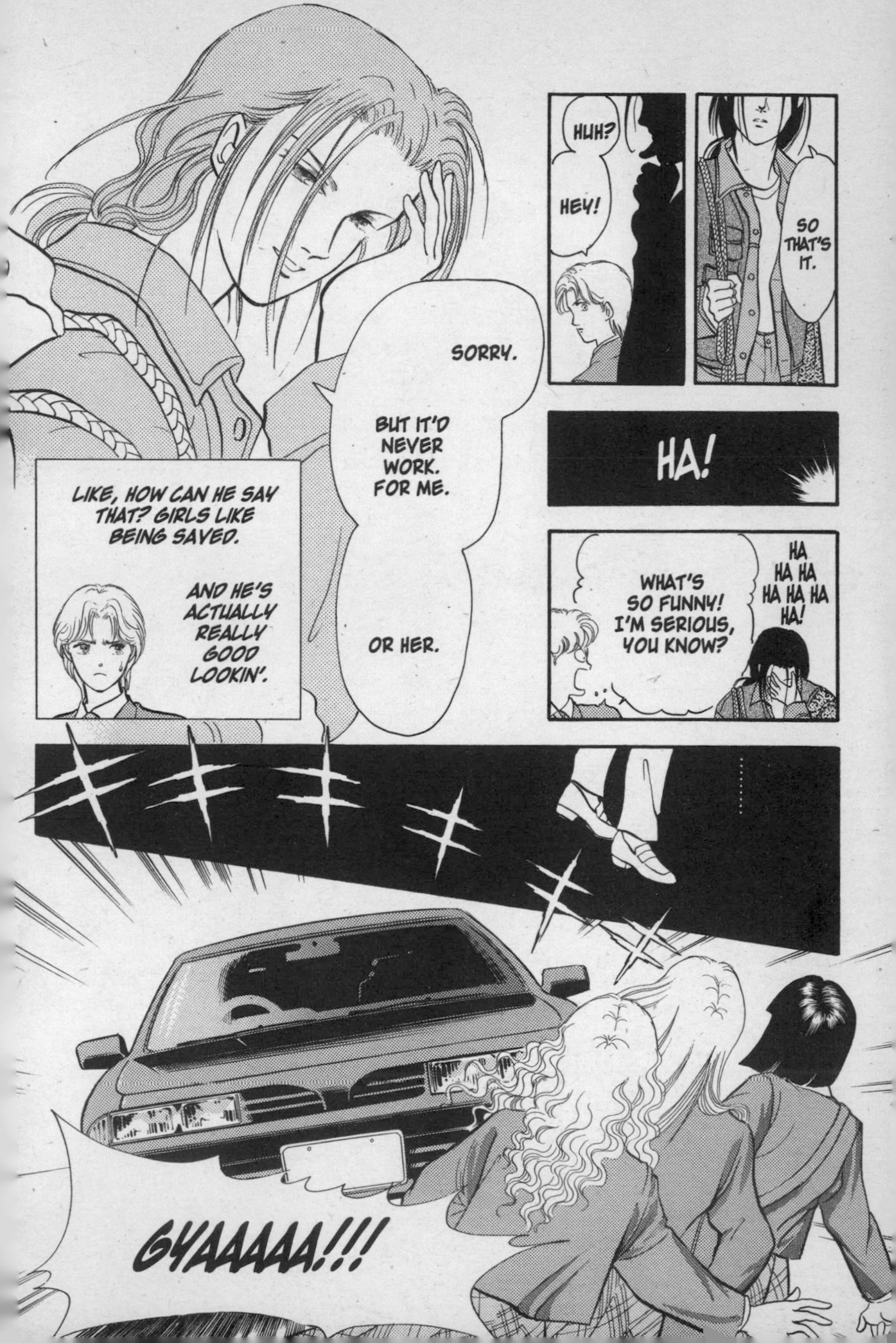
SO THAT'S IT.
HUH?
HEY!
HA!
HA HA HA HA HA HA HA!
WHAT'S SO FUNNY! I'M SERIOUS, YOU KNOW?
SORRY.
BUT IT'D NEVER WORK. FOR ME.
OR HER.
LIKE, HOW CAN HE SAY THAT? GIRLS LIKE BEING SAVED.
AND HE'S ACTUALLY REALLY GOOD LOOKIN'.
......
GYAAAAA!!!

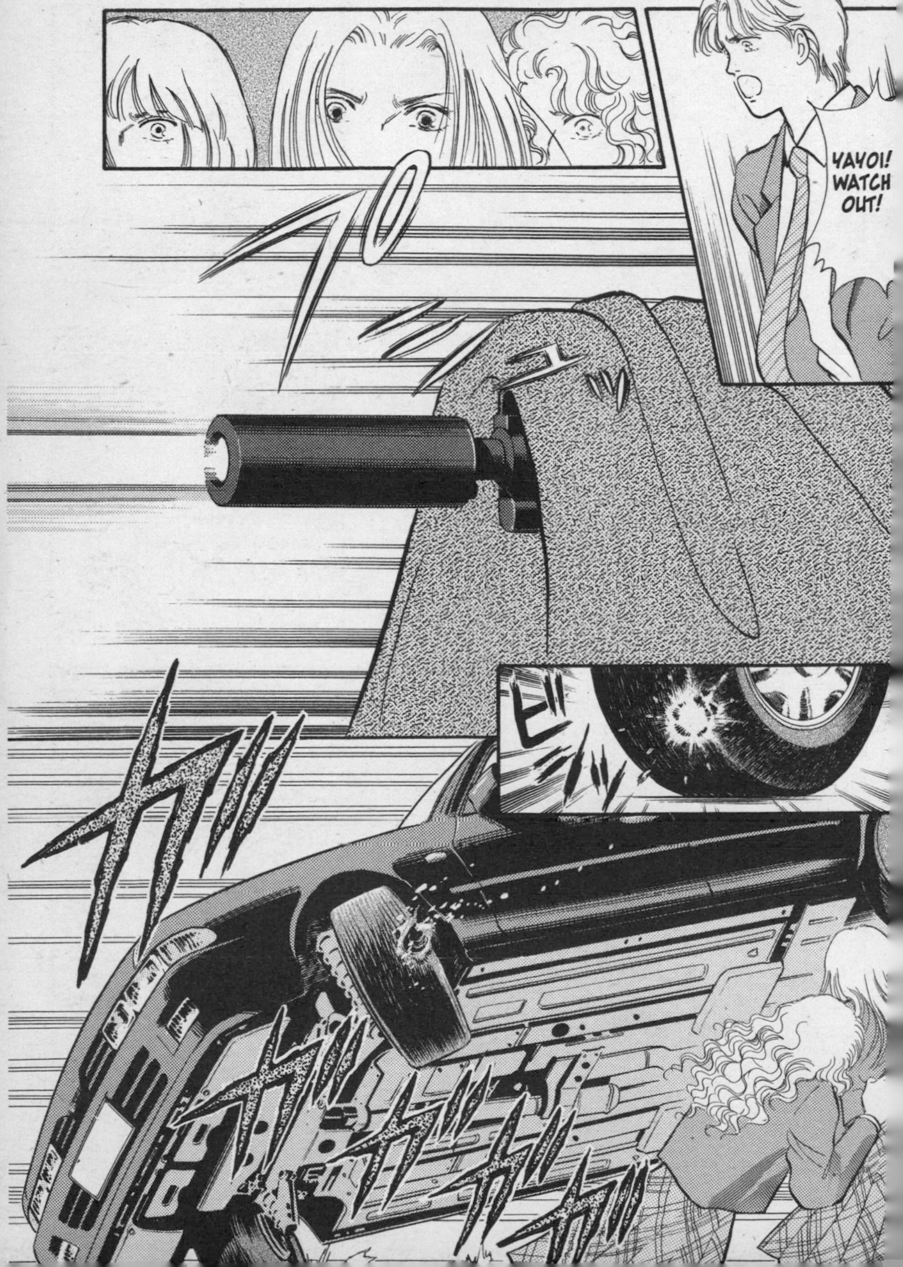
YAYOI! WATCH OUT!

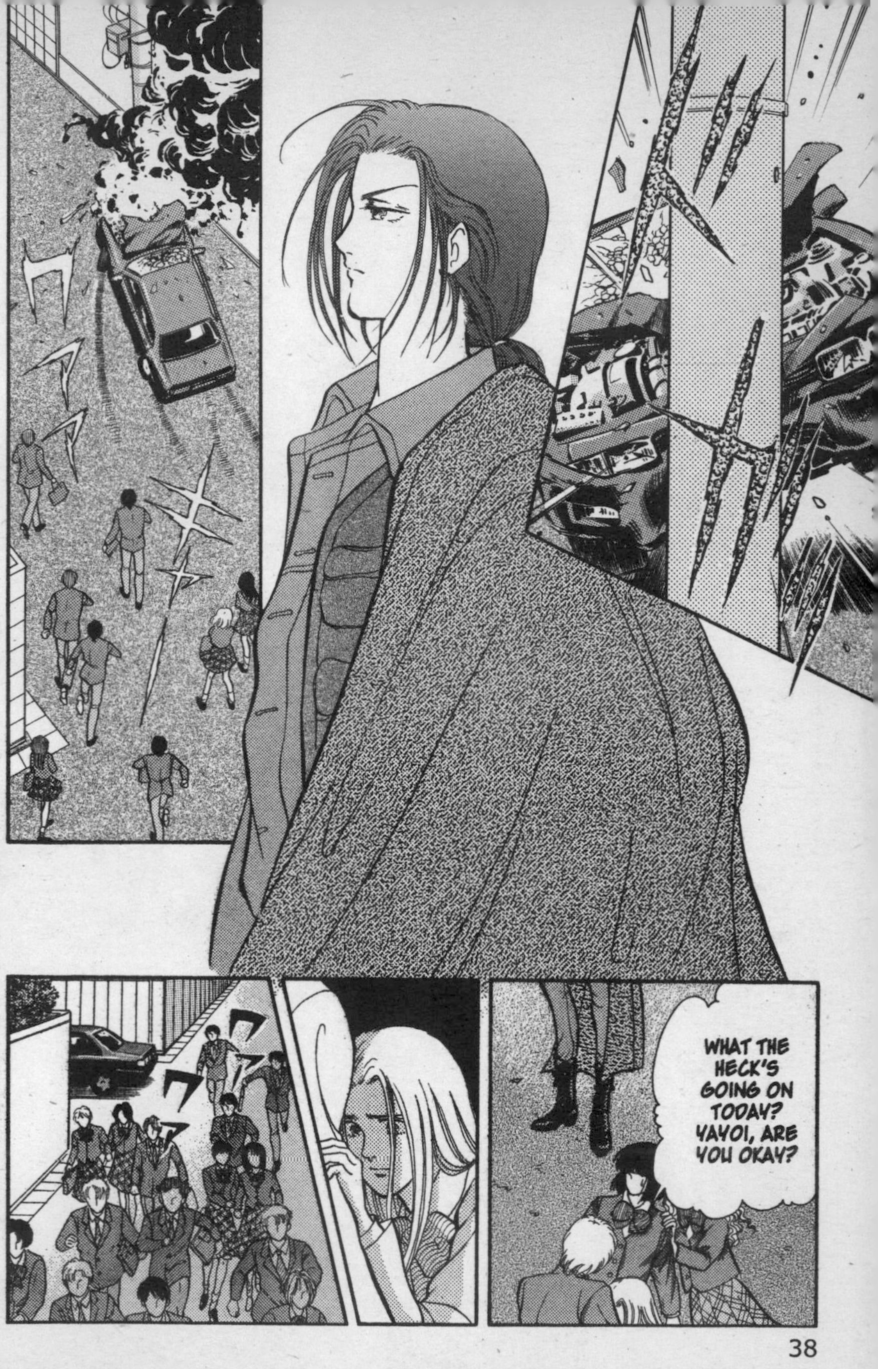
WHAT THE HECK'S GOING ON TODAY? YAYOI, ARE YOU OKAY?

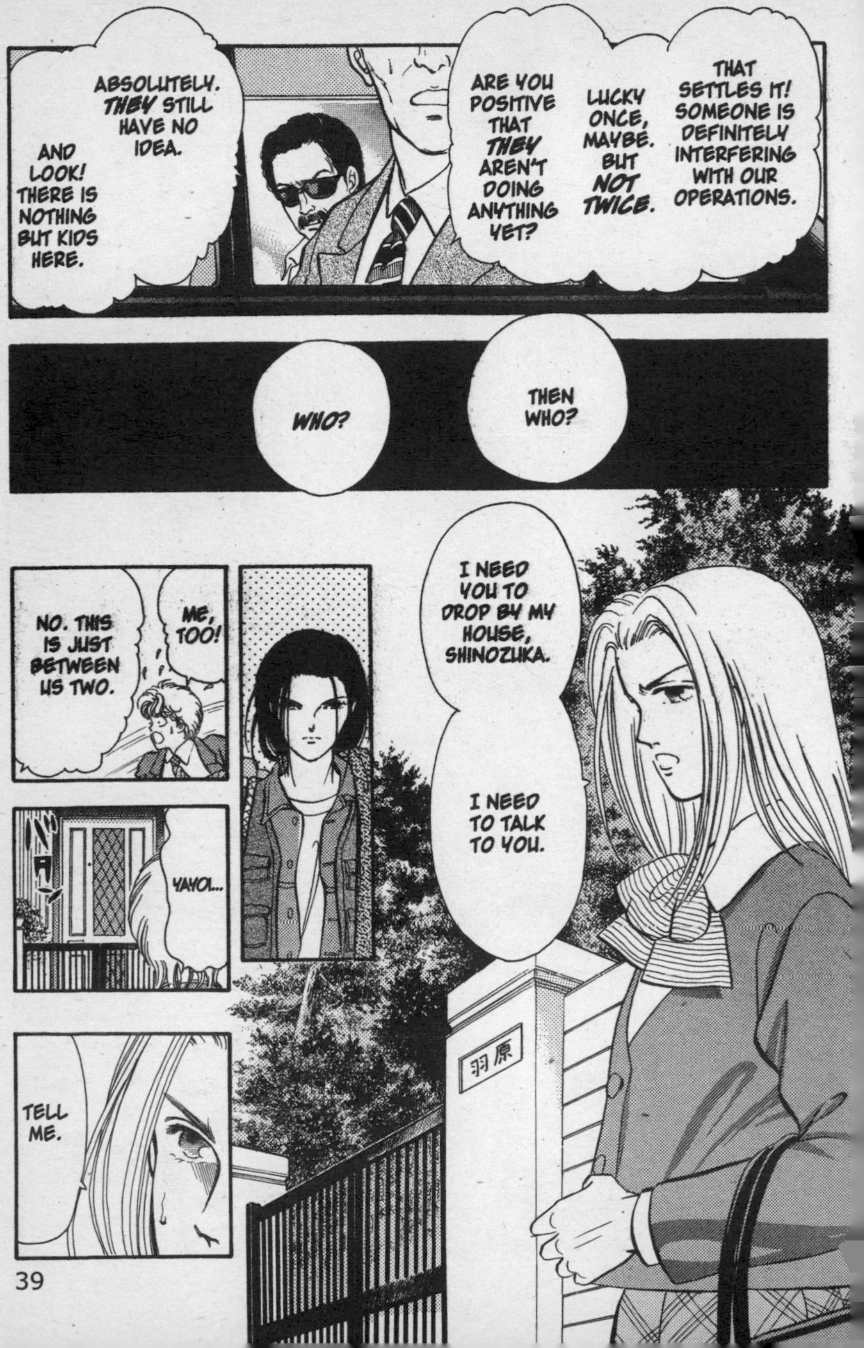
THAT SETTLES IT! SOMEONE IS DEFINITELY INTERFERING WITH OUR OPERATIONS.
LUCKY ONCE, MAYBE. BUT NOT TWICE.
ARE YOU POSITIVE THAT THEY AREN'T DOING ANYTHING YET?
ABSOLUTELY. THEY STILL HAVE NO IDEA.
AND LOOK! THERE IS NOTHING BUT KIDS HERE.
THEN WHO?
WHO?
I NEED YOU TO DROP BY MY HOUSE, SHINOZUKA.
I NEED TO TALK TO YOU.
羽原
ME, TOO!
NO. THIS IS JUST BETWEEN US TWO.
YAYOI...
TELL ME.

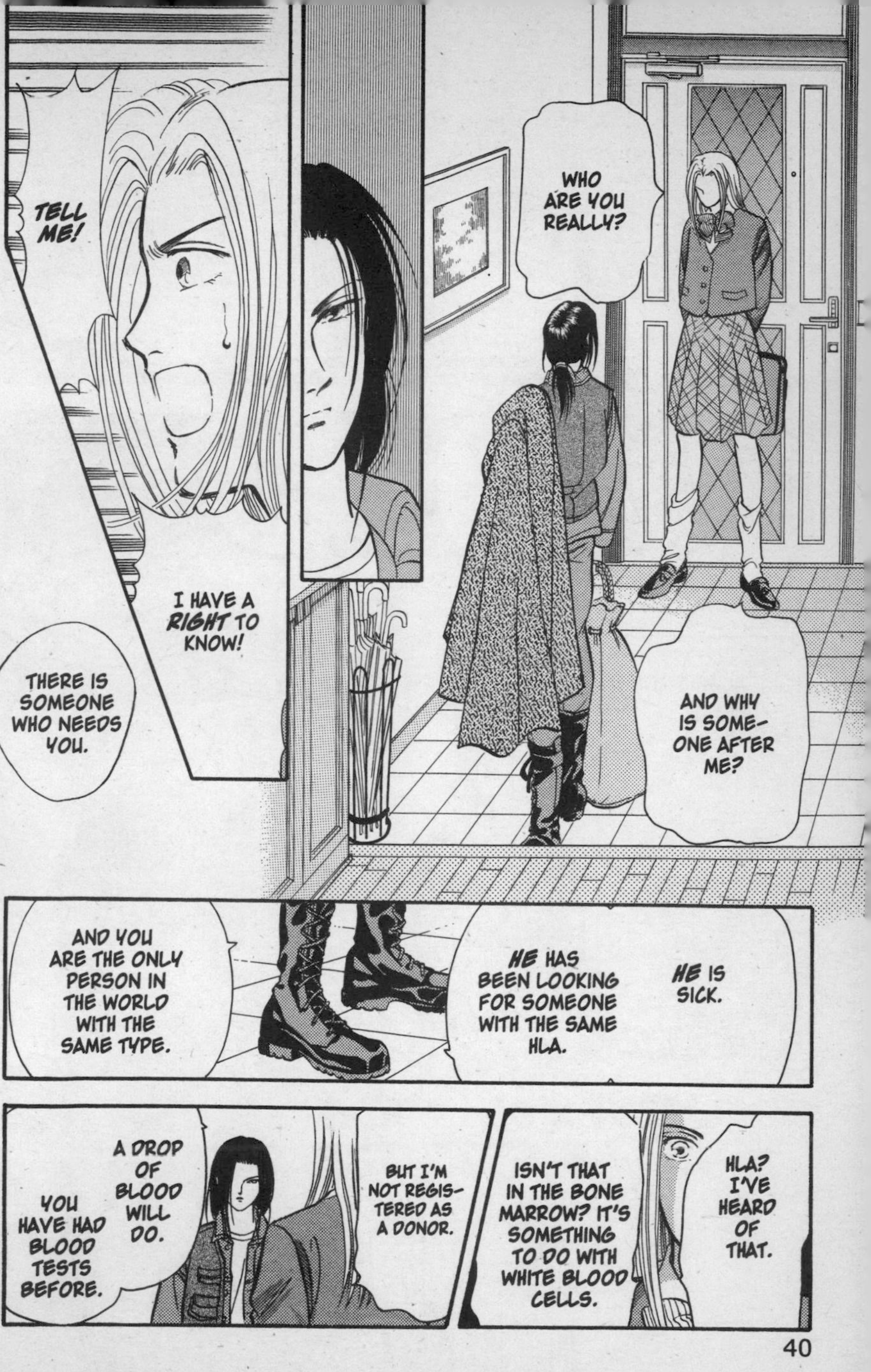
WHO ARE YOU REALLY?
AND WHY IS SOME-ONE AFTER ME?
TELL ME!
I HAVE A RIGHT TO KNOW!
THERE IS SOMEONE WHO NEEDS YOU.
HE IS SICK.
HE HAS BEEN LOOKING FOR SOMEONE WITH THE SAME HLA.
AND YOU ARE THE ONLY PERSON IN THE WORLD WITH THE SAME TYPE.
HLA? I'VE HEARD OF THAT.
ISN'T THAT IN THE BONE MARROW? IT'S SOMETHING TO DO WITH WHITE BLOOD CELLS.
BUT I'M NOT REGIS-TERED AS A DONOR.
A DROP OF BLOOD WILL DO.
YOU HAVE HAD BLOOD TESTS BEFORE.

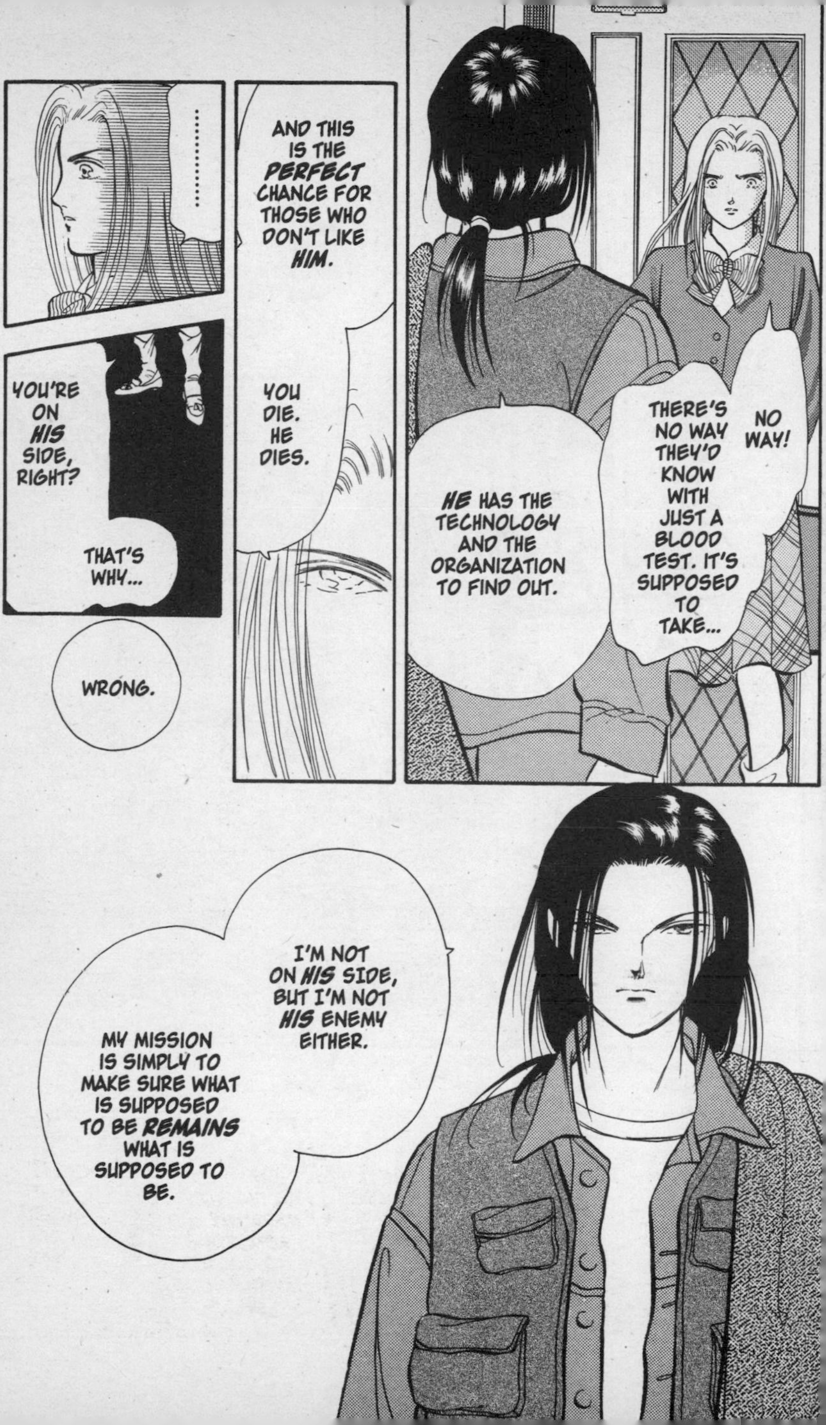
NO WAY!
THERE'S NO WAY THEY'D KNOW WITH JUST A BLOOD TEST. IT'S SUPPOSED TO TAKE...
HE HAS THE TECHNOLOGY AND THE ORGANIZATION TO FIND OUT.
AND THIS IS THE PERFECT CHANCE FOR THOSE WHO DON'T LIKE HIM.
YOU DIE. HE DIES.
......
YOU'RE ON HIS SIDE, RIGHT?
THAT'S WHY...
WRONG.
I'M NOT ON HIS SIDE, BUT I'M NOT HIS ENEMY EITHER.
MY MISSION IS SIMPLY TO MAKE SURE WHAT IS SUPPOSED TO BE REMAINS WHAT IS SUPPOSED TO BE.

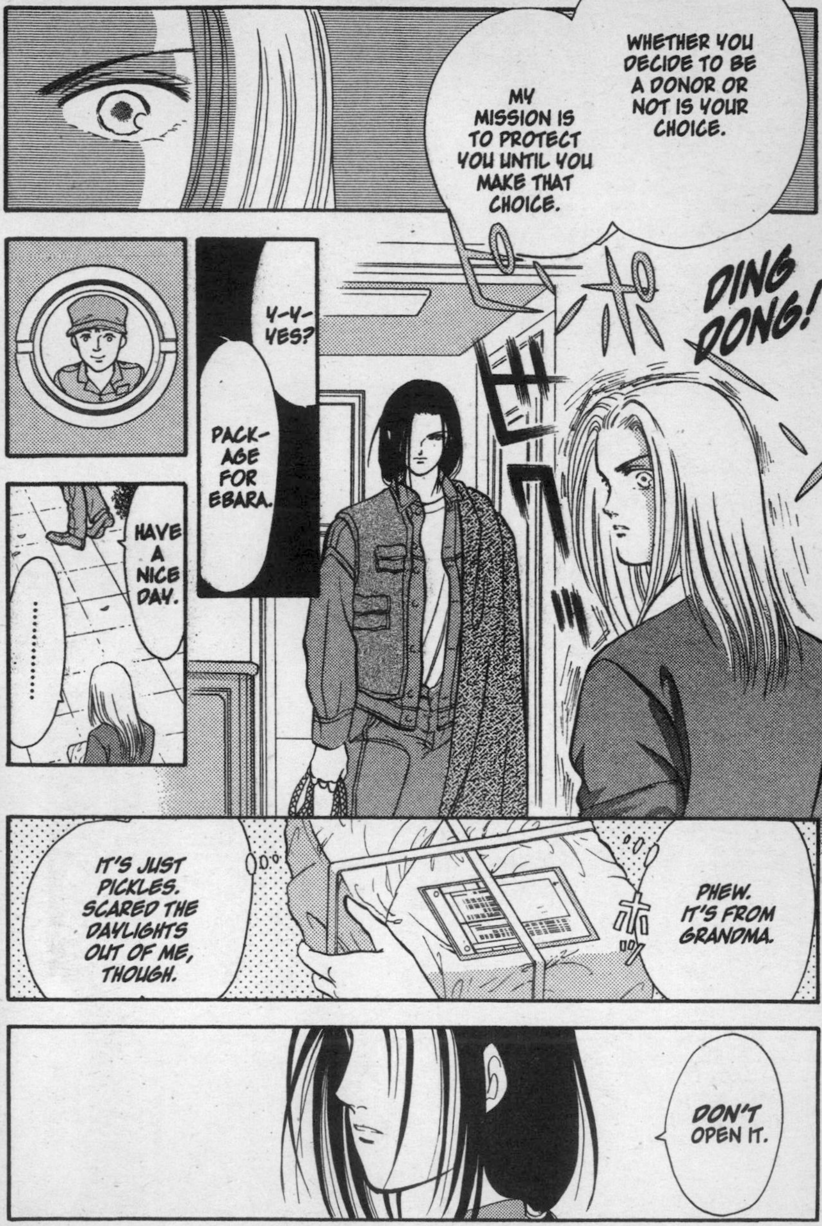
WHETHER YOU DECIDE TO BE A DONOR OR NOT IS YOUR CHOICE.
MY MISSION IS TO PROTECT YOU UNTIL YOU MAKE THAT CHOICE.
DING DONG!
Y-Y-YES?
PACKAGE FOR EBARA.
HAVE A NICE DAY.
......
PHEW. IT'S FROM GRANDMA.
IT'S JUST PICKLES. SCARED THE DAYLIGHTS OUT OF ME, THOUGH.
DON'T OPEN IT.

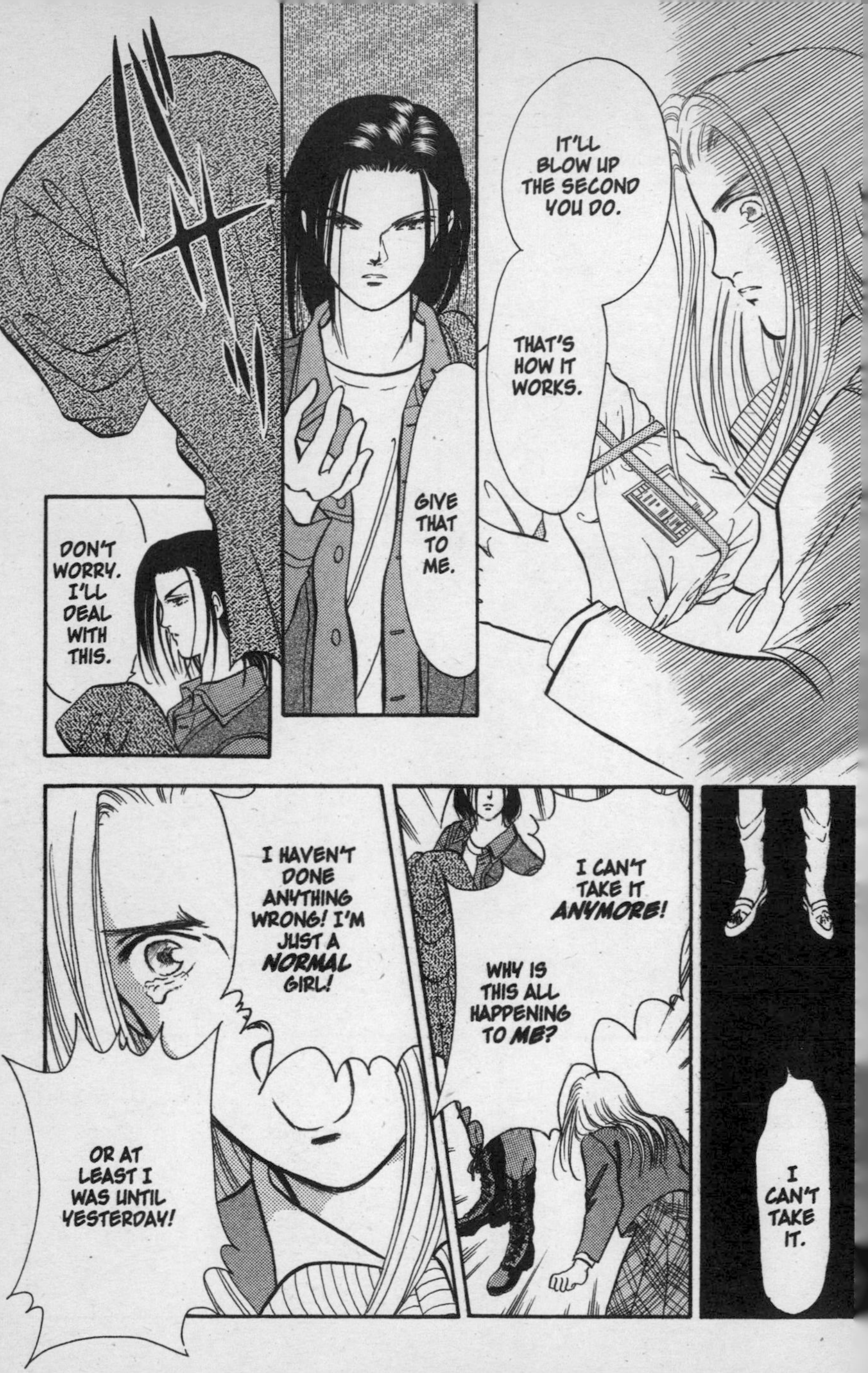
IT'LL BLOW UP THE SECOND YOU DO.
THAT'S HOW IT WORKS.
GIVE THAT TO ME.
DON'T WORRY. I'LL DEAL WITH THIS.
I CAN'T TAKE IT.
I CAN'T TAKE IT ANYMORE!
WHY IS THIS ALL HAPPENING TO ME?
I HAVEN'T DONE ANYTHING WRONG! I'M JUST A NORMAL GIRL!
OR AT LEAST I WAS UNTIL YESTERDAY!

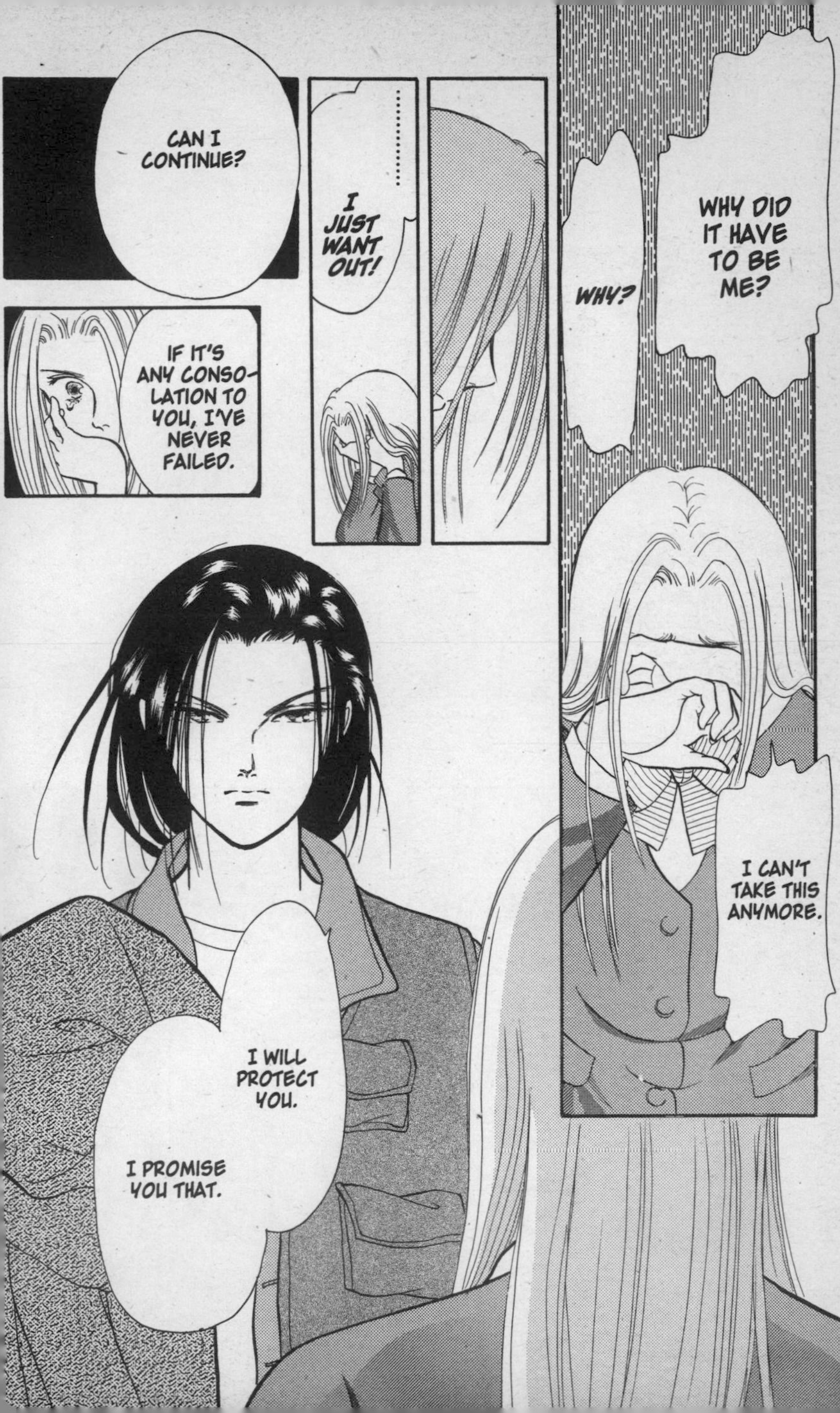
WHY DID IT HAVE TO BE ME?
WHY?
I CAN'T TAKE THIS ANYMORE.
...... I JUST WANT OUT!
CAN I CONTINUE?
IF IT'S ANY CONSOLATION TO YOU, I'VE NEVER FAILED.
I WILL PROTECT YOU.
I PROMISE YOU THAT.

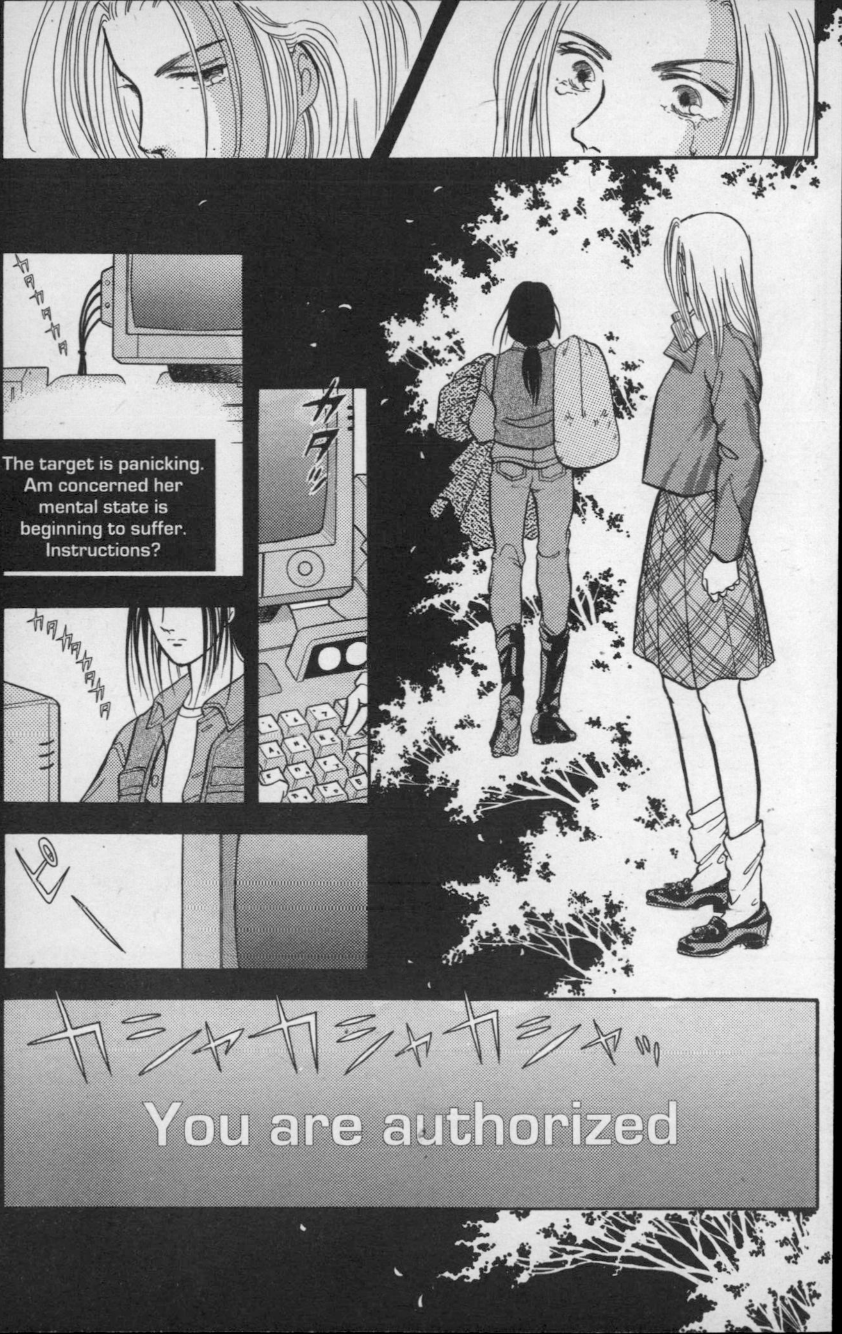
The target is panicking.
Am concerned her
mental state is
beginning to suffer.
Instructions?
カシャカシャカシャ
You are authorized

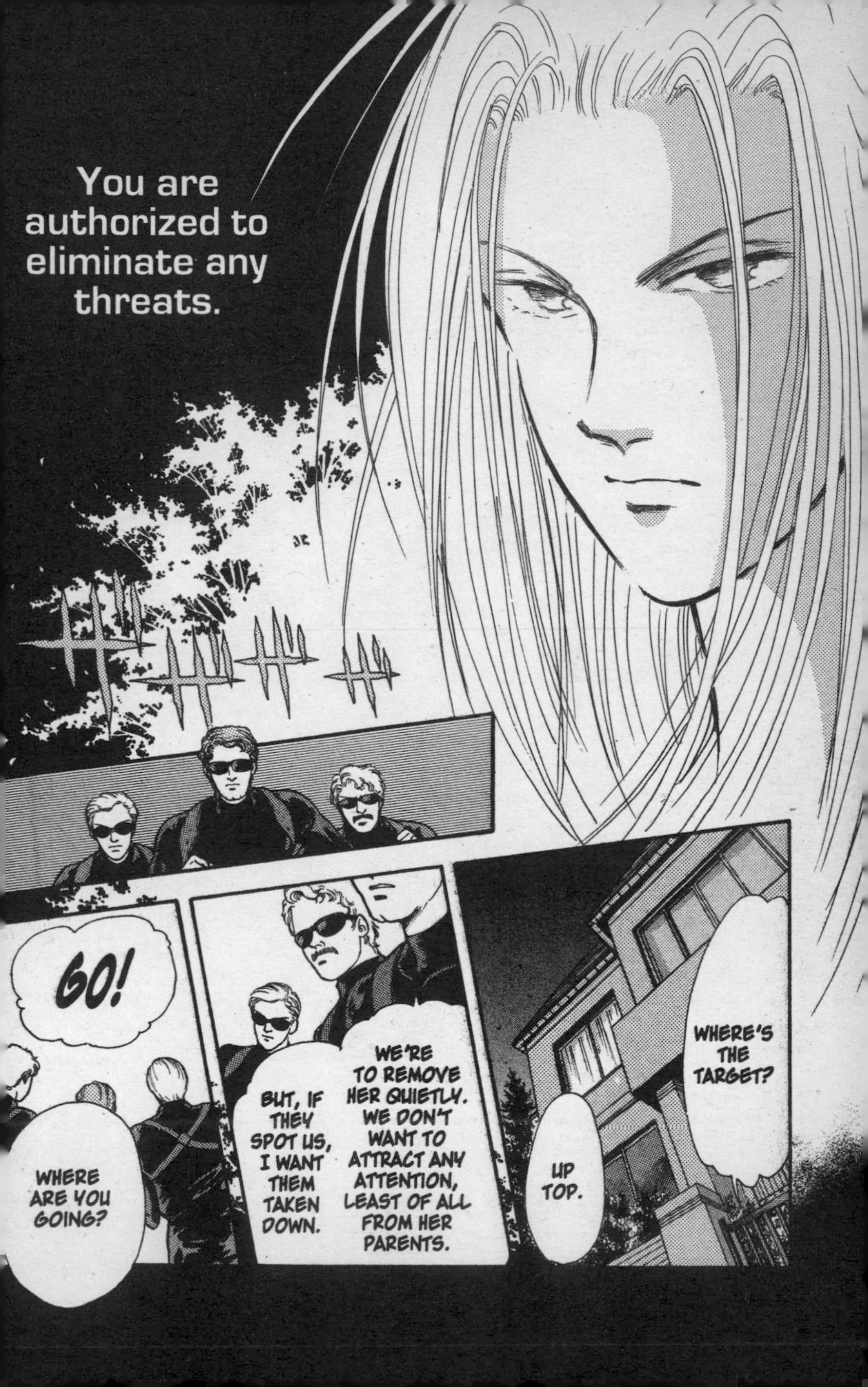
You are authorized to eliminate any threats.
WHERE'S THE TARGET?
UP TOP.
WE'RE TO REMOVE HER QUIETLY. WE DON'T WANT TO ATTRACT ANY ATTENTION, LEAST OF ALL FROM HER PARENTS.
BUT, IF THEY SPOT US, I WANT THEM TAKEN DOWN.
GO!
WHERE ARE YOU GOING?

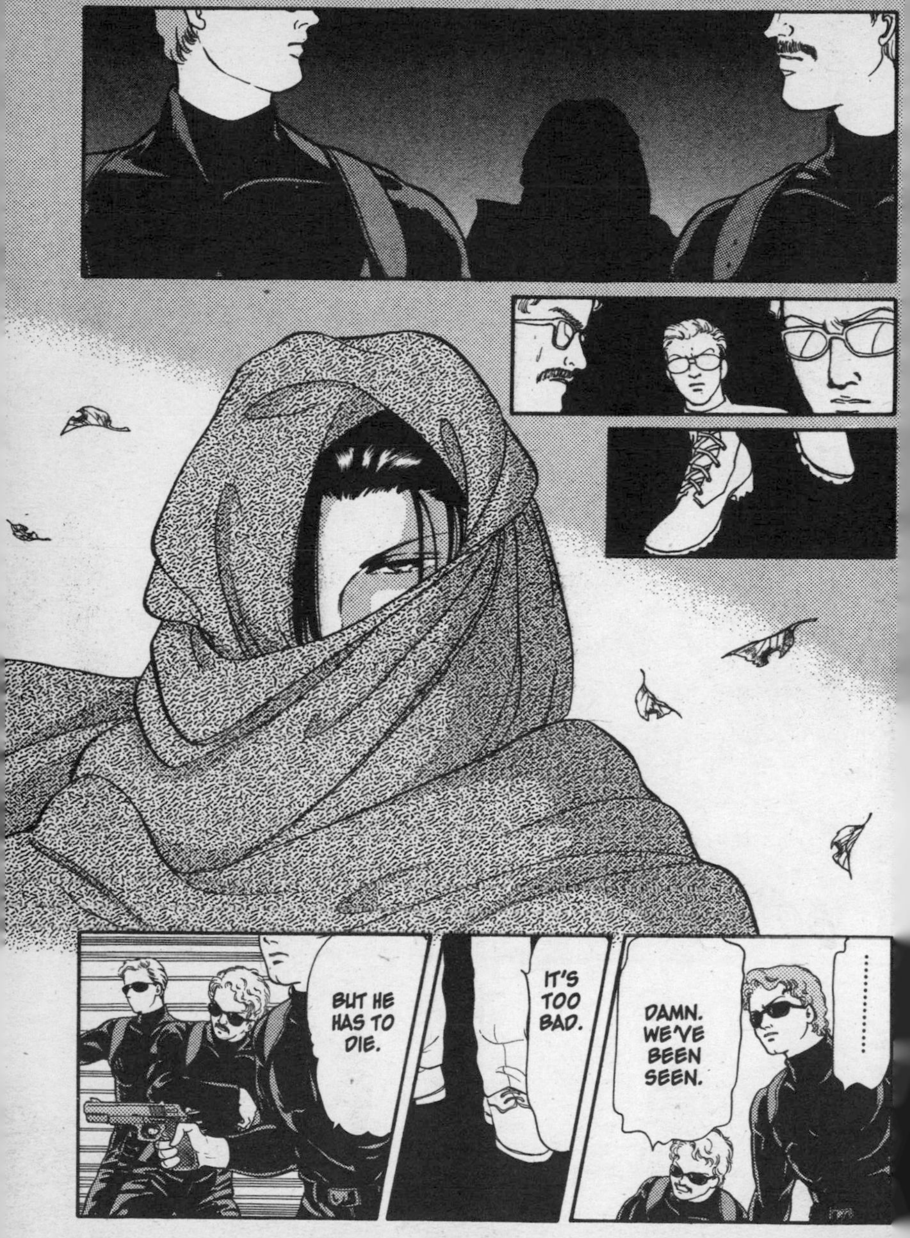
......
DAMN. WE'VE BEEN SEEN.
IT'S TOO BAD.
BUT HE HAS TO DIE.

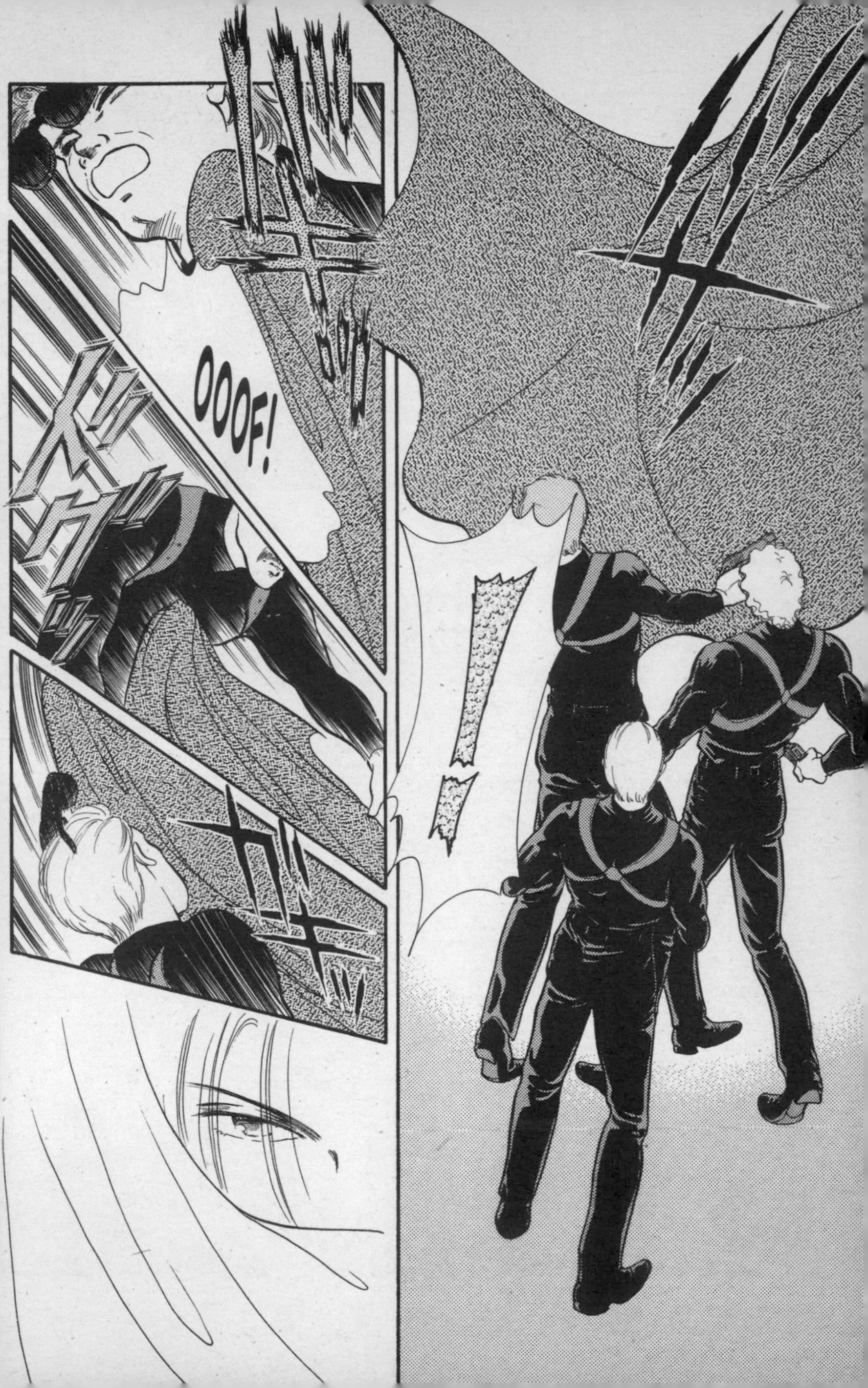
OOOF!

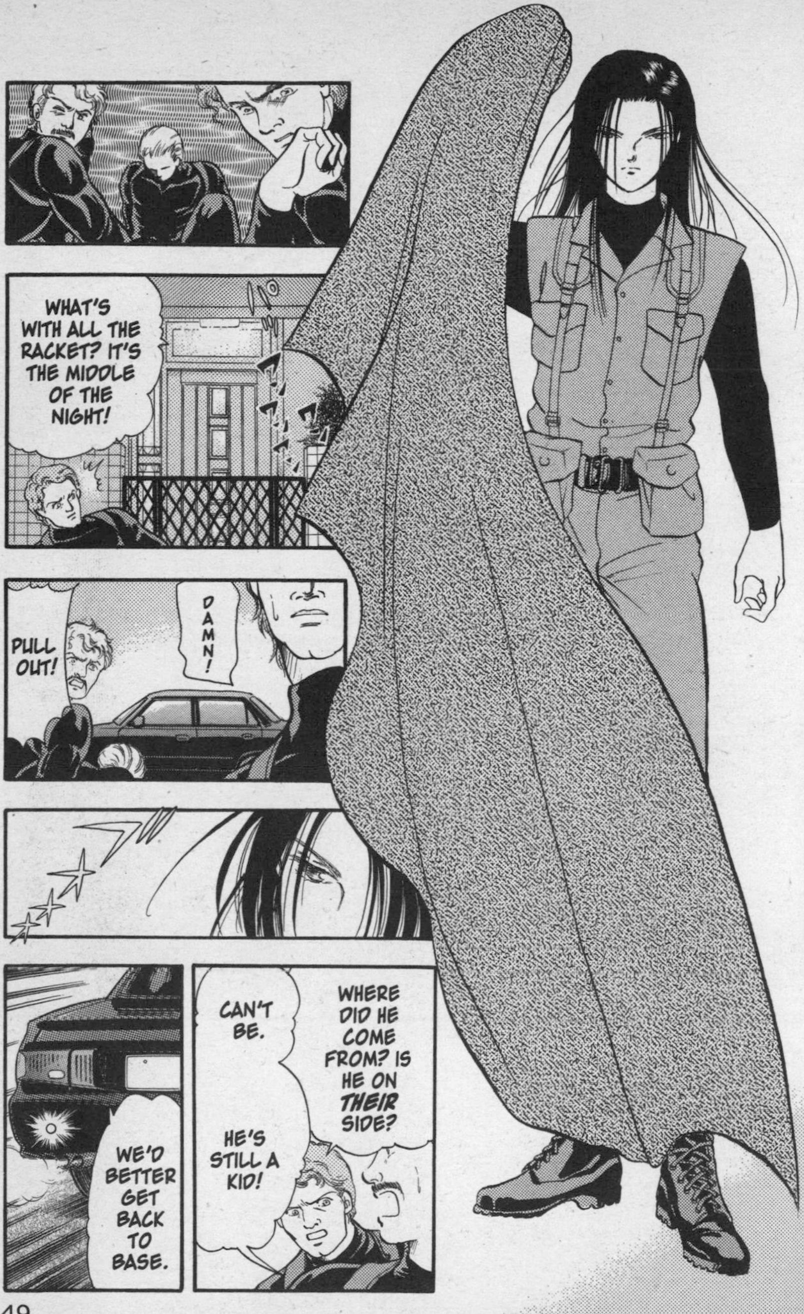
WHAT'S WITH ALL THE RACKET? IT'S THE MIDDLE OF THE NIGHT!
DAMN!
PULL OUT!
WHERE DID HE COME FROM? IS HE ON *THEIR* SIDE?
CAN'T BE.
HE'S STILL A KID!
WE'D BETTER GET BACK TO BASE.

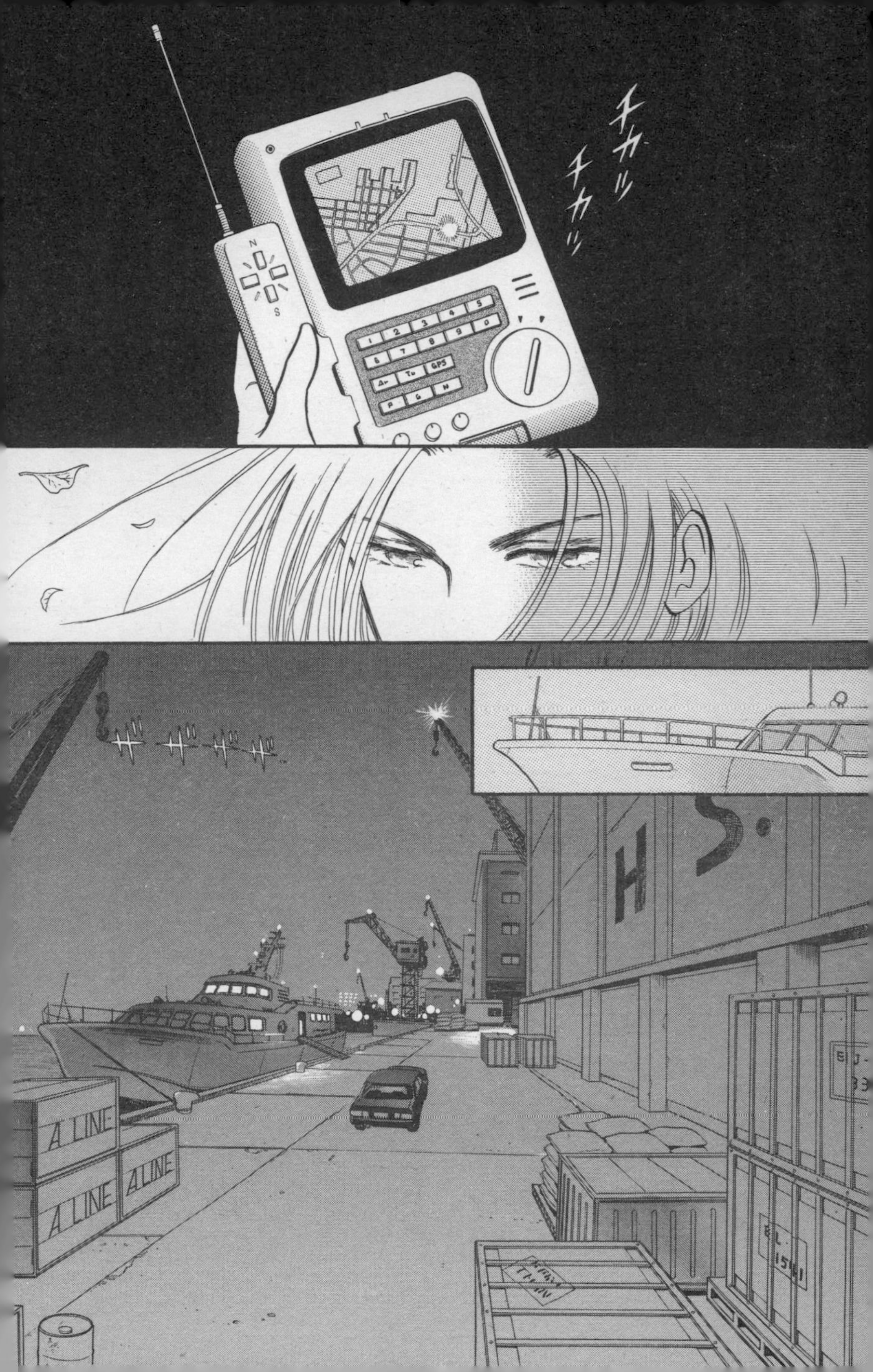
チカッ
チカッ
N
S
GPS
A LINE
A LINE
A LINE

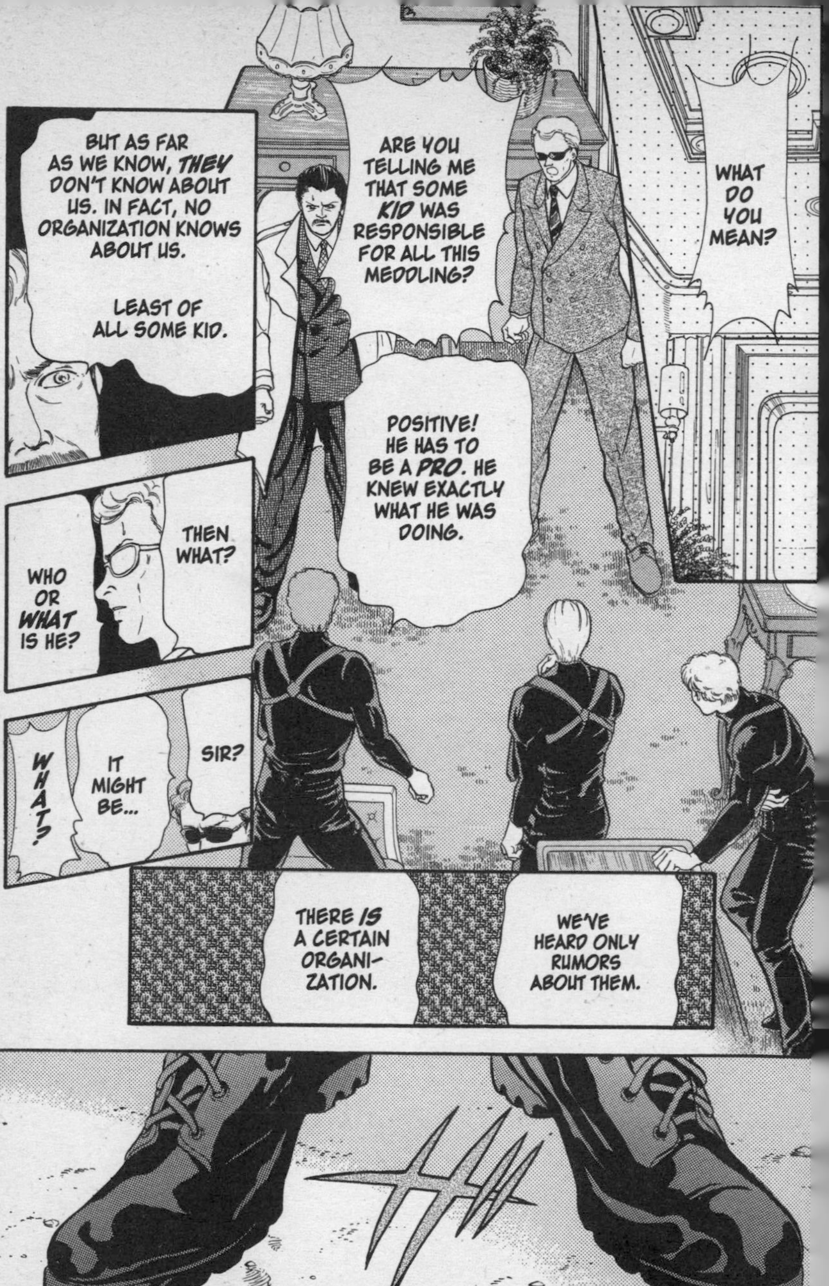
WHAT DO YOU MEAN?
ARE YOU TELLING ME THAT SOME KID WAS RESPONSIBLE FOR ALL THIS MEDDLING?
POSITIVE! HE HAS TO BE A PRO. HE KNEW EXACTLY WHAT HE WAS DOING.
BUT AS FAR AS WE KNOW, THEY DON'T KNOW ABOUT US. IN FACT, NO ORGANIZATION KNOWS ABOUT US.
LEAST OF ALL SOME KID.
THEN WHAT?
WHO OR WHAT IS HE?
SIR?
IT MIGHT BE...
WHAT?
THERE IS A CERTAIN ORGANIZATION.
WE'VE HEARD ONLY RUMORS ABOUT THEM.

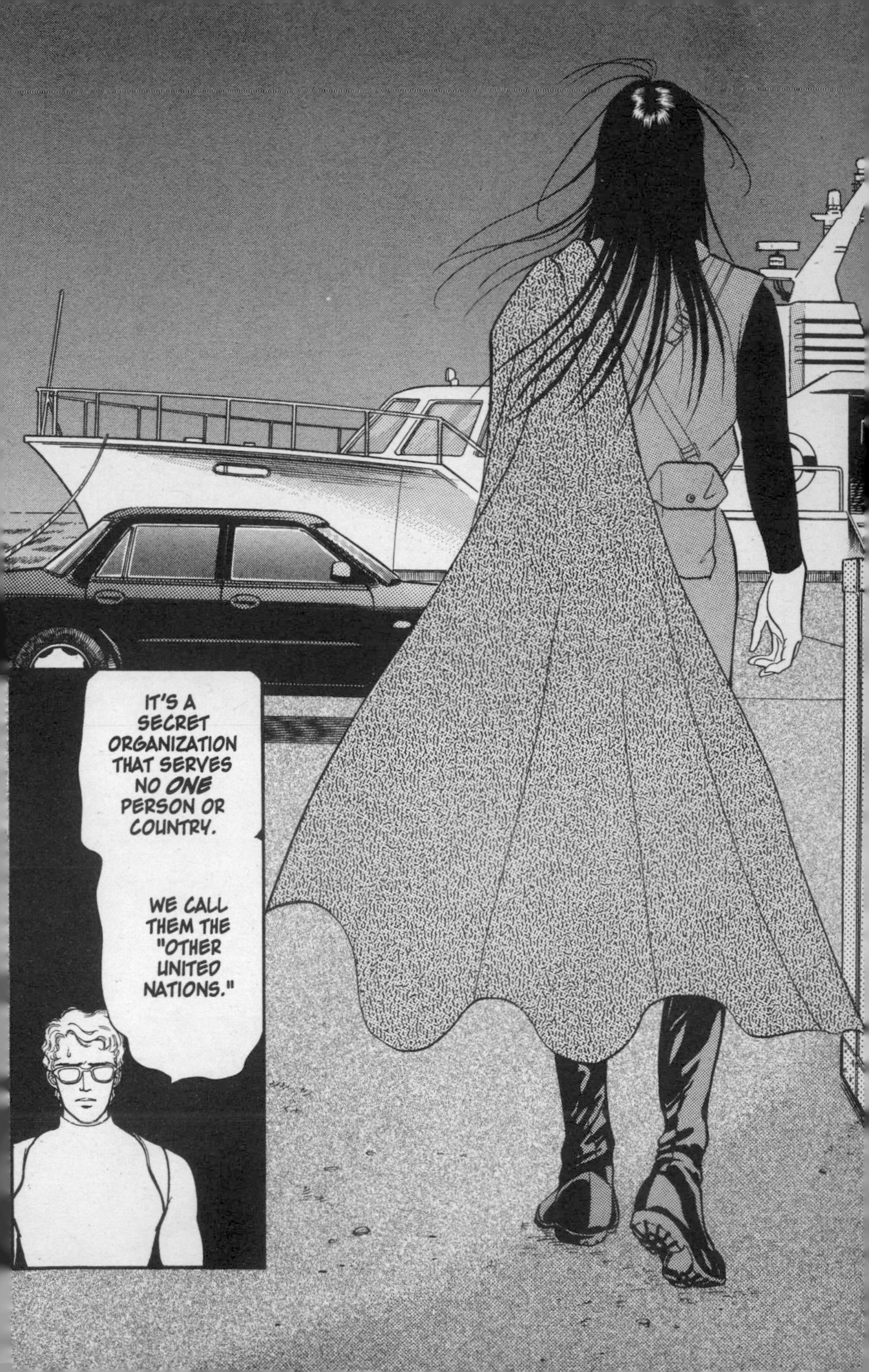
IT'S A SECRET ORGANIZATION THAT SERVES NO *ONE* PERSON OR COUNTRY.
WE CALL THEM THE "OTHER UNITED NATIONS."

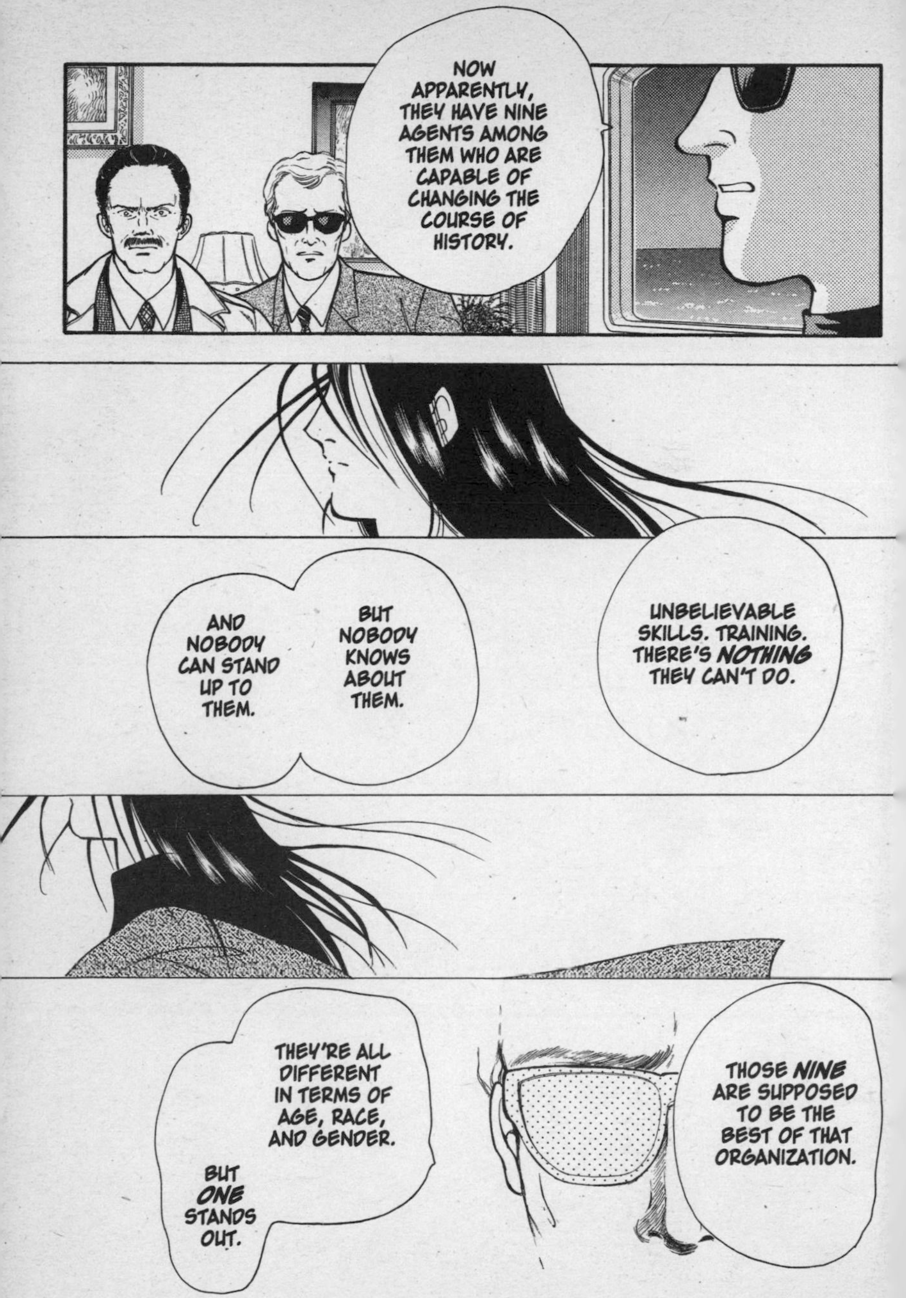
NOW APPARENTLY, THEY HAVE NINE AGENTS AMONG THEM WHO ARE CAPABLE OF CHANGING THE COURSE OF HISTORY.
UNBELIEVABLE SKILLS. TRAINING. THERE'S *NOTHING* THEY CAN'T DO.
BUT NOBODY KNOWS ABOUT THEM.
AND NOBODY CAN STAND UP TO THEM.
THOSE *NINE* ARE SUPPOSED TO BE THE BEST OF THAT ORGANIZATION.
THEY'RE ALL DIFFERENT IN TERMS OF AGE, RACE, AND GENDER.
BUT *ONE* STANDS OUT.

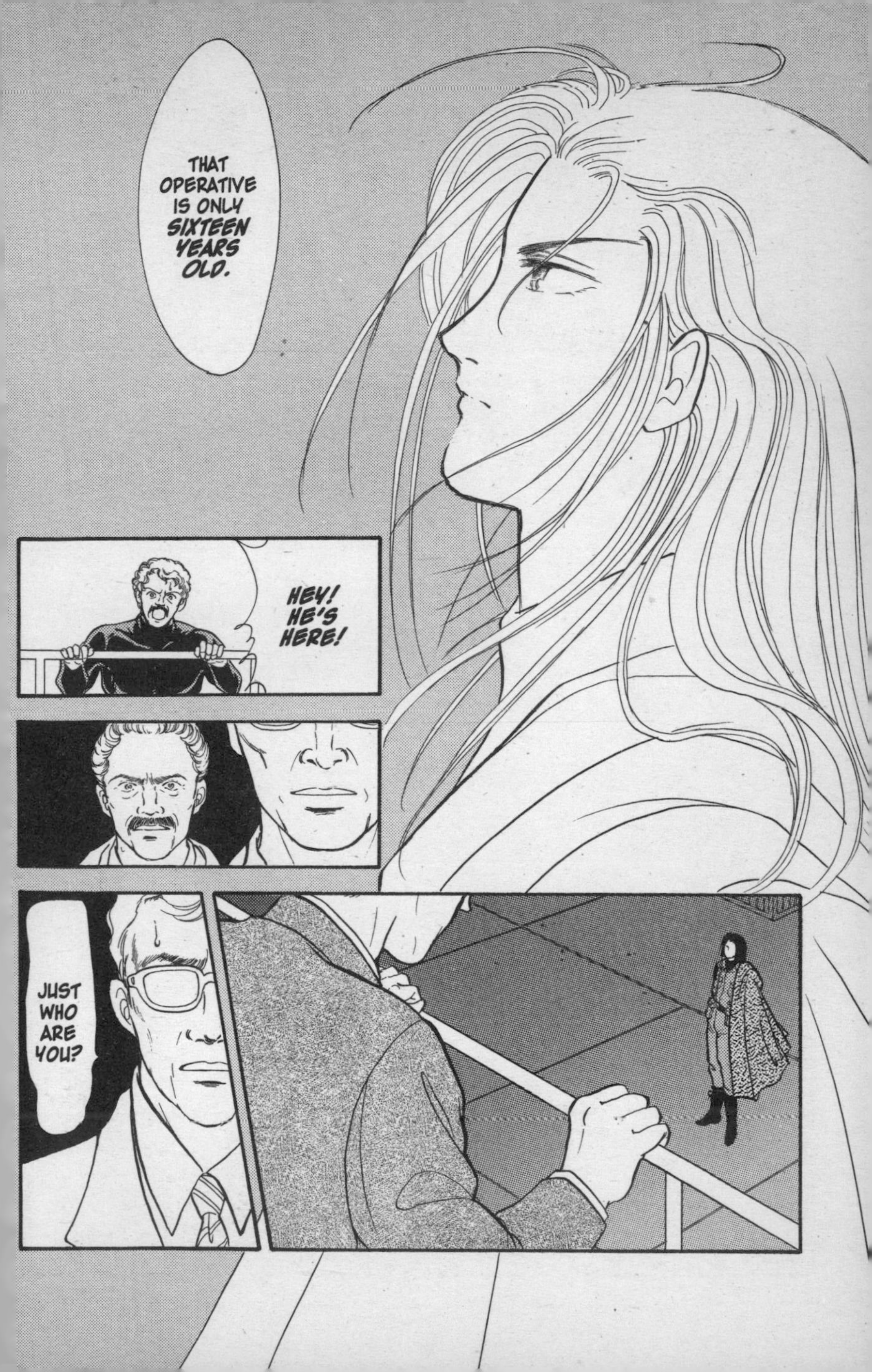
THAT OPERATIVE IS ONLY SIXTEEN YEARS OLD.
HEY! HE'S HERE!
JUST WHO ARE YOU?

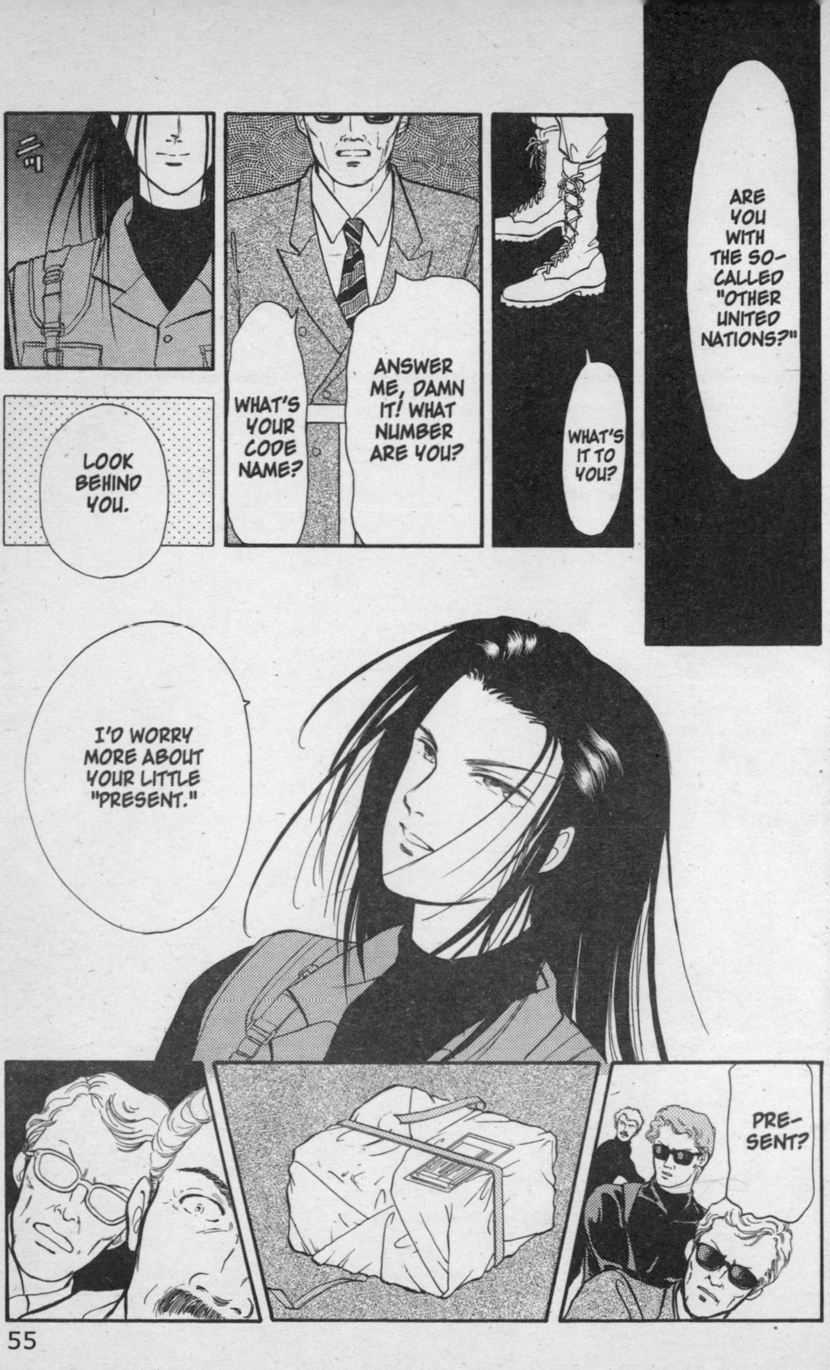
ARE YOU WITH THE SO-CALLED "OTHER UNITED NATIONS?"
WHAT'S IT TO YOU?
ANSWER ME, DAMN IT! WHAT NUMBER ARE YOU?
WHAT'S YOUR CODE NAME?
ニッ
LOOK BEHIND YOU.
I'D WORRY MORE ABOUT YOUR LITTLE "PRESENT."
PRE-SENT?

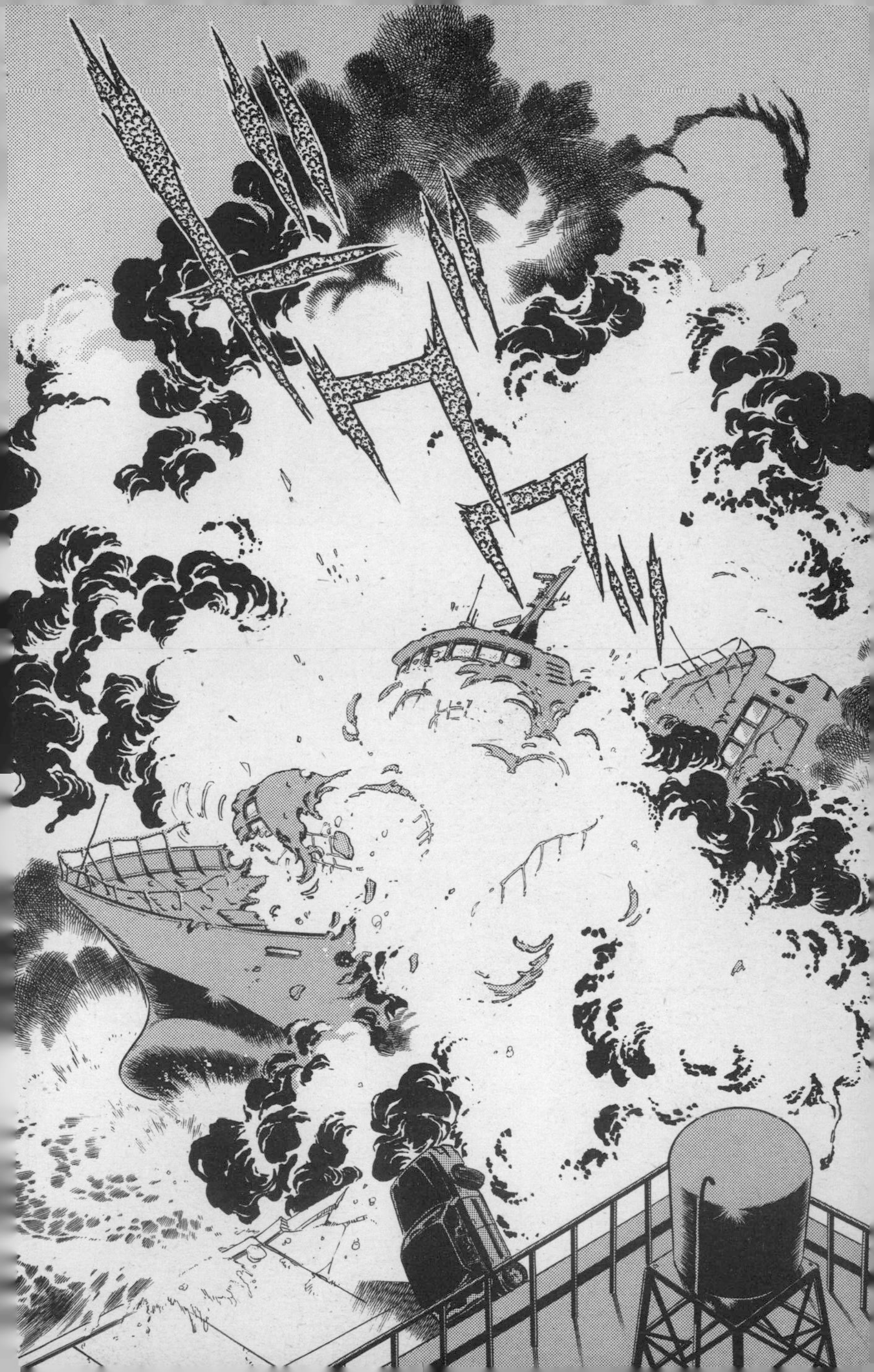

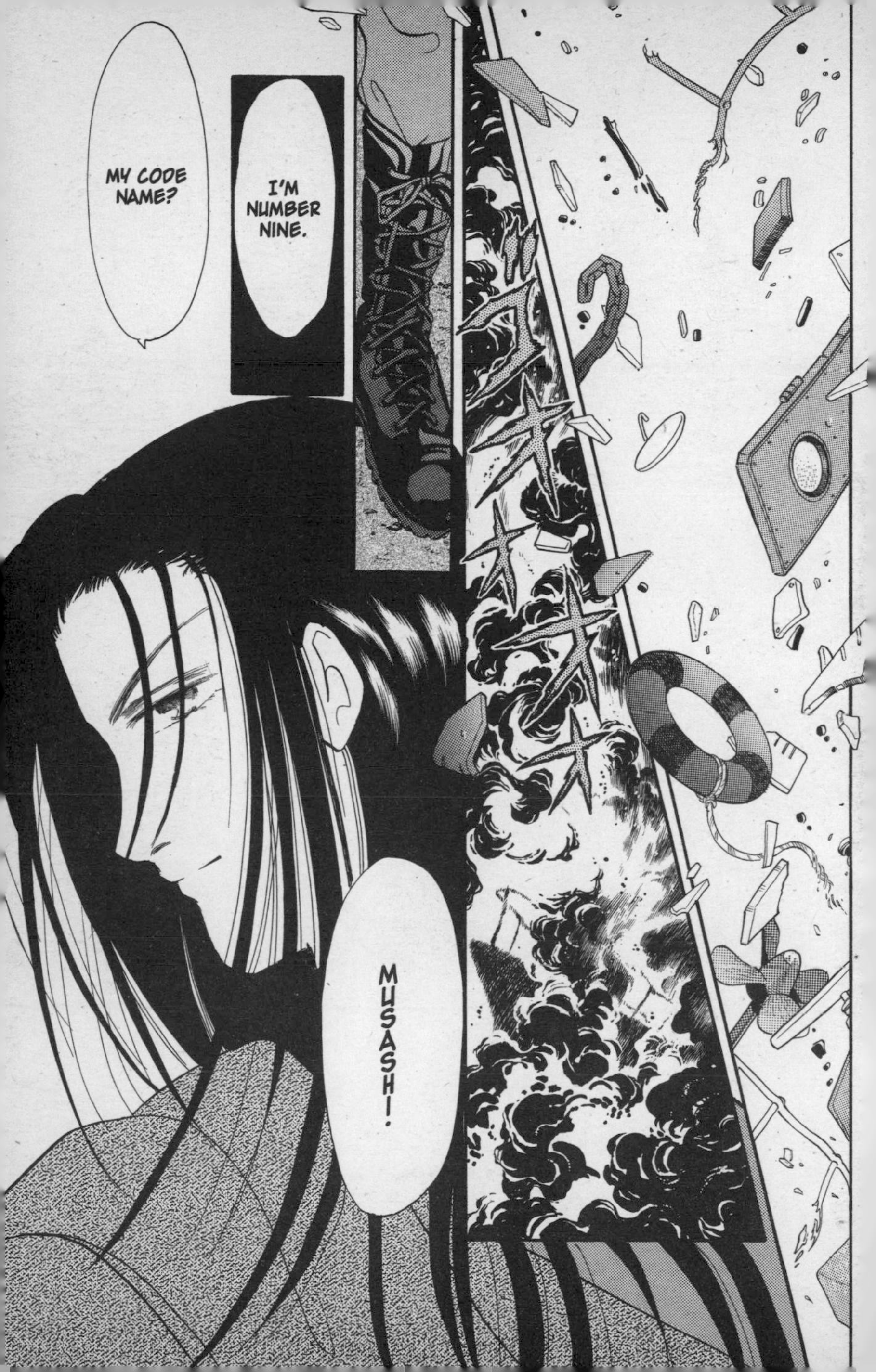
MY CODE NAME?
I'M NUMBER NINE.
MUSASHI!

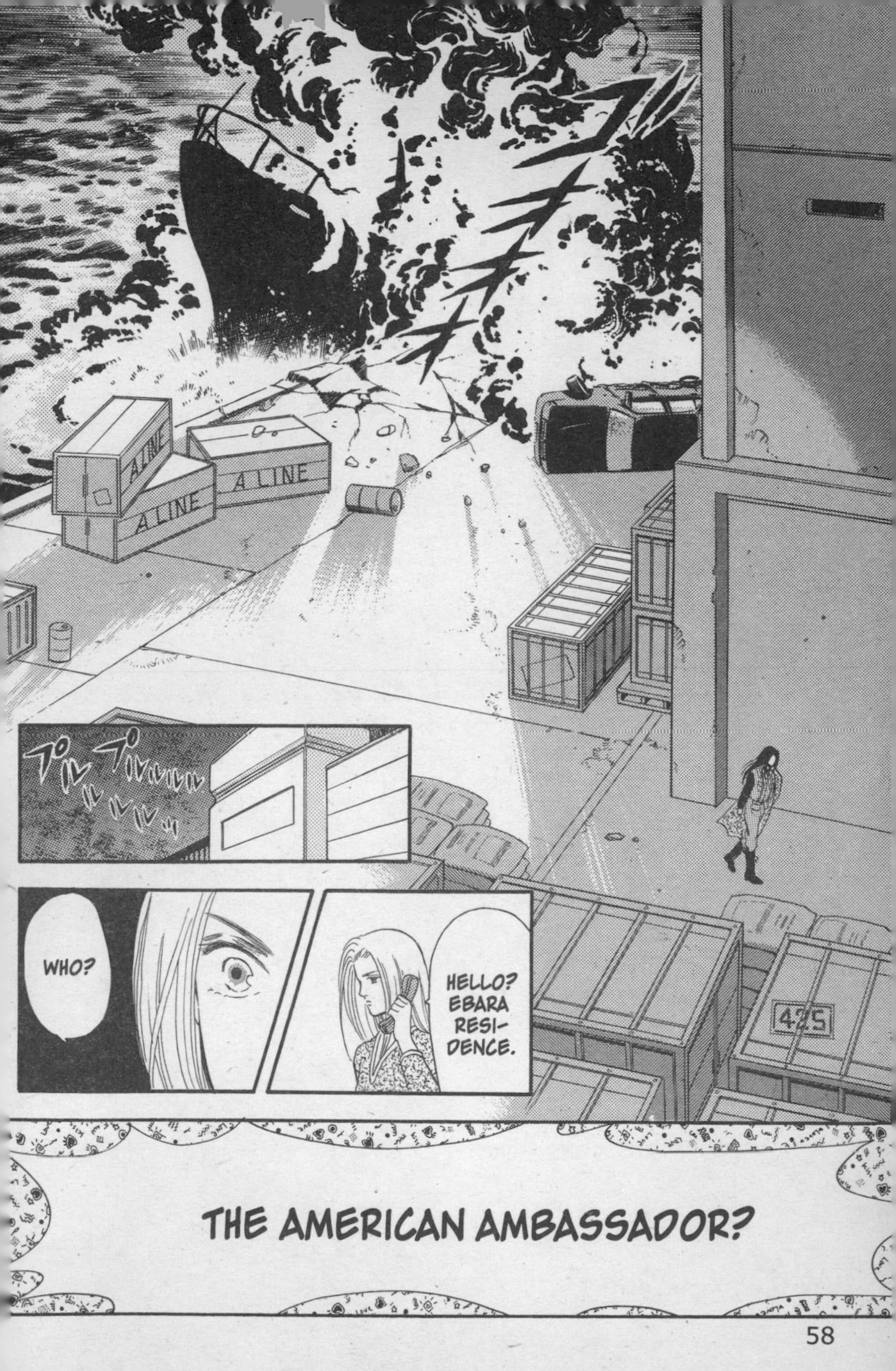
HELLO? EBARA RESIDENCE.
WHO?
THE AMERICAN AMBASSADOR?

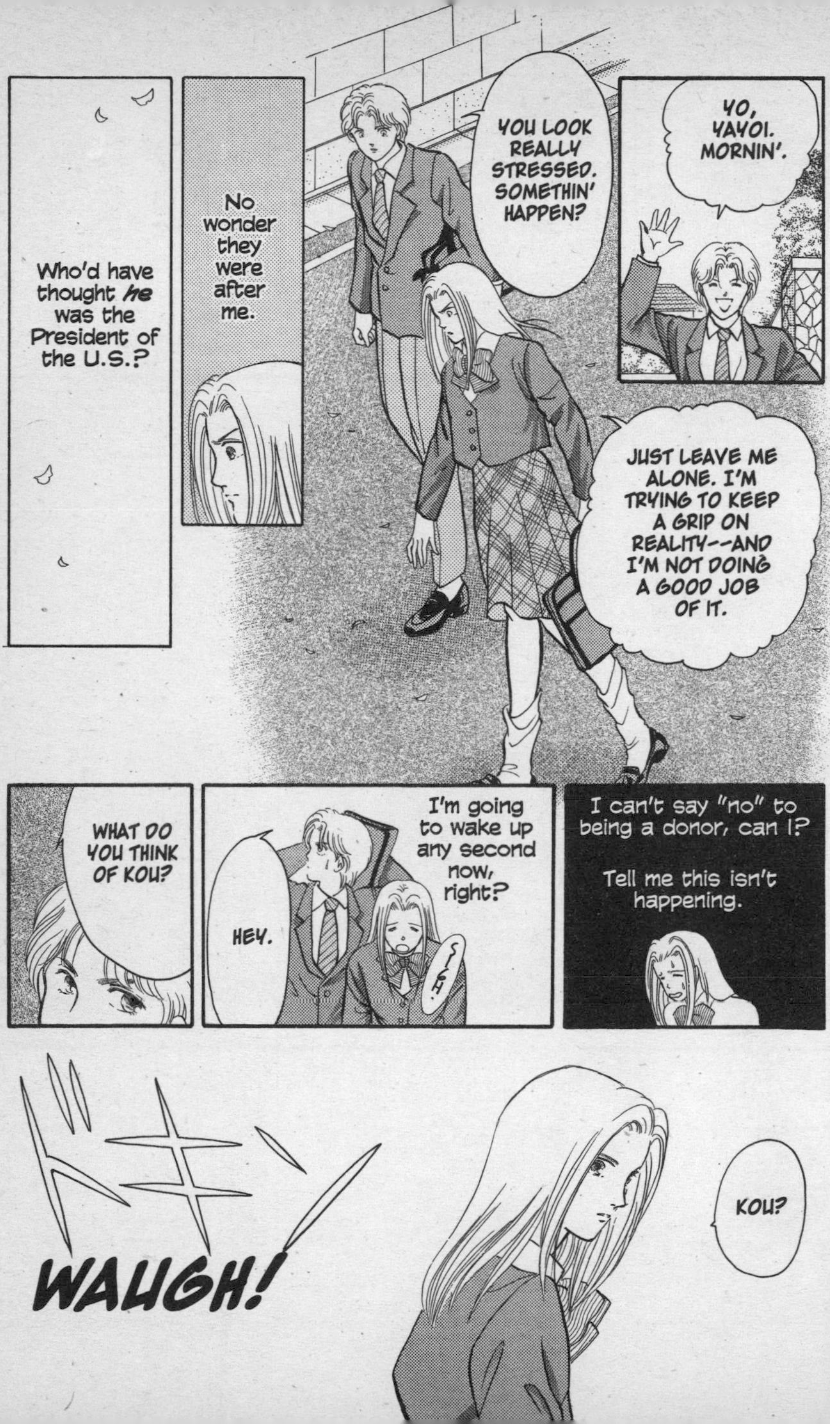
YO, YAYOI. MORNIN'.
YOU LOOK REALLY STRESSED. SOMETHIN' HAPPEN?
JUST LEAVE ME ALONE. I'M TRYING TO KEEP A GRIP ON REALITY--AND I'M NOT DOING A GOOD JOB OF IT.
No wonder they were after me.
Who'd have thought *he* was the President of the U.S.?
I can't say "no" to being a donor, can I?
Tell me this isn't happening.
I'm going to wake up any second now, right?
SIGH.
HEY.
WHAT DO YOU THINK OF KOU?
KOU?
WAUGH!

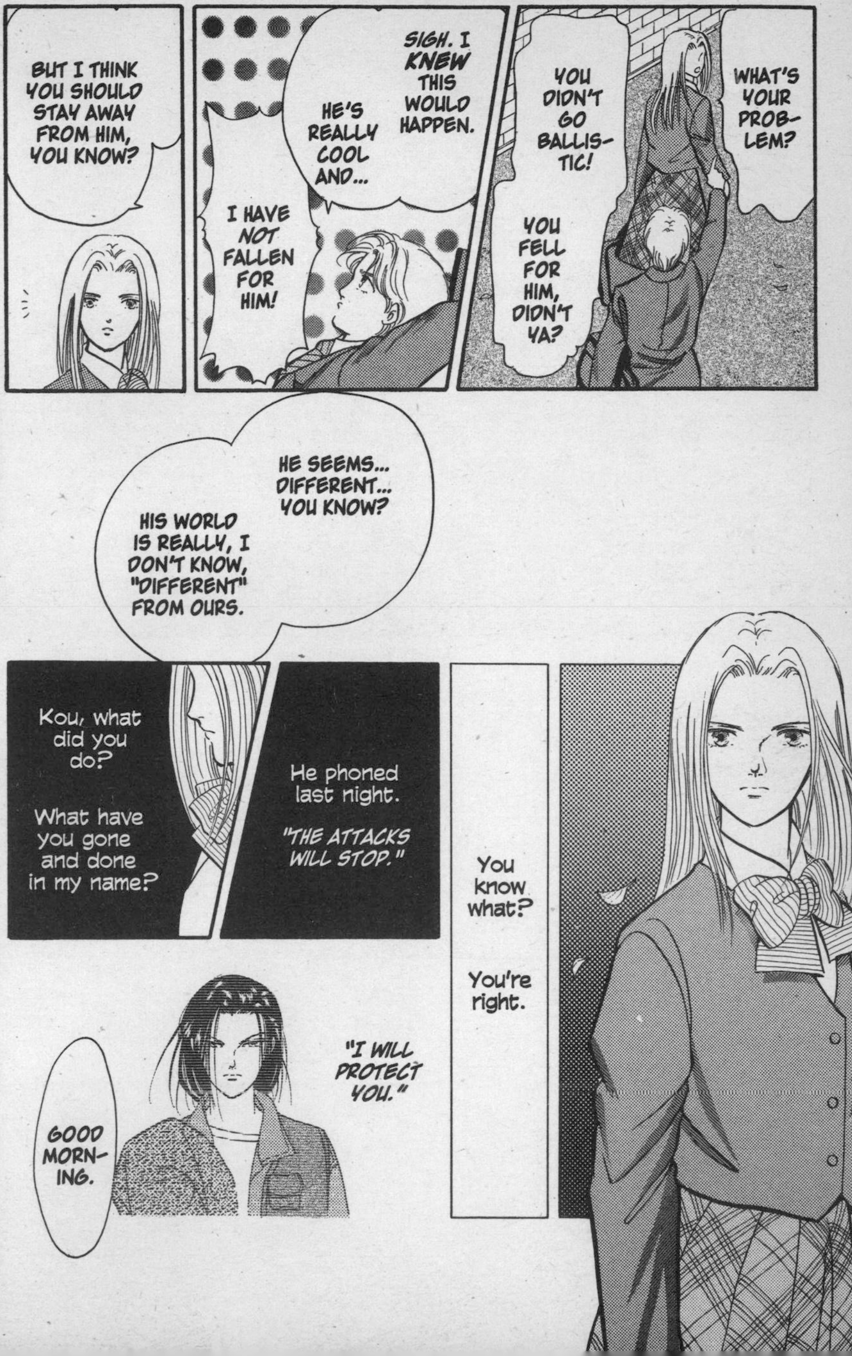
WHAT'S YOUR PROB-LEM?
YOU DIDN'T GO BALLIS-TIC!
YOU FELL FOR HIM, DIDN'T YA?
SIGH. I KNEW THIS WOULD HAPPEN.
HE'S REALLY COOL AND...
I HAVE NOT FALLEN FOR HIM!
BUT I THINK YOU SHOULD STAY AWAY FROM HIM, YOU KNOW?
HE SEEMS... DIFFERENT... YOU KNOW?
HIS WORLD IS REALLY, I DON'T KNOW, "DIFFERENT" FROM OURS.
You know what?
You're right.
He phoned last night.
"THE ATTACKS WILL STOP."
Kou, what did you do?
What have you gone and done in my name?
"I WILL PROTECT YOU."
GOOD MORN-ING.

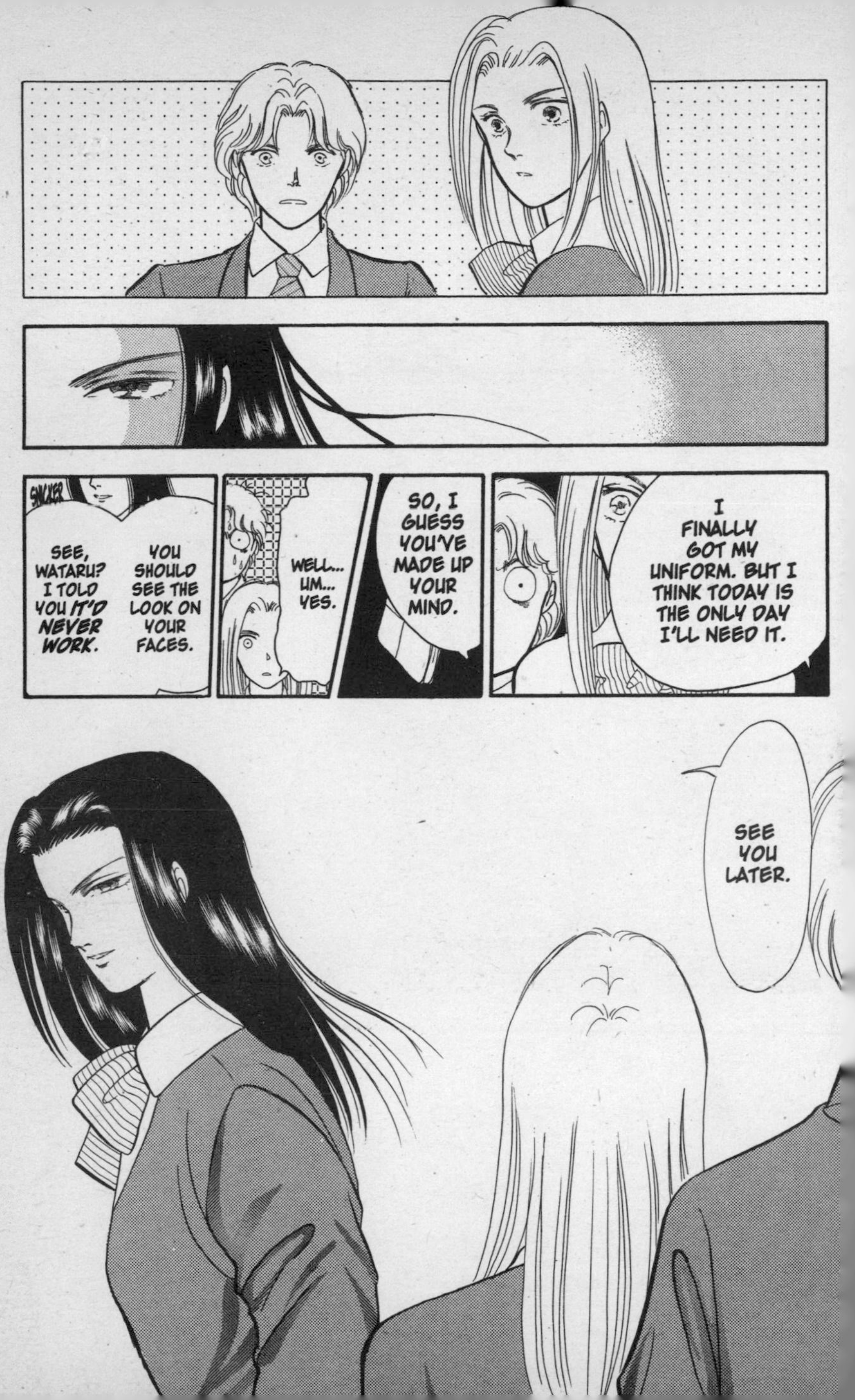
I FINALLY GOT MY UNIFORM. BUT I THINK TODAY IS THE ONLY DAY I'LL NEED IT.
SO, I GUESS YOU'VE MADE UP YOUR MIND.
WELL... UM... YES.
SNICKER
SEE, WATARU? I TOLD YOU *IT'D NEVER WORK.*
YOU SHOULD SEE THE LOOK ON YOUR FACES.
SEE YOU LATER.

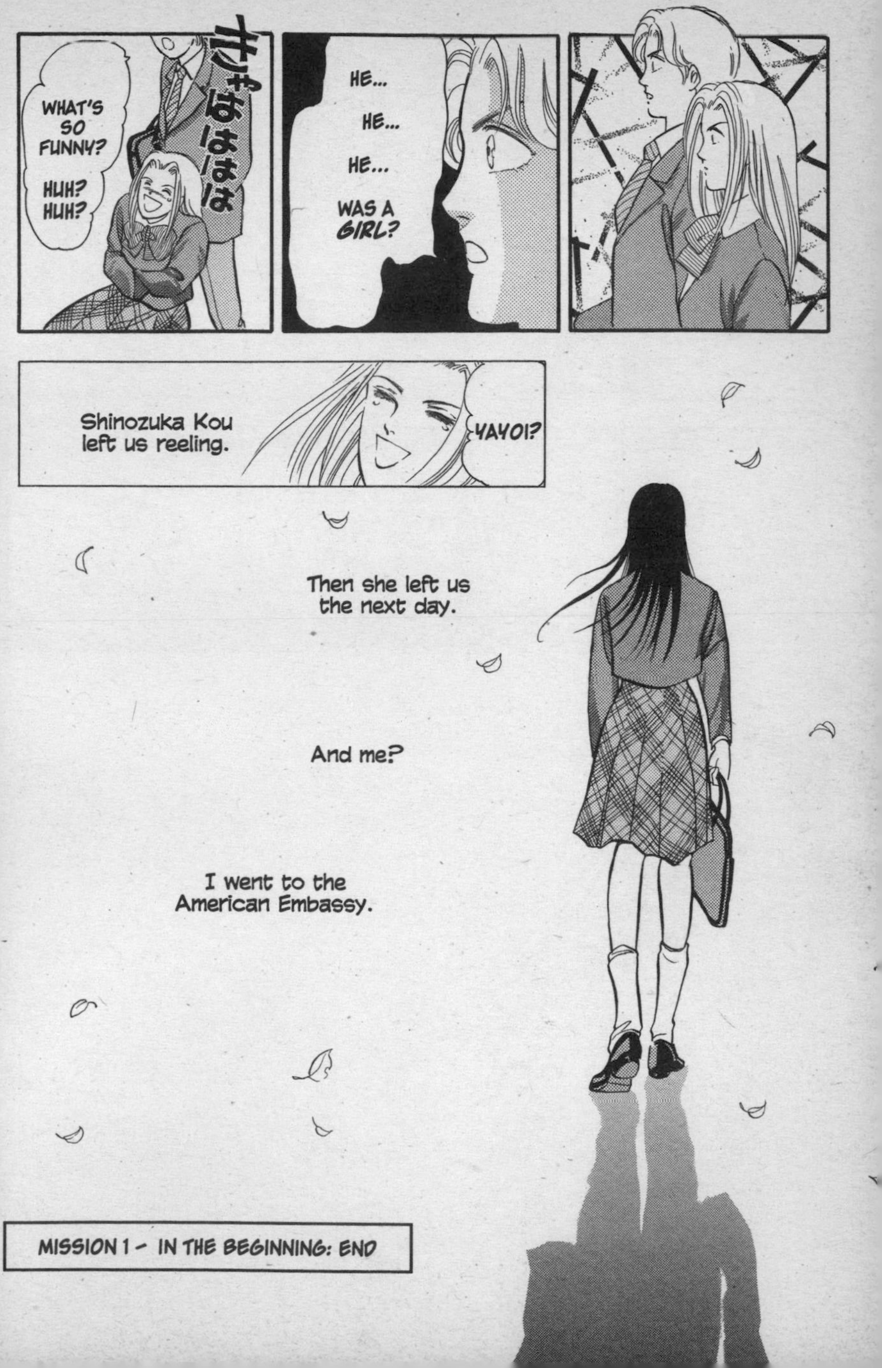
HE... HE... HE... WAS A GIRL?
きゃははは
WHAT'S SO FUNNY?
HUH? HUH?
YAYOI?
Shinozuka Kou left us reeling.
Then she left us the next day.
And me?
I went to the American Embassy.
MISSION 1 - IN THE BEGINNING: END

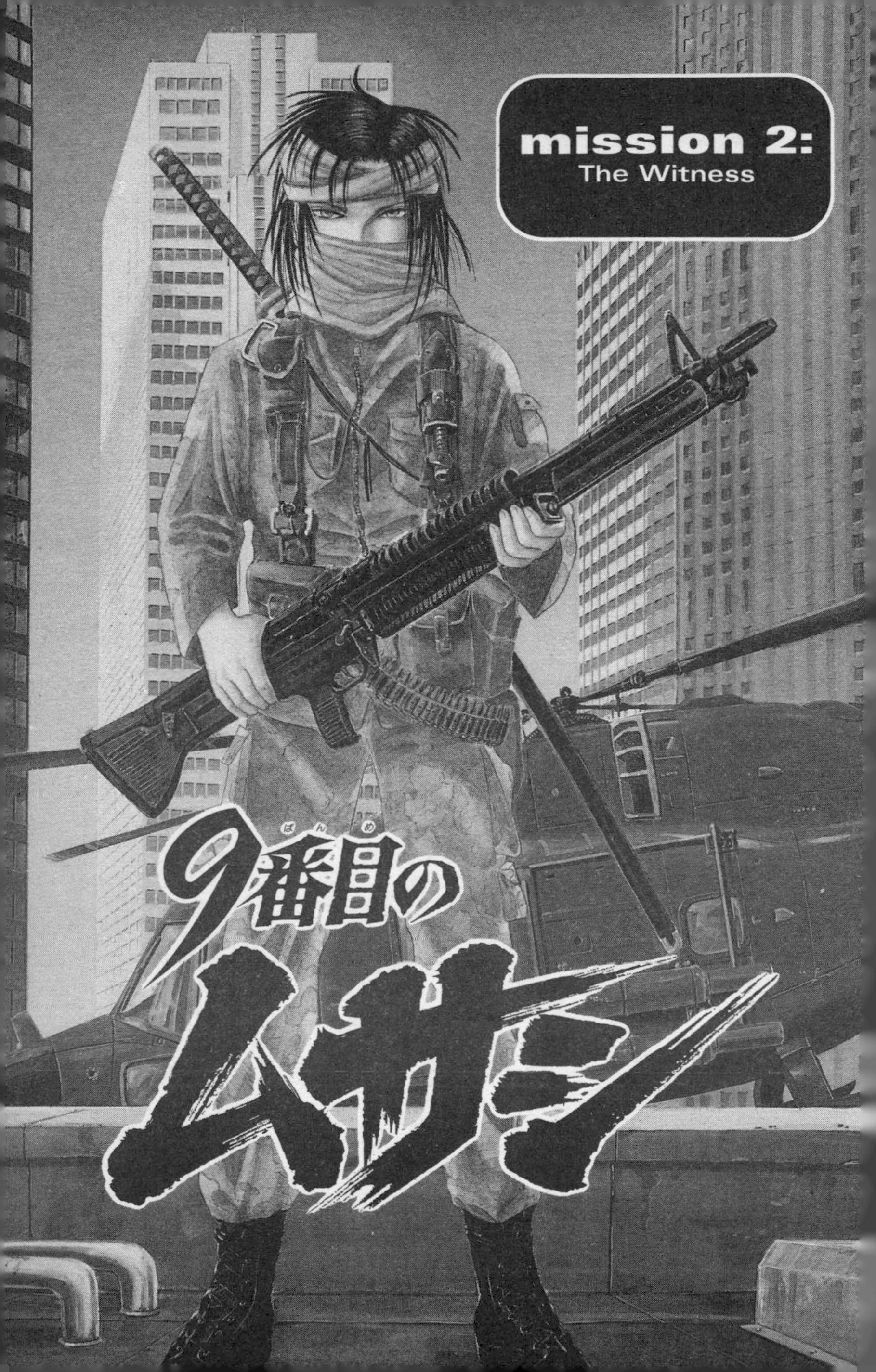
mission 2:
The Witness
9番目のムサシ

The history of mankind has
been one of wars. Race.
Religion. Philosophy. The
causes are untold.

The combatants have their own
justifications, but on occasion
some create a volatile situation
that threatens to destroy
the world.

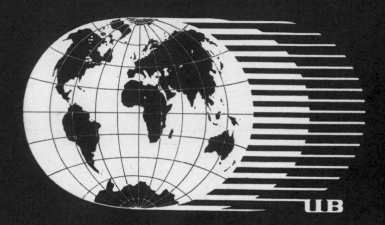

Ultimate Blue.

An organization shrouded in complete
secrecy. Also known as the "other
United Nations." Nobody knows
when it was created. Nobody knows
where it is based.

The Blue of the Seas.
The Blue of the Skies.
The Blue of the Earth.

The last line of defense against chaos.

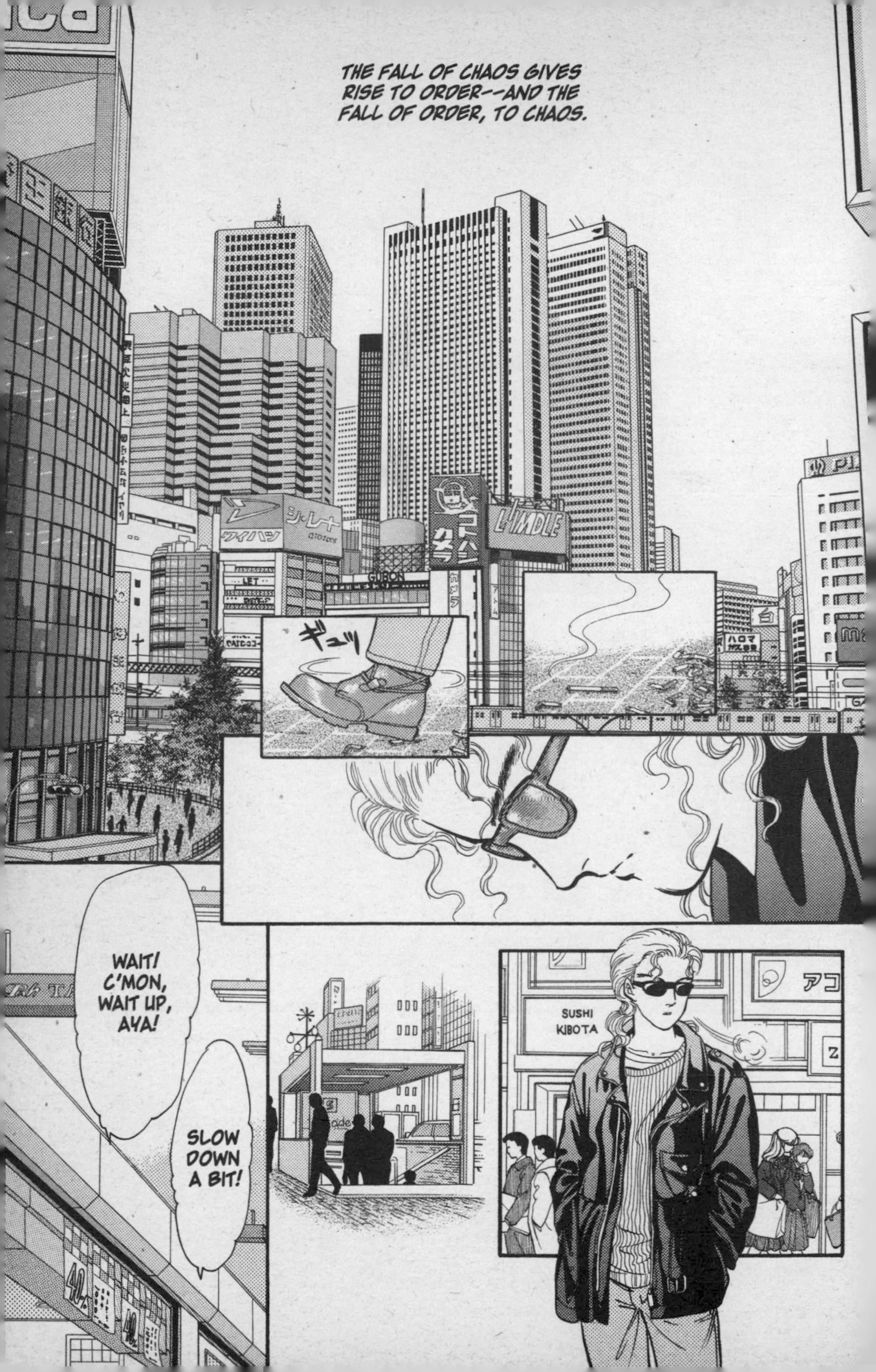
THE FALL OF CHAOS GIVES RISE TO ORDER--AND THE FALL OF ORDER, TO CHAOS.
ギュッ
SUSHI KIBOTA
WAIT! C'MON, WAIT UP, AYA!
SLOW DOWN A BIT!

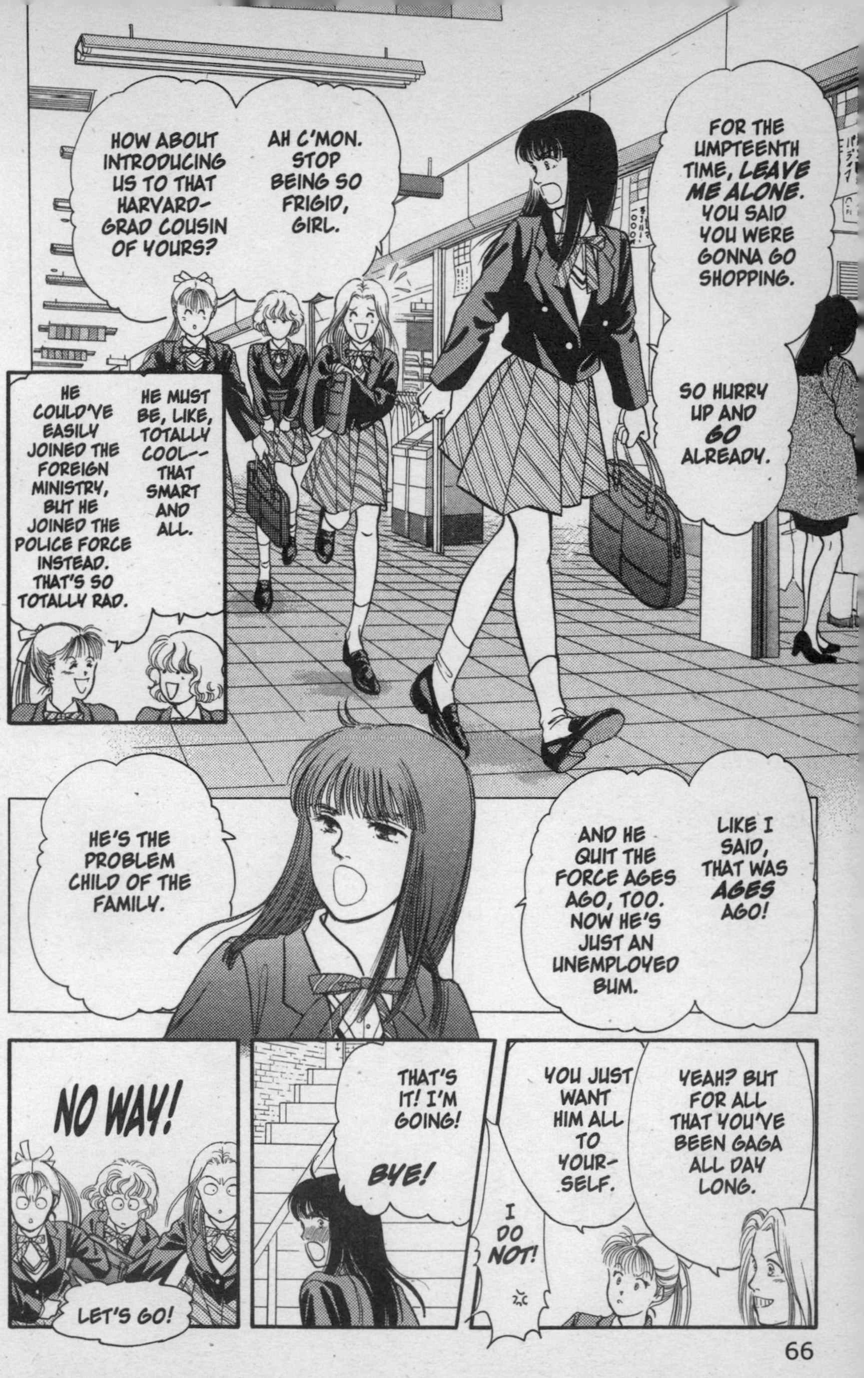
FOR THE UMPTEENTH TIME, LEAVE ME ALONE. YOU SAID YOU WERE GONNA GO SHOPPING.
SO HURRY UP AND GO ALREADY.
AH C'MON. STOP BEING SO FRIGID, GIRL.
HOW ABOUT INTRODUCING US TO THAT HARVARD-GRAD COUSIN OF YOURS?
HE MUST BE, LIKE, TOTALLY COOL--THAT SMART AND ALL.
HE COULD'VE EASILY JOINED THE FOREIGN MINISTRY, BUT HE JOINED THE POLICE FORCE INSTEAD. THAT'S SO TOTALLY RAD.
LIKE I SAID, THAT WAS AGES AGO!
AND HE QUIT THE FORCE AGES AGO, TOO. NOW HE'S JUST AN UNEMPLOYED BUM.
HE'S THE PROBLEM CHILD OF THE FAMILY.
YEAH? BUT FOR ALL THAT YOU'VE BEEN GAGA ALL DAY LONG.
YOU JUST WANT HIM ALL TO YOUR-SELF.
I DO NOT!
THAT'S IT! I'M GOING!
BYE!
NO WAY!
LET'S GO!

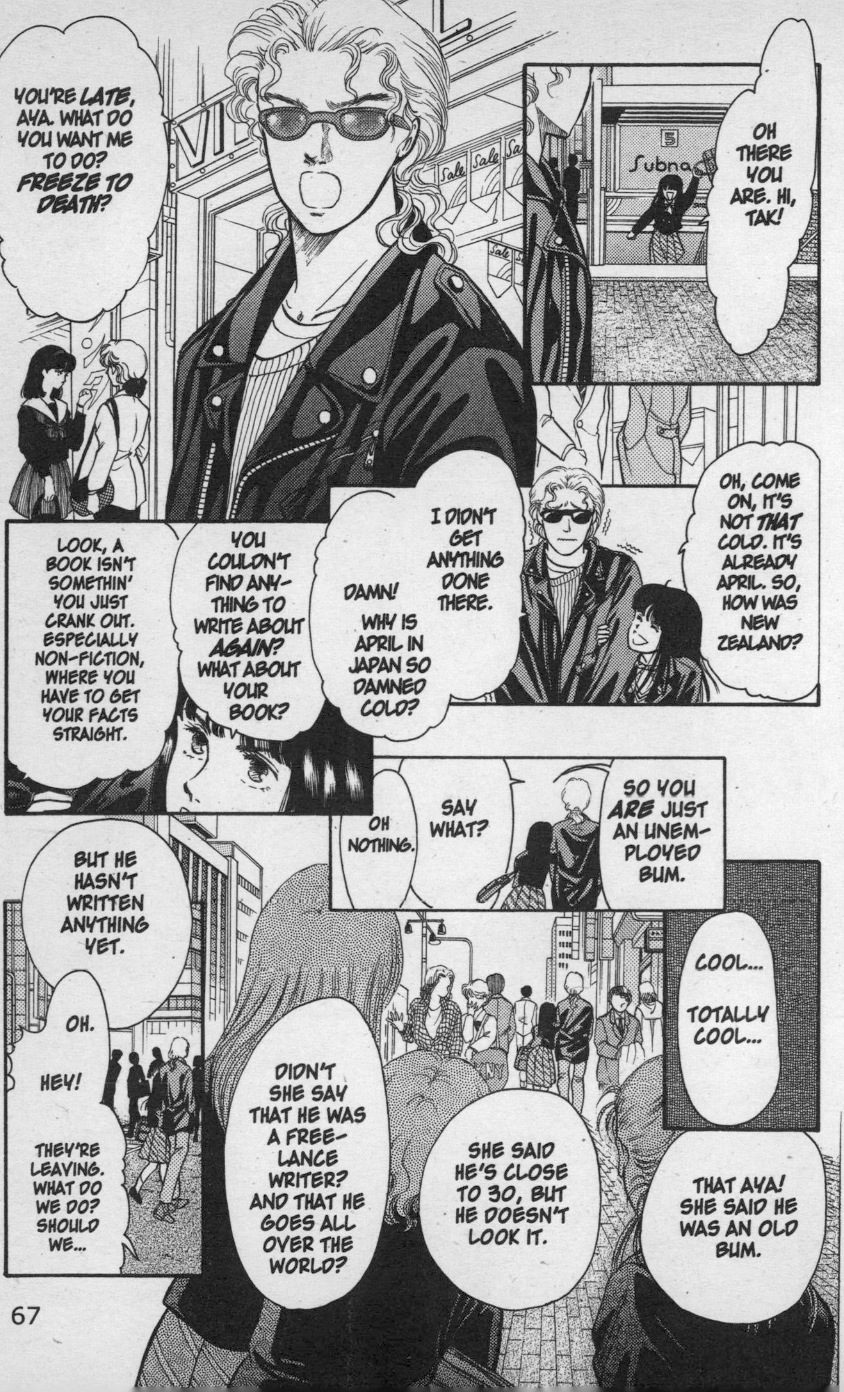
OH THERE YOU ARE. HI, TAK!
YOU'RE *LATE*, AYA. WHAT DO YOU WANT ME TO DO? *FREEZE TO DEATH?*
OH, COME ON, IT'S NOT *THAT* COLD. IT'S ALREADY APRIL. SO, HOW WAS NEW ZEALAND?
I DIDN'T GET ANYTHING DONE THERE.
DAMN! WHY IS APRIL IN JAPAN SO DAMNED COLD?
YOU COULDN'T FIND ANY-THING TO WRITE ABOUT *AGAIN?* WHAT ABOUT YOUR BOOK?
LOOK, A BOOK ISN'T SOMETHIN' YOU JUST CRANK OUT. ESPECIALLY NON-FICTION, WHERE YOU HAVE TO GET YOUR FACTS STRAIGHT.
SO YOU **ARE** JUST AN UNEM-PLOYED BUM.
SAY WHAT?
OH NOTHING.
COOL... TOTALLY COOL...
THAT AYA! SHE SAID HE WAS AN OLD BUM.
SHE SAID HE'S CLOSE TO 30, BUT HE DOESN'T LOOK IT.
DIDN'T SHE SAY THAT HE WAS A FREE-LANCE WRITER? AND THAT HE GOES ALL OVER THE WORLD?
BUT HE HASN'T WRITTEN ANYTHING YET.
OH.
HEY!
THEY'RE LEAVING. WHAT DO WE DO? SHOULD WE...

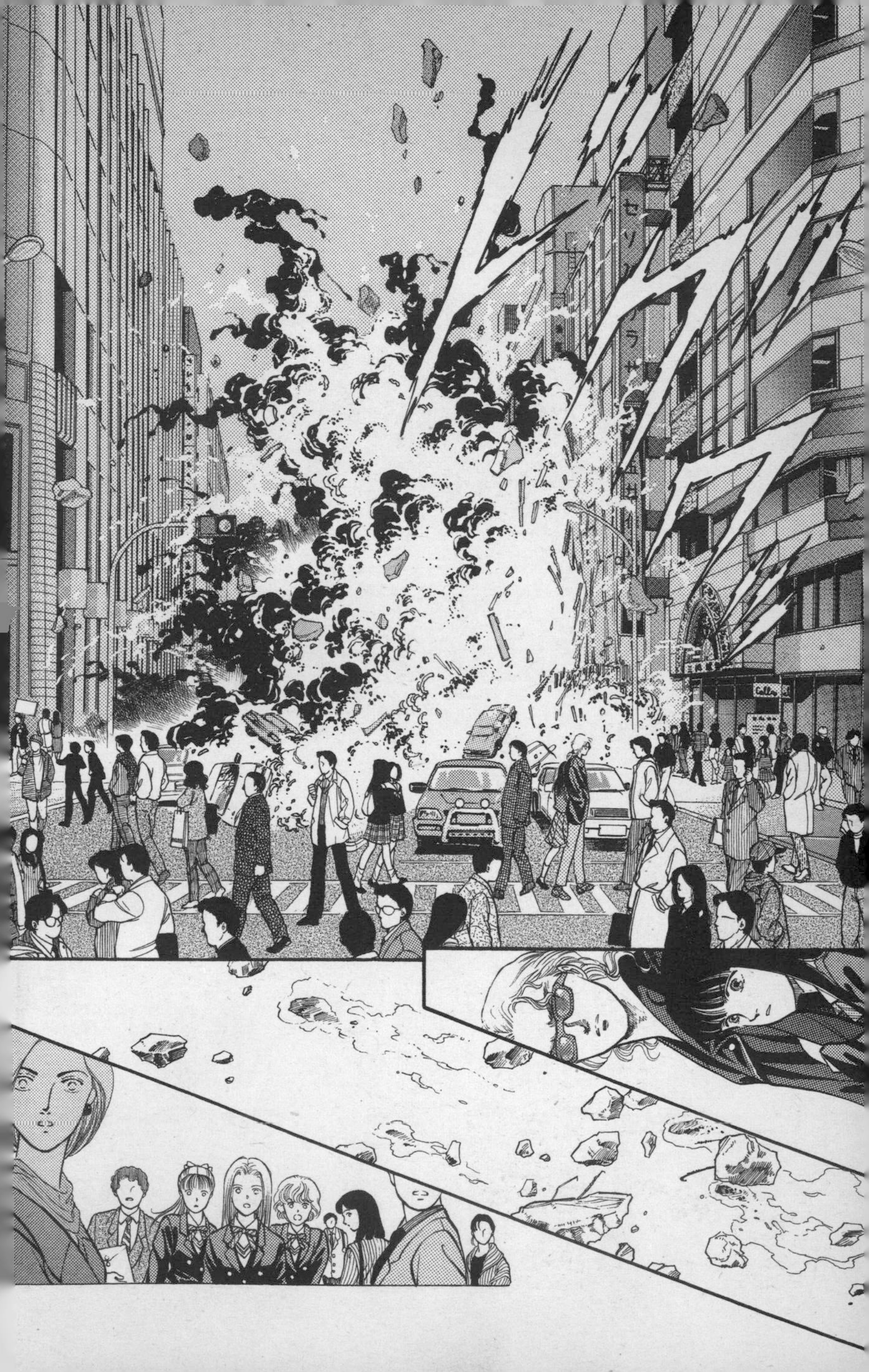

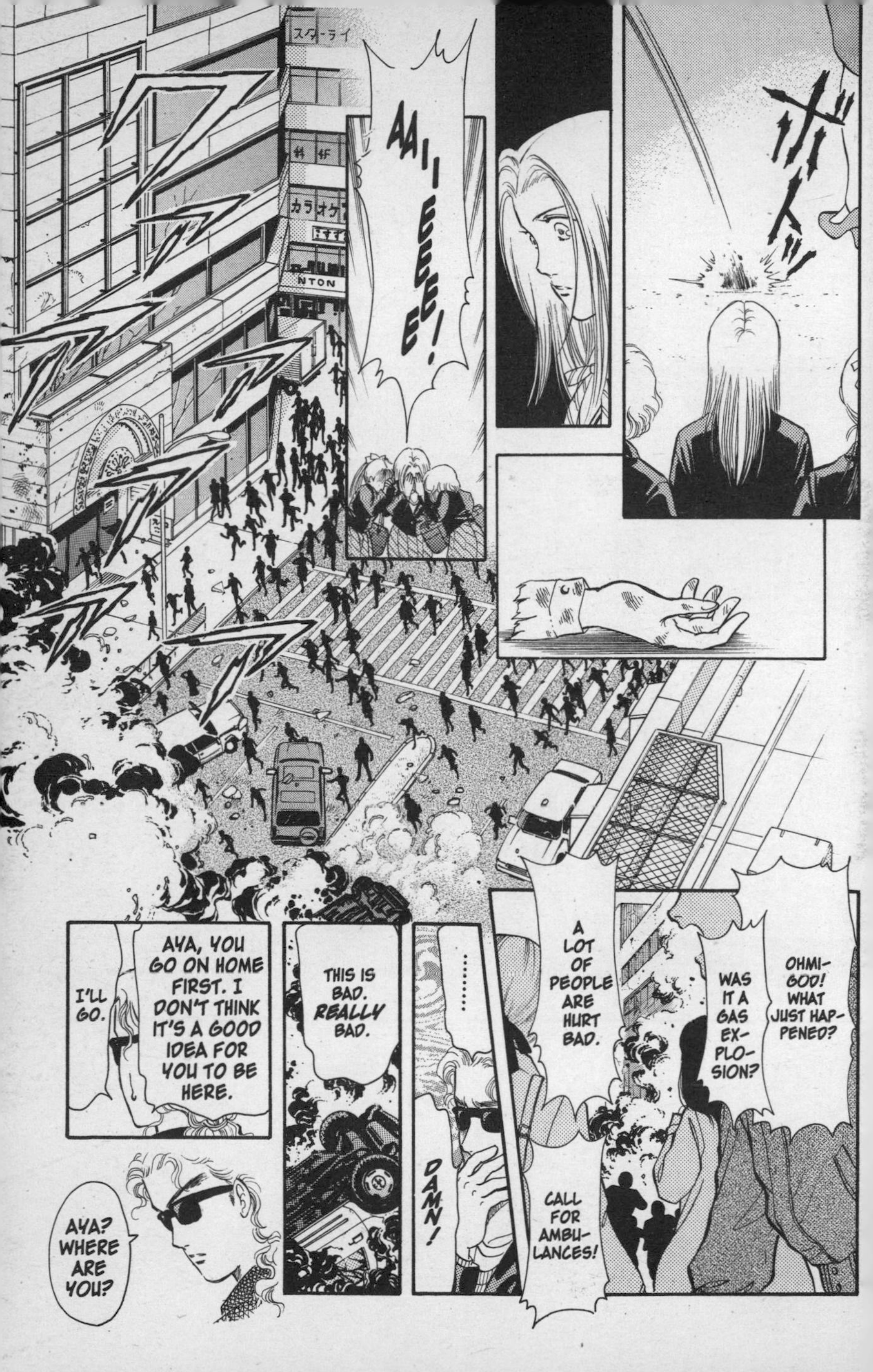
AAIIEEEE!
OHMI-GOD! WHAT JUST HAPPENED?
WAS IT A GAS EXPLOSION?
A LOT OF PEOPLE ARE HURT BAD.
CALL FOR AMBULANCES!
......
DAMN!
THIS IS BAD. REALLY BAD.
AYA, YOU GO ON HOME FIRST. I DON'T THINK IT'S A GOOD IDEA FOR YOU TO BE HERE.
I'LL GO.
AYA? WHERE ARE YOU?

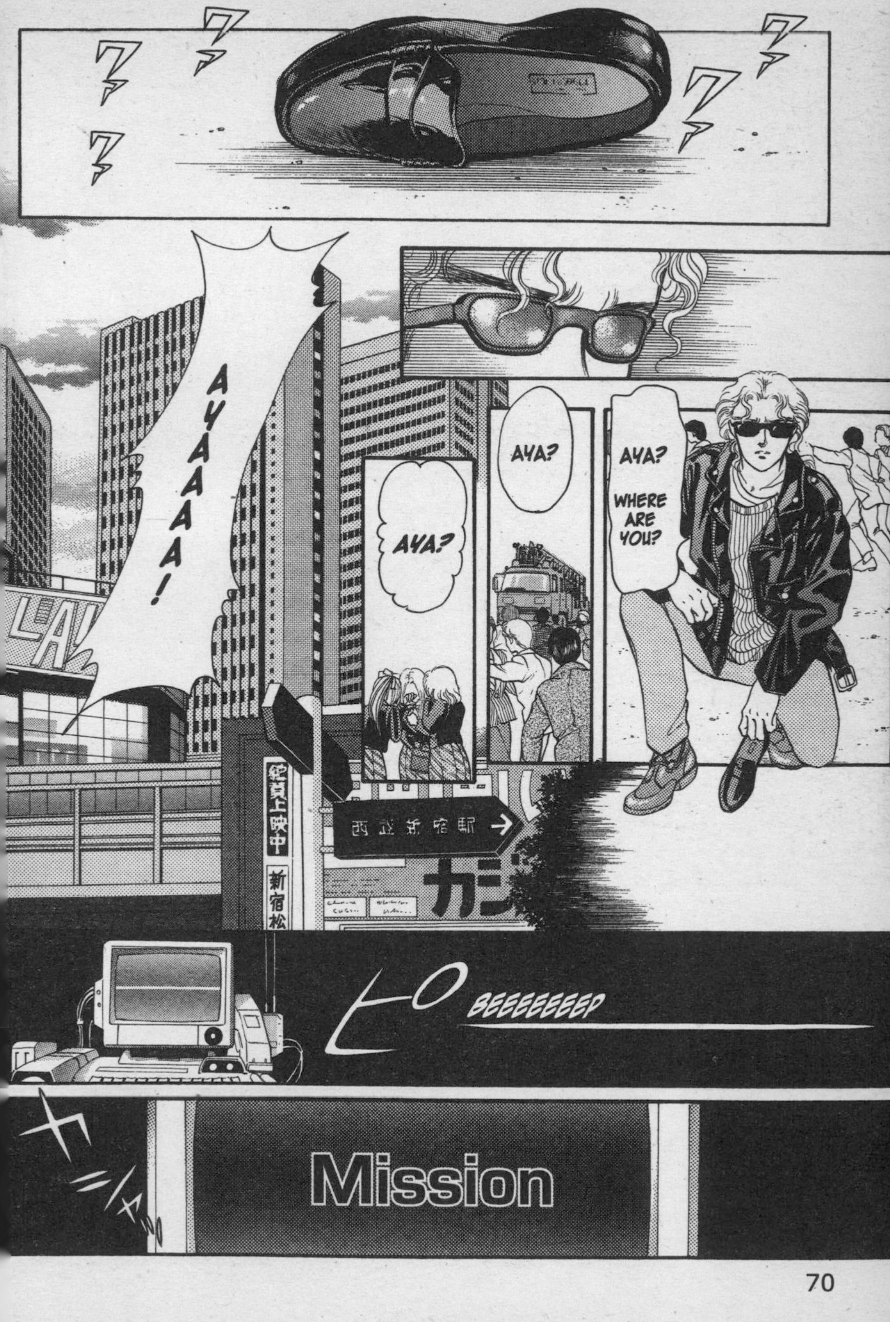
AYA? WHERE ARE YOU?
AYA?
AYA?
AYAAAAA!
西武新宿駅
BEEEEEEEP
Mission

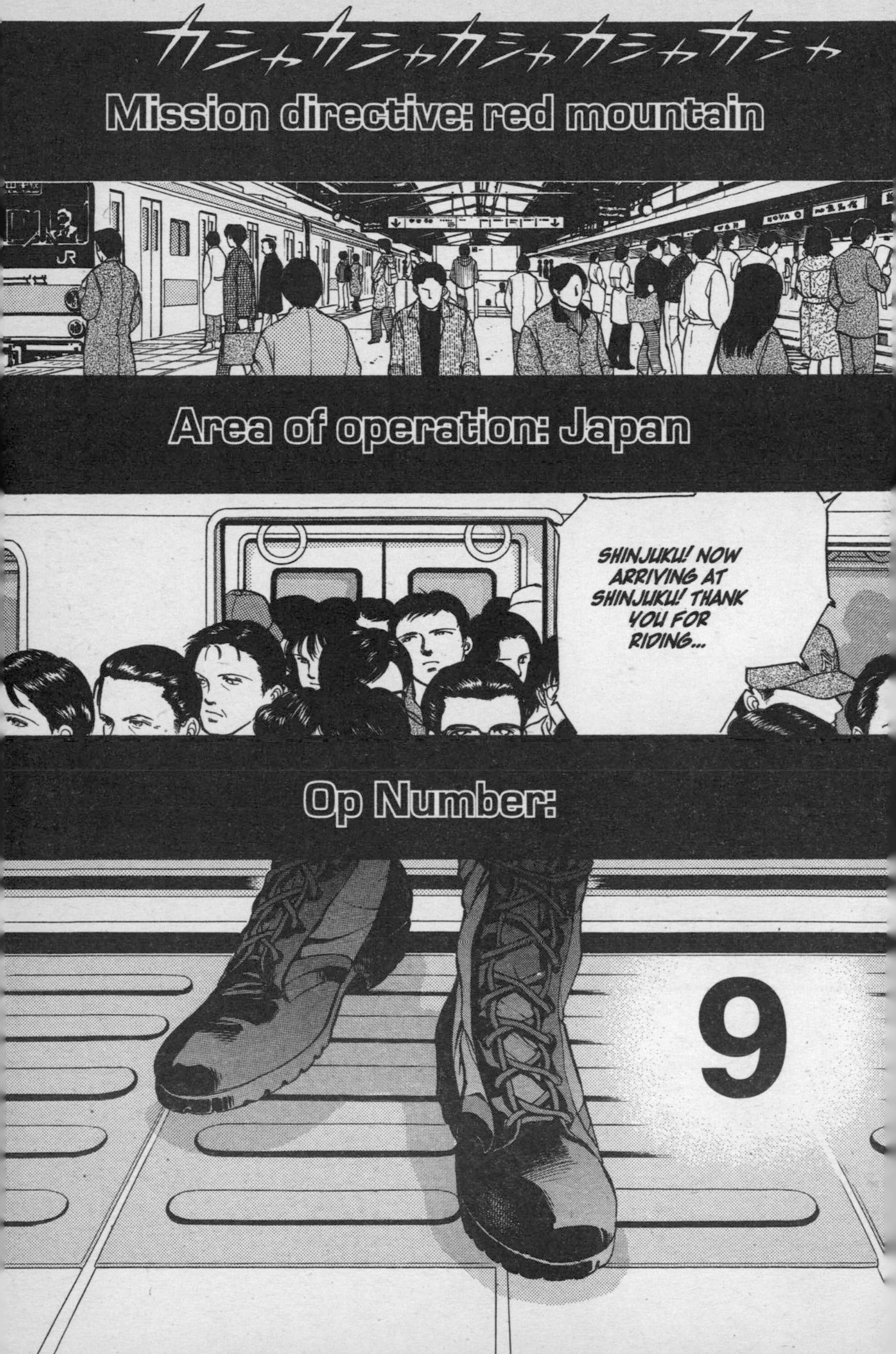
カシャカシャカシャカシャカシャ
Mission directive: red mountain
Area of operation: Japan
SHINJUKU! NOW ARRIVING AT SHINJUKU! THANK YOU FOR RIDING...
Op Number:
9

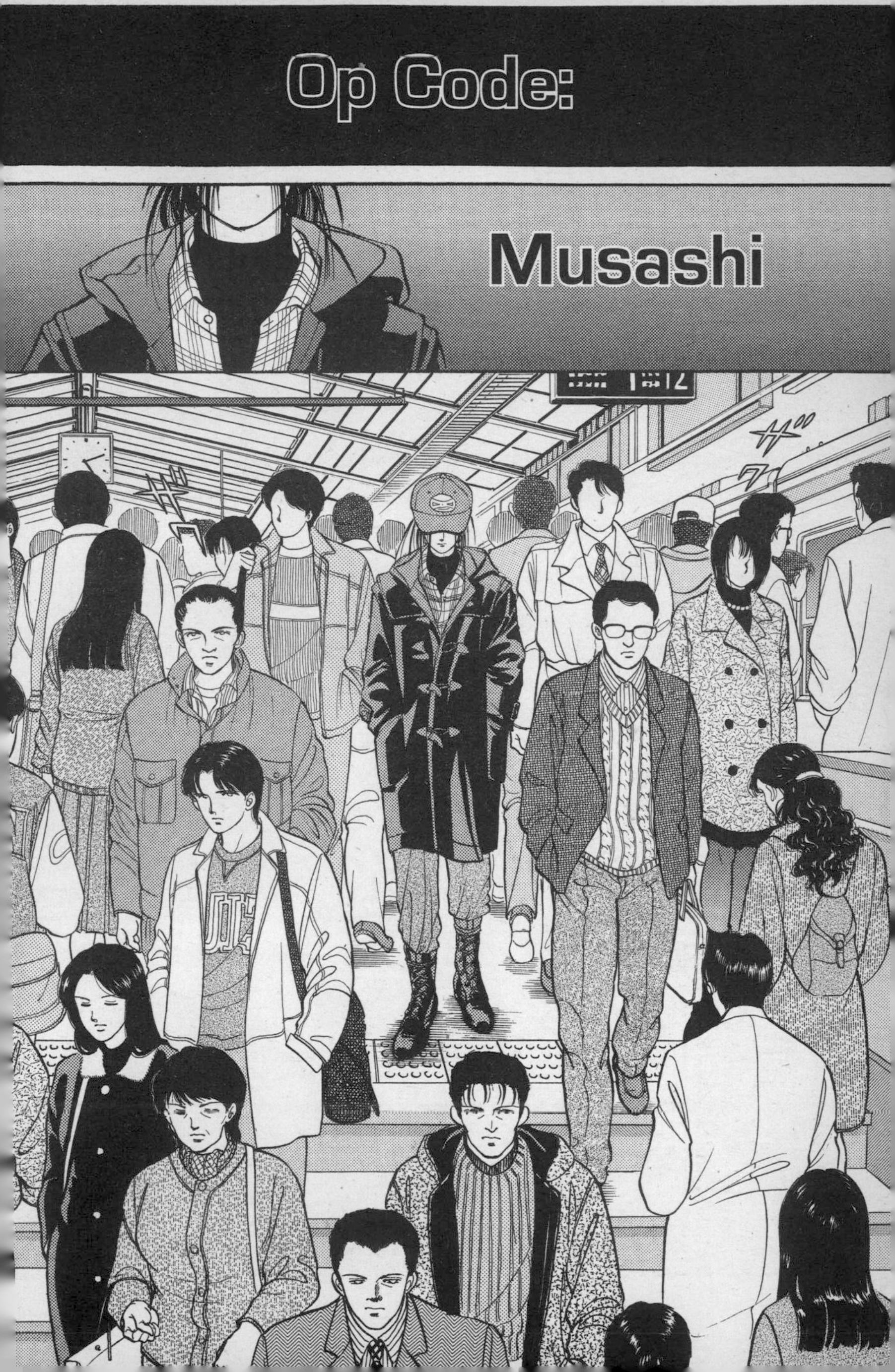
Op Code:
Musashi

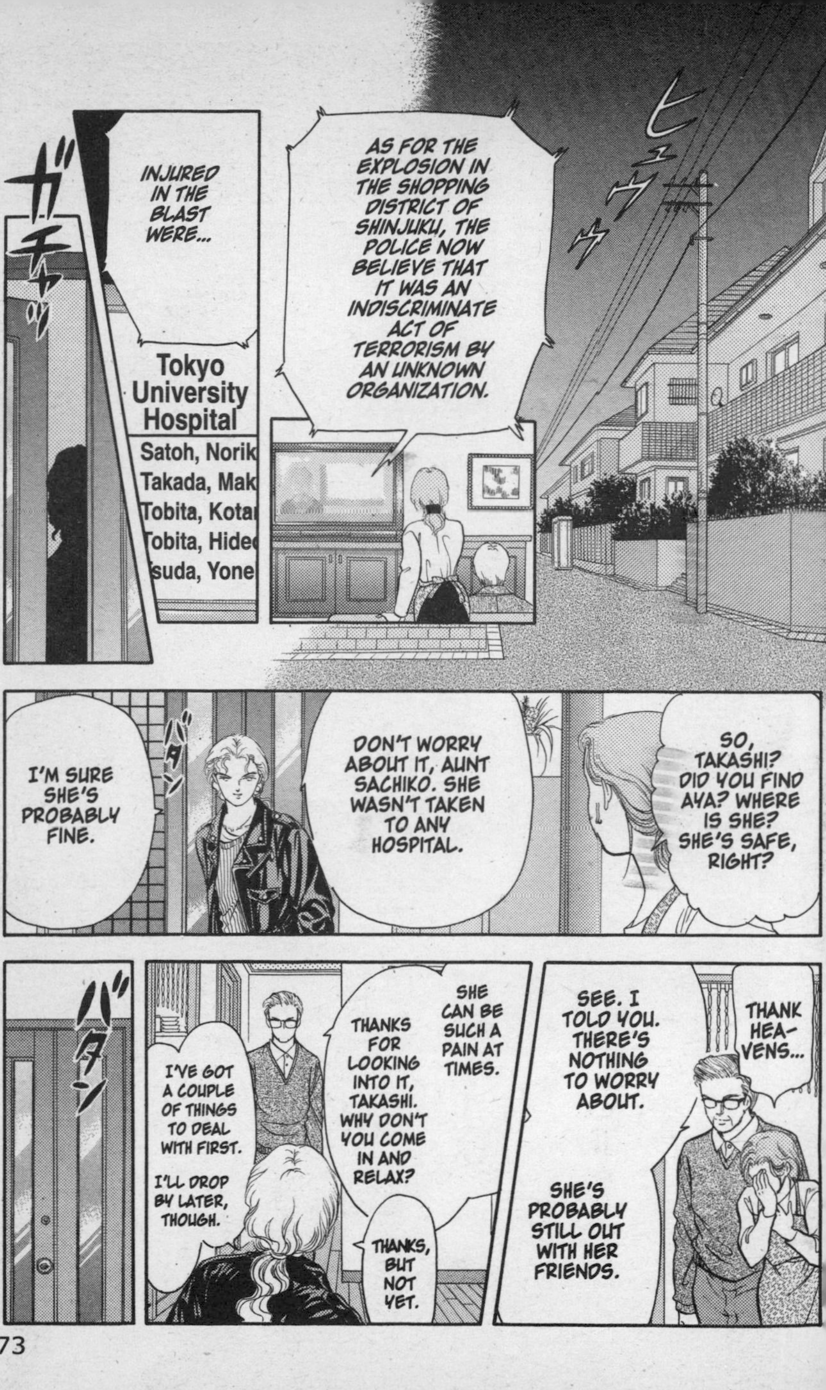
ヒュウウ
AS FOR THE EXPLOSION IN THE SHOPPING DISTRICT OF SHINJUKU, THE POLICE NOW BELIEVE THAT IT WAS AN INDISCRIMINATE ACT OF TERRORISM BY AN UNKNOWN ORGANIZATION.
INJURED IN THE BLAST WERE...
Tokyo University Hospital
Satoh, Norik
Takada, Mak
Tobita, Kotar
Tobita, Hided
Tsuda, Yone
ガチャッ
SO, TAKASHI? DID YOU FIND AYA? WHERE IS SHE? SHE'S SAFE, RIGHT?
DON'T WORRY ABOUT IT, AUNT SACHIKO. SHE WASN'T TAKEN TO ANY HOSPITAL.
バタン
I'M SURE SHE'S PROBABLY FINE.
THANK HEA-VENS...
SEE. I TOLD YOU. THERE'S NOTHING TO WORRY ABOUT.
SHE'S PROBABLY STILL OUT WITH HER FRIENDS.
SHE CAN BE SUCH A PAIN AT TIMES.
THANKS FOR LOOKING INTO IT, TAKASHI. WHY DON'T YOU COME IN AND RELAX?
THANKS, BUT NOT YET.
I'VE GOT A COUPLE OF THINGS TO DEAL WITH FIRST.
I'LL DROP BY LATER, THOUGH.
バターン

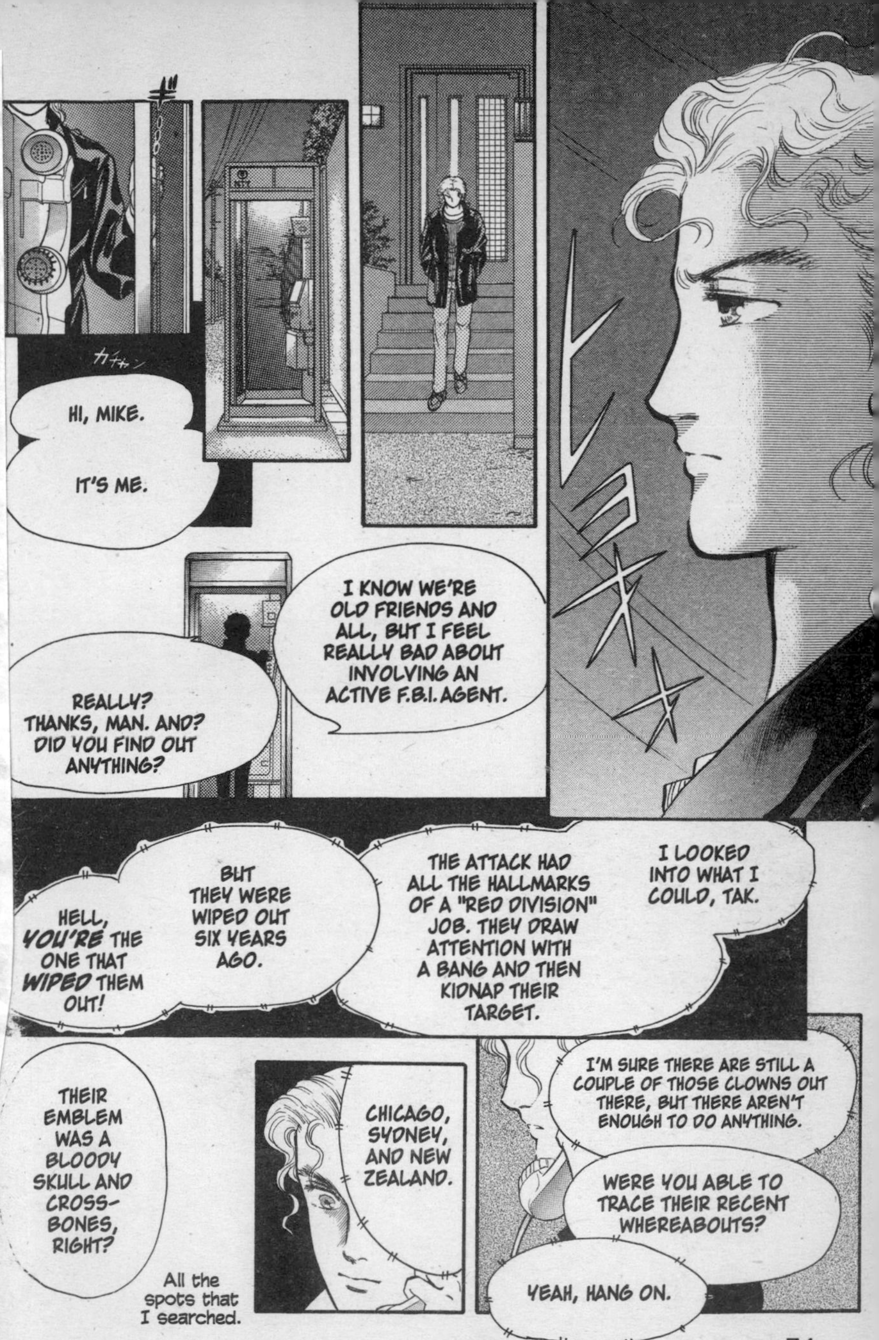
HI, MIKE.
IT'S ME.
I KNOW WE'RE OLD FRIENDS AND ALL, BUT I FEEL REALLY BAD ABOUT INVOLVING AN ACTIVE F.B.I. AGENT.
REALLY? THANKS, MAN. AND? DID YOU FIND OUT ANYTHING?
I LOOKED INTO WHAT I COULD, TAK.
THE ATTACK HAD ALL THE HALLMARKS OF A "RED DIVISION" JOB. THEY DRAW ATTENTION WITH A BANG AND THEN KIDNAP THEIR TARGET.
BUT THEY WERE WIPED OUT SIX YEARS AGO.
HELL, ***YOU'RE*** THE ONE THAT ***WIPED*** THEM OUT!
I'M SURE THERE ARE STILL A COUPLE OF THOSE CLOWNS OUT THERE, BUT THERE AREN'T ENOUGH TO DO ANYTHING.
WERE YOU ABLE TO TRACE THEIR RECENT WHEREABOUTS?
YEAH, HANG ON.
CHICAGO, SYDNEY, AND NEW ZEALAND.
All the spots that I searched.
THEIR EMBLEM WAS A BLOODY SKULL AND CROSS-BONES, RIGHT?

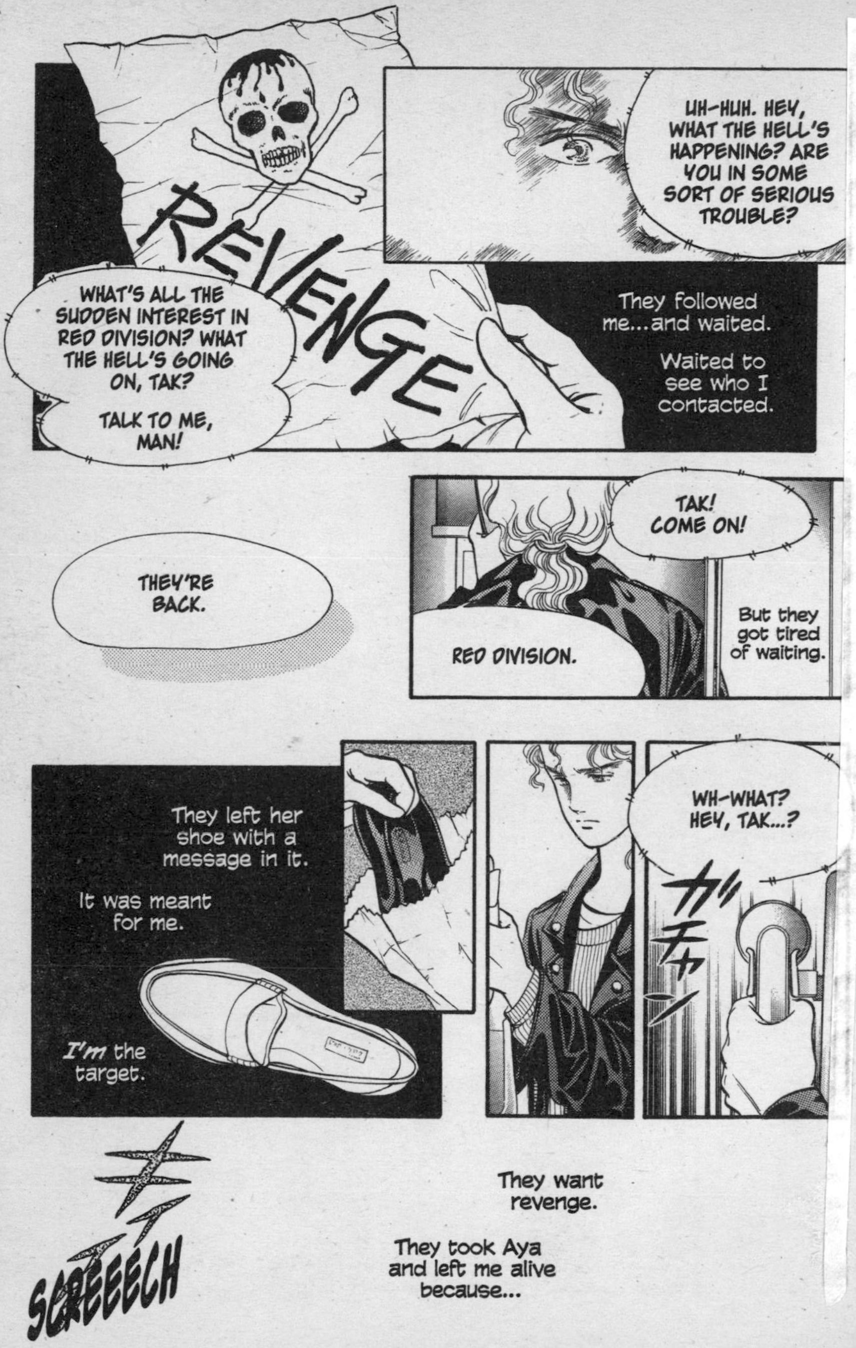
UH-HUH. HEY, WHAT THE HELL'S HAPPENING? ARE YOU IN SOME SORT OF SERIOUS TROUBLE?
REVENGE
They followed me...and waited.
Waited to see who I contacted.
WHAT'S ALL THE SUDDEN INTEREST IN RED DIVISION? WHAT THE HELL'S GOING ON, TAK?
TALK TO ME, MAN!
TAK! COME ON!
But they got tired of waiting.
RED DIVISION.
THEY'RE BACK.
WH-WHAT? HEY, TAK...?
ガチャン
They left her shoe with a message in it.
It was meant for me.
I'm the target.
They want revenge.
They took Aya and left me alive because...
SCREEECH

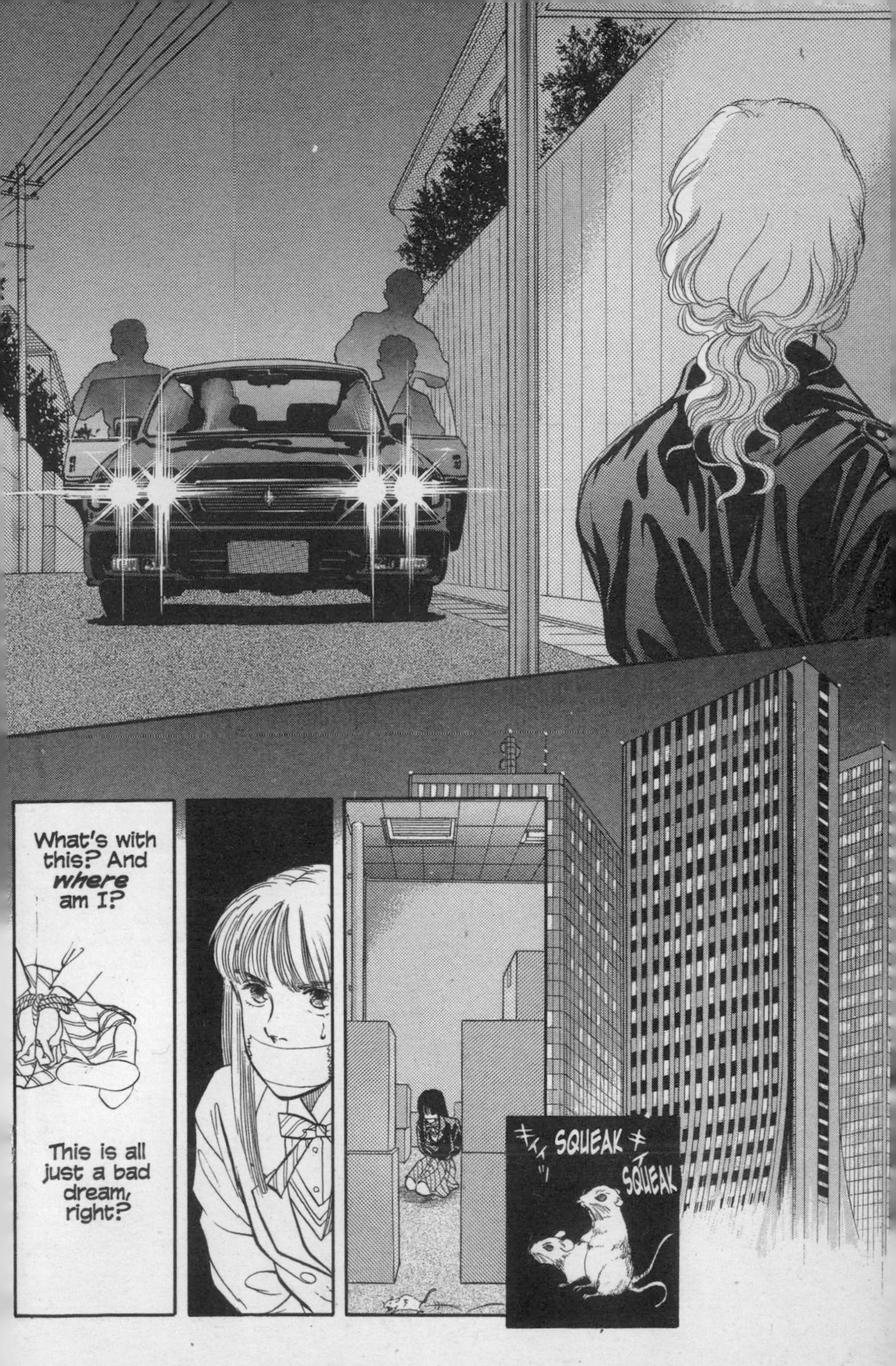
SQUEAK
SQUEAK
What's with this? And *where* am I?
This is all just a bad dream, right?

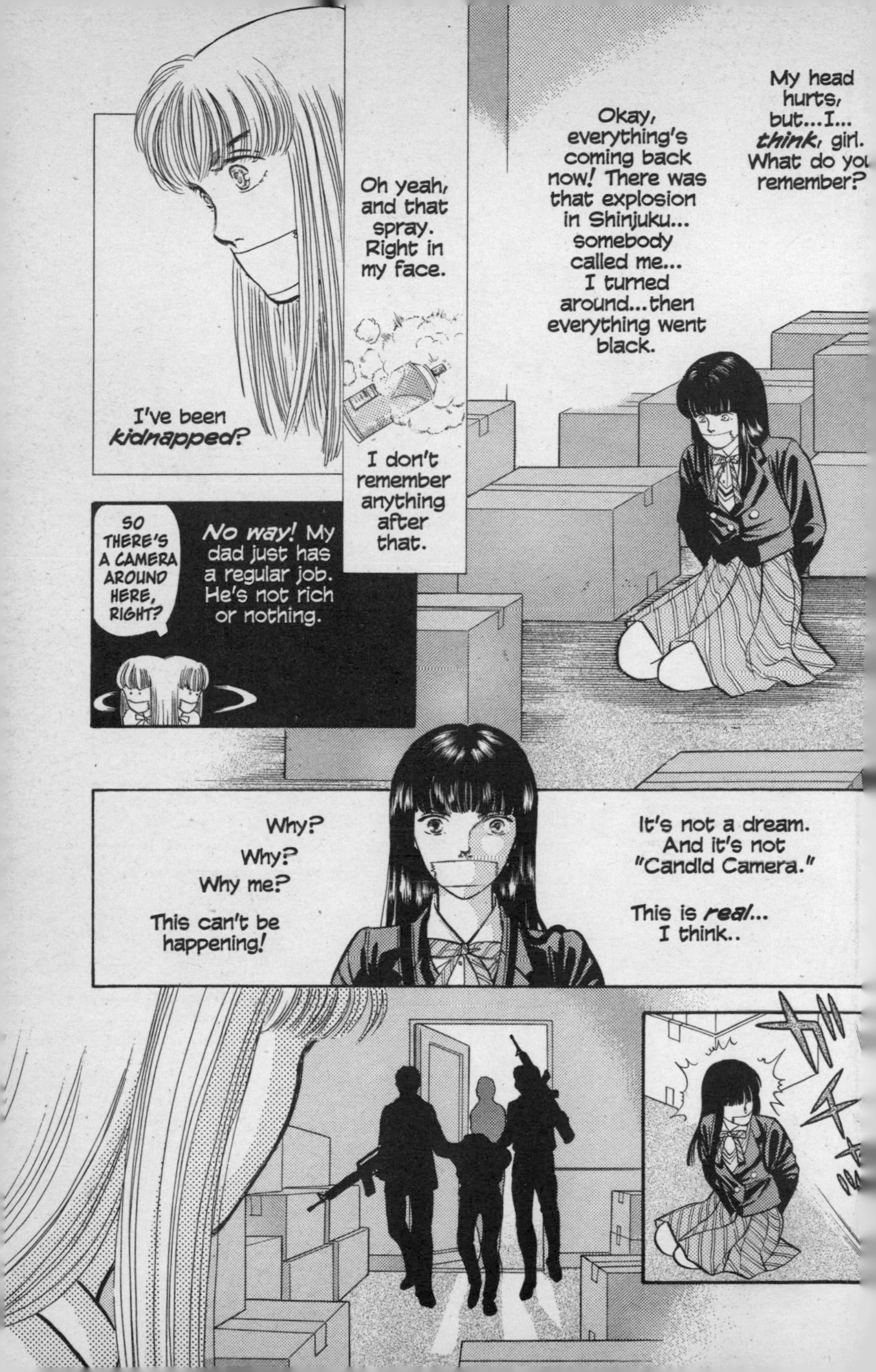
My head hurts, but...I... *think*, girl. What do you remember?
Okay, everything's coming back now! There was that explosion in Shinjuku... somebody called me... I turned around...then everything went black.
Oh yeah, and that spray. Right in my face.
I don't remember anything after that.
I've been *kidnapped?*
No way! My dad just has a regular job. He's not rich or nothing.
SO THERE'S A CAMERA AROUND HERE, RIGHT?
It's not a dream. And it's not "Candid Camera."
This is *real*... I think..
Why?
Why?
Why me?
This can't be happening!

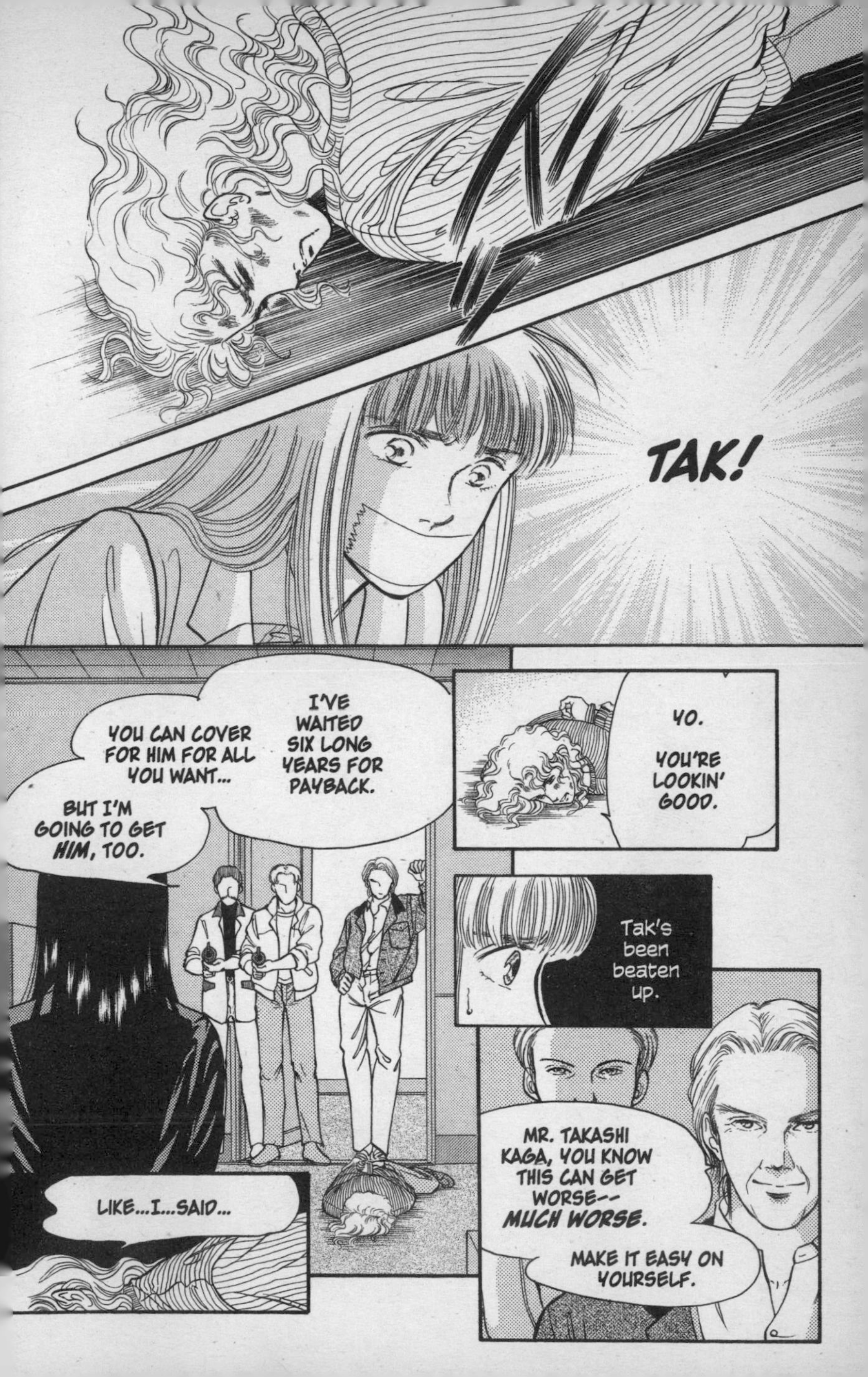
TAK!
YO.
YOU'RE LOOKIN' GOOD.
Tak's been beaten up.
MR. TAKASHI KAGA, YOU KNOW THIS CAN GET WORSE-- *MUCH WORSE*.
MAKE IT EASY ON YOURSELF.
I'VE WAITED SIX LONG YEARS FOR PAYBACK.
YOU CAN COVER FOR HIM FOR ALL YOU WANT...
BUT I'M GOING TO GET *HIM*, TOO.
LIKE...I...SAID...

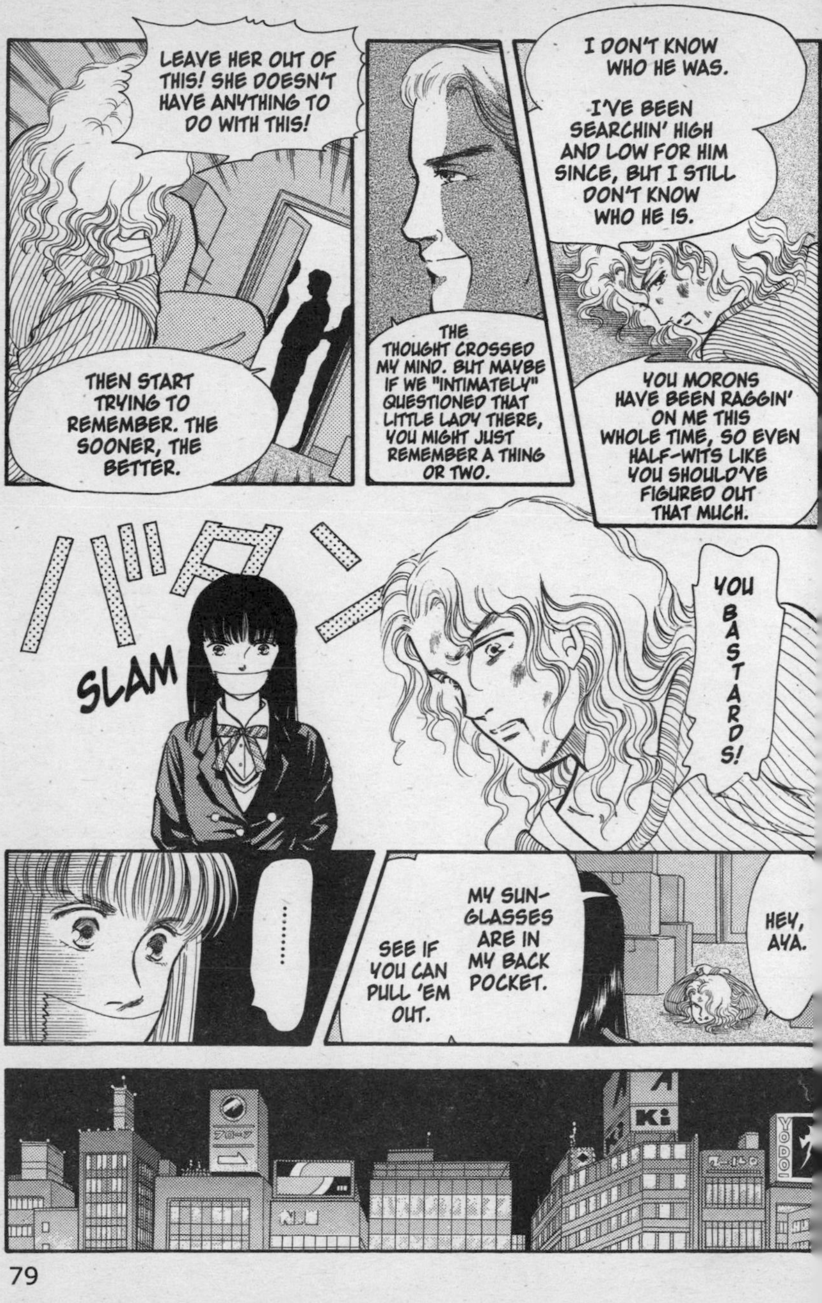
I DON'T KNOW WHO HE WAS.
I'VE BEEN SEARCHIN' HIGH AND LOW FOR HIM SINCE, BUT I STILL DON'T KNOW WHO HE IS.
YOU MORONS HAVE BEEN RAGGIN' ON ME THIS WHOLE TIME, SO EVEN HALF-WITS LIKE YOU SHOULD'VE FIGURED OUT THAT MUCH.
THE THOUGHT CROSSED MY MIND. BUT MAYBE IF WE "INTIMATELY" QUESTIONED THAT LITTLE LADY THERE, YOU MIGHT JUST REMEMBER A THING OR TWO.
LEAVE HER OUT OF THIS! SHE DOESN'T HAVE ANYTHING TO DO WITH THIS!
THEN START TRYING TO REMEMBER. THE SOONER, THE BETTER.
YOU BASTARDS!
バタン
SLAM
HEY, AYA.
MY SUN-GLASSES ARE IN MY BACK POCKET.
SEE IF YOU CAN PULL 'EM OUT.
......

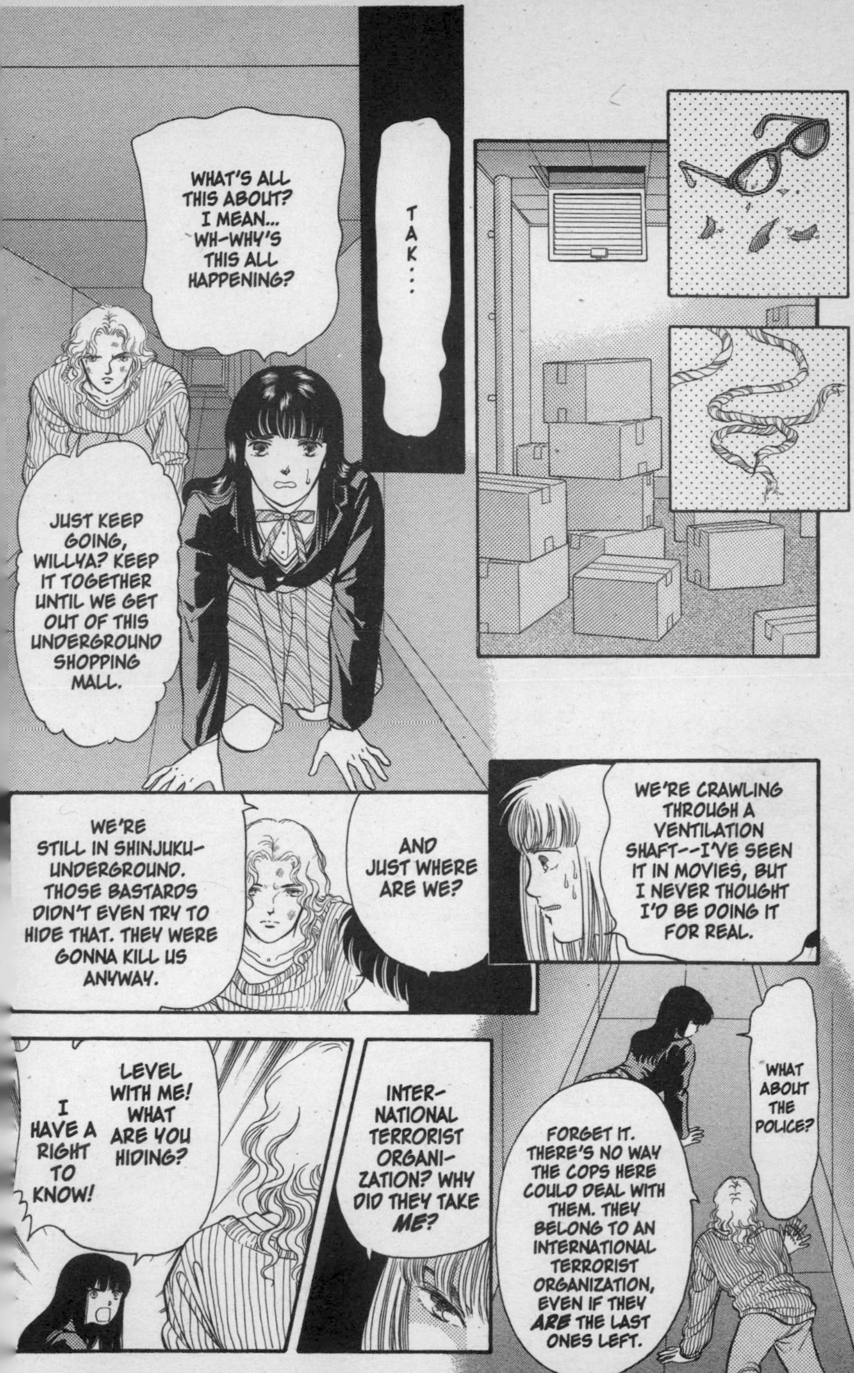

TAK...
WHAT'S ALL THIS ABOUT? I MEAN... WH-WHY'S THIS ALL HAPPENING?
JUST KEEP GOING, WILLYA? KEEP IT TOGETHER UNTIL WE GET OUT OF THIS UNDERGROUND SHOPPING MALL.
WE'RE CRAWLING THROUGH A VENTILATION SHAFT--I'VE SEEN IT IN MOVIES, BUT I NEVER THOUGHT I'D BE DOING IT FOR REAL.
AND JUST WHERE ARE WE?
WE'RE STILL IN SHINJUKU-UNDERGROUND. THOSE BASTARDS DIDN'T EVEN TRY TO HIDE THAT. THEY WERE GONNA KILL US ANYWAY.
WHAT ABOUT THE POLICE?
FORGET IT. THERE'S NO WAY THE COPS HERE COULD DEAL WITH THEM. THEY BELONG TO AN INTERNATIONAL TERRORIST ORGANIZATION, EVEN IF THEY *ARE* THE LAST ONES LEFT.
INTER-NATIONAL TERRORIST ORGANI-ZATION? WHY DID THEY TAKE *ME*?
LEVEL WITH ME! WHAT ARE YOU HIDING?
I HAVE A RIGHT TO KNOW!

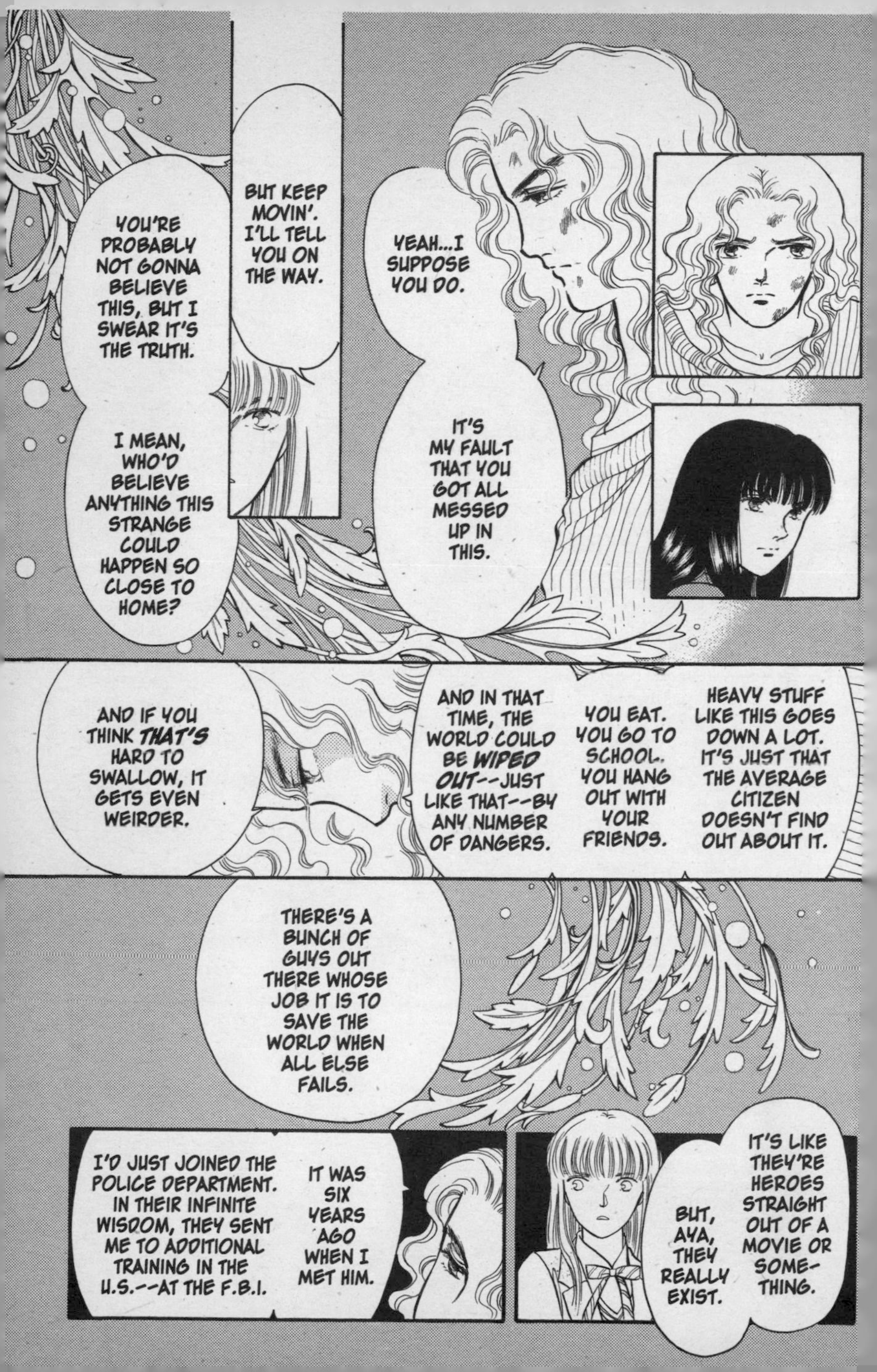
YEAH...I SUPPOSE YOU DO.
IT'S MY FAULT THAT YOU GOT ALL MESSED UP IN THIS.
BUT KEEP MOVIN'. I'LL TELL YOU ON THE WAY.
YOU'RE PROBABLY NOT GONNA BELIEVE THIS, BUT I SWEAR IT'S THE TRUTH.
I MEAN, WHO'D BELIEVE ANYTHING THIS STRANGE COULD HAPPEN SO CLOSE TO HOME?
HEAVY STUFF LIKE THIS GOES DOWN A LOT. IT'S JUST THAT THE AVERAGE CITIZEN DOESN'T FIND OUT ABOUT IT.
YOU EAT. YOU GO TO SCHOOL. YOU HANG OUT WITH YOUR FRIENDS.
AND IN THAT TIME, THE WORLD COULD BE *WIPED OUT*--JUST LIKE THAT--BY ANY NUMBER OF DANGERS.
AND IF YOU THINK *THAT'S* HARD TO SWALLOW, IT GETS EVEN WEIRDER.
THERE'S A BUNCH OF GUYS OUT THERE WHOSE JOB IT IS TO SAVE THE WORLD WHEN ALL ELSE FAILS.
IT'S LIKE THEY'RE HEROES STRAIGHT OUT OF A MOVIE OR SOME-THING.
BUT, AYA, THEY REALLY EXIST.
IT WAS SIX YEARS AGO WHEN I MET HIM.
I'D JUST JOINED THE POLICE DEPARTMENT. IN THEIR INFINITE WISDOM, THEY SENT ME TO ADDITIONAL TRAINING IN THE U.S.--AT THE F.B.I.

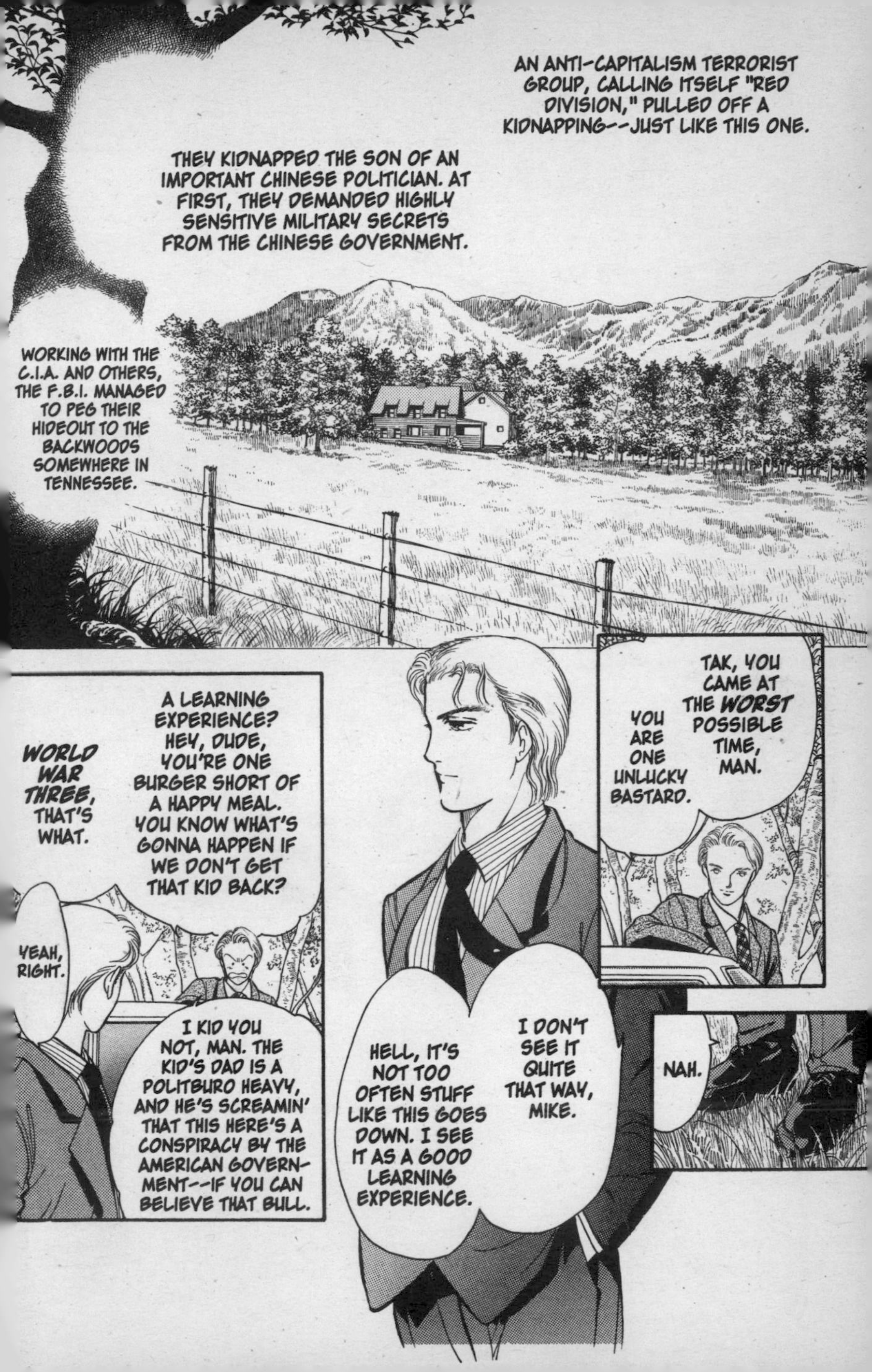
AN ANTI-CAPITALISM TERRORIST GROUP, CALLING ITSELF "RED DIVISION," PULLED OFF A KIDNAPPING--JUST LIKE THIS ONE.
THEY KIDNAPPED THE SON OF AN IMPORTANT CHINESE POLITICIAN. AT FIRST, THEY DEMANDED HIGHLY SENSITIVE MILITARY SECRETS FROM THE CHINESE GOVERNMENT.
WORKING WITH THE C.I.A. AND OTHERS, THE F.B.I. MANAGED TO PEG THEIR HIDEOUT TO THE BACKWOODS SOMEWHERE IN TENNESSEE.
TAK, YOU CAME AT THE *WORST* POSSIBLE TIME, MAN.
YOU ARE ONE UNLUCKY BASTARD.
NAH.
I DON'T SEE IT QUITE THAT WAY, MIKE.
HELL, IT'S NOT TOO OFTEN STUFF LIKE THIS GOES DOWN. I SEE IT AS A GOOD LEARNING EXPERIENCE.
A LEARNING EXPERIENCE? HEY, DUDE, YOU'RE ONE BURGER SHORT OF A HAPPY MEAL. YOU KNOW WHAT'S GONNA HAPPEN IF WE DON'T GET THAT KID BACK?
WORLD WAR THREE, THAT'S WHAT.
YEAH, RIGHT.
I KID YOU NOT, MAN. THE KID'S DAD IS A POLITBURO HEAVY, AND HE'S SCREAMIN' THAT THIS HERE'S A CONSPIRACY BY THE AMERICAN GOVERNMENT--IF YOU CAN BELIEVE THAT BULL.

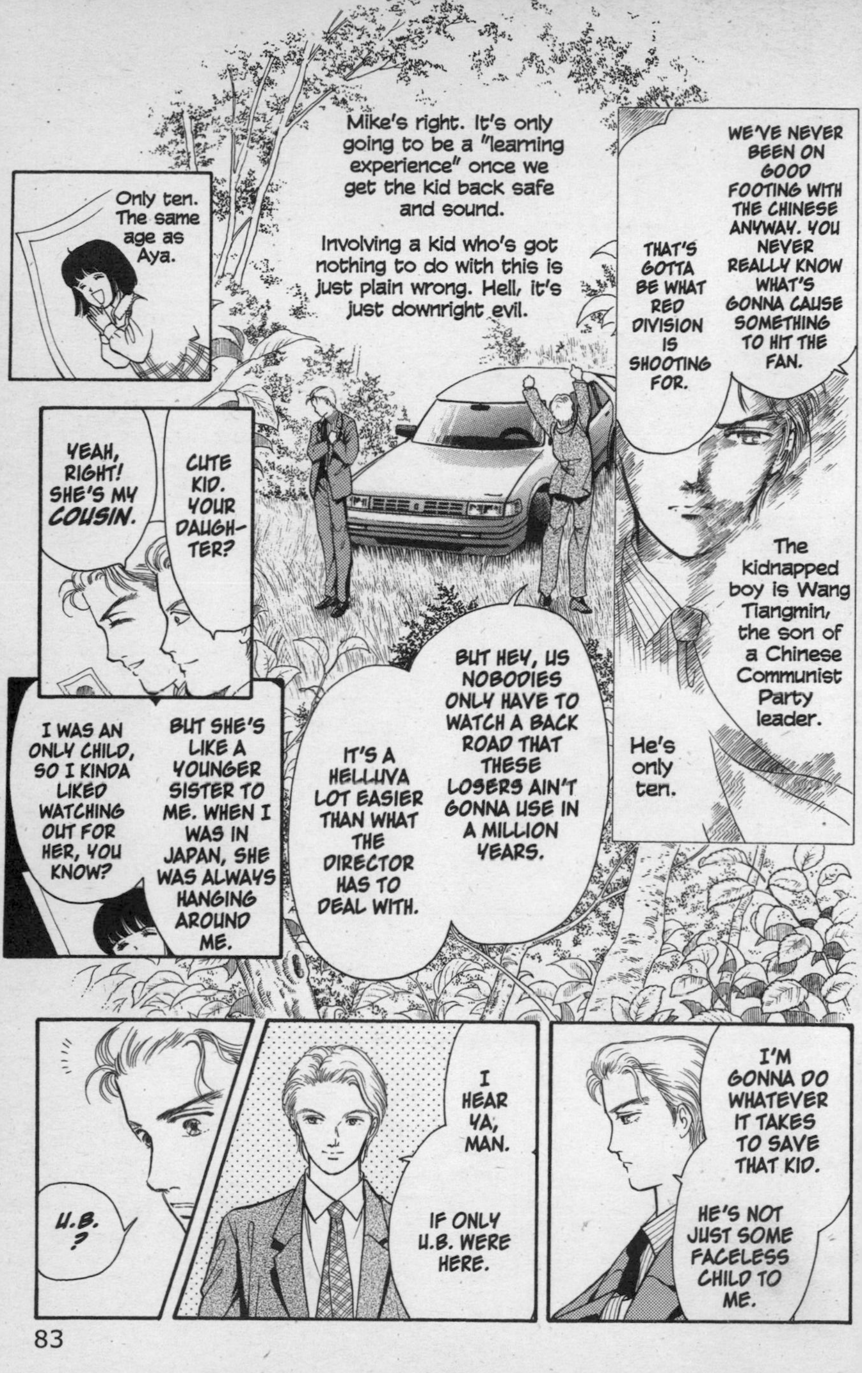
WE'VE NEVER BEEN ON GOOD FOOTING WITH THE CHINESE ANYWAY. YOU NEVER REALLY KNOW WHAT'S GONNA CAUSE SOMETHING TO HIT THE FAN.
THAT'S GOTTA BE WHAT RED DIVISION IS SHOOTING FOR.
The kidnapped boy is Wang Tiangmin, the son of a Chinese Communist Party leader.
He's only ten.
Mike's right. It's only going to be a "learning experience" once we get the kid back safe and sound.
Involving a kid who's got nothing to do with this is just plain wrong. Hell, it's just downright evil.
BUT HEY, US NOBODIES ONLY HAVE TO WATCH A BACK ROAD THAT THESE LOSERS AIN'T GONNA USE IN A MILLION YEARS.
IT'S A HELLUVA LOT EASIER THAN WHAT THE DIRECTOR HAS TO DEAL WITH.
Only ten. The same age as Aya.
CUTE KID. YOUR DAUGHTER?
YEAH, RIGHT! SHE'S MY COUSIN.
BUT SHE'S LIKE A YOUNGER SISTER TO ME. WHEN I WAS IN JAPAN, SHE WAS ALWAYS HANGING AROUND ME.
I WAS AN ONLY CHILD, SO I KINDA LIKED WATCHING OUT FOR HER, YOU KNOW?
I'M GONNA DO WHATEVER IT TAKES TO SAVE THAT KID.
HE'S NOT JUST SOME FACELESS CHILD TO ME.
I HEAR YA, MAN.
IF ONLY U.B. WERE HERE.
U.B.?

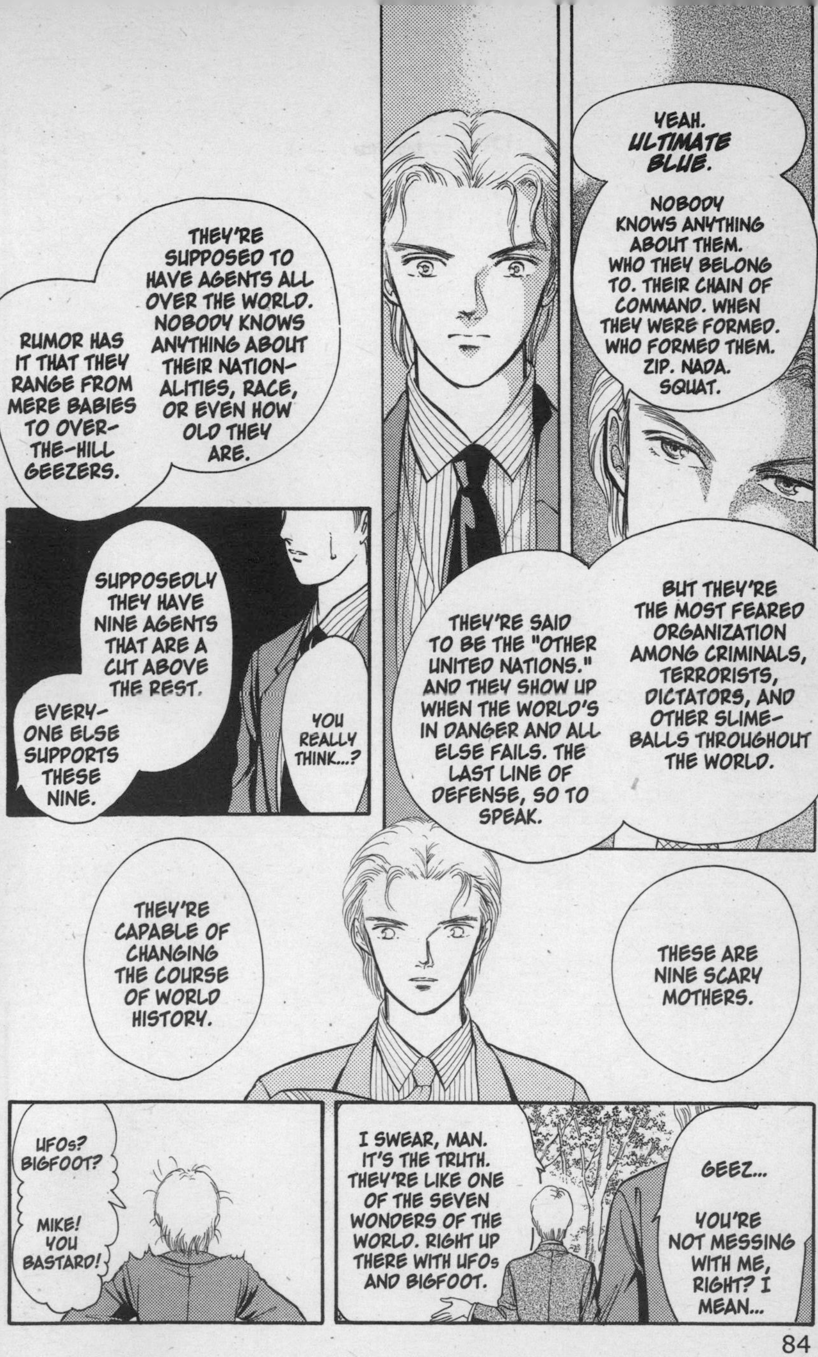
YEAH. *ULTIMATE BLUE.*
NOBODY KNOWS ANYTHING ABOUT THEM. WHO THEY BELONG TO. THEIR CHAIN OF COMMAND. WHEN THEY WERE FORMED. WHO FORMED THEM. ZIP. NADA. SQUAT.
THEY'RE SAID TO BE THE "OTHER UNITED NATIONS." AND THEY SHOW UP WHEN THE WORLD'S IN DANGER AND ALL ELSE FAILS. THE LAST LINE OF DEFENSE, SO TO SPEAK.
BUT THEY'RE THE MOST FEARED ORGANIZATION AMONG CRIMINALS, TERRORISTS, DICTATORS, AND OTHER SLIME-BALLS THROUGHOUT THE WORLD.
THEY'RE SUPPOSED TO HAVE AGENTS ALL OVER THE WORLD. NOBODY KNOWS ANYTHING ABOUT THEIR NATION-ALITIES, RACE, OR EVEN HOW OLD THEY ARE.
RUMOR HAS IT THAT THEY RANGE FROM MERE BABIES TO OVER-THE-HILL GEEZERS.
YOU REALLY THINK...?
SUPPOSEDLY THEY HAVE NINE AGENTS THAT ARE A CUT ABOVE THE REST.
EVERY-ONE ELSE SUPPORTS THESE NINE.
THEY'RE CAPABLE OF CHANGING THE COURSE OF WORLD HISTORY.
THESE ARE NINE SCARY MOTHERS.
GEEZ...
YOU'RE NOT MESSING WITH ME, RIGHT? I MEAN...
I SWEAR, MAN. IT'S THE TRUTH. THEY'RE LIKE ONE OF THE SEVEN WONDERS OF THE WORLD. RIGHT UP THERE WITH UFOs AND BIGFOOT.
UFOs? BIGFOOT?
MIKE! YOU BASTARD!

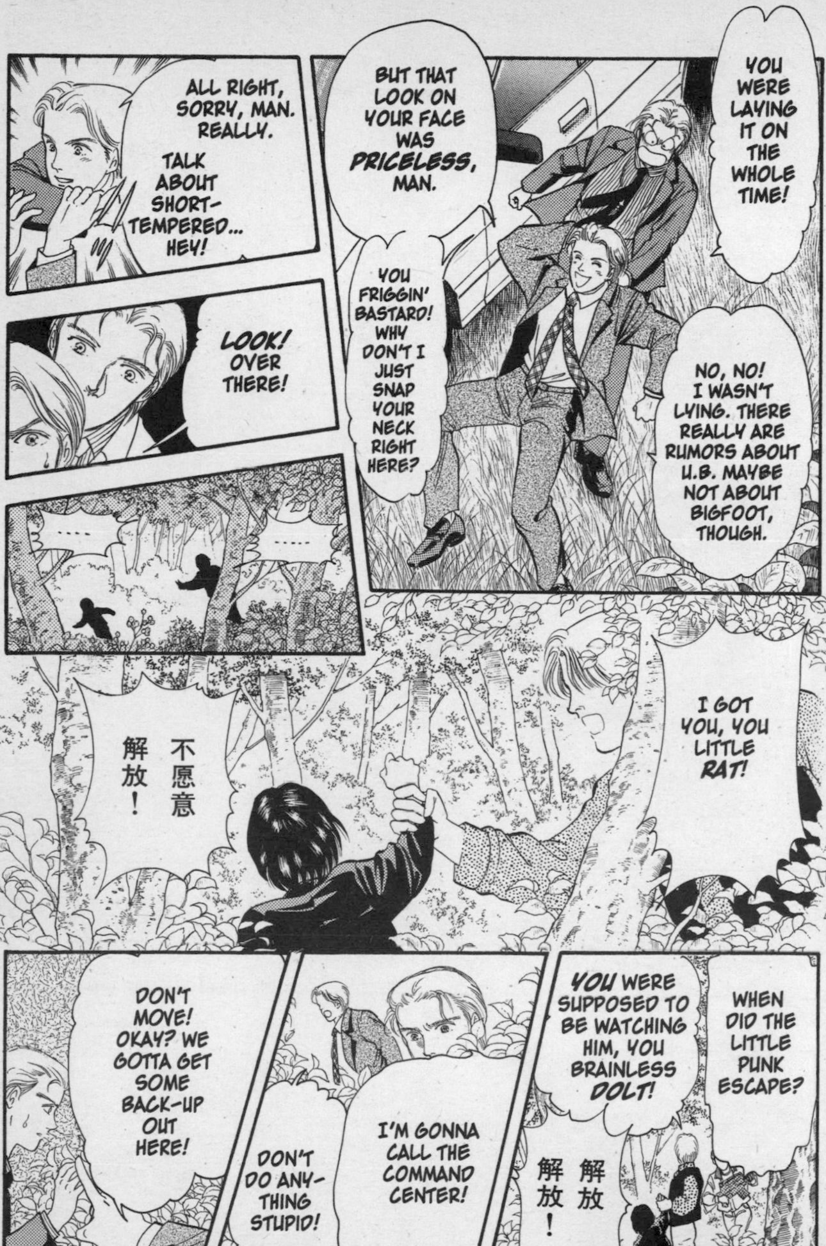
YOU WERE LAYING IT ON THE WHOLE TIME!
NO, NO! I WASN'T LYING. THERE REALLY ARE RUMORS ABOUT U.B. MAYBE NOT ABOUT BIGFOOT, THOUGH.
BUT THAT LOOK ON YOUR FACE WAS *PRICELESS*, MAN.
YOU FRIGGIN' BASTARD! WHY DON'T I JUST SNAP YOUR NECK RIGHT HERE?
ALL RIGHT, SORRY, MAN. REALLY.
TALK ABOUT SHORT-TEMPERED... HEY!
LOOK! OVER THERE!
....
.....
I GOT YOU, YOU LITTLE *RAT!*
不愿意解放！
WHEN DID THE LITTLE PUNK ESCAPE?
YOU WERE SUPPOSED TO BE WATCHING HIM, YOU BRAINLESS *DOLT!*
解放解放！
I'M GONNA CALL THE COMMAND CENTER!
DON'T DO ANYTHING STUPID!
DON'T MOVE! OKAY? WE GOTTA GET SOME BACK-UP OUT HERE!

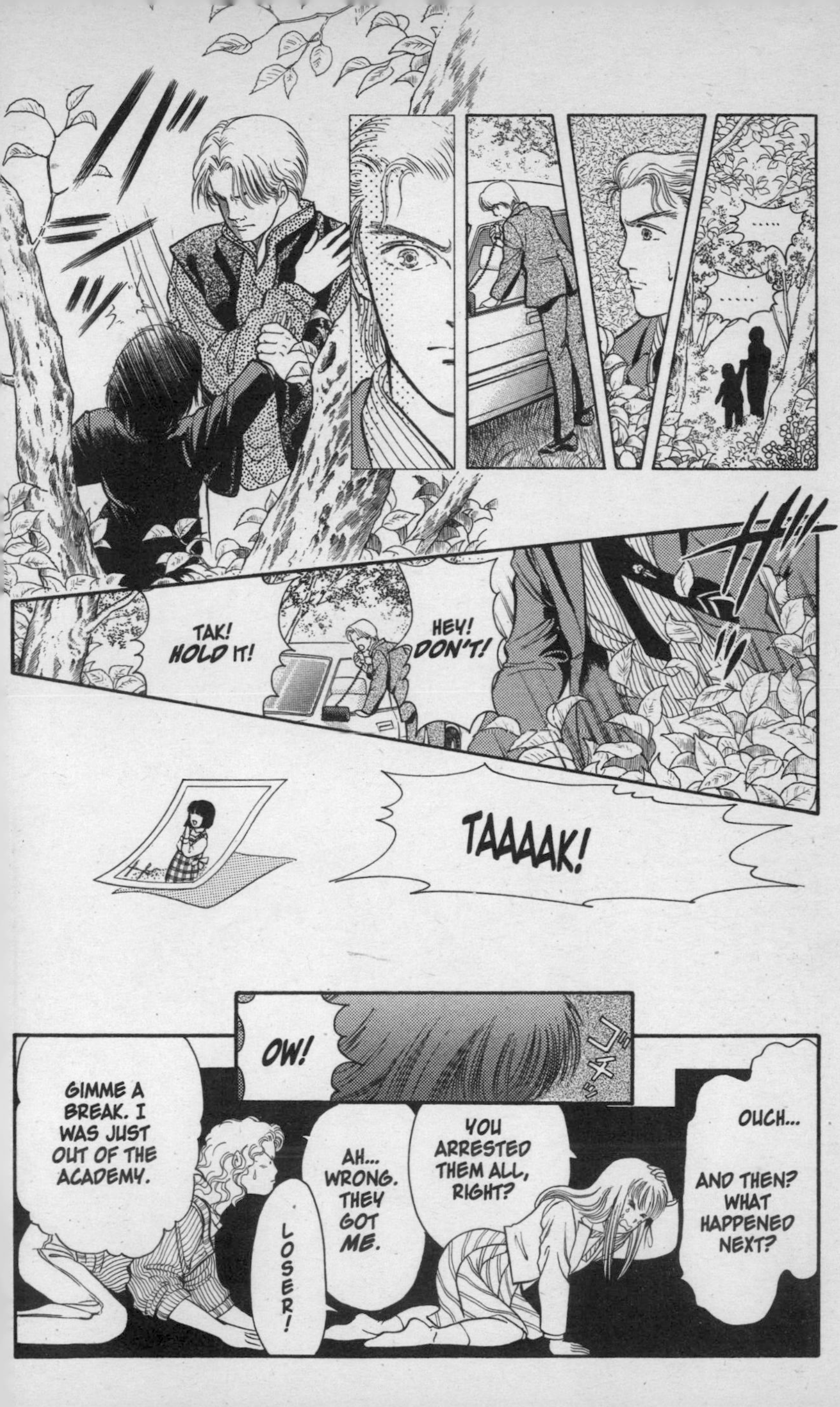
.....
......
HEY! DON'T!
TAK! HOLD IT!
TAAAAK!
OW!
OUCH...
AND THEN? WHAT HAPPENED NEXT?
YOU ARRESTED THEM ALL, RIGHT?
AH... WRONG. THEY GOT ME.
LOSER!
GIMME A BREAK. I WAS JUST OUT OF THE ACADEMY.

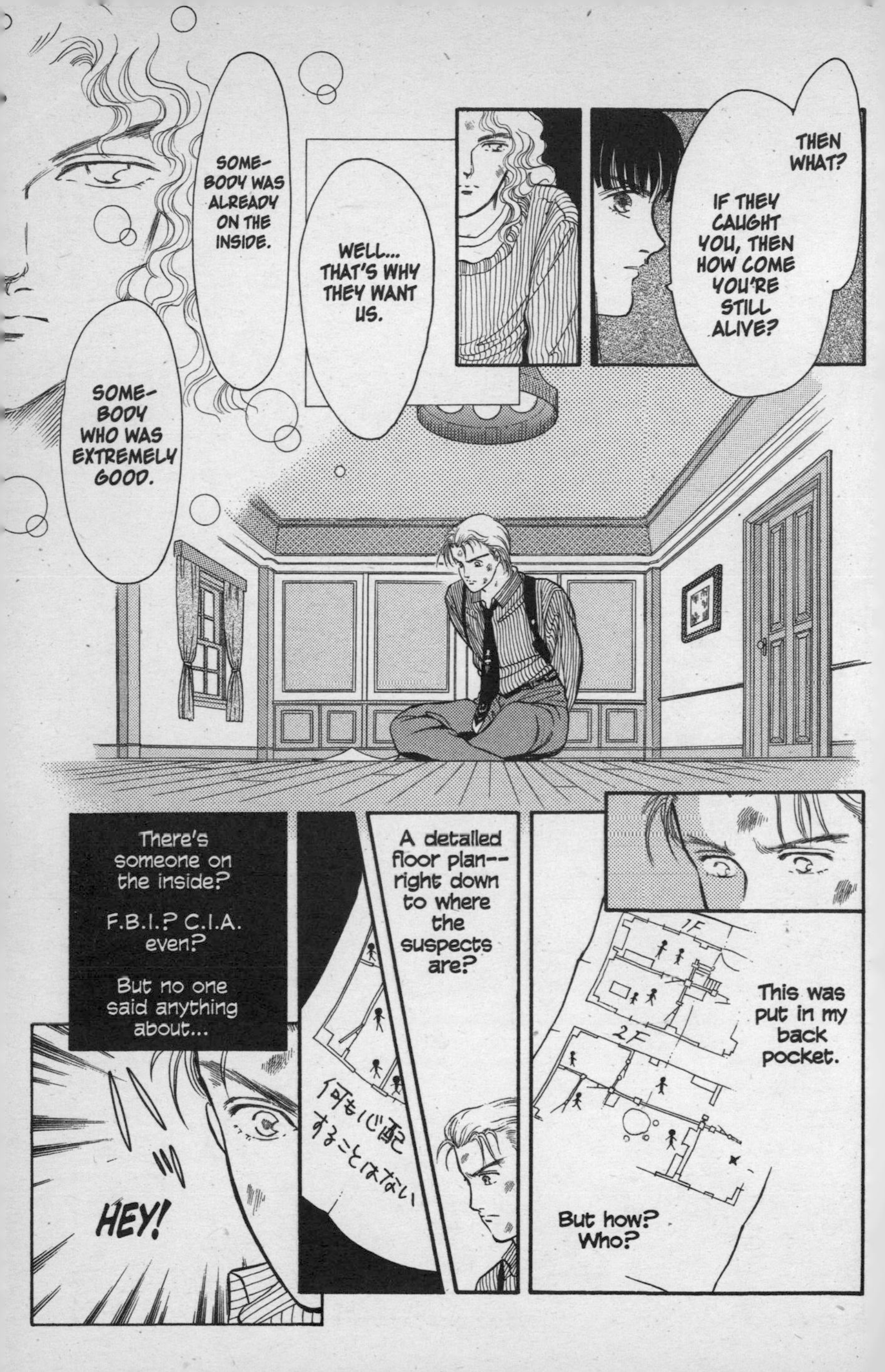
THEN WHAT?
IF THEY CAUGHT YOU, THEN HOW COME YOU'RE STILL ALIVE?
WELL... THAT'S WHY THEY WANT US.
SOME-BODY WAS ALREADY ON THE INSIDE.
SOME-BODY WHO WAS EXTREMELY GOOD.
This was put in my back pocket.
But how? Who?
A detailed floor plan-- right down to where the suspects are?
何も心配することはない
There's someone on the inside?
F.B.I.? C.I.A. even?
But no one said anything about...
HEY!

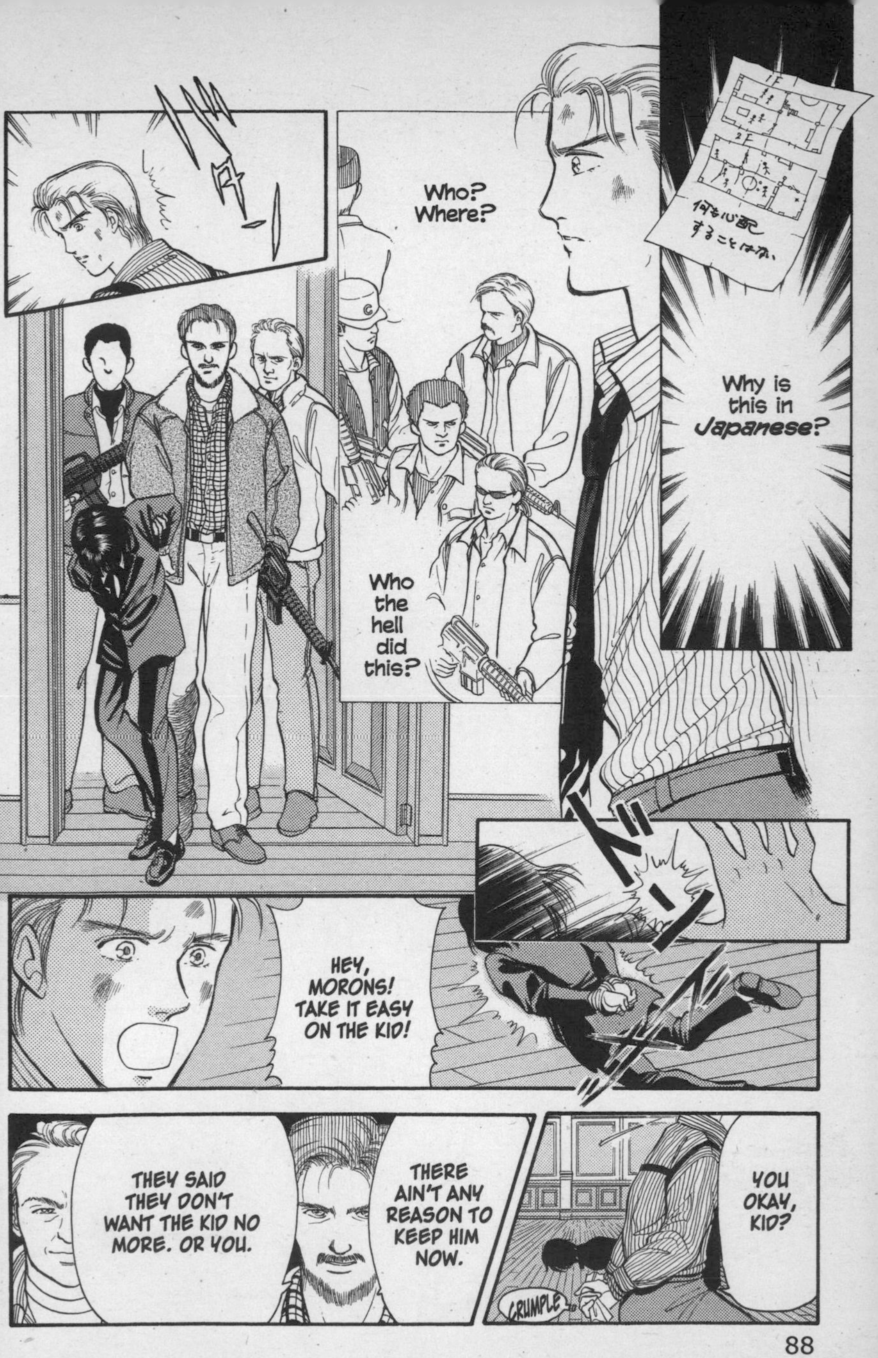
1F
2F
何も心配
することはない
Why is this in Japanese?
Who? Where?
Who the hell did this?
HEY, MORONS! TAKE IT EASY ON THE KID!
YOU OKAY, KID?
CRUMPLE
THERE AIN'T ANY REASON TO KEEP HIM NOW.
THEY SAID THEY DON'T WANT THE KID NO MORE. OR YOU.

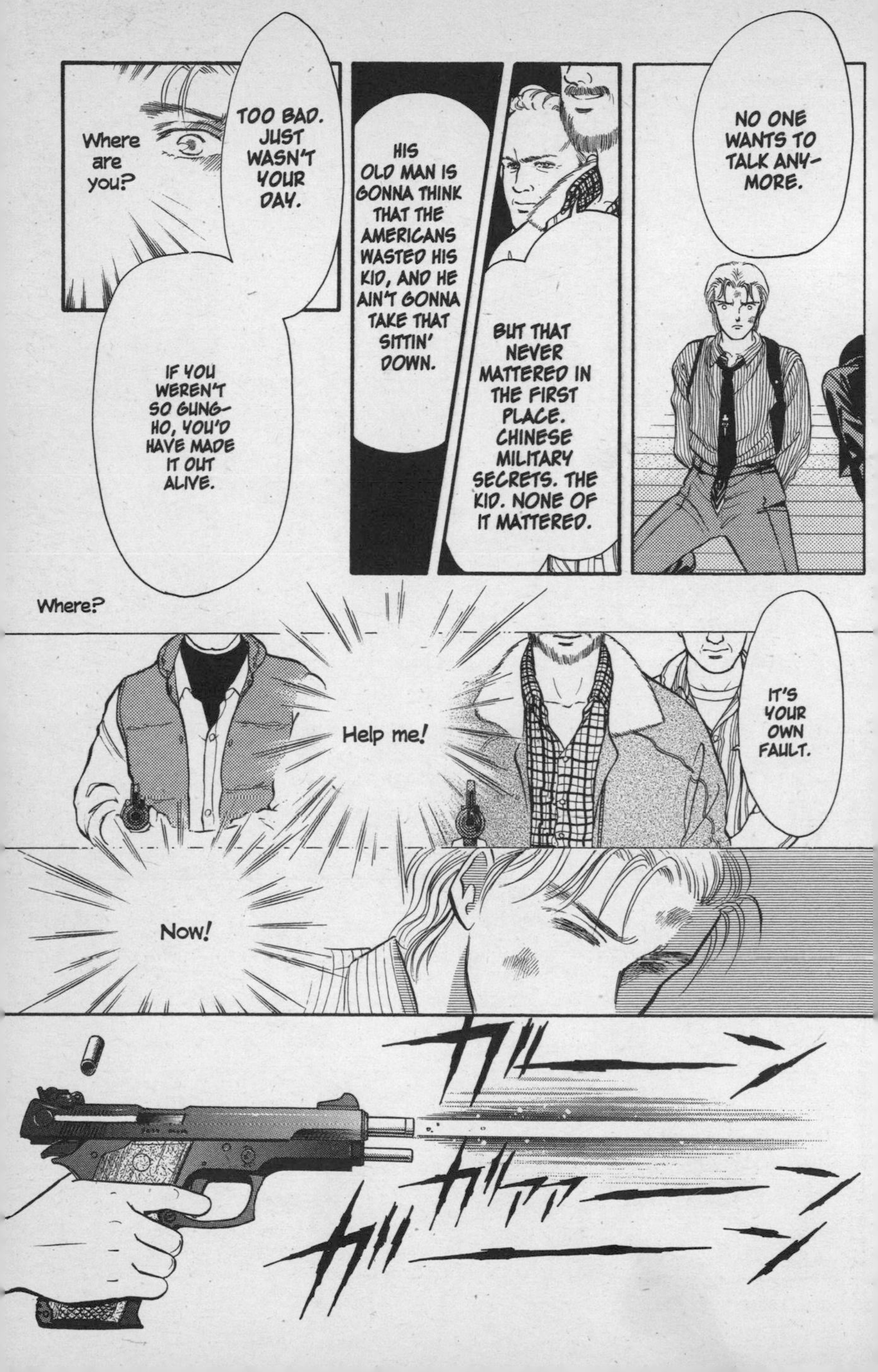
NO ONE WANTS TO TALK ANY-MORE.
HIS OLD MAN IS GONNA THINK THAT THE AMERICANS WASTED HIS KID, AND HE AIN'T GONNA TAKE THAT SITTIN' DOWN.
BUT THAT NEVER MATTERED IN THE FIRST PLACE. CHINESE MILITARY SECRETS. THE KID. NONE OF IT MATTERED.
TOO BAD. JUST WASN'T YOUR DAY.
Where are you?
IF YOU WEREN'T SO GUNG-HO, YOU'D HAVE MADE IT OUT ALIVE.
Where?
IT'S YOUR OWN FAULT.
Help me!
Now!

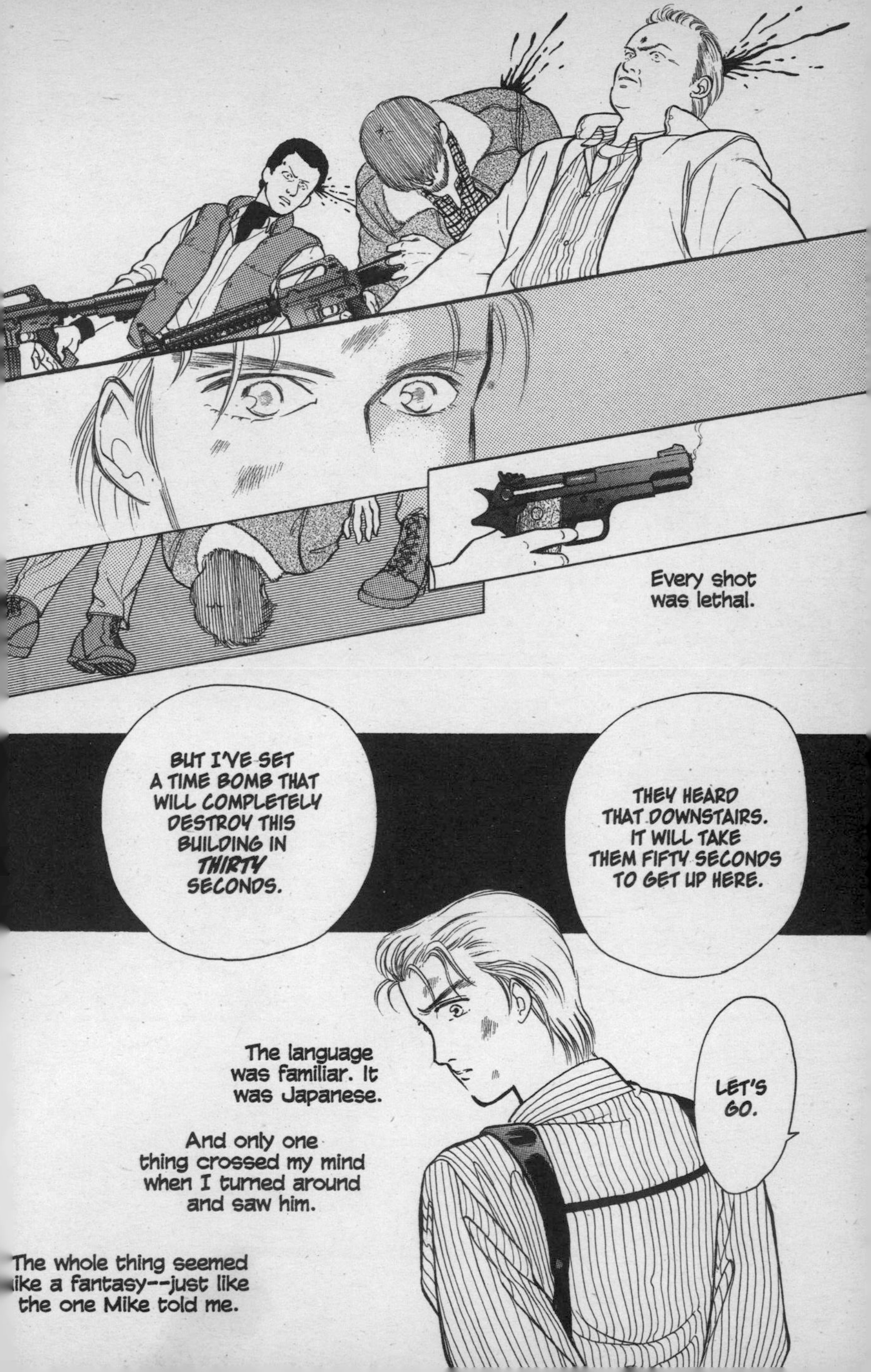
Every shot was lethal.
THEY HEARD THAT DOWNSTAIRS. IT WILL TAKE THEM FIFTY SECONDS TO GET UP HERE.
BUT I'VE SET A TIME BOMB THAT WILL COMPLETELY DESTROY THIS BUILDING IN THIRTY SECONDS.
LET'S GO.
The language was familiar. It was Japanese.
And only one thing crossed my mind when I turned around and saw him.
The whole thing seemed like a fantasy--just like the one Mike told me.

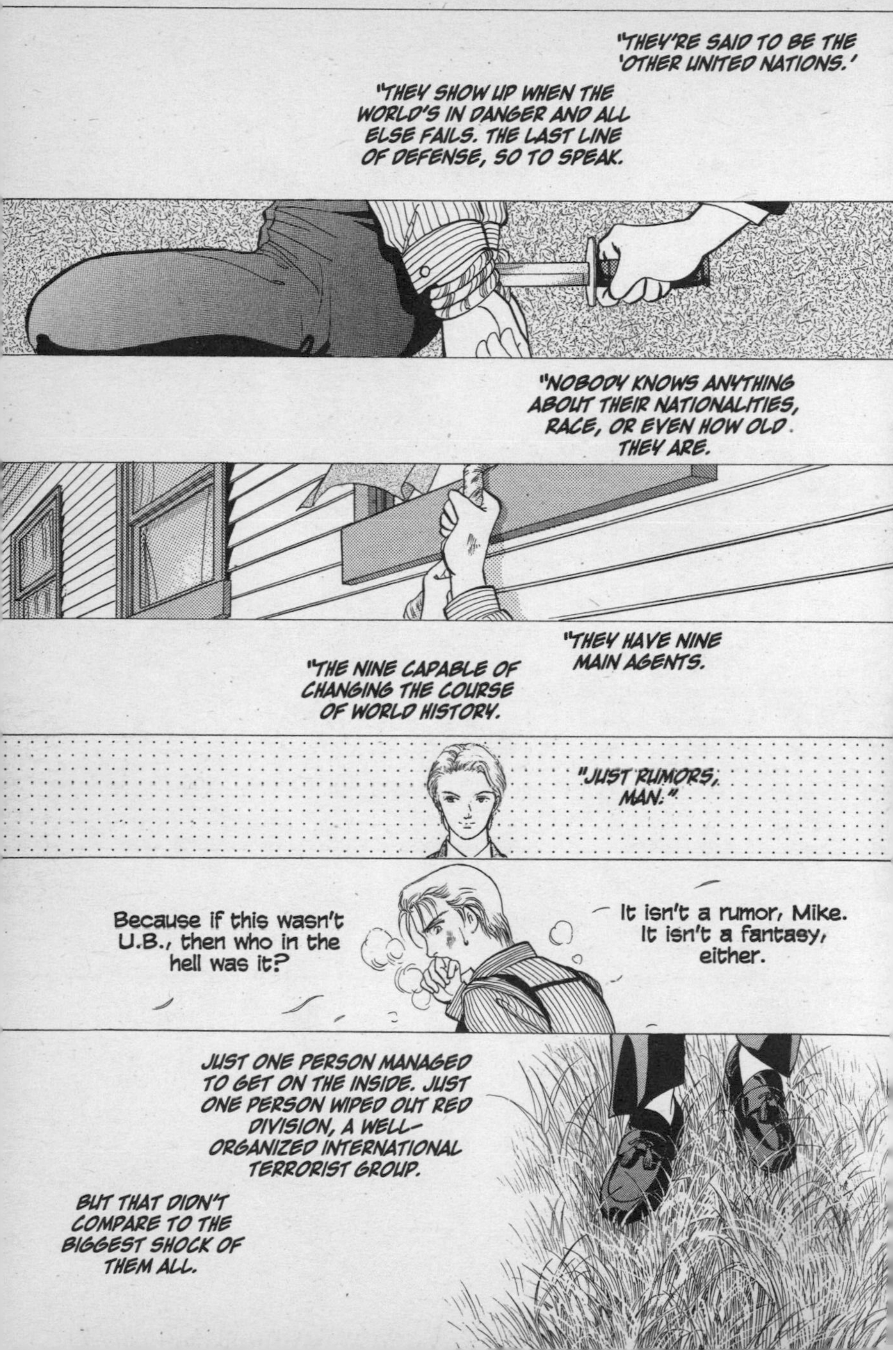
"THEY'RE SAID TO BE THE 'OTHER UNITED NATIONS.'
"THEY SHOW UP WHEN THE WORLD'S IN DANGER AND ALL ELSE FAILS. THE LAST LINE OF DEFENSE, SO TO SPEAK.
"NOBODY KNOWS ANYTHING ABOUT THEIR NATIONALITIES, RACE, OR EVEN HOW OLD THEY ARE.
"THEY HAVE NINE MAIN AGENTS.
"THE NINE CAPABLE OF CHANGING THE COURSE OF WORLD HISTORY.
"JUST RUMORS, MAN."
It isn't a rumor, Mike. It isn't a fantasy, either.
Because if this wasn't U.B., then who in the hell was it?
JUST ONE PERSON MANAGED TO GET ON THE INSIDE. JUST ONE PERSON WIPED OUT RED DIVISION, A WELL-ORGANIZED INTERNATIONAL TERRORIST GROUP.
BUT THAT DIDN'T COMPARE TO THE BIGGEST SHOCK OF THEM ALL.

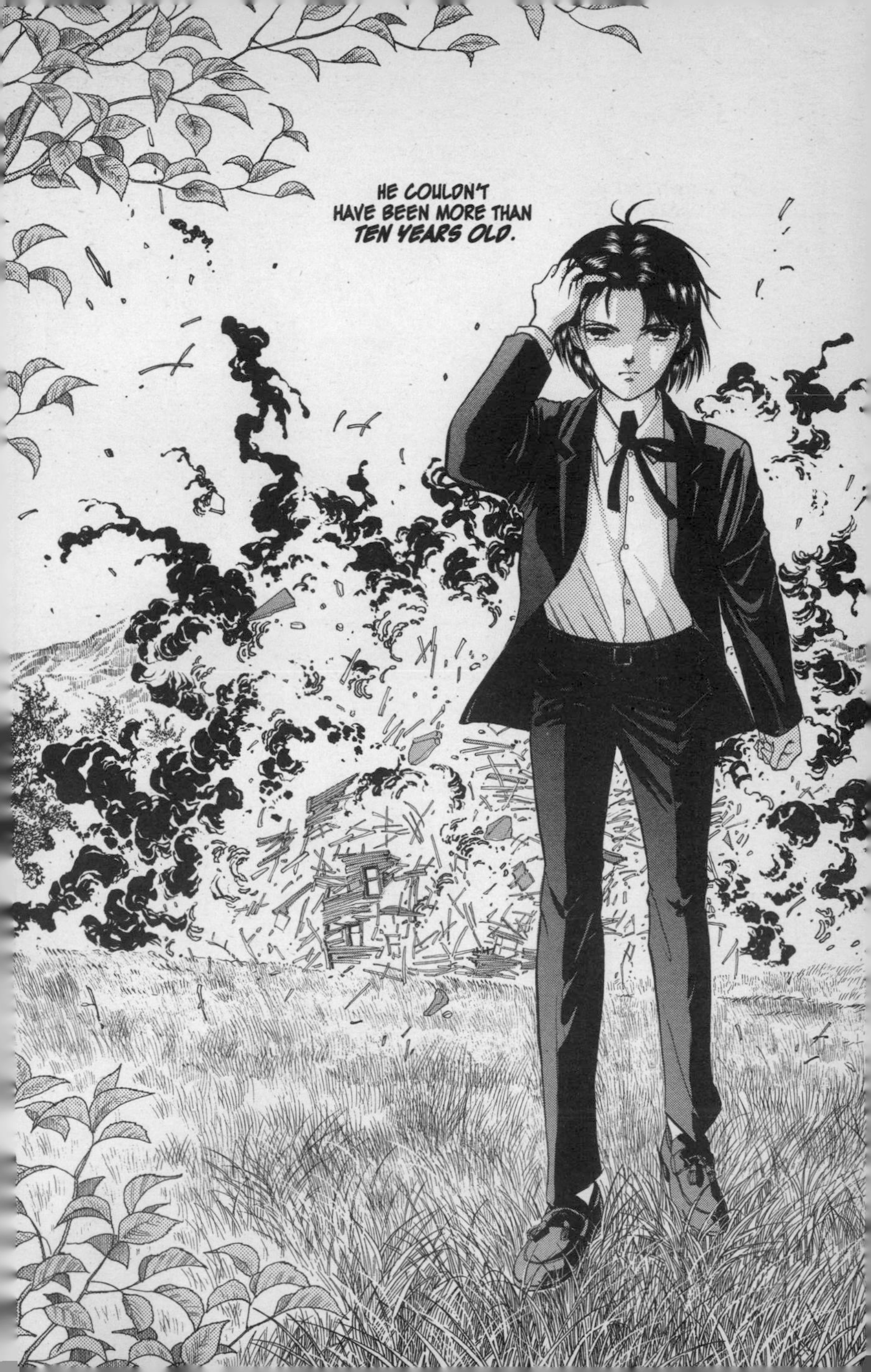
HE COULDN'T HAVE BEEN MORE THAN TEN YEARS OLD.

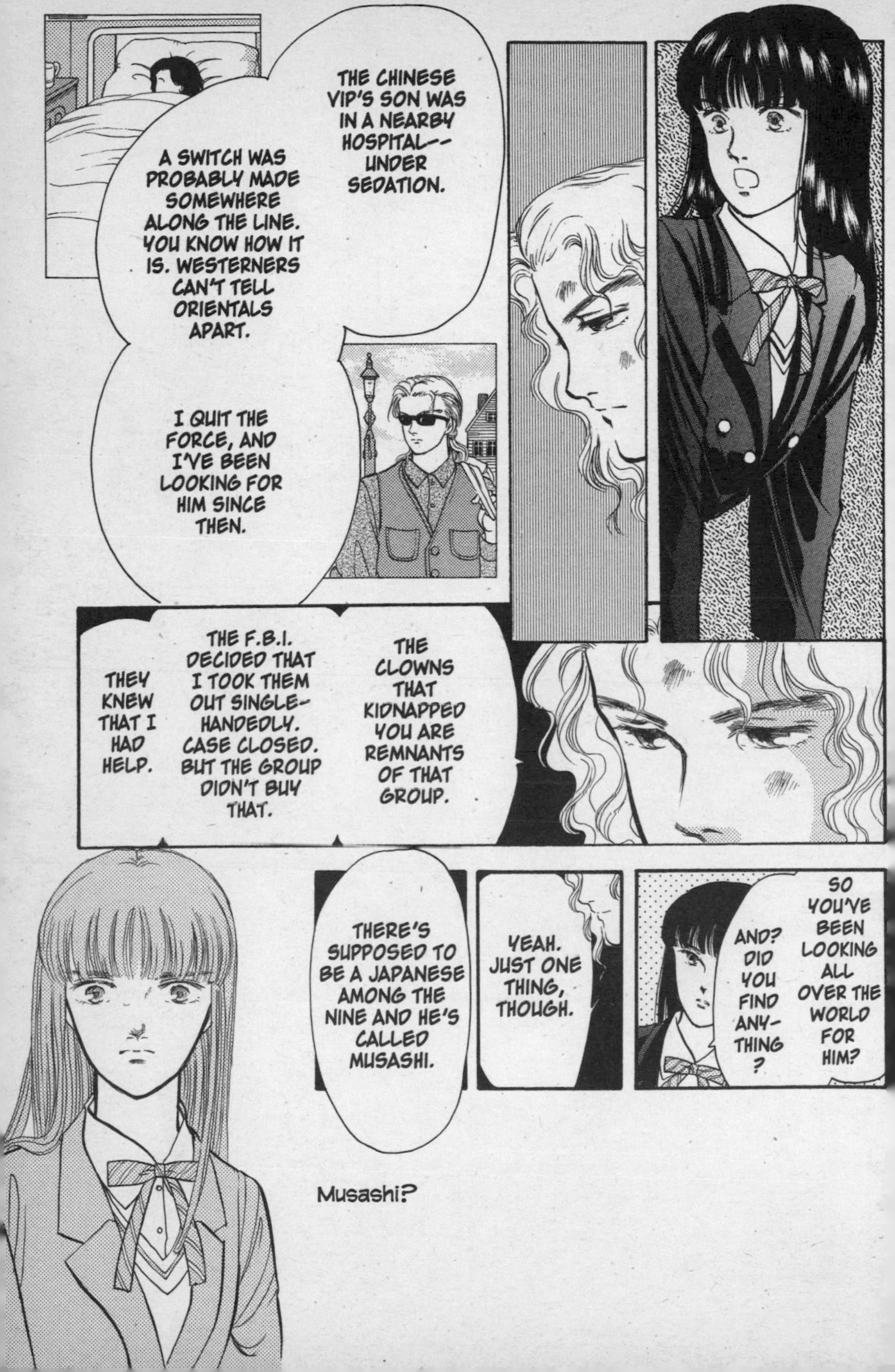
THE CHINESE VIP'S SON WAS IN A NEARBY HOSPITAL-- UNDER SEDATION.
A SWITCH WAS PROBABLY MADE SOMEWHERE ALONG THE LINE. YOU KNOW HOW IT IS. WESTERNERS CAN'T TELL ORIENTALS APART.
I QUIT THE FORCE, AND I'VE BEEN LOOKING FOR HIM SINCE THEN.
THE F.B.I. DECIDED THAT I TOOK THEM OUT SINGLE-HANDEDLY. CASE CLOSED. BUT THE GROUP DIDN'T BUY THAT.
THEY KNEW THAT I HAD HELP.
THE CLOWNS THAT KIDNAPPED YOU ARE REMNANTS OF THAT GROUP.
SO YOU'VE BEEN LOOKING ALL OVER THE WORLD FOR HIM?
AND? DID YOU FIND ANY-THING?
YEAH. JUST ONE THING, THOUGH.
THERE'S SUPPOSED TO BE A JAPANESE AMONG THE NINE AND HE'S CALLED MUSASHI.
Musashi?

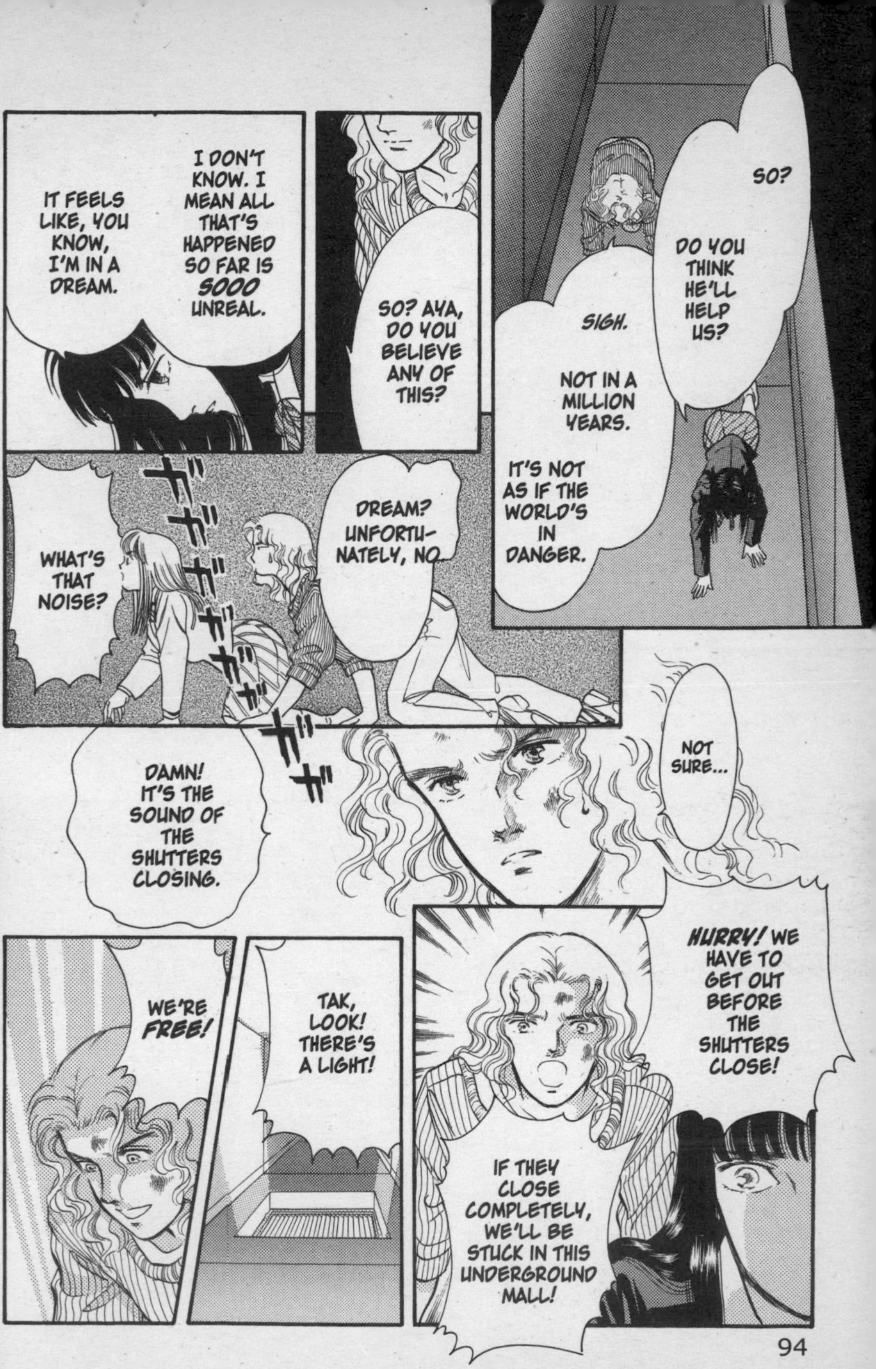
SO?
DO YOU THINK HE'LL HELP US?
SIGH.
NOT IN A MILLION YEARS.
IT'S NOT AS IF THE WORLD'S IN DANGER.
SO? AYA, DO YOU BELIEVE ANY OF THIS?
I DON'T KNOW. I MEAN ALL THAT'S HAPPENED SO FAR IS SOOO UNREAL.
IT FEELS LIKE, YOU KNOW, I'M IN A DREAM.
DREAM? UNFORTUNATELY, NO.
ガガガガガガガ
WHAT'S THAT NOISE?
ガガ
NOT SURE...
DAMN! IT'S THE SOUND OF THE SHUTTERS CLOSING.
HURRY! WE HAVE TO GET OUT BEFORE THE SHUTTERS CLOSE!
IF THEY CLOSE COMPLETELY, WE'LL BE STUCK IN THIS UNDERGROUND MALL!
TAK, LOOK! THERE'S A LIGHT!
WE'RE FREE!

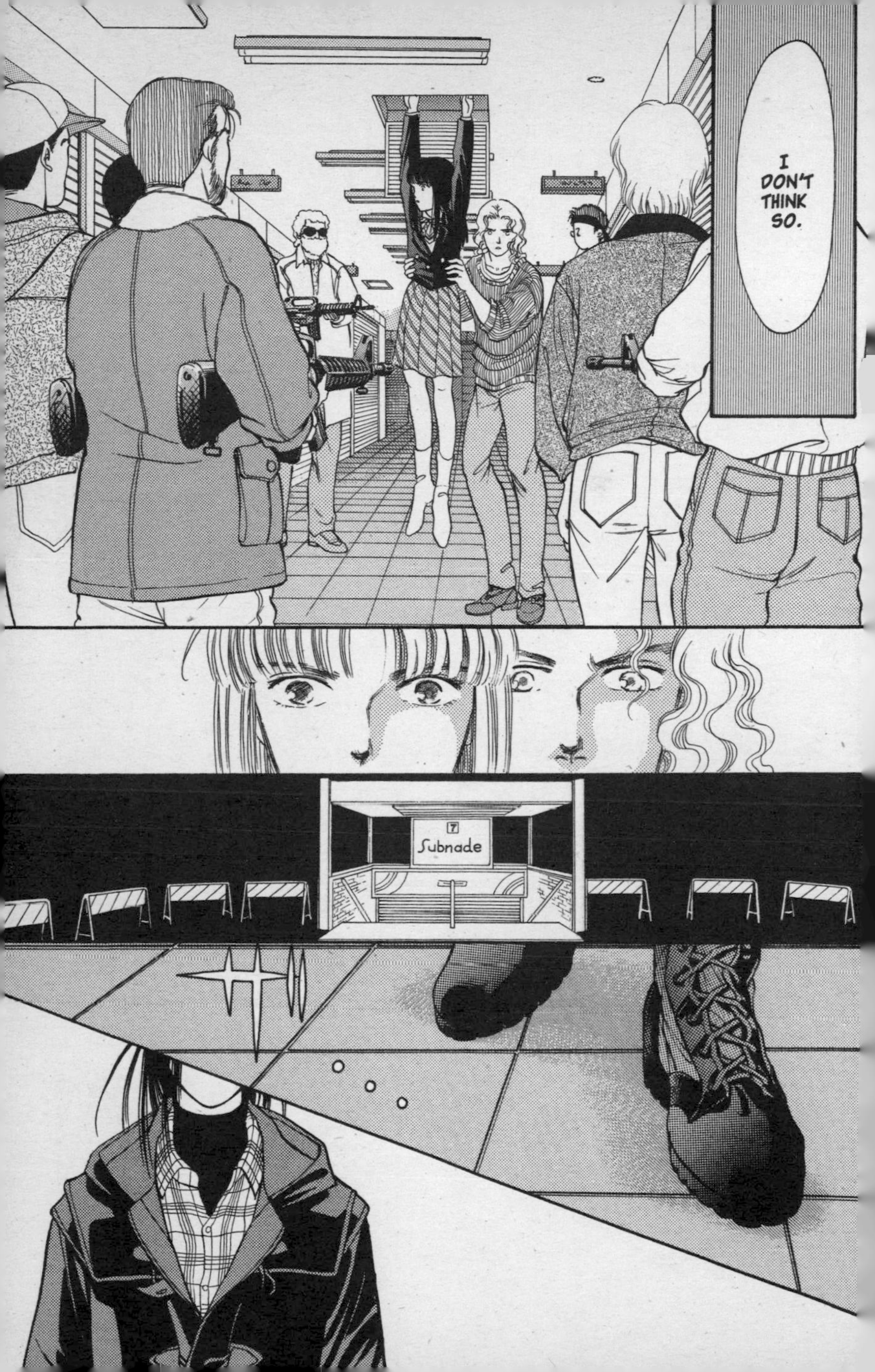
I DON'T THINK SO.
7
Subnade

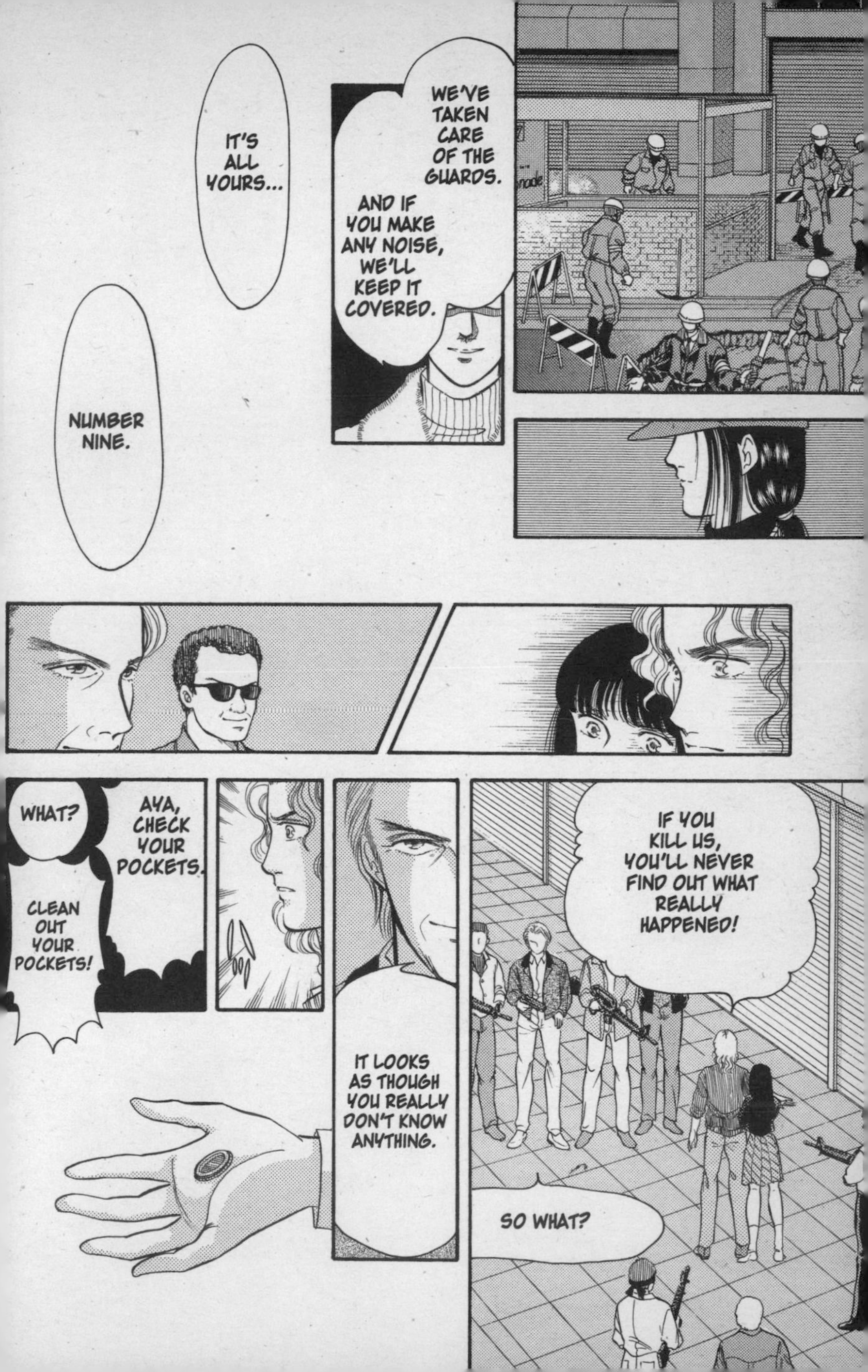
WE'VE TAKEN CARE OF THE GUARDS.
AND IF YOU MAKE ANY NOISE, WE'LL KEEP IT COVERED.
IT'S ALL YOURS...
NUMBER NINE.
IF YOU KILL US, YOU'LL NEVER FIND OUT WHAT REALLY HAPPENED!
SO WHAT?
IT LOOKS AS THOUGH YOU REALLY DON'T KNOW ANYTHING.
AYA, CHECK YOUR POCKETS.
WHAT?
CLEAN OUT YOUR POCKETS!

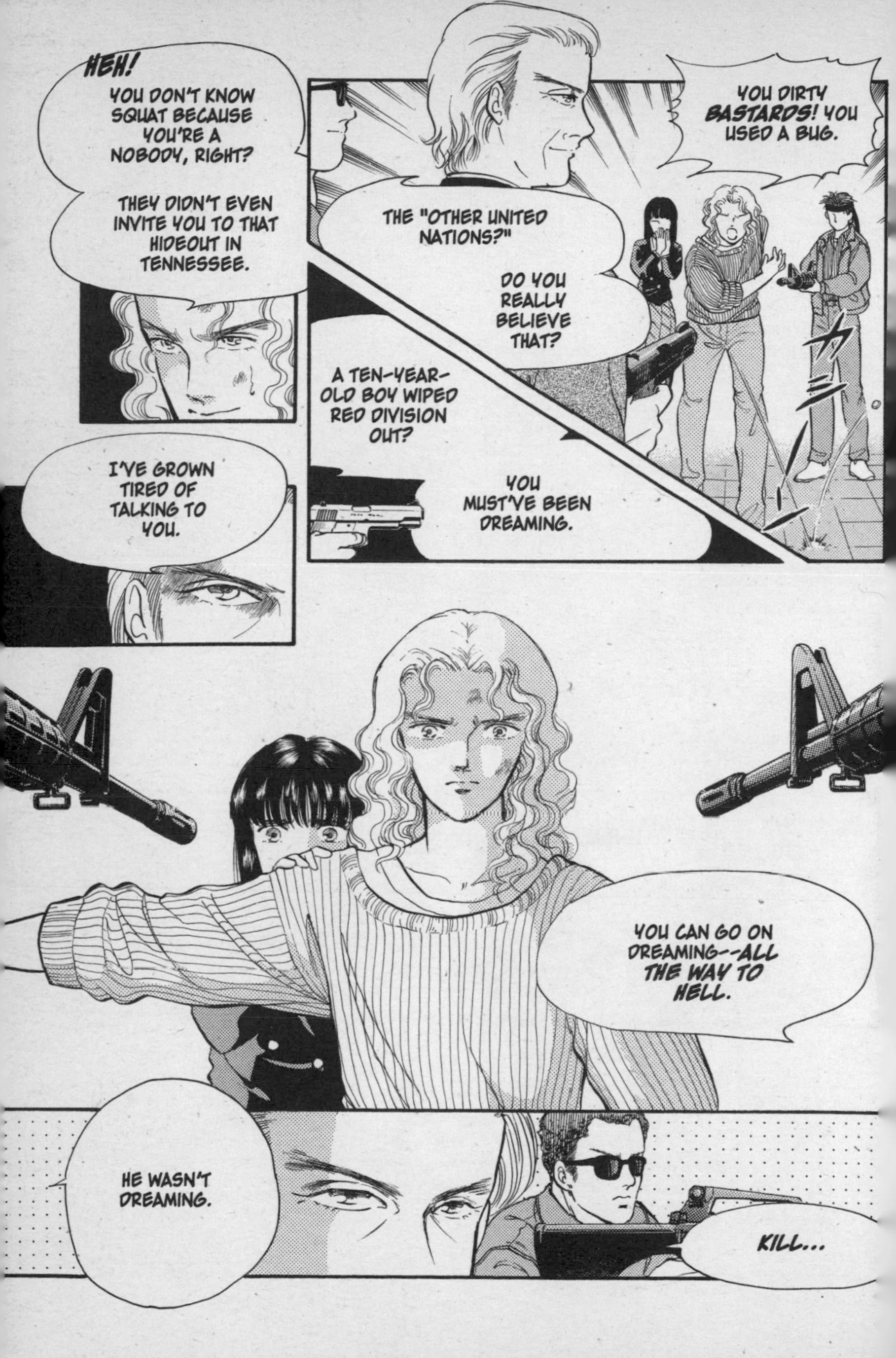
YOU DIRTY BASTARDS! YOU USED A BUG.
THE "OTHER UNITED NATIONS?"
DO YOU REALLY BELIEVE THAT?
A TEN-YEAR-OLD BOY WIPED RED DIVISION OUT?
YOU MUST'VE BEEN DREAMING.
HEH! YOU DON'T KNOW SQUAT BECAUSE YOU'RE A NOBODY, RIGHT?
THEY DIDN'T EVEN INVITE YOU TO THAT HIDEOUT IN TENNESSEE.
I'VE GROWN TIRED OF TALKING TO YOU.
YOU CAN GO ON DREAMING--ALL THE WAY TO HELL.
KILL...
HE WASN'T DREAMING.

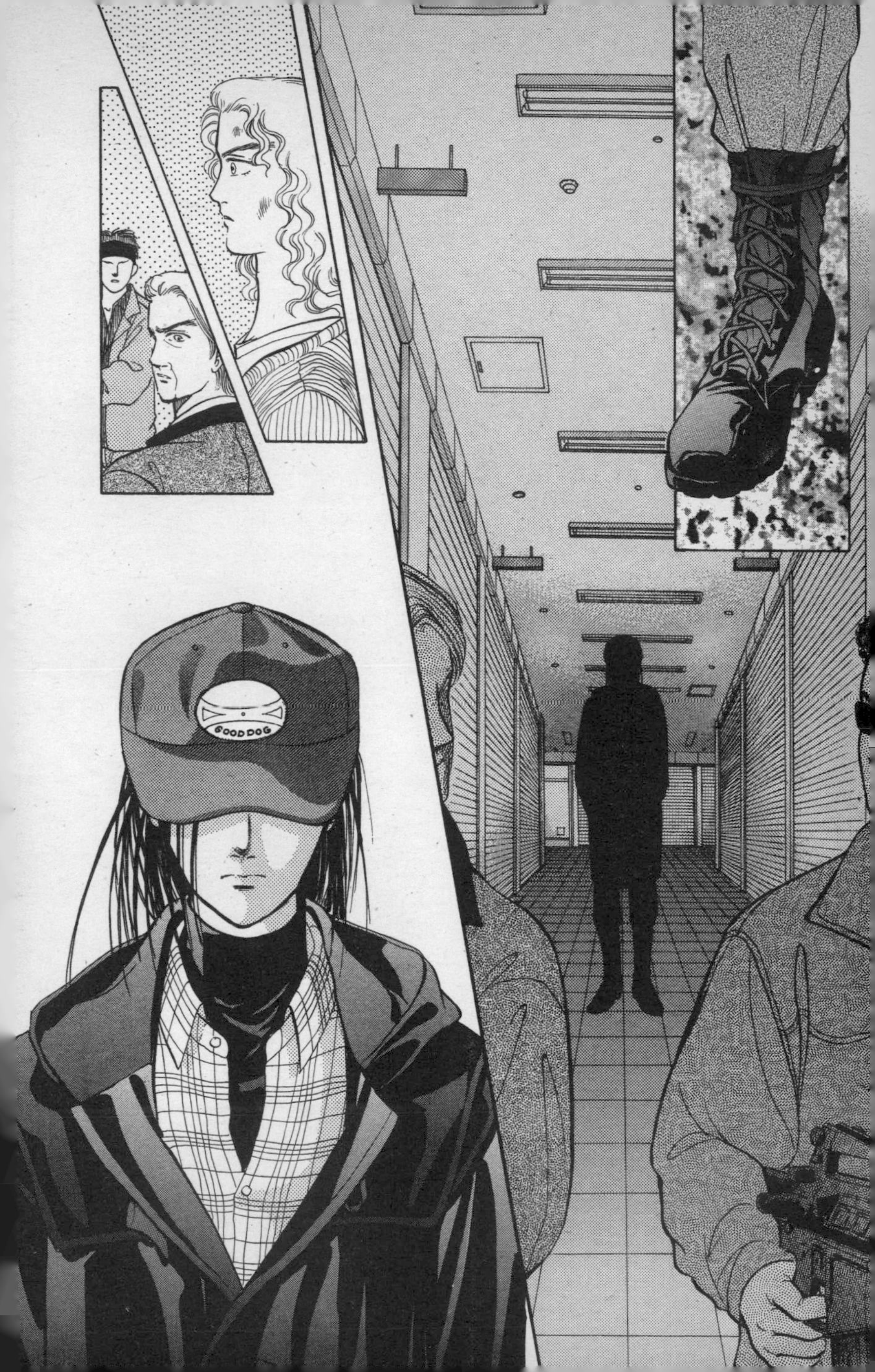
GOOD DOG

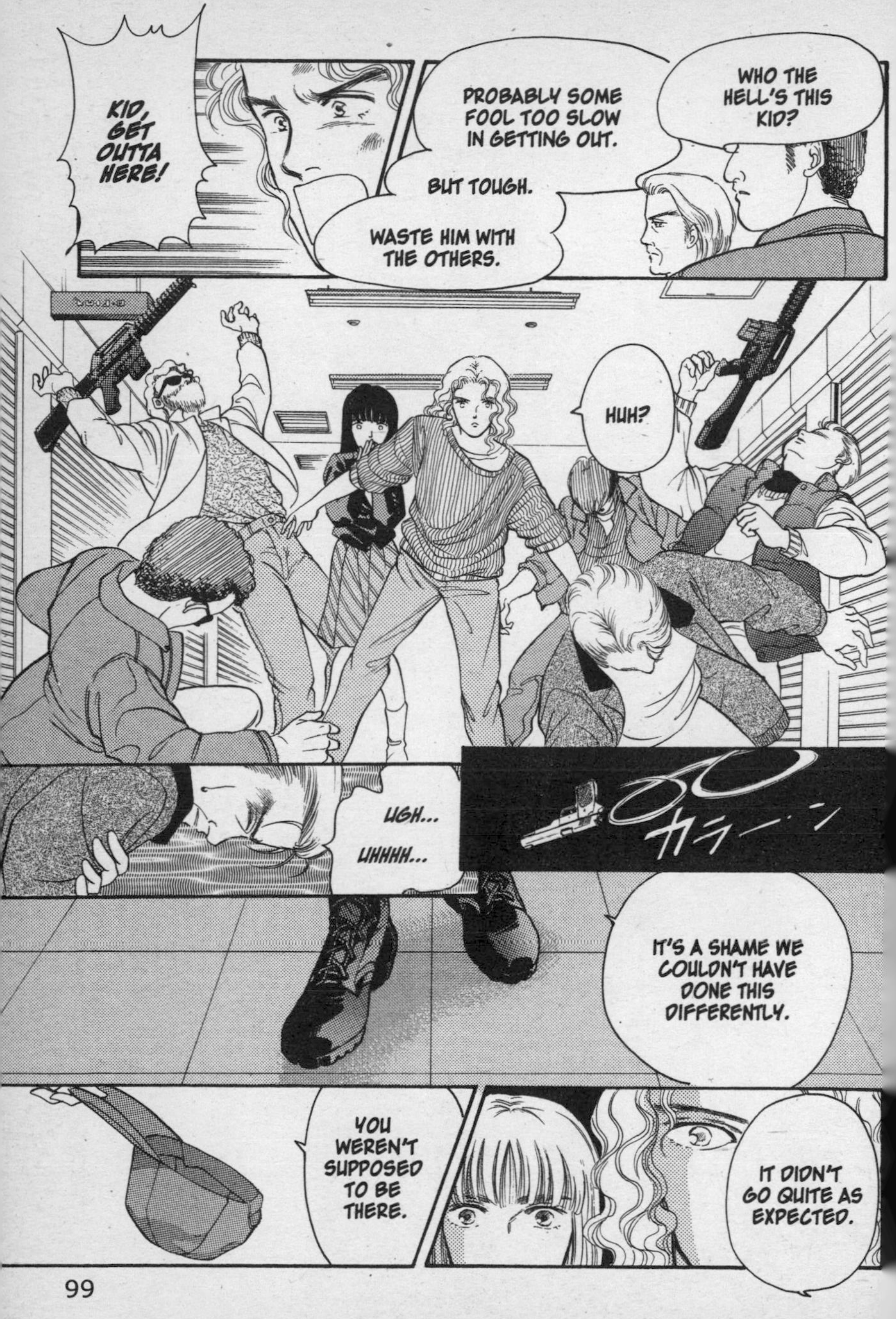
WHO THE HELL'S THIS KID?
PROBABLY SOME FOOL TOO SLOW IN GETTING OUT.
BUT TOUGH.
WASTE HIM WITH THE OTHERS.
KID, GET OUTTA HERE!
HUH?
カラーン
UGH...
UHHHH...
IT'S A SHAME WE COULDN'T HAVE DONE THIS DIFFERENTLY.
IT DIDN'T GO QUITE AS EXPECTED.
YOU WEREN'T SUPPOSED TO BE THERE.

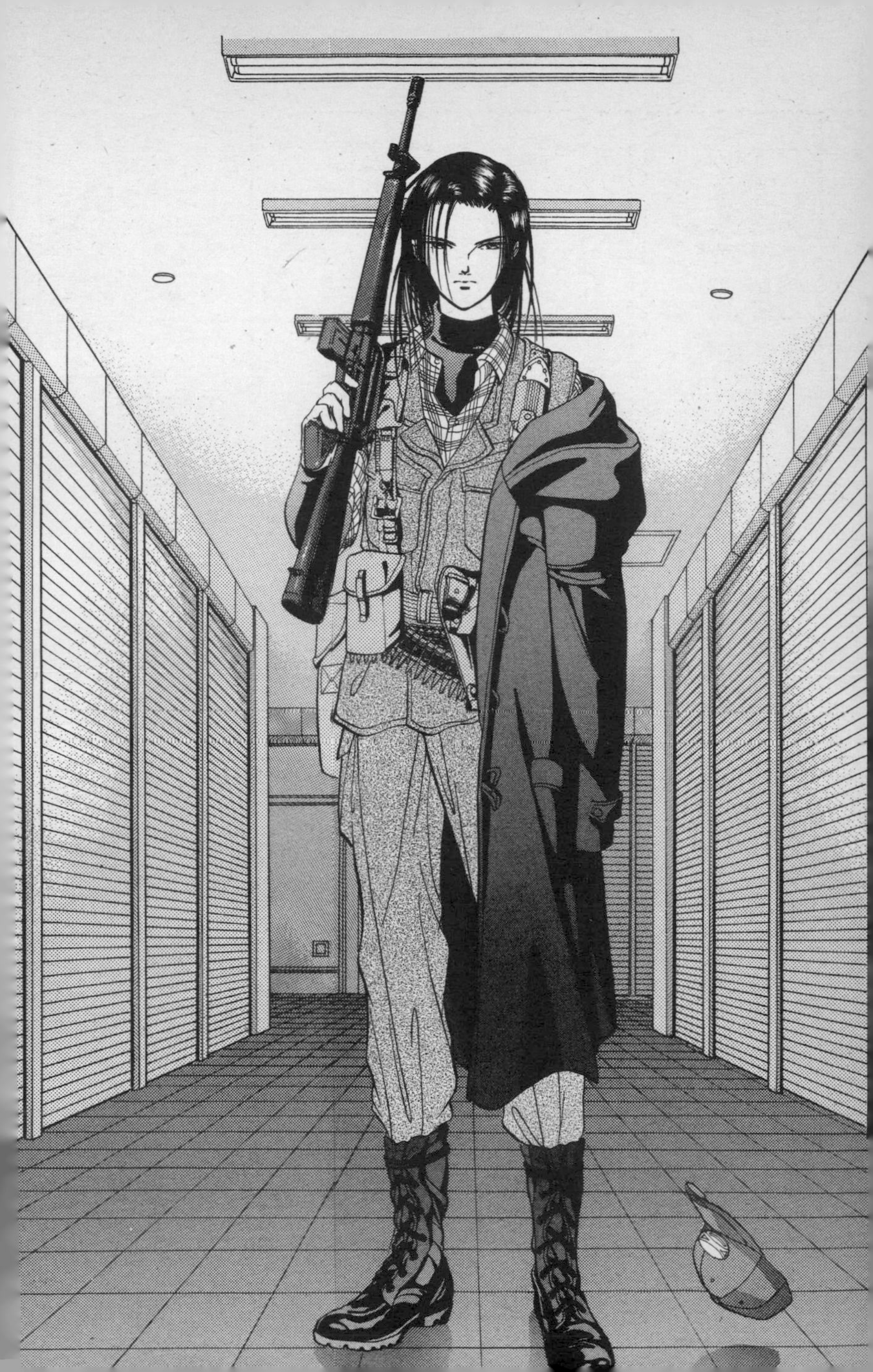

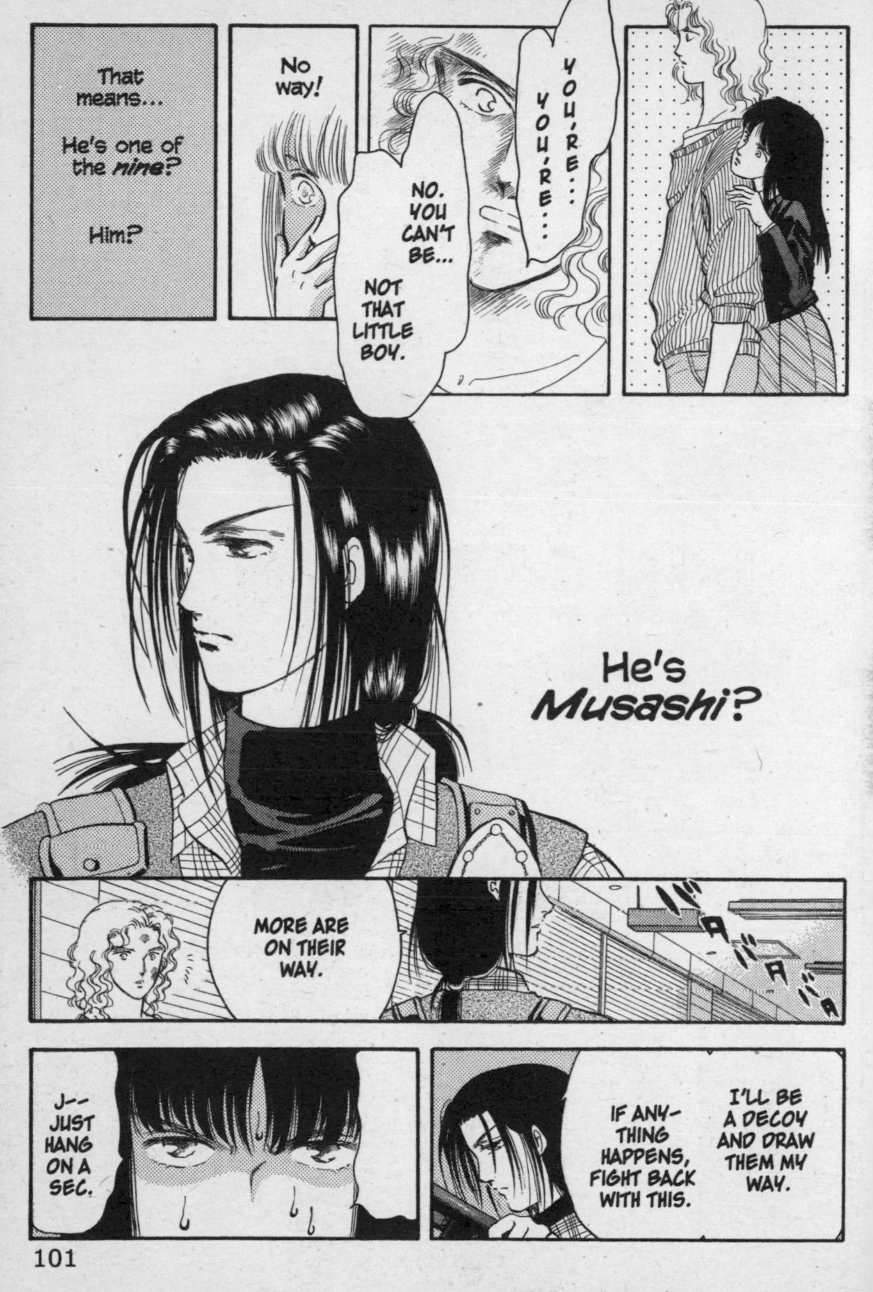
YOU'RE... YOU'RE...
NO. YOU CAN'T BE... NOT THAT LITTLE BOY.
No way!
That means... He's one of the *nine*? Him?
He's *Musashi*?
MORE ARE ON THEIR WAY.
I'LL BE A DECOY AND DRAW THEM MY WAY.
IF ANY- THING HAPPENS, FIGHT BACK WITH THIS.
J-- JUST HANG ON A SEC.

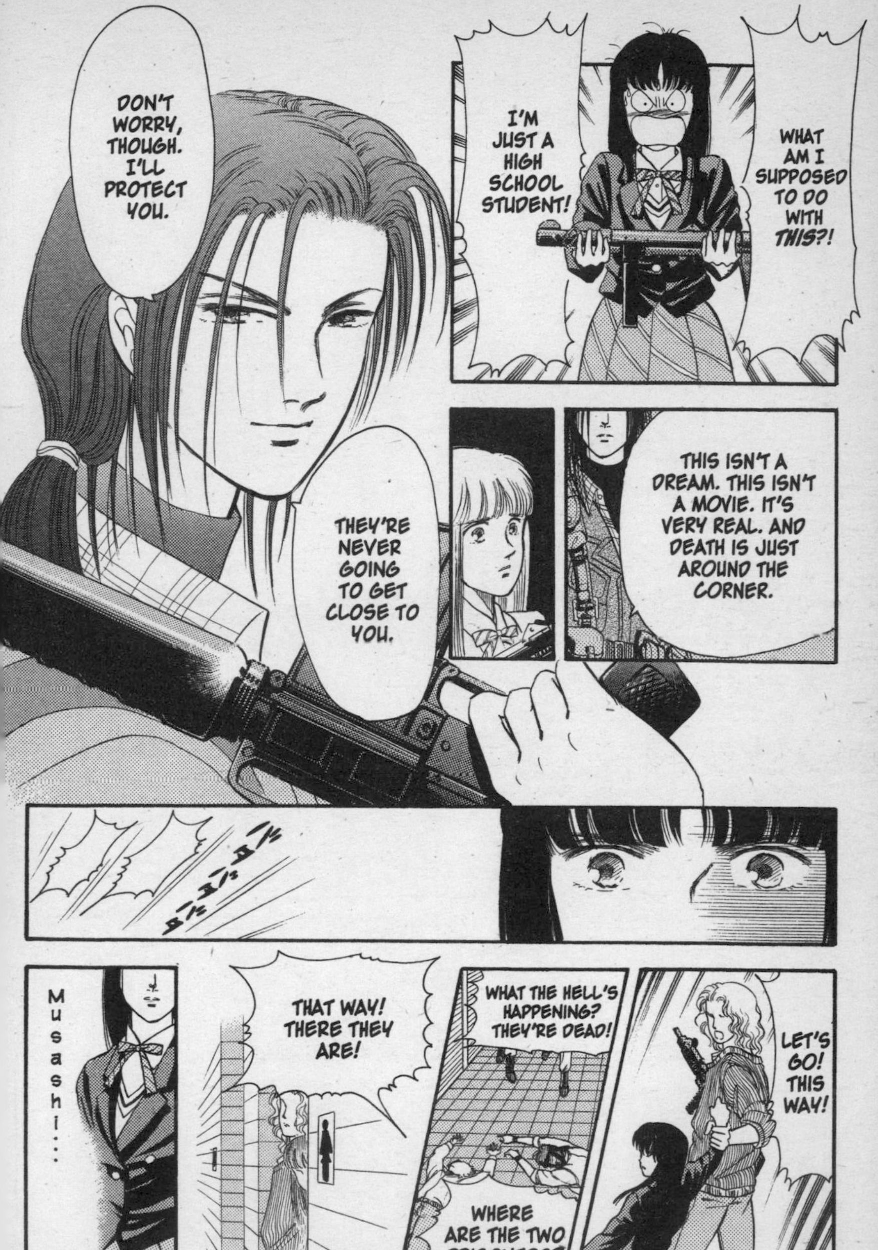
WHAT AM I SUPPOSED TO DO WITH *THIS?!*
I'M JUST A HIGH SCHOOL STUDENT!
THIS ISN'T A DREAM. THIS ISN'T A MOVIE. IT'S VERY REAL. AND DEATH IS JUST AROUND THE CORNER.
DON'T WORRY, THOUGH. I'LL PROTECT YOU.
THEY'RE NEVER GOING TO GET CLOSE TO YOU.
LET'S GO! THIS WAY!
WHAT THE HELL'S HAPPENING? THEY'RE DEAD!
WHERE ARE THE TWO PRISONERS?
THAT WAY! THERE THEY ARE!
Musashi...

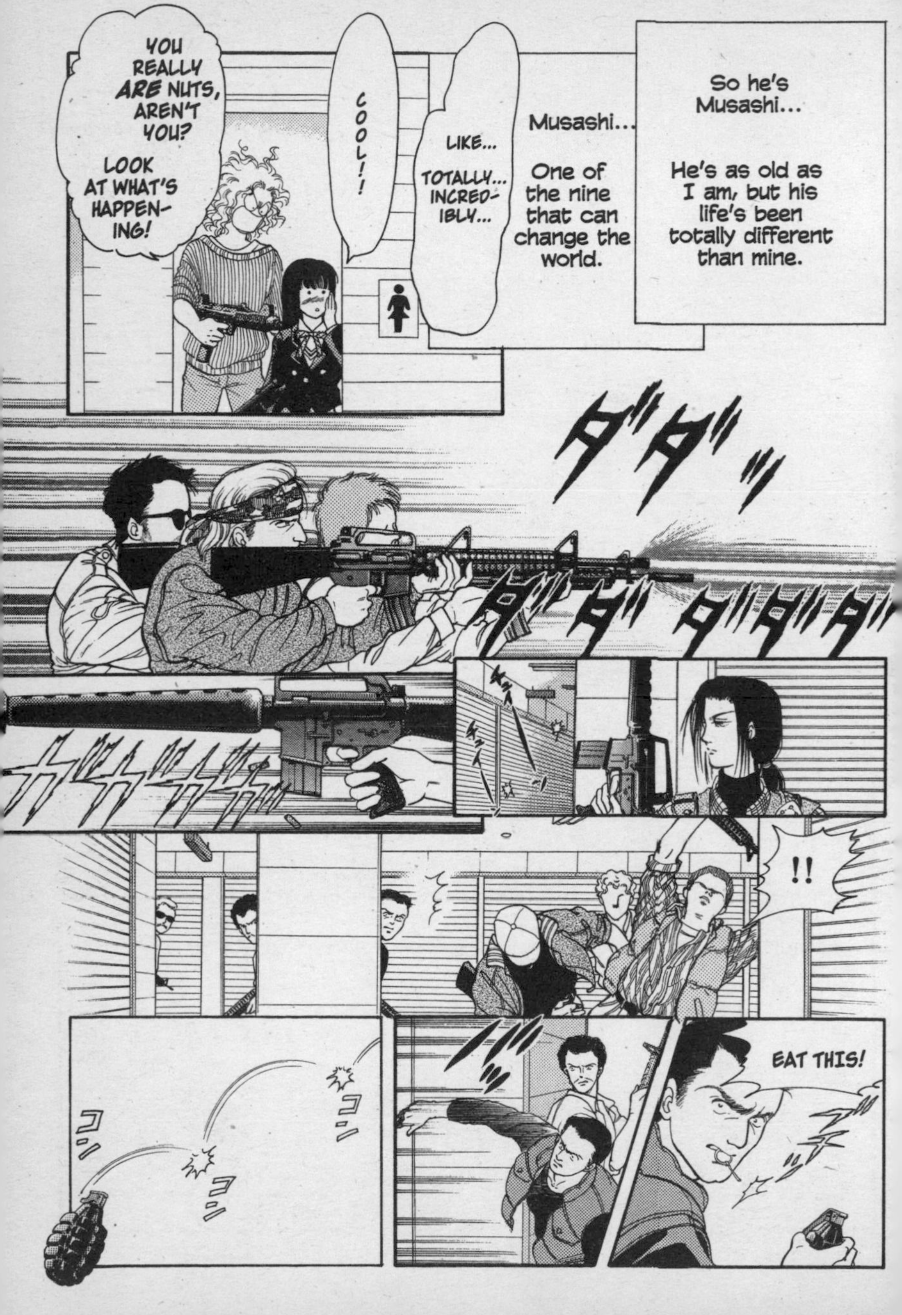

So he's Musashi...
He's as old as I am, but his life's been totally different than mine.
Musashi...
One of the nine that can change the world.
LIKE...
TOTALLY... INCRED-IBLY...
COOL!!
YOU REALLY ARE NUTS, AREN'T YOU?
LOOK AT WHAT'S HAPPEN-ING!
!!
EAT THIS!

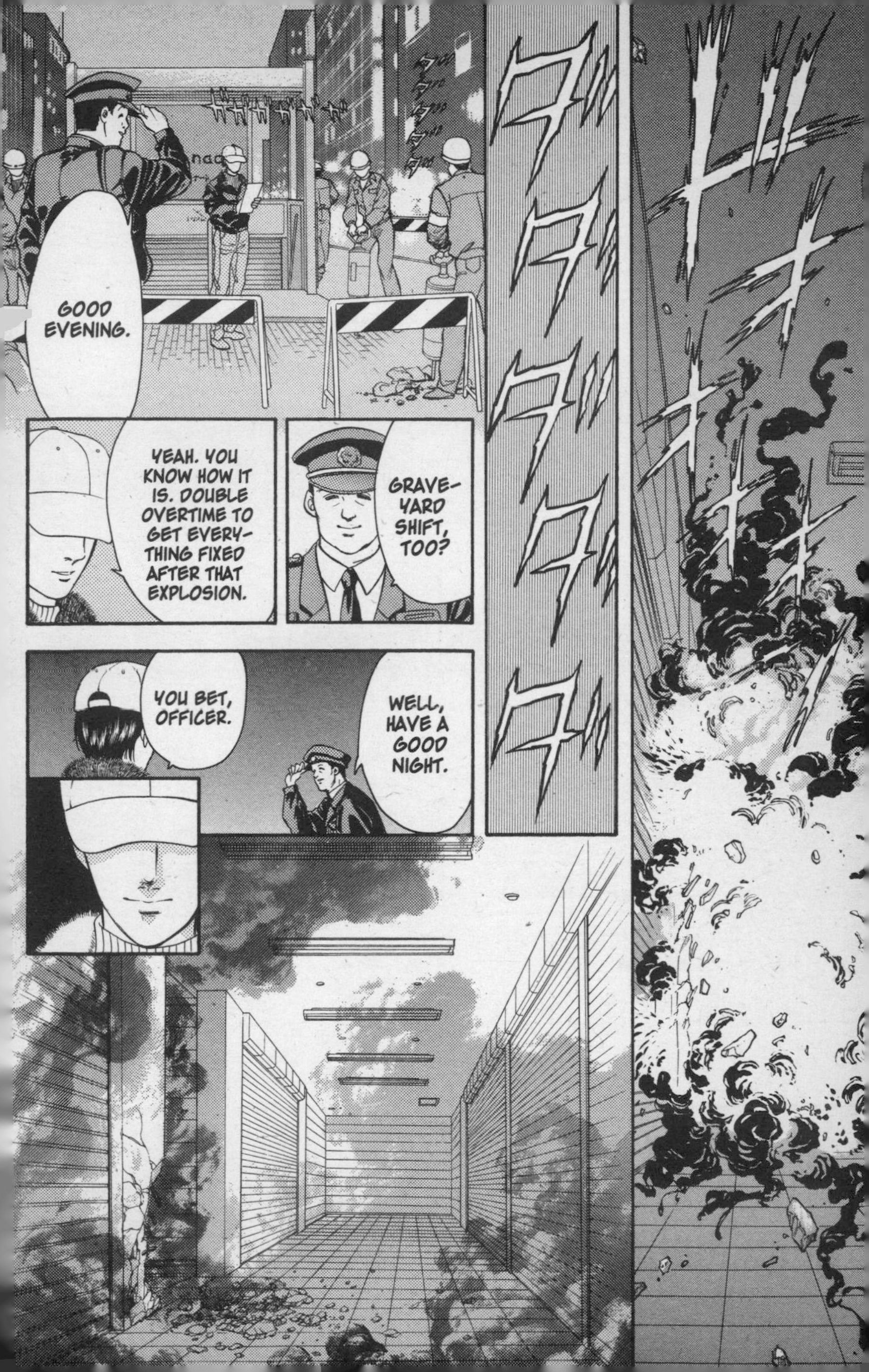
GOOD EVENING.
GRAVE-YARD SHIFT, TOO?
YEAH. YOU KNOW HOW IT IS. DOUBLE OVERTIME TO GET EVERY-THING FIXED AFTER THAT EXPLOSION.
WELL, HAVE A GOOD NIGHT.
YOU BET, OFFICER.

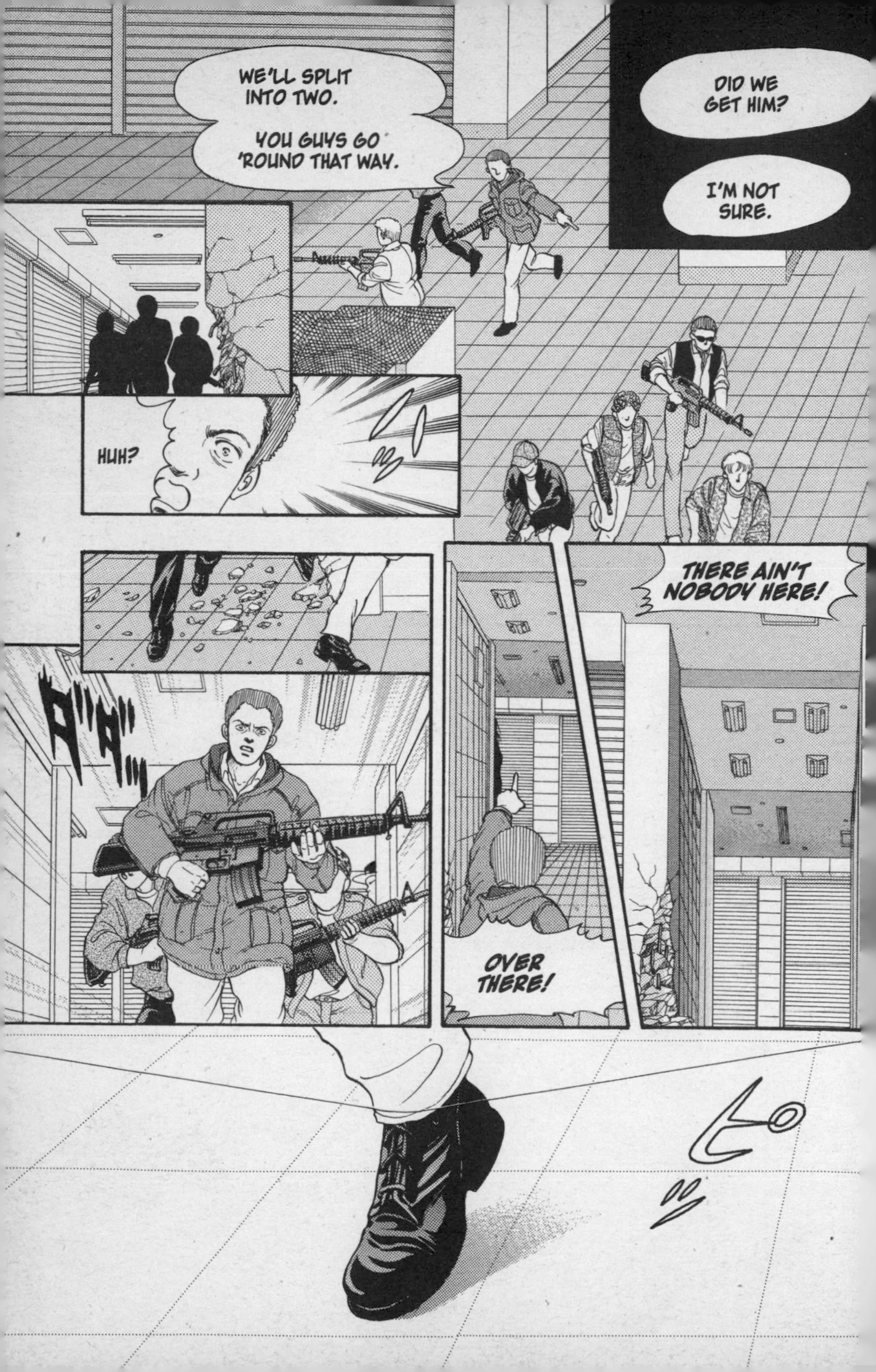
DID WE GET HIM?
I'M NOT SURE.
WE'LL SPLIT INTO TWO.
YOU GUYS GO 'ROUND THAT WAY.
HUH?
THERE AIN'T NOBODY HERE!
OVER THERE!

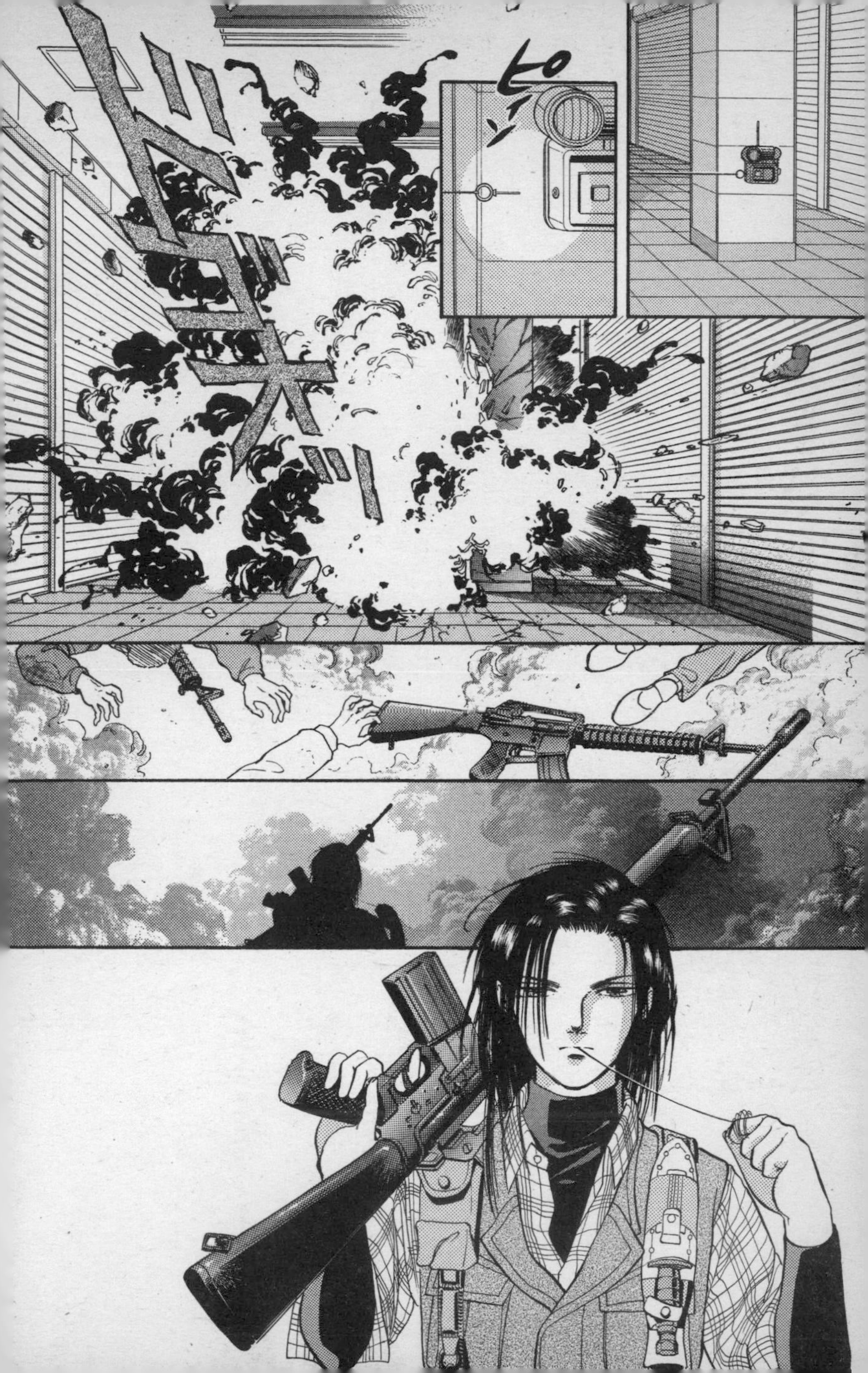
ピン
ズゴオ

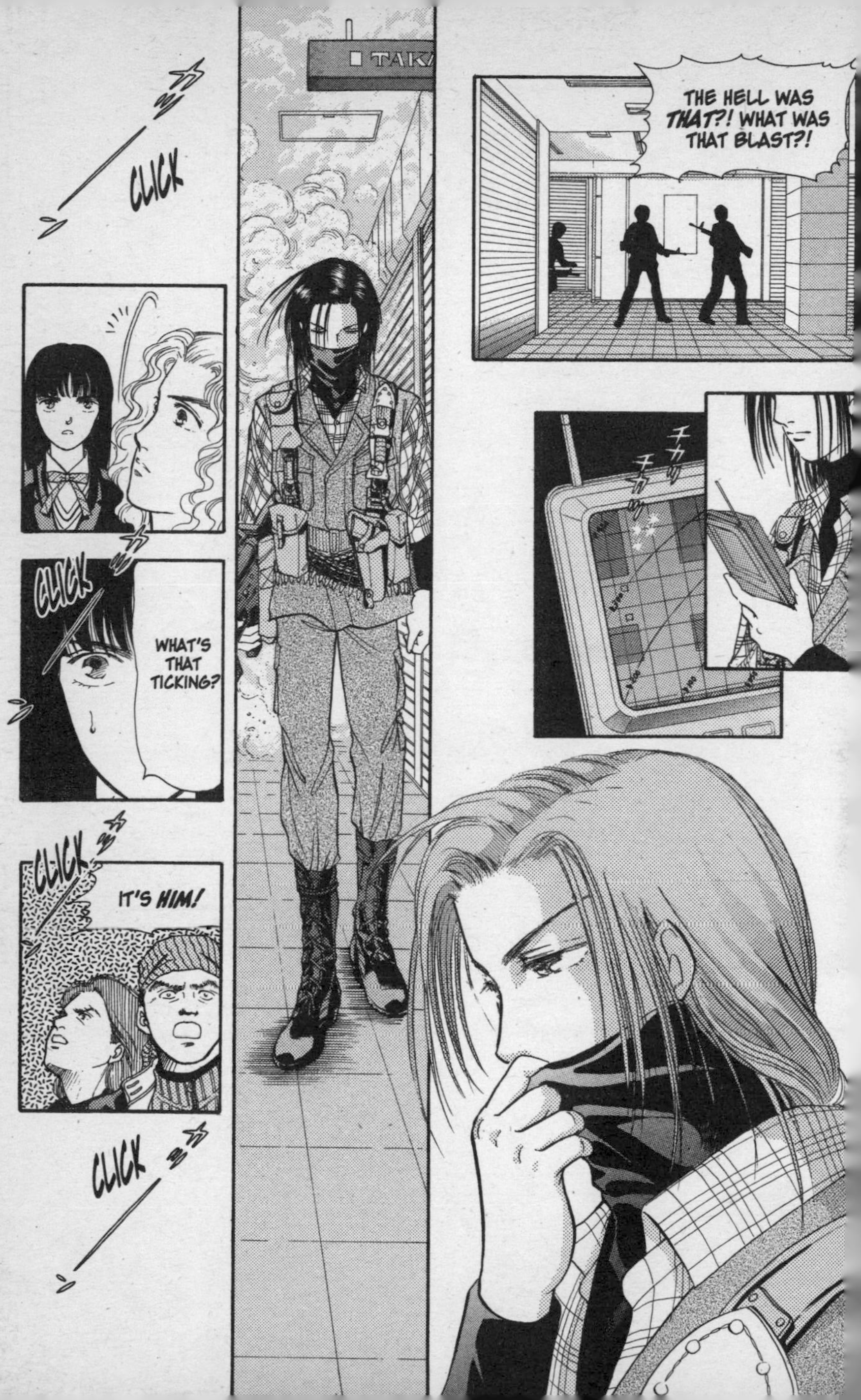
THE HELL WAS *THAT?!* WHAT WAS THAT BLAST?!
TAKA
CLICK
CLICK
WHAT'S THAT TICKING?
CLICK
IT'S *HIM!*
CLICK

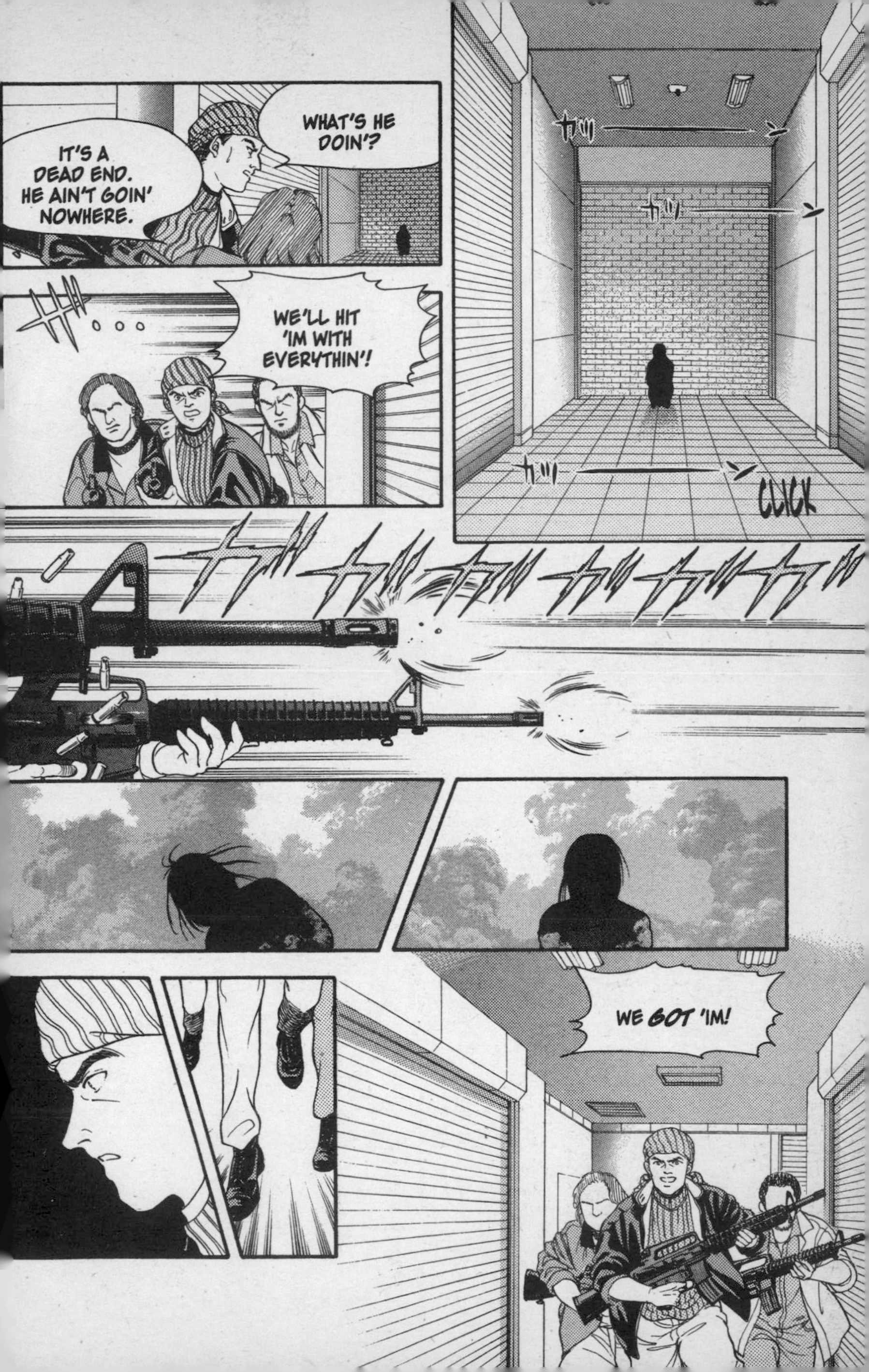
CLICK
WHAT'S HE DOIN'?
IT'S A DEAD END. HE AIN'T GOIN' NOWHERE.
WE'LL HIT 'IM WITH EVERYTHIN'!
WE GOT 'IM!

カチッ

カ カチッ

カ゛゛———ン

CLICK

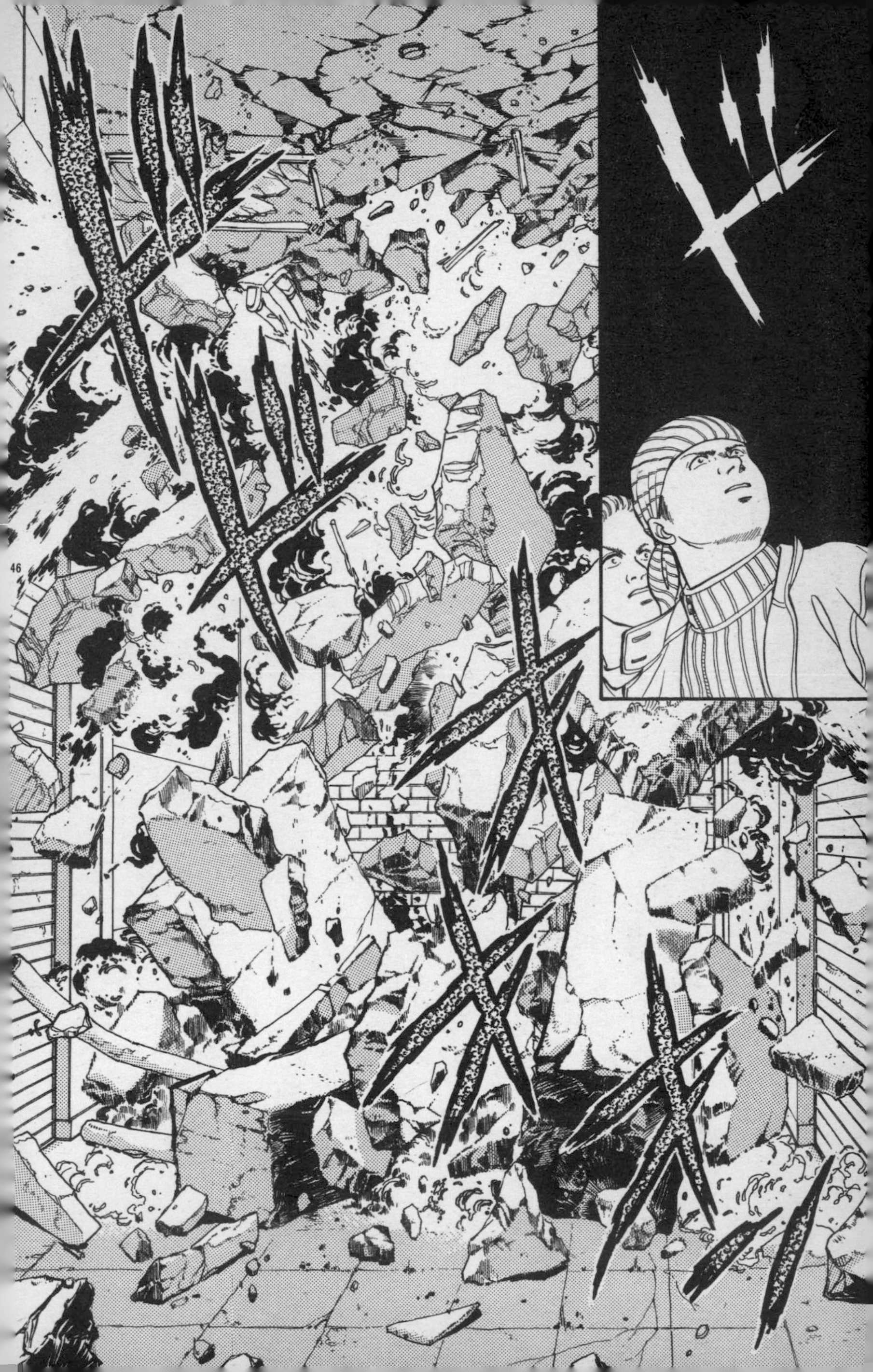

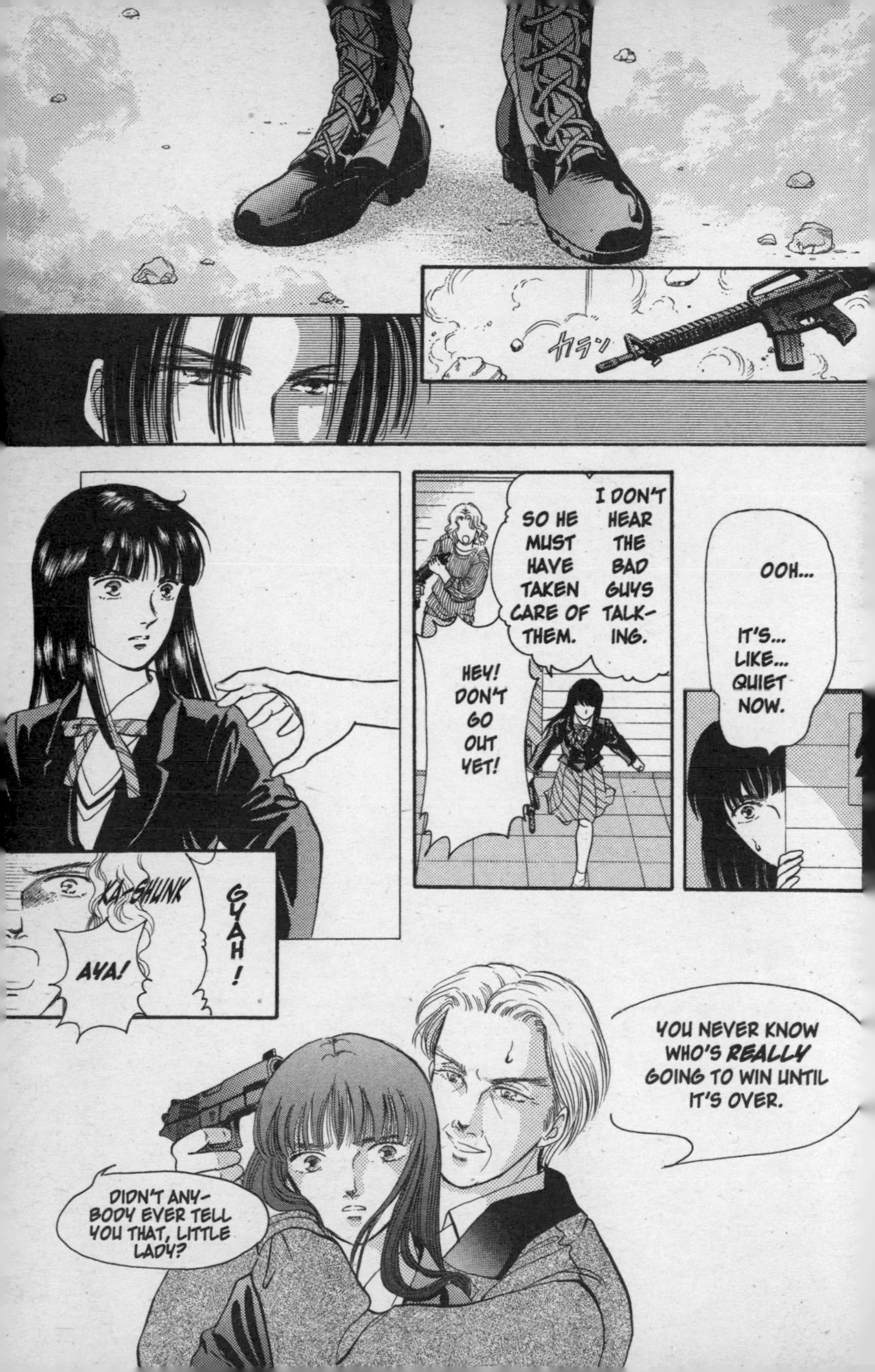
カラン
OOH... IT'S... LIKE... QUIET NOW.
I DON'T HEAR THE BAD GUYS TALKING.
SO HE MUST HAVE TAKEN CARE OF THEM.
HEY! DON'T GO OUT YET!
GUAH!
KA-SHUNK
AYA!
YOU NEVER KNOW WHO'S **REALLY** GOING TO WIN UNTIL IT'S OVER.
DIDN'T ANYBODY EVER TELL YOU THAT, LITTLE LADY?

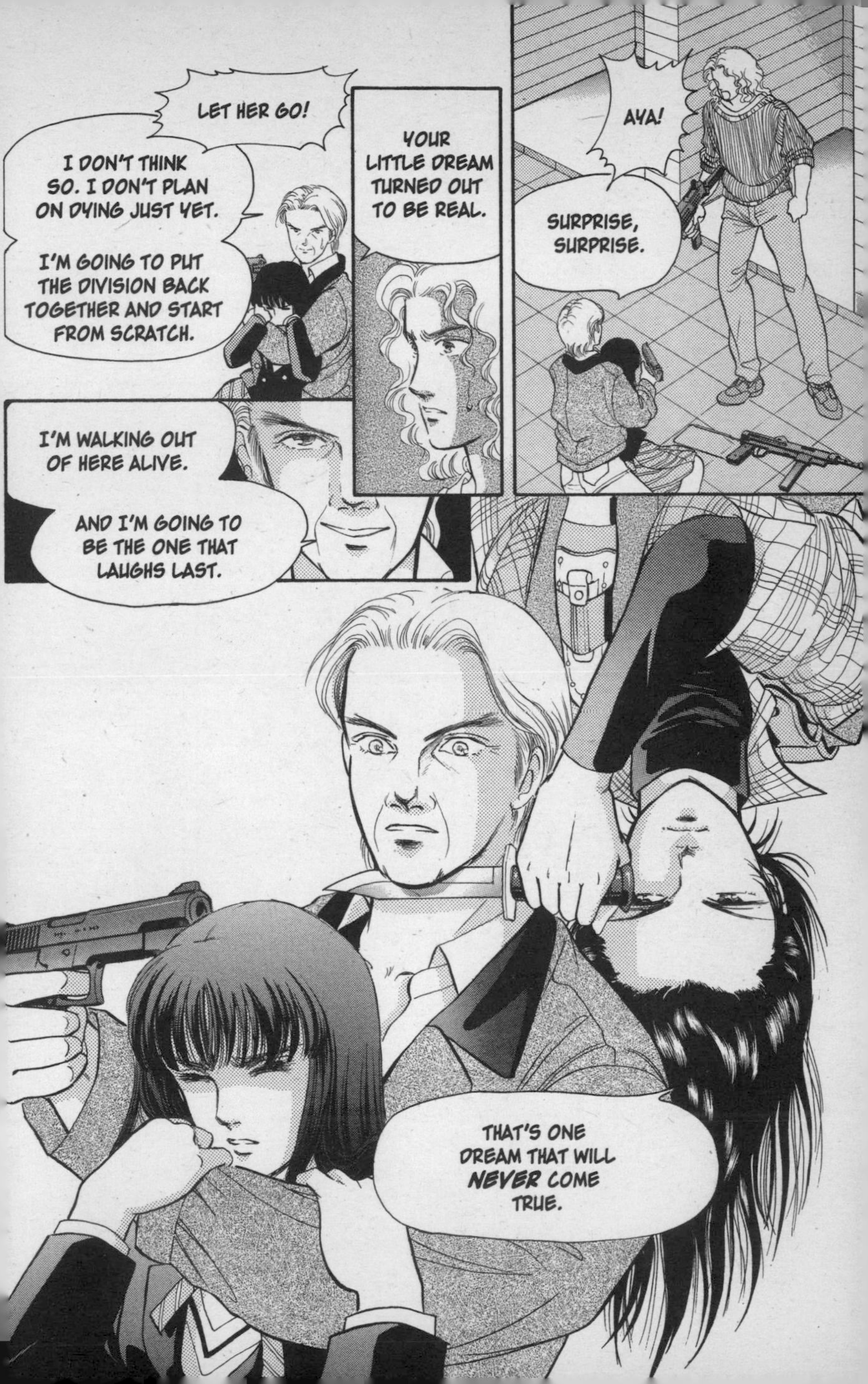
AYA!
SURPRISE, SURPRISE.
YOUR LITTLE DREAM TURNED OUT TO BE REAL.
LET HER GO!
I DON'T THINK SO. I DON'T PLAN ON DYING JUST YET.
I'M GOING TO PUT THE DIVISION BACK TOGETHER AND START FROM SCRATCH.
I'M WALKING OUT OF HERE ALIVE.
AND I'M GOING TO BE THE ONE THAT LAUGHS LAST.
THAT'S ONE DREAM THAT WILL *NEVER* COME TRUE.

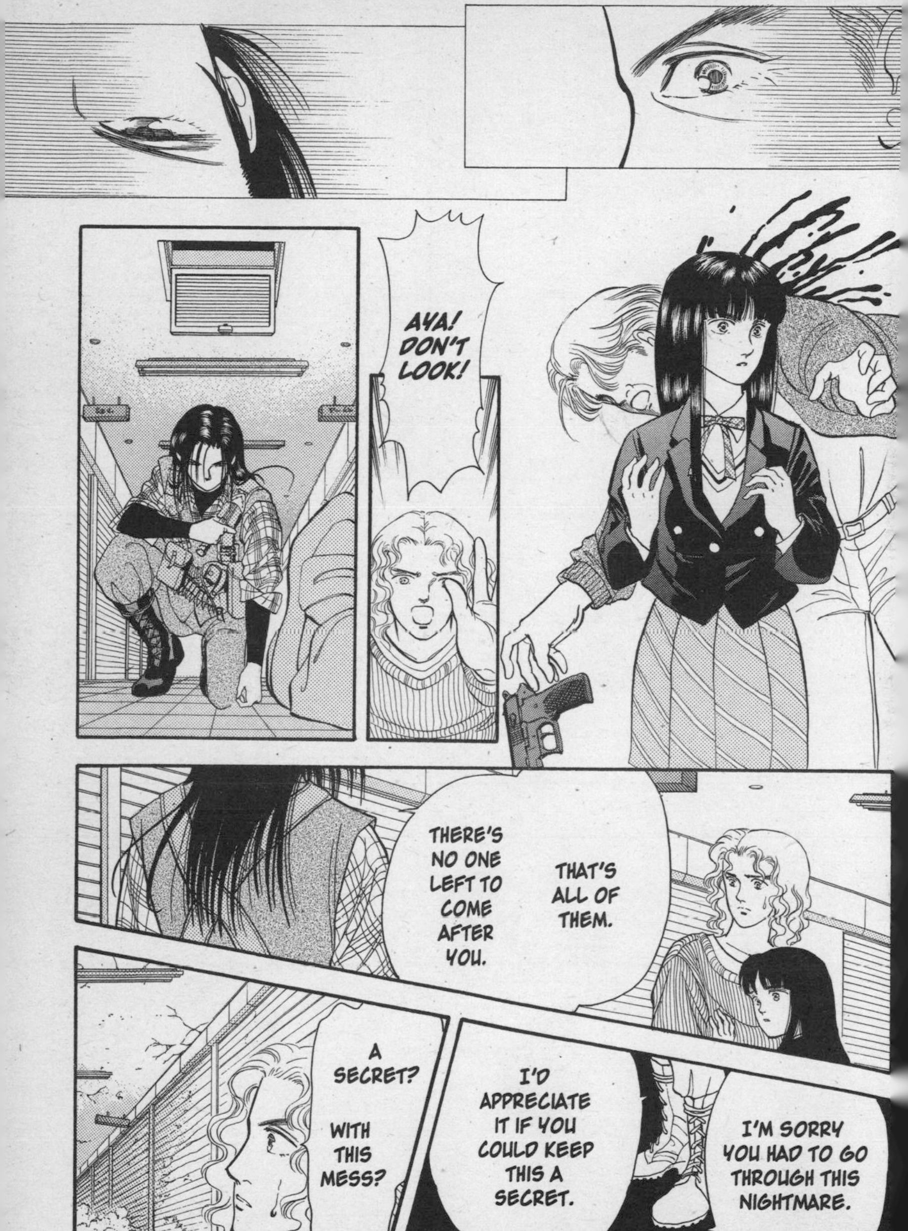
AYA! DON'T LOOK!
THAT'S ALL OF THEM.
THERE'S NO ONE LEFT TO COME AFTER YOU.
I'M SORRY YOU HAD TO GO THROUGH THIS NIGHTMARE.
I'D APPRECIATE IT IF YOU COULD KEEP THIS A SECRET.
A SECRET?
WITH THIS MESS?

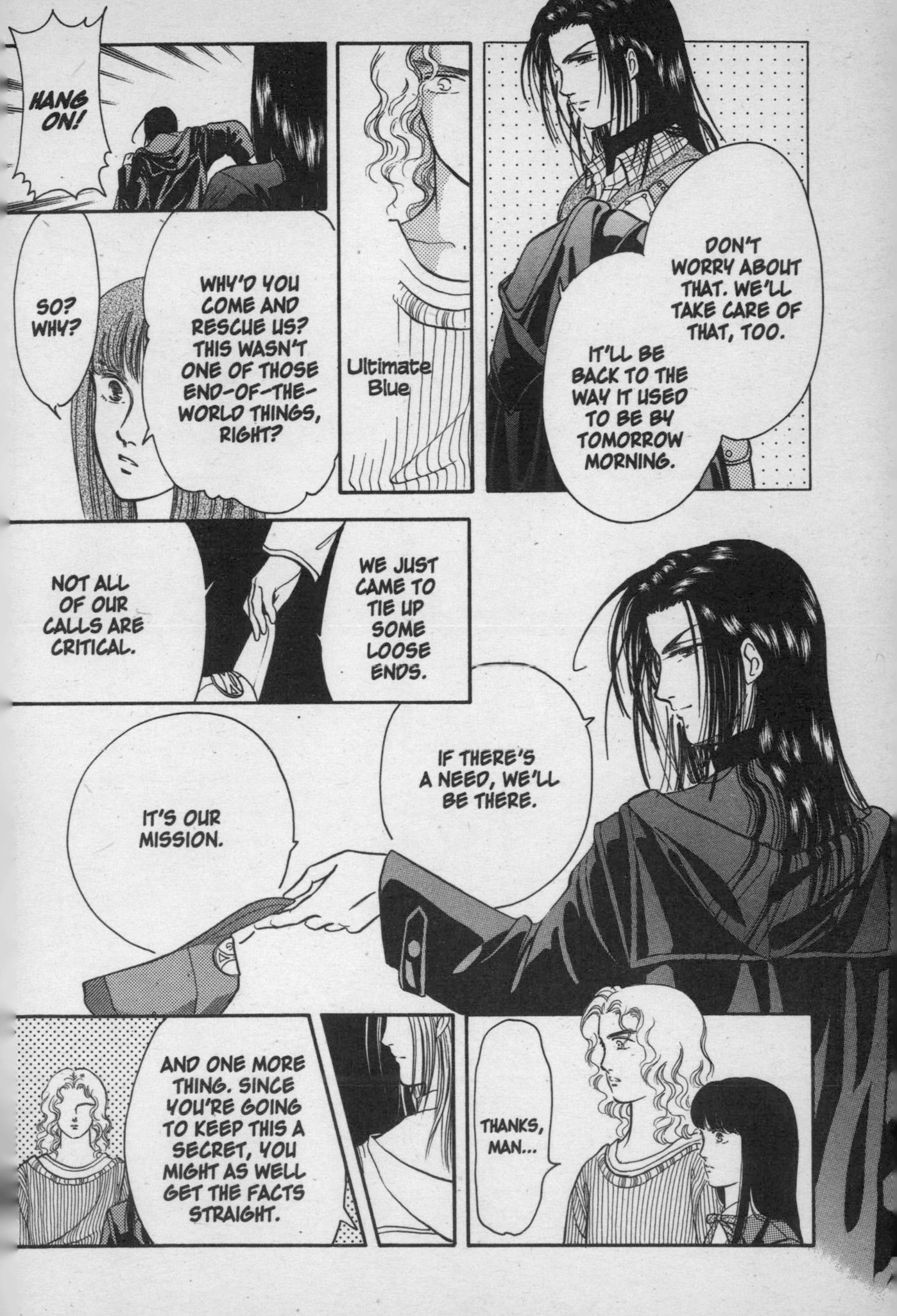
DON'T WORRY ABOUT THAT. WE'LL TAKE CARE OF THAT, TOO.
IT'LL BE BACK TO THE WAY IT USED TO BE BY TOMORROW MORNING.
Ultimate Blue
HANG ON!
WHY'D YOU COME AND RESCUE US? THIS WASN'T ONE OF THOSE END-OF-THE-WORLD THINGS, RIGHT?
SO? WHY?
WE JUST CAME TO TIE UP SOME LOOSE ENDS.
NOT ALL OF OUR CALLS ARE CRITICAL.
IF THERE'S A NEED, WE'LL BE THERE.
IT'S OUR MISSION.
THANKS, MAN...
AND ONE MORE THING. SINCE YOU'RE GOING TO KEEP THIS A SECRET, YOU MIGHT AS WELL GET THE FACTS STRAIGHT.

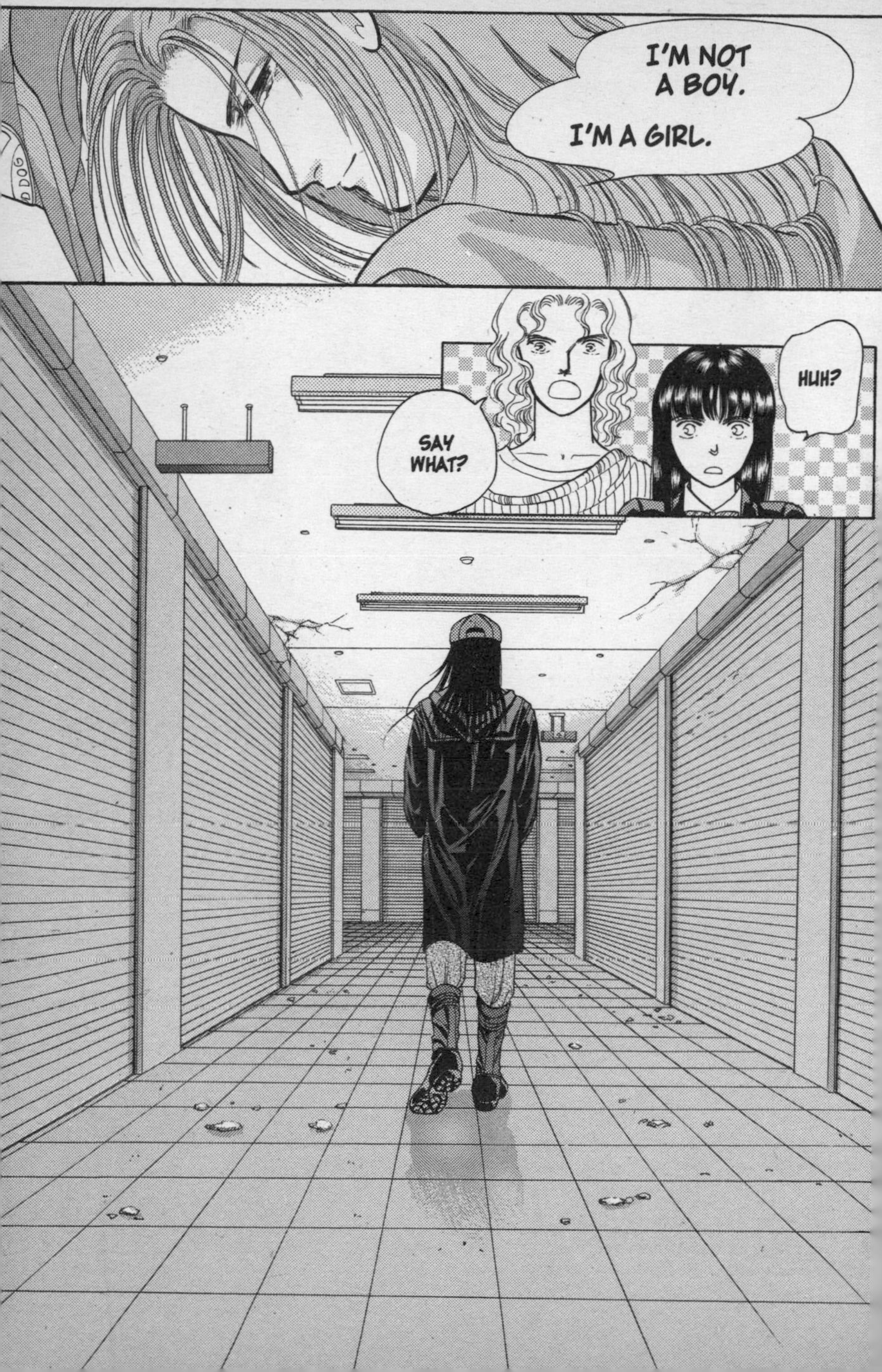
I'M NOT A BOY.
I'M A GIRL.
HUH?
SAY WHAT?

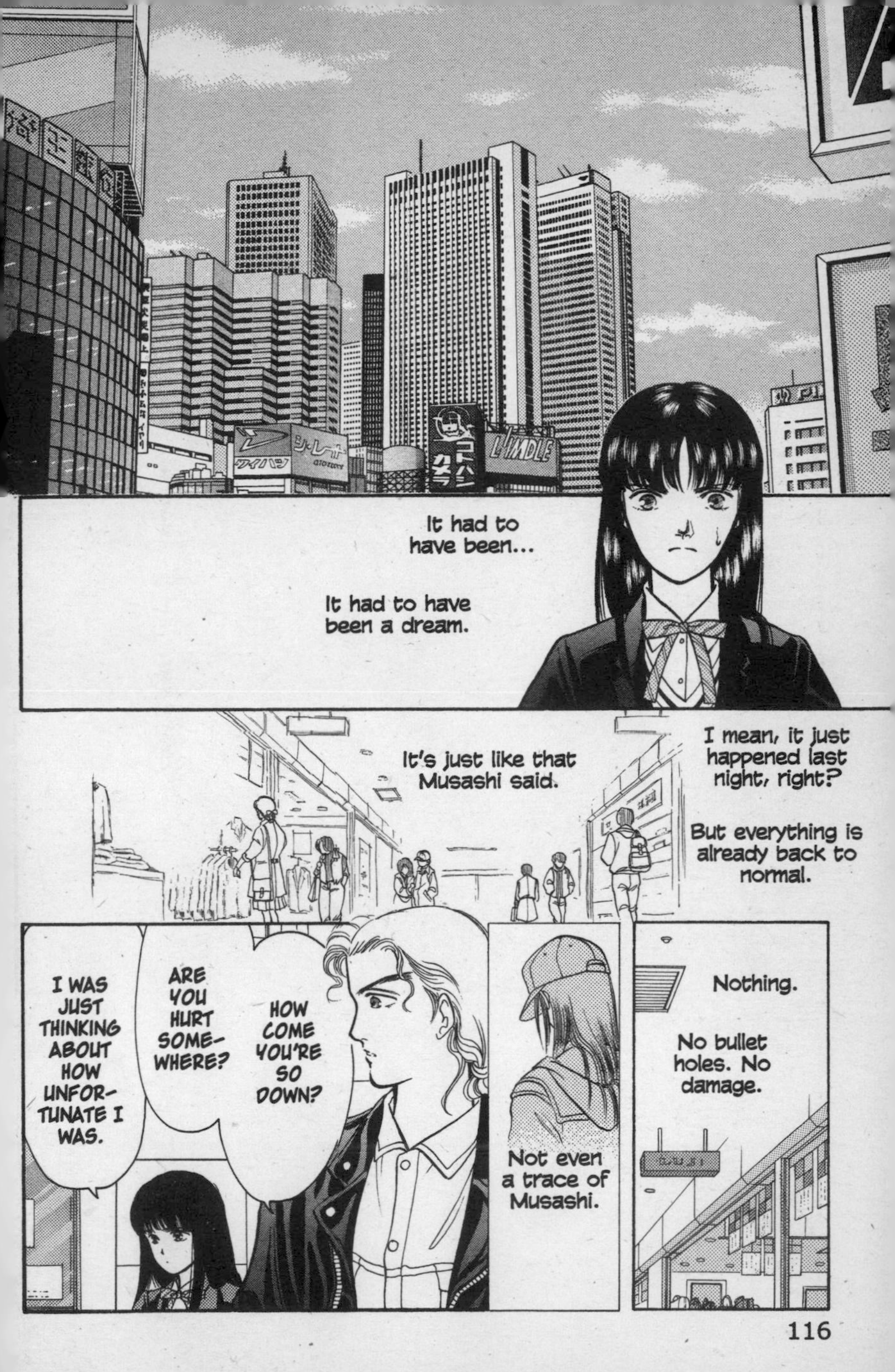
It had to have been...
It had to have been a dream.
I mean, it just happened last night, right?
But everything is already back to normal.
It's just like that Musashi said.
Nothing.
No bullet holes. No damage.
Not even a trace of Musashi.
HOW COME YOU'RE SO DOWN?
ARE YOU HURT SOMEWHERE?
I WAS JUST THINKING ABOUT HOW UNFORTUNATE I WAS.

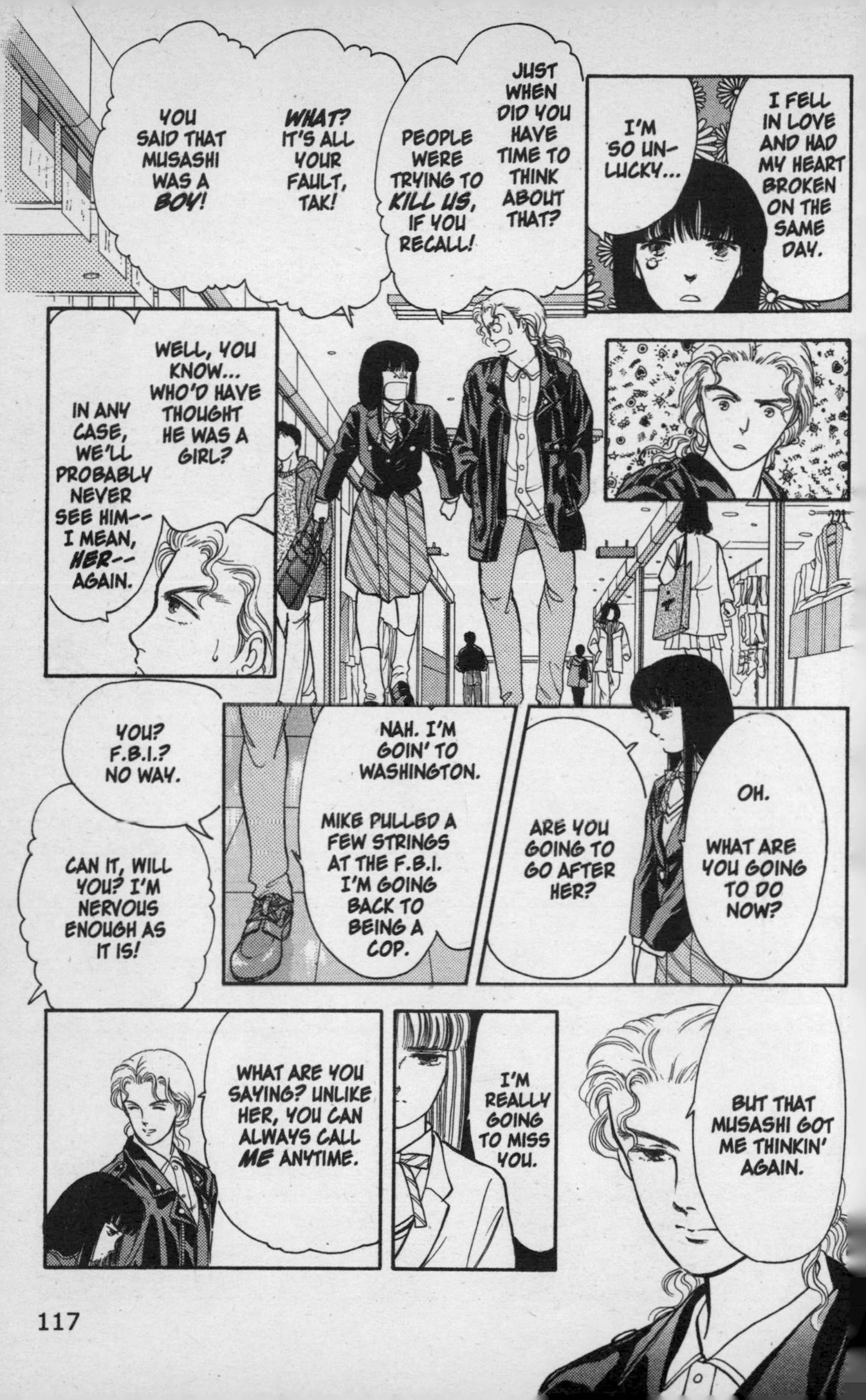
I FELL IN LOVE AND HAD MY HEART BROKEN ON THE SAME DAY.
I'M SO UNLUCKY...
JUST WHEN DID YOU HAVE TIME TO THINK ABOUT THAT?
PEOPLE WERE TRYING TO **KILL US**, IF YOU RECALL!
WHAT? IT'S ALL YOUR FAULT, TAK!
YOU SAID THAT MUSASHI WAS A **BOY**!
WELL, YOU KNOW... WHO'D HAVE THOUGHT HE WAS A GIRL?
IN ANY CASE, WE'LL PROBABLY NEVER SEE HIM-- I MEAN, **HER**-- AGAIN.
OH.
WHAT ARE YOU GOING TO DO NOW?
ARE YOU GOING TO GO AFTER HER?
NAH. I'M GOIN' TO WASHINGTON.
MIKE PULLED A FEW STRINGS AT THE F.B.I. I'M GOING BACK TO BEING A COP.
YOU? F.B.I.? NO WAY.
CAN IT, WILL YOU? I'M NERVOUS ENOUGH AS IT IS!
BUT THAT MUSASHI GOT ME THINKIN' AGAIN.
I'M REALLY GOING TO MISS YOU.
WHAT ARE YOU SAYING? UNLIKE HER, YOU CAN ALWAYS CALL **ME** ANYTIME.

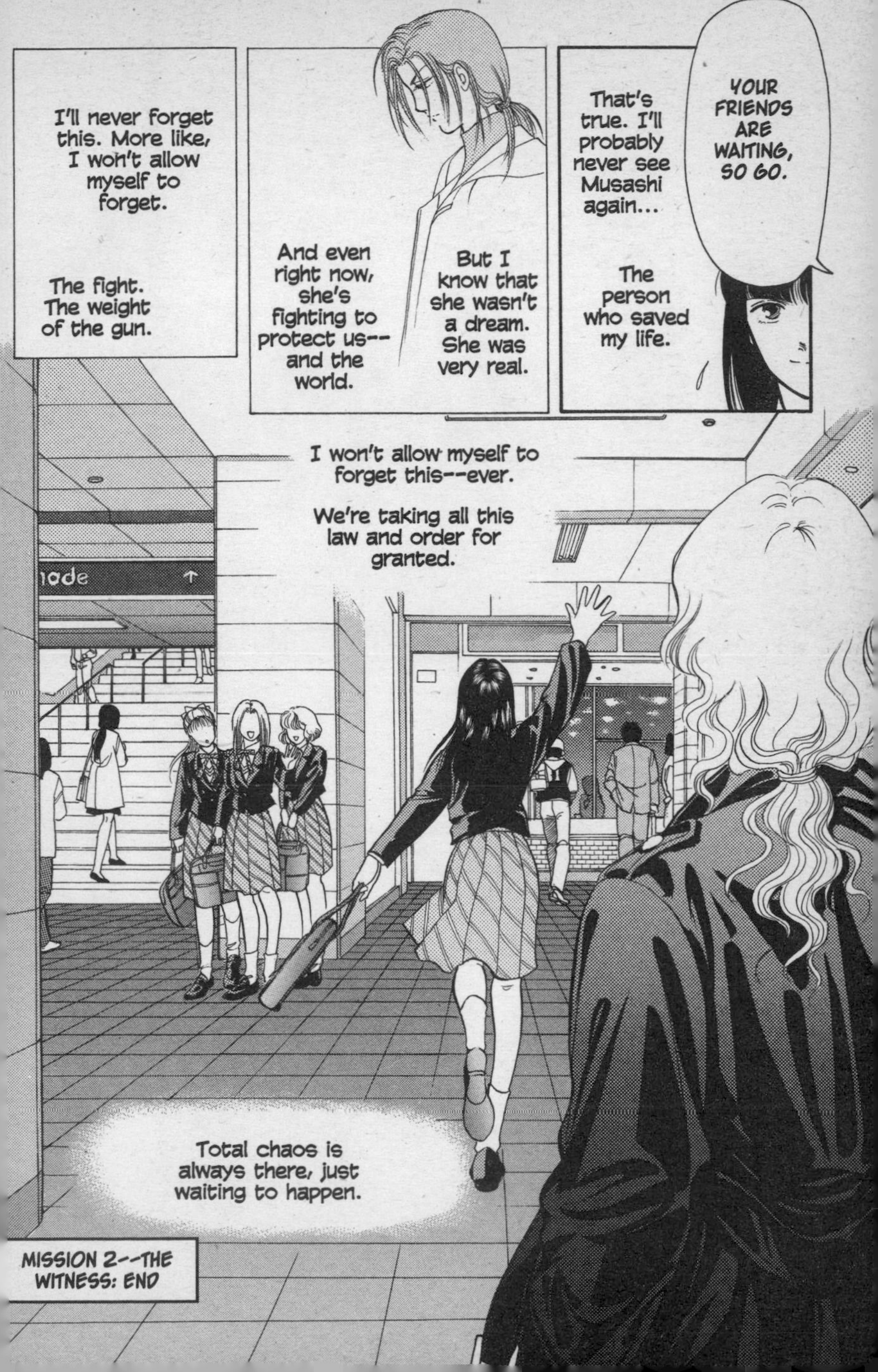
YOUR FRIENDS ARE WAITING, SO GO.
That's true. I'll probably never see Musashi again...
The person who saved my life.
But I know that she wasn't a dream. She was very real.
And even right now, she's fighting to protect us--and the world.
I'll never forget this. More like, I won't allow myself to forget.
The fight. The weight of the gun.
I won't allow myself to forget this--ever.
We're taking all this law and order for granted.
Total chaos is always there, just waiting to happen.
MISSION 2--THE WITNESS: END

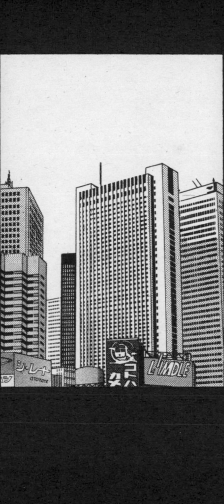

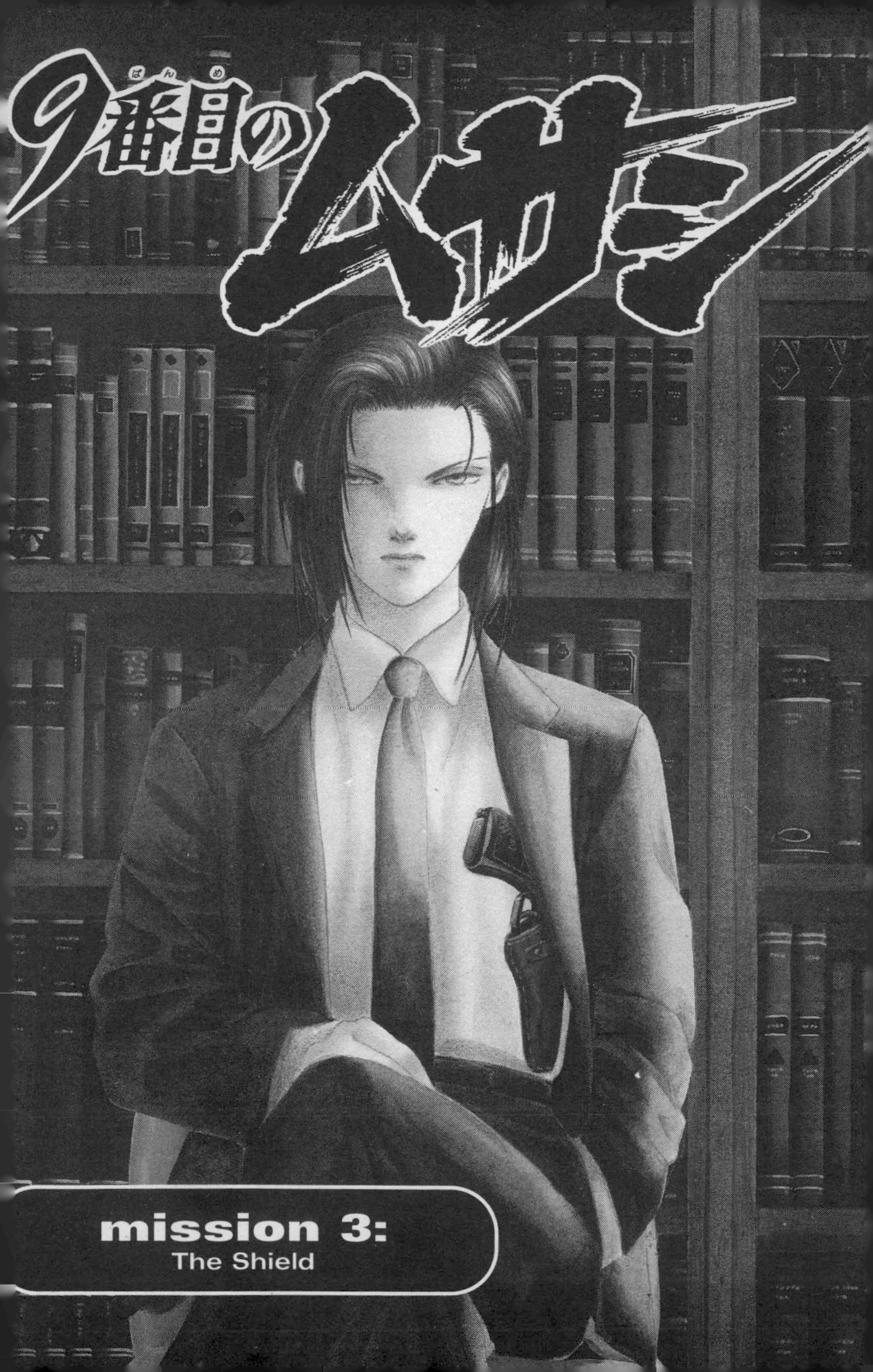
9番目のムサシ
mission 3:
The Shield

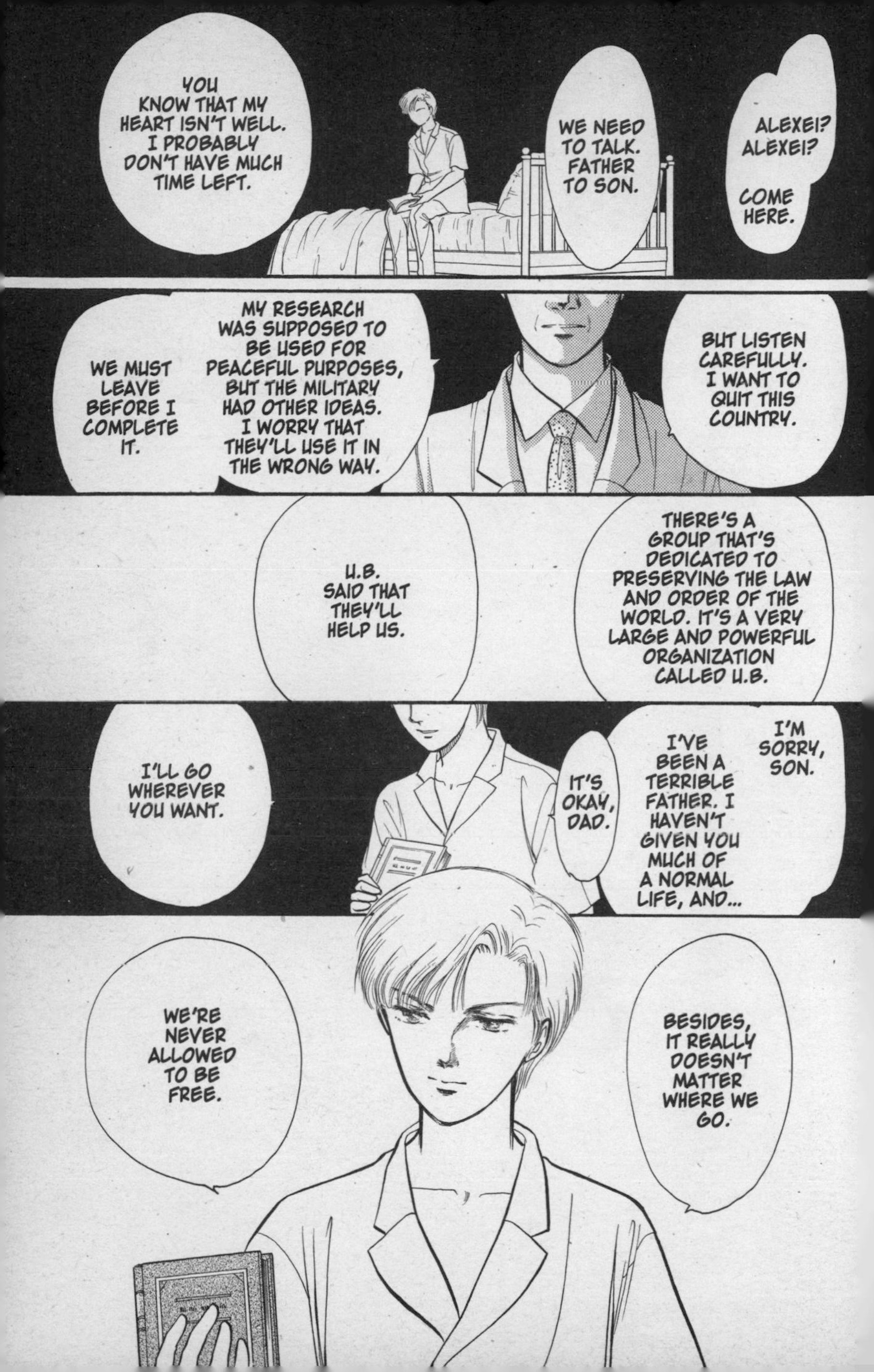
ALEXEI? ALEXEI? COME HERE.
WE NEED TO TALK. FATHER TO SON.
YOU KNOW THAT MY HEART ISN'T WELL. I PROBABLY DON'T HAVE MUCH TIME LEFT.
BUT LISTEN CAREFULLY. I WANT TO QUIT THIS COUNTRY.
MY RESEARCH WAS SUPPOSED TO BE USED FOR PEACEFUL PURPOSES, BUT THE MILITARY HAD OTHER IDEAS. I WORRY THAT THEY'LL USE IT IN THE WRONG WAY.
WE MUST LEAVE BEFORE I COMPLETE IT.
THERE'S A GROUP THAT'S DEDICATED TO PRESERVING THE LAW AND ORDER OF THE WORLD. IT'S A VERY LARGE AND POWERFUL ORGANIZATION CALLED U.B.
U.B. SAID THAT THEY'LL HELP US.
I'M SORRY, SON.
I'VE BEEN A TERRIBLE FATHER. I HAVEN'T GIVEN YOU MUCH OF A NORMAL LIFE, AND...
IT'S OKAY, DAD.
I'LL GO WHEREVER YOU WANT.
BESIDES, IT REALLY DOESN'T MATTER WHERE WE GO.
WE'RE NEVER ALLOWED TO BE FREE.

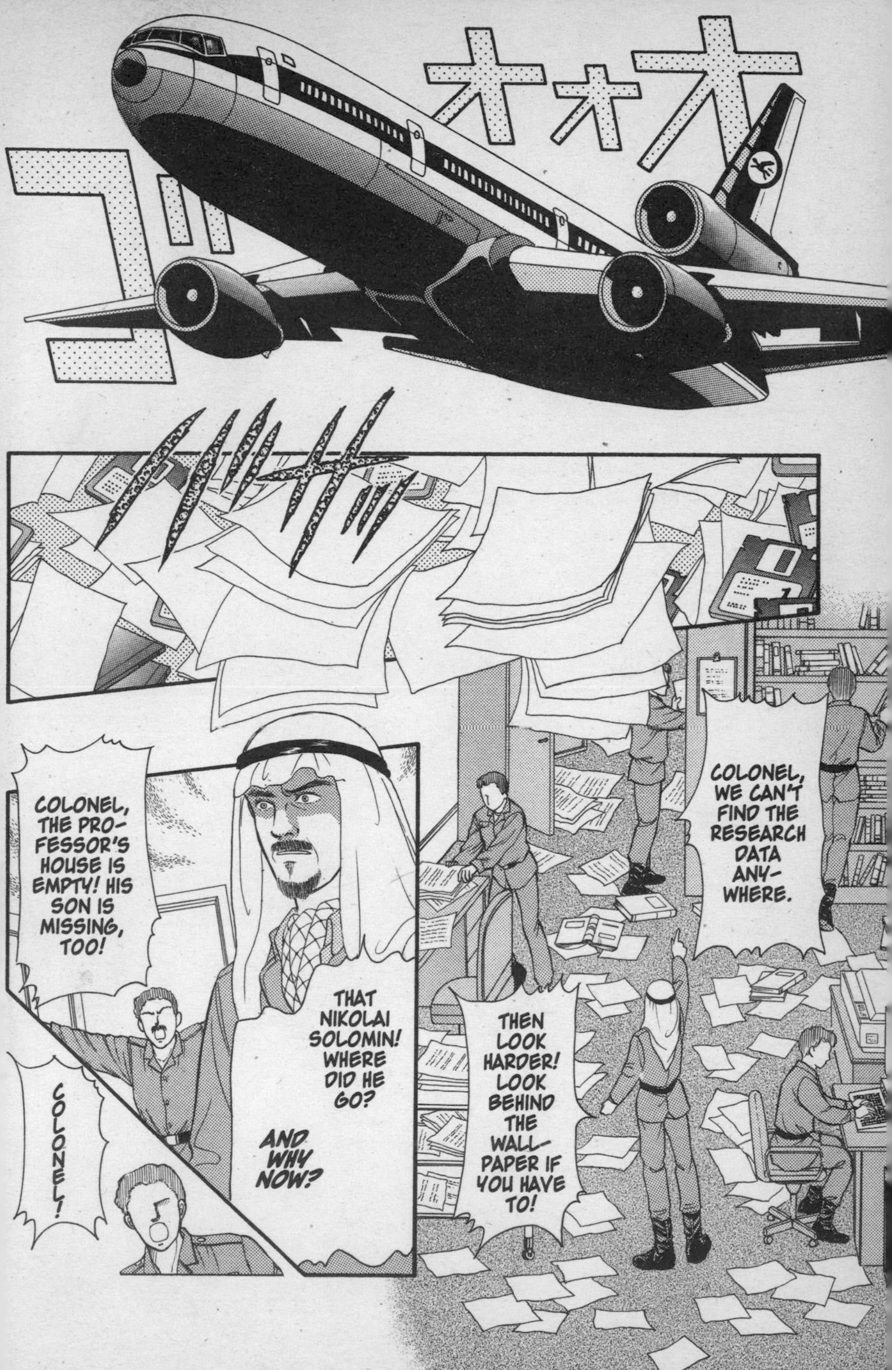
COLONEL, WE CAN'T FIND THE RESEARCH DATA ANY-WHERE.
THEN LOOK HARDER! LOOK BEHIND THE WALL-PAPER IF YOU HAVE TO!
THAT NIKOLAI SOLOMIN! WHERE DID HE GO?
AND WHY NOW?
COLONEL, THE PRO-FESSOR'S HOUSE IS EMPTY! HIS SON IS MISSING, TOO!
COLONEL!

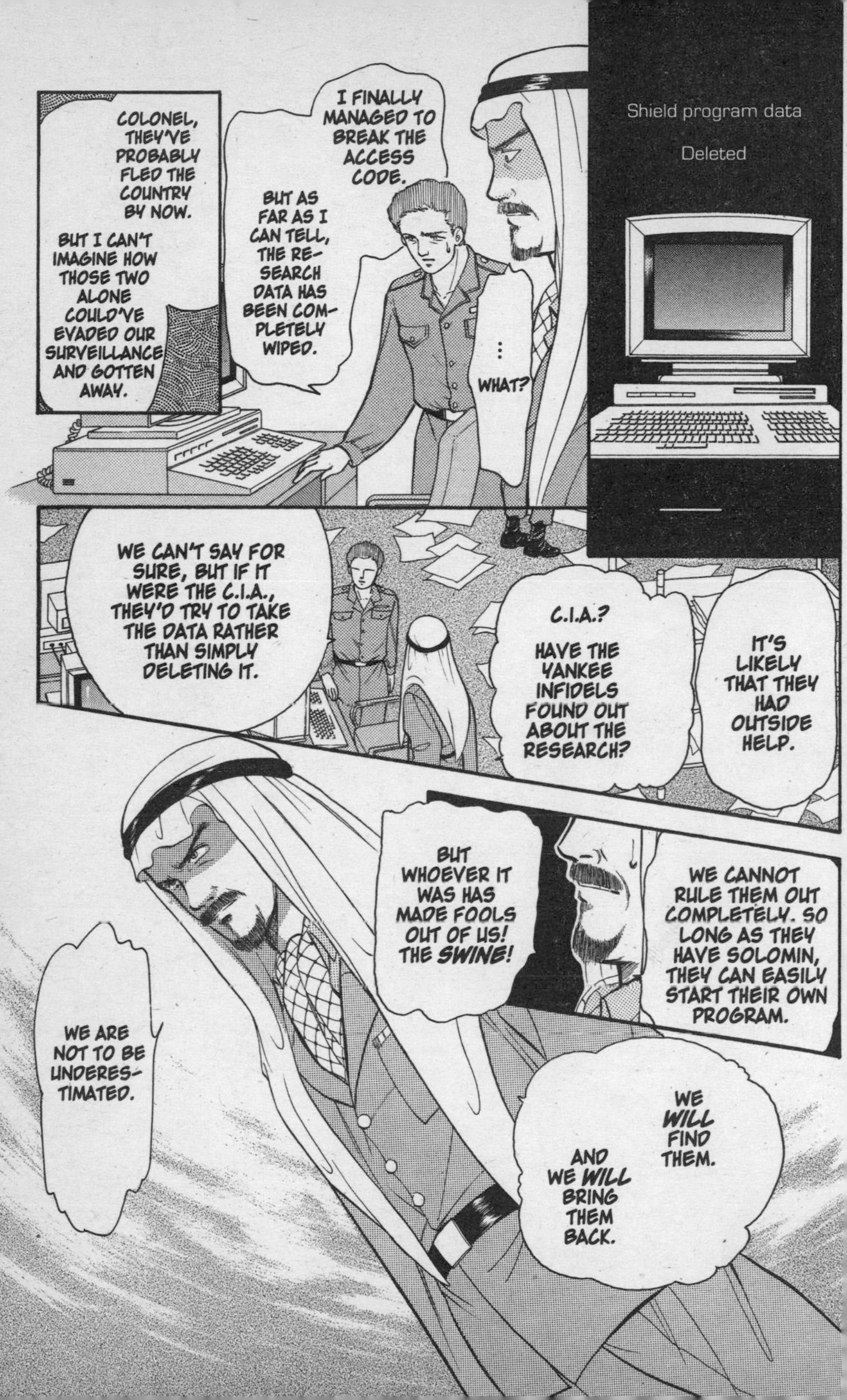
Shield program data
Deleted
I FINALLY MANAGED TO BREAK THE ACCESS CODE.
BUT AS FAR AS I CAN TELL, THE RE-SEARCH DATA HAS BEEN COM-PLETELY WIPED.
...
WHAT?
COLONEL, THEY'VE PROBABLY FLED THE COUNTRY BY NOW.
BUT I CAN'T IMAGINE HOW THOSE TWO ALONE COULD'VE EVADED OUR SURVEILLANCE AND GOTTEN AWAY.
IT'S LIKELY THAT THEY HAD OUTSIDE HELP.
C.I.A.?
HAVE THE YANKEE INFIDELS FOUND OUT ABOUT THE RESEARCH?
WE CAN'T SAY FOR SURE, BUT IF IT WERE THE C.I.A., THEY'D TRY TO TAKE THE DATA RATHER THAN SIMPLY DELETING IT.
WE CANNOT RULE THEM OUT COMPLETELY. SO LONG AS THEY HAVE SOLOMIN, THEY CAN EASILY START THEIR OWN PROGRAM.
BUT WHOEVER IT WAS HAS MADE FOOLS OUT OF US! THE SWINE!
WE WILL FIND THEM.
AND WE WILL BRING THEM BACK.
WE ARE NOT TO BE UNDERES-TIMATED.

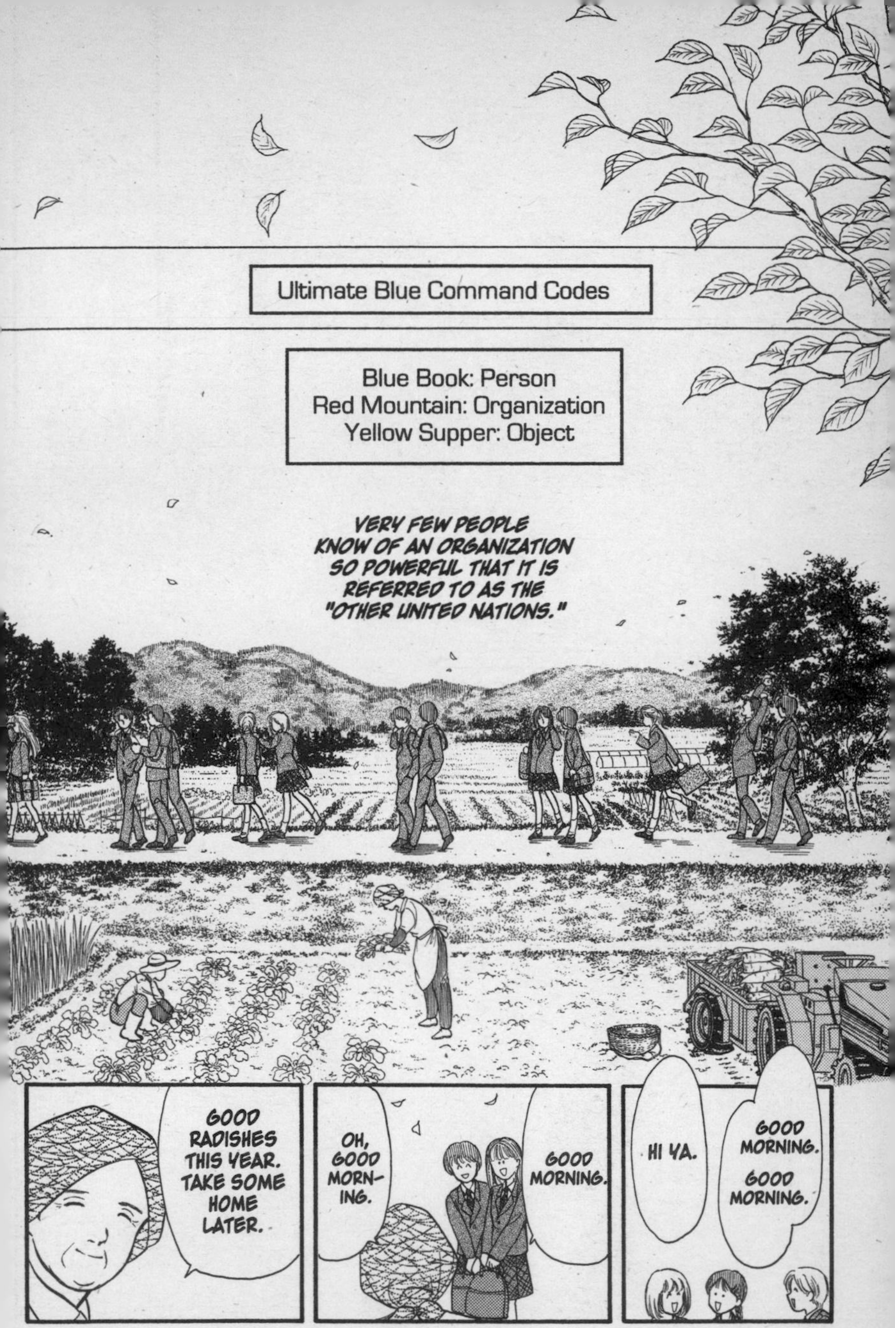
Ultimate Blue Command Codes
Blue Book: Person
Red Mountain: Organization
Yellow Supper: Object
VERY FEW PEOPLE KNOW OF AN ORGANIZATION SO POWERFUL THAT IT IS REFERRED TO AS THE "OTHER UNITED NATIONS."
GOOD MORNING.
GOOD MORNING.
HI YA.
GOOD MORNING.
OH, GOOD MORN-ING.
GOOD RADISHES THIS YEAR. TAKE SOME HOME LATER.

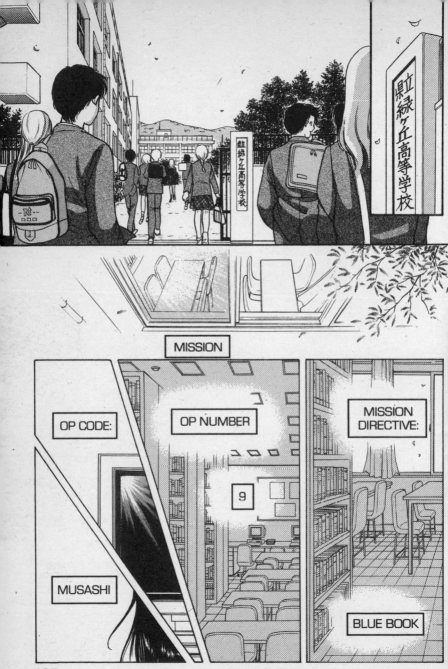

MISSION

OP CODE:

OP NUMBER

9

MUSASHI

MISSION DIRECTIVE:

BLUE BOOK

125

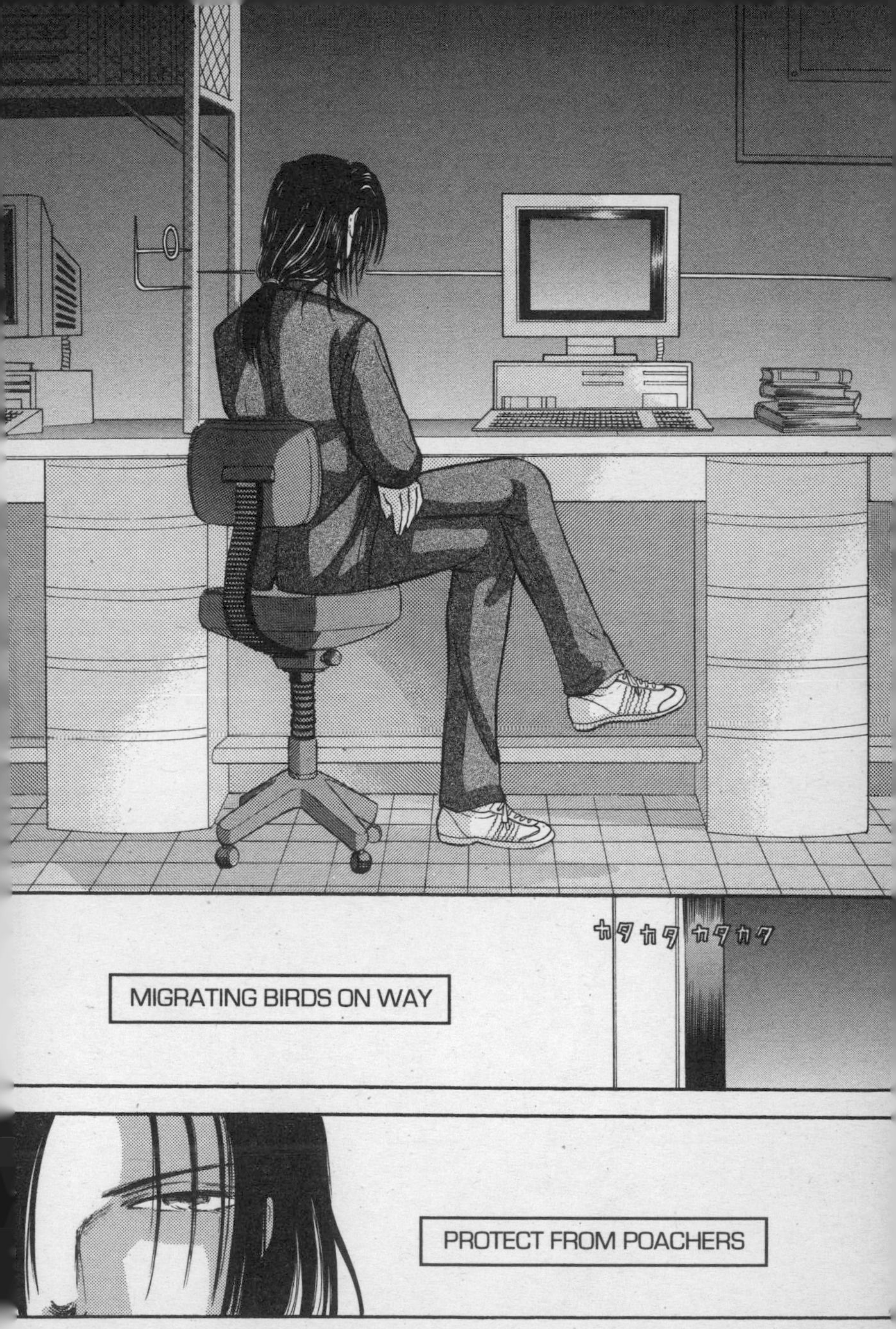
カタカタ カタカタ
MIGRATING BIRDS ON WAY
PROTECT FROM POACHERS

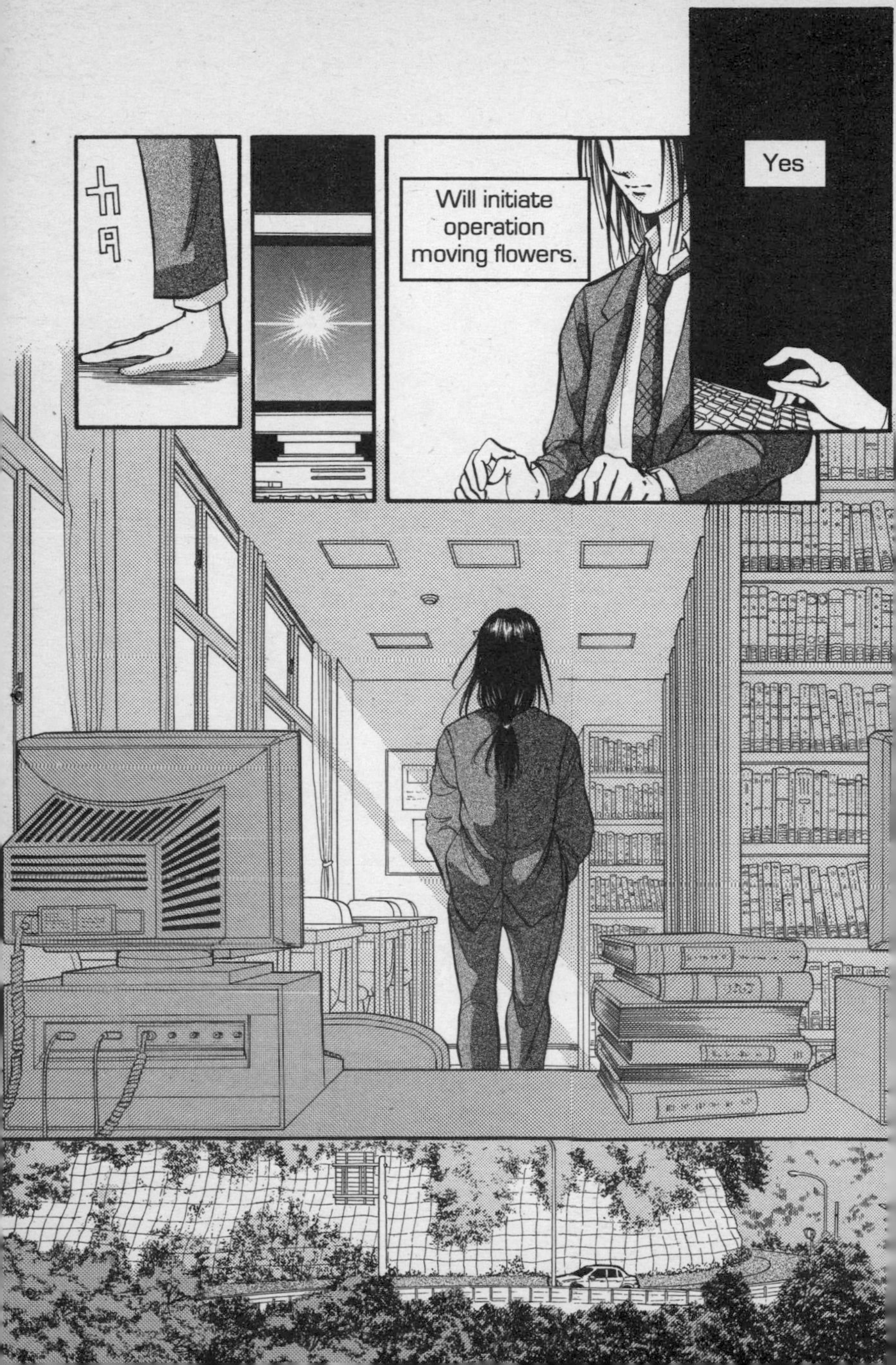
Yes
Will initiate operation moving flowers.

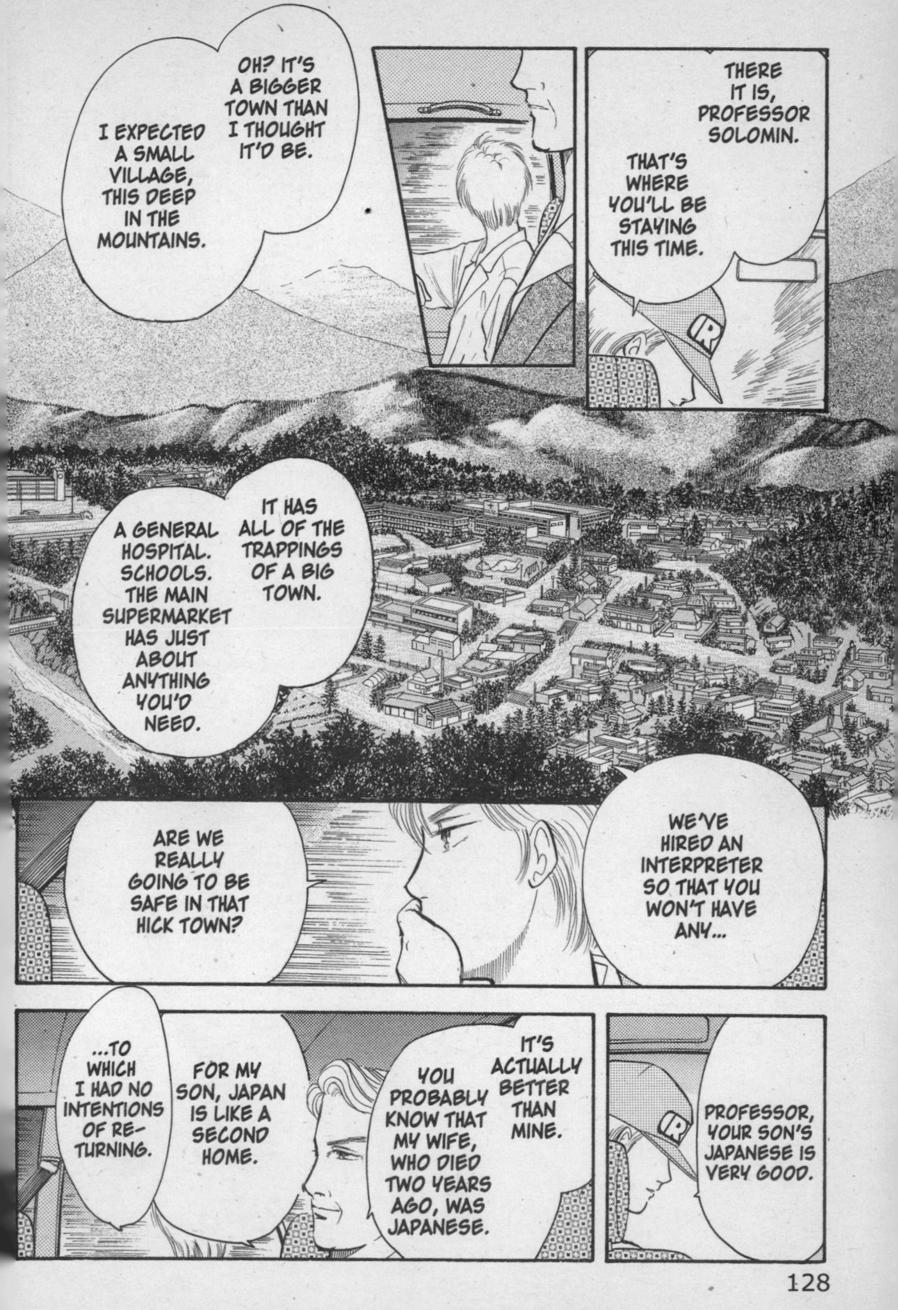
THERE IT IS, PROFESSOR SOLOMIN.
THAT'S WHERE YOU'LL BE STAYING THIS TIME.
OH? IT'S A BIGGER TOWN THAN I THOUGHT IT'D BE.
I EXPECTED A SMALL VILLAGE, THIS DEEP IN THE MOUNTAINS.
IT HAS ALL OF THE TRAPPINGS OF A BIG TOWN.
A GENERAL HOSPITAL. SCHOOLS. THE MAIN SUPERMARKET HAS JUST ABOUT ANYTHING YOU'D NEED.
WE'VE HIRED AN INTERPRETER SO THAT YOU WON'T HAVE ANY...
ARE WE REALLY GOING TO BE SAFE IN THAT HICK TOWN?
PROFESSOR, YOUR SON'S JAPANESE IS VERY GOOD.
IT'S ACTUALLY BETTER THAN MINE.
YOU PROBABLY KNOW THAT MY WIFE, WHO DIED TWO YEARS AGO, WAS JAPANESE.
FOR MY SON, JAPAN IS LIKE A SECOND HOME.
...TO WHICH I HAD NO INTENTIONS OF RE-TURNING.

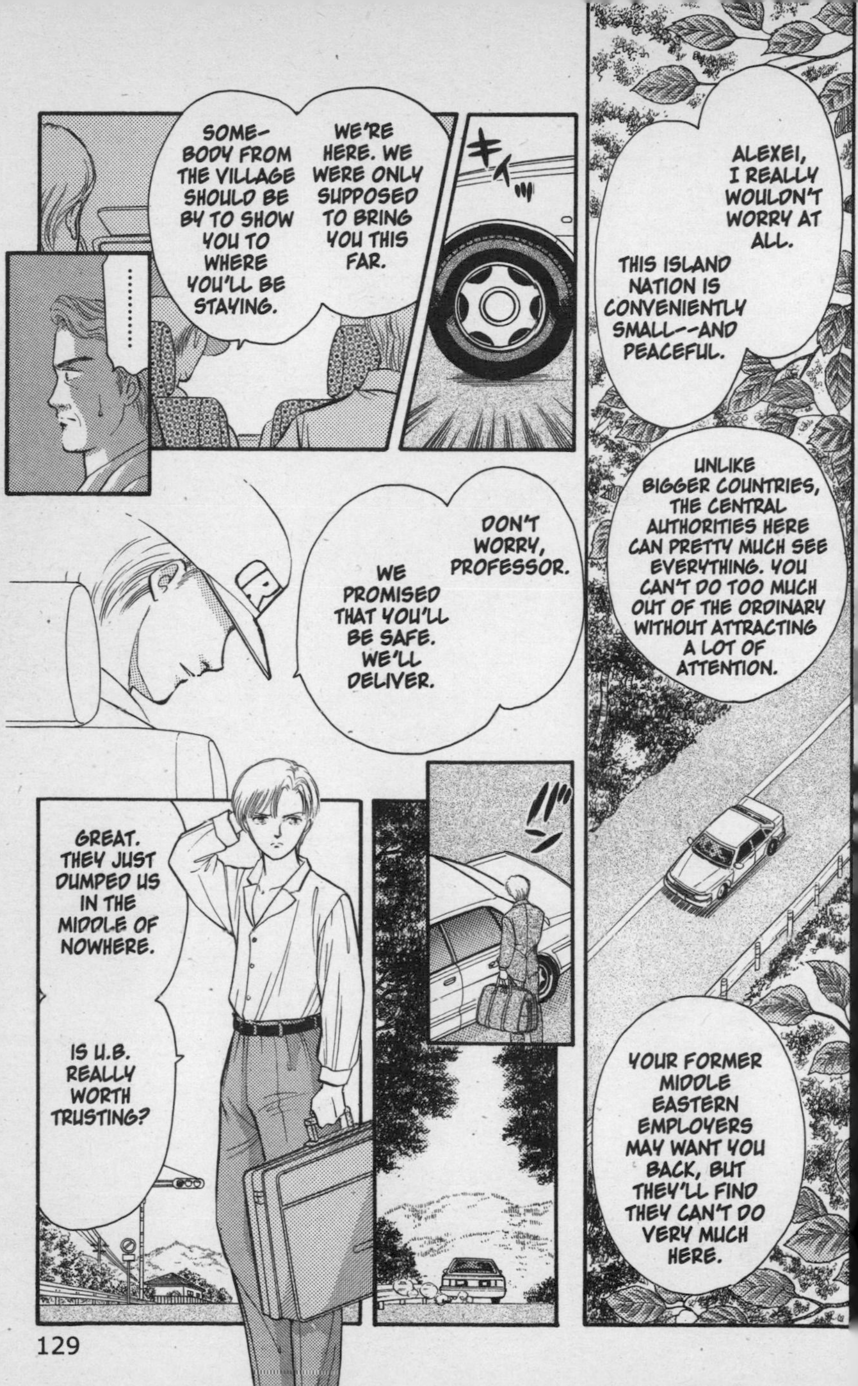
ALEXEI, I REALLY WOULDN'T WORRY AT ALL.
THIS ISLAND NATION IS CONVENIENTLY SMALL--AND PEACEFUL.
UNLIKE BIGGER COUNTRIES, THE CENTRAL AUTHORITIES HERE CAN PRETTY MUCH SEE EVERYTHING. YOU CAN'T DO TOO MUCH OUT OF THE ORDINARY WITHOUT ATTRACTING A LOT OF ATTENTION.
YOUR FORMER MIDDLE EASTERN EMPLOYERS MAY WANT YOU BACK, BUT THEY'LL FIND THEY CAN'T DO VERY MUCH HERE.
キィ
WE'RE HERE. WE WERE ONLY SUPPOSED TO BRING YOU THIS FAR.
SOME-BODY FROM THE VILLAGE SHOULD BE BY TO SHOW YOU TO WHERE YOU'LL BE STAYING.
......
DON'T WORRY, PROFESSOR.
WE PROMISED THAT YOU'LL BE SAFE. WE'LL DELIVER.
GREAT. THEY JUST DUMPED US IN THE MIDDLE OF NOWHERE.
IS U.B. REALLY WORTH TRUSTING?

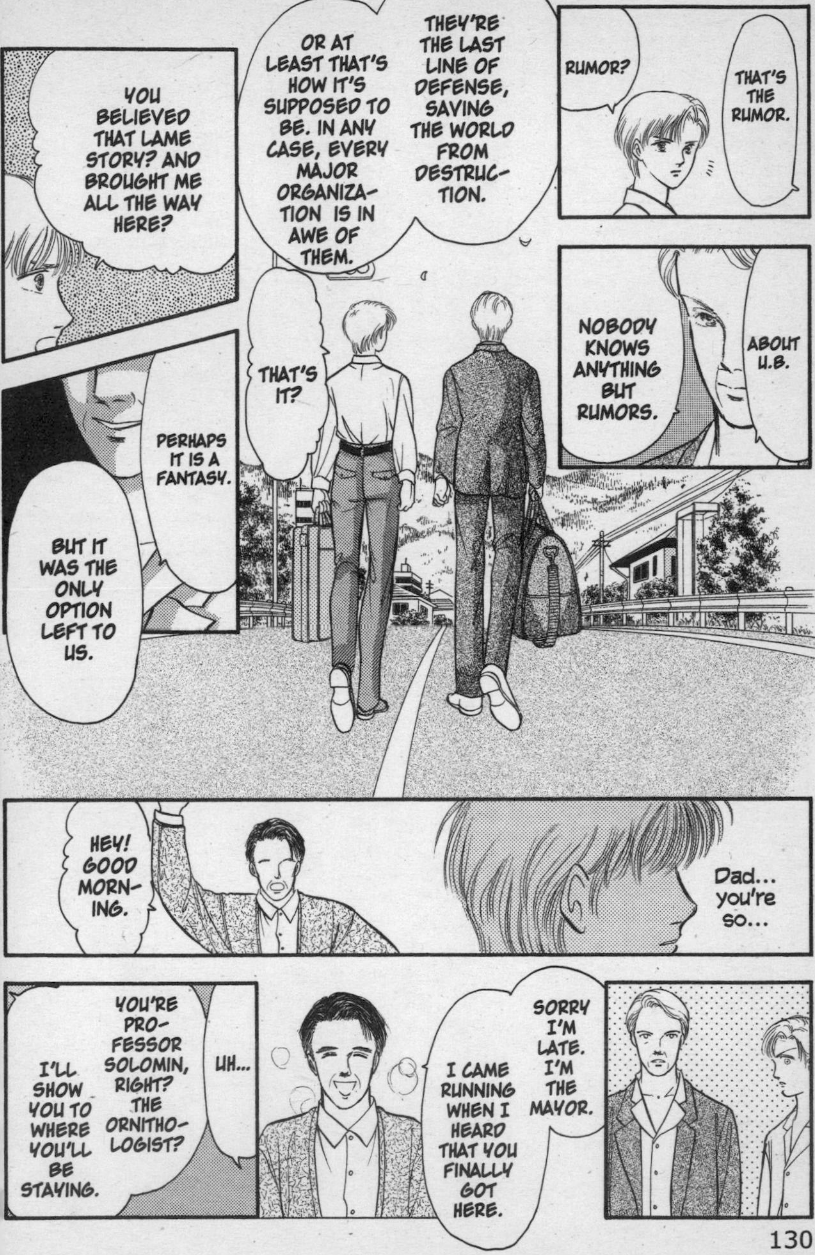
THAT'S THE RUMOR.
RUMOR?
THEY'RE THE LAST LINE OF DEFENSE, SAVING THE WORLD FROM DESTRUC-TION.
OR AT LEAST THAT'S HOW IT'S SUPPOSED TO BE. IN ANY CASE, EVERY MAJOR ORGANIZA-TION IS IN AWE OF THEM.
YOU BELIEVED THAT LAME STORY? AND BROUGHT ME ALL THE WAY HERE?
ABOUT U.B.
NOBODY KNOWS ANYTHING BUT RUMORS.
THAT'S IT?
PERHAPS IT IS A FANTASY.
BUT IT WAS THE ONLY OPTION LEFT TO US.
Dad... you're so...
HEY! GOOD MORN-ING.
SORRY I'M LATE. I'M THE MAYOR.
I CAME RUNNING WHEN I HEARD THAT YOU FINALLY GOT HERE.
UH...
YOU'RE PRO-FESSOR SOLOMIN, RIGHT? THE ORNITHO-LOGIST?
I'LL SHOW YOU TO WHERE YOU'LL BE STAYING.

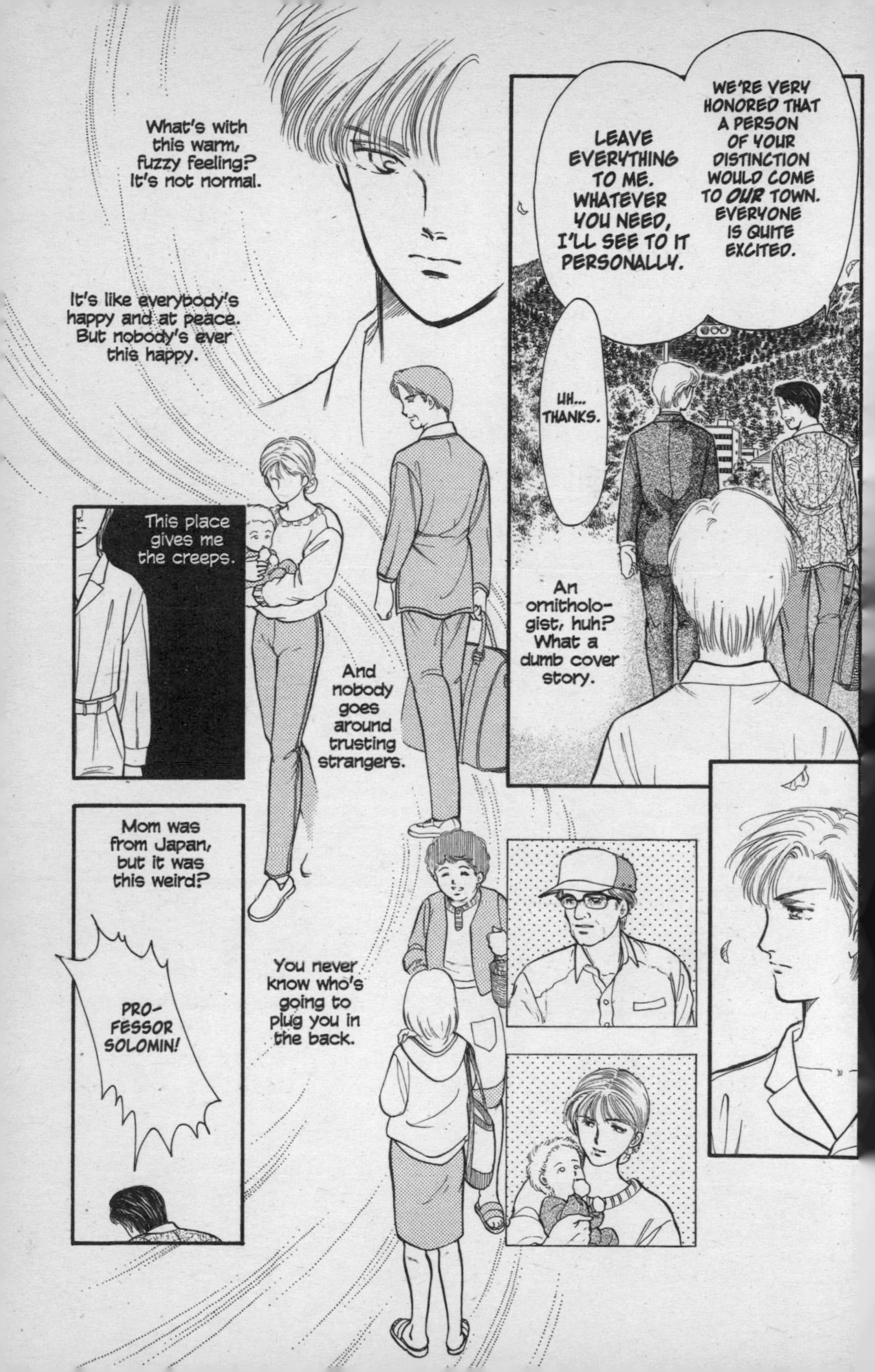
WE'RE VERY HONORED THAT A PERSON OF YOUR DISTINCTION WOULD COME TO OUR TOWN. EVERYONE IS QUITE EXCITED.
LEAVE EVERYTHING TO ME. WHATEVER YOU NEED, I'LL SEE TO IT PERSONALLY.
UH... THANKS.
An ornitholo-gist, huh? What a dumb cover story.
What's with this warm, fuzzy feeling? It's not normal.
It's like everybody's happy and at peace. But nobody's ever this happy.
This place gives me the creeps.
And nobody goes around trusting strangers.
You never know who's going to plug you in the back.
Mom was from Japan, but it was this weird?
PRO-FESSOR SOLOMIN!

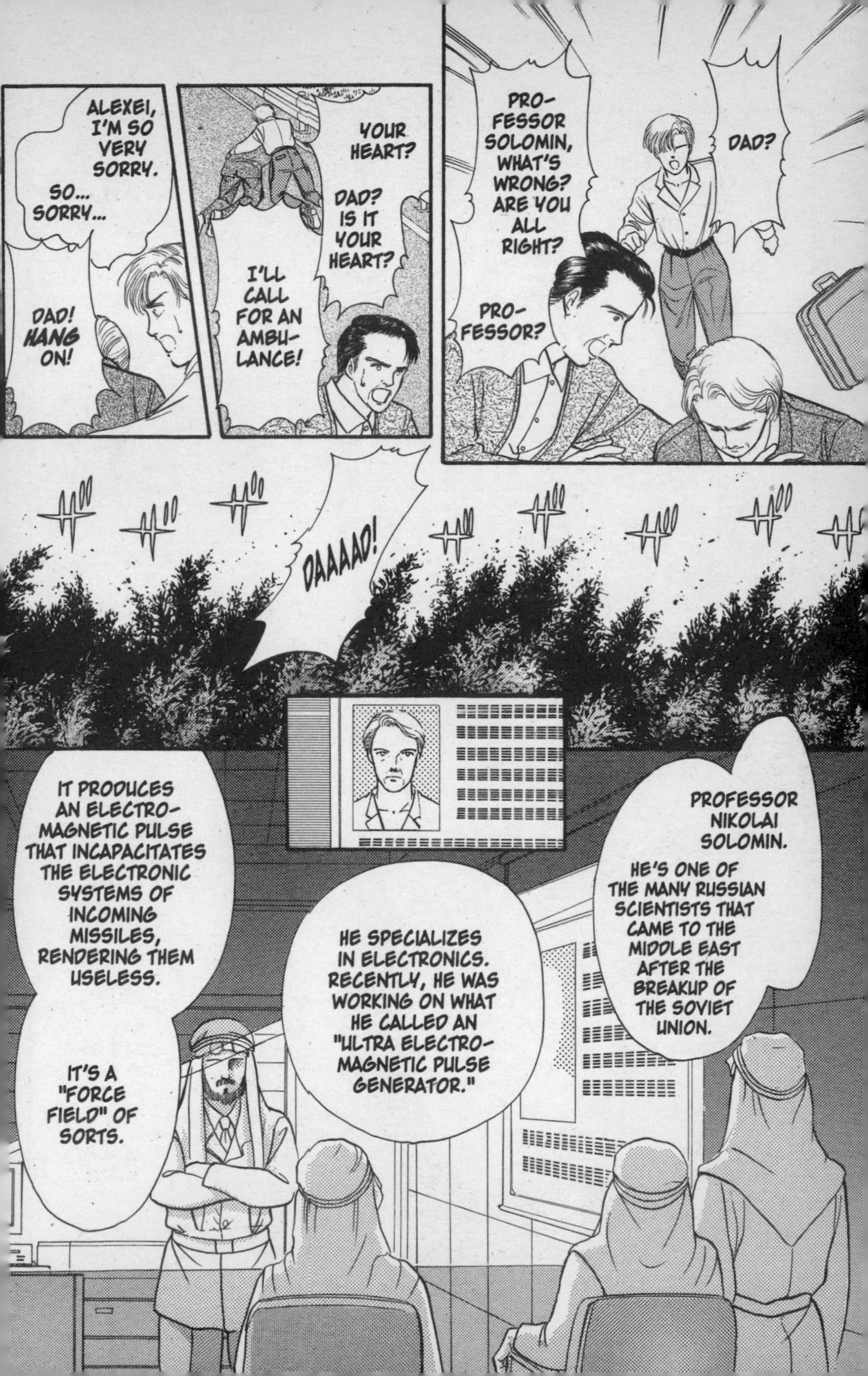
DAD?
PROFESSOR SOLOMIN, WHAT'S WRONG? ARE YOU ALL RIGHT?
PROFESSOR?
YOUR HEART?
DAD? IS IT YOUR HEART?
I'LL CALL FOR AN AMBULANCE!
ALEXEI, I'M SO VERY SORRY.
SO... SORRY...
DAD! HANG ON!
DAAAAD!
PROFESSOR NIKOLAI SOLOMIN.
HE'S ONE OF THE MANY RUSSIAN SCIENTISTS THAT CAME TO THE MIDDLE EAST AFTER THE BREAKUP OF THE SOVIET UNION.
HE SPECIALIZES IN ELECTRONICS. RECENTLY, HE WAS WORKING ON WHAT HE CALLED AN "ULTRA ELECTRO-MAGNETIC PULSE GENERATOR."
IT PRODUCES AN ELECTRO-MAGNETIC PULSE THAT INCAPACITATES THE ELECTRONIC SYSTEMS OF INCOMING MISSILES, RENDERING THEM USELESS.
IT'S A "FORCE FIELD" OF SORTS.

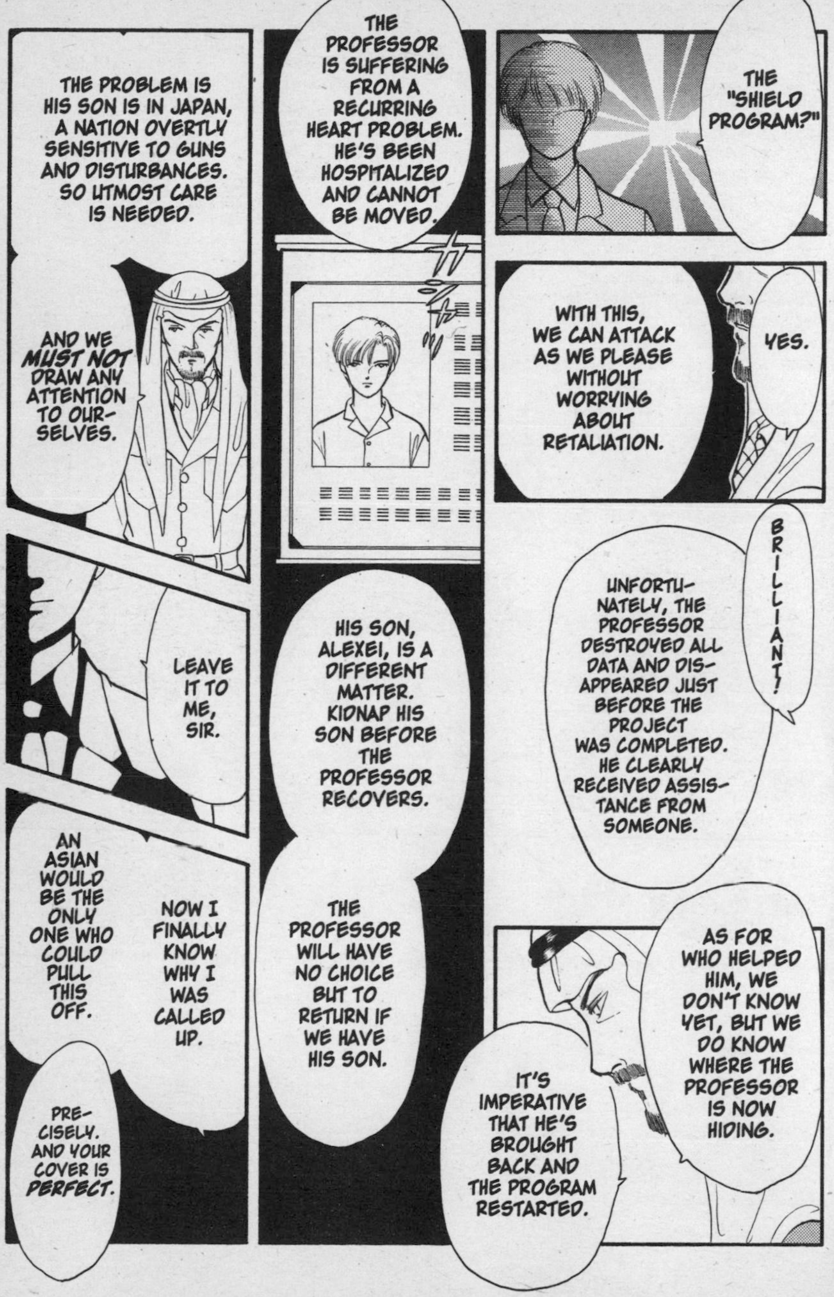
THE "SHIELD PROGRAM?"
YES.
WITH THIS, WE CAN ATTACK AS WE PLEASE WITHOUT WORRYING ABOUT RETALIATION.
BRILLIANT!
UNFORTUNATELY, THE PROFESSOR DESTROYED ALL DATA AND DISAPPEARED JUST BEFORE THE PROJECT WAS COMPLETED. HE CLEARLY RECEIVED ASSISTANCE FROM SOMEONE.
AS FOR WHO HELPED HIM, WE DON'T KNOW YET, BUT WE DO KNOW WHERE THE PROFESSOR IS NOW HIDING.
IT'S IMPERATIVE THAT HE'S BROUGHT BACK AND THE PROGRAM RESTARTED.
THE PROFESSOR IS SUFFERING FROM A RECURRING HEART PROBLEM. HE'S BEEN HOSPITALIZED AND CANNOT BE MOVED.
HIS SON, ALEXEI, IS A DIFFERENT MATTER. KIDNAP HIS SON BEFORE THE PROFESSOR RECOVERS.
THE PROFESSOR WILL HAVE NO CHOICE BUT TO RETURN IF WE HAVE HIS SON.
THE PROBLEM IS HIS SON IS IN JAPAN, A NATION OVERTLY SENSITIVE TO GUNS AND DISTURBANCES. SO UTMOST CARE IS NEEDED.
AND WE *MUST NOT* DRAW ANY ATTENTION TO OURSELVES.
LEAVE IT TO ME, SIR.
NOW I FINALLY KNOW WHY I WAS CALLED UP.
AN ASIAN WOULD BE THE ONLY ONE WHO COULD PULL THIS OFF.
PRECISELY. AND YOUR COVER IS *PERFECT*.

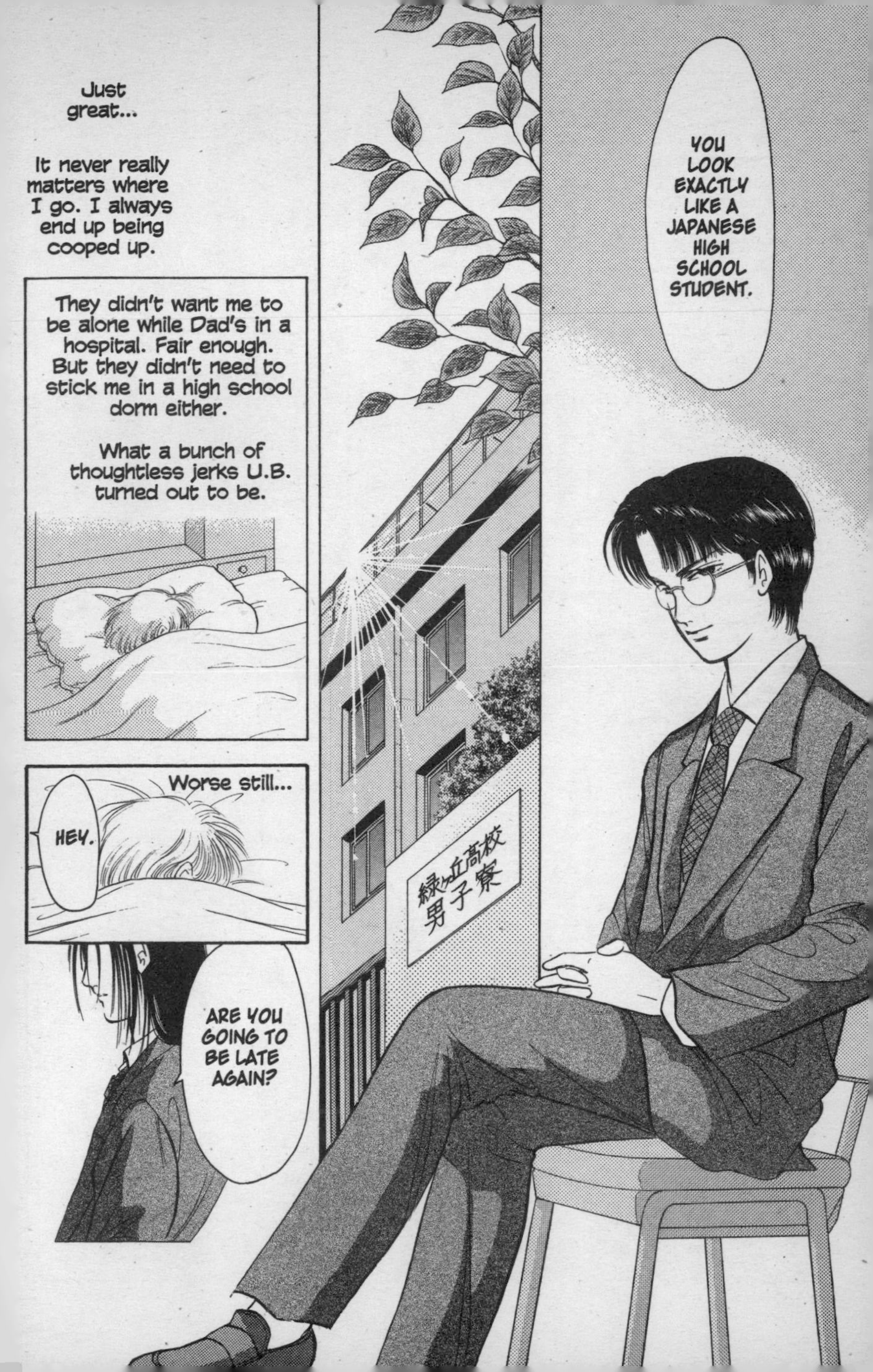
YOU LOOK EXACTLY LIKE A JAPANESE HIGH SCHOOL STUDENT.
緑ヶ丘高校 男子寮
Just great...
It never really matters where I go. I always end up being cooped up.
They didn't want me to be alone while Dad's in a hospital. Fair enough. But they didn't need to stick me in a high school dorm either.
What a bunch of thoughtless jerks U.B. turned out to be.
Worse still...
HEY.
ARE YOU GOING TO BE LATE AGAIN?

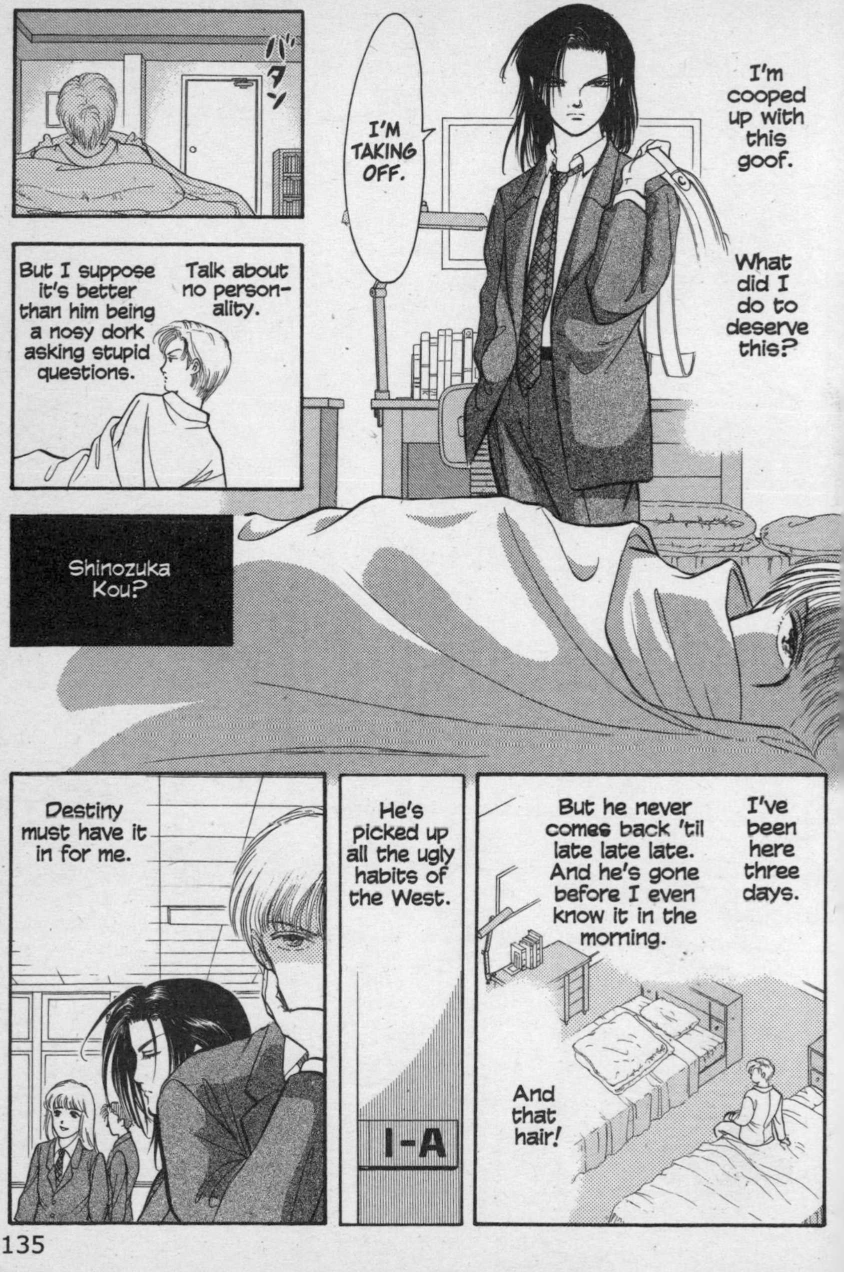
I'm cooped up with this goof.
What did I do to deserve this?
I'M TAKING OFF.
Shinozuka Kou?
バタン
Talk about no personality.
But I suppose it's better than him being a nosy dork asking stupid questions.
I've been here three days.
But he never comes back 'til late late late. And he's gone before I even know it in the morning.
And that hair!
He's picked up all the ugly habits of the West.
I-A
Destiny must have it in for me.

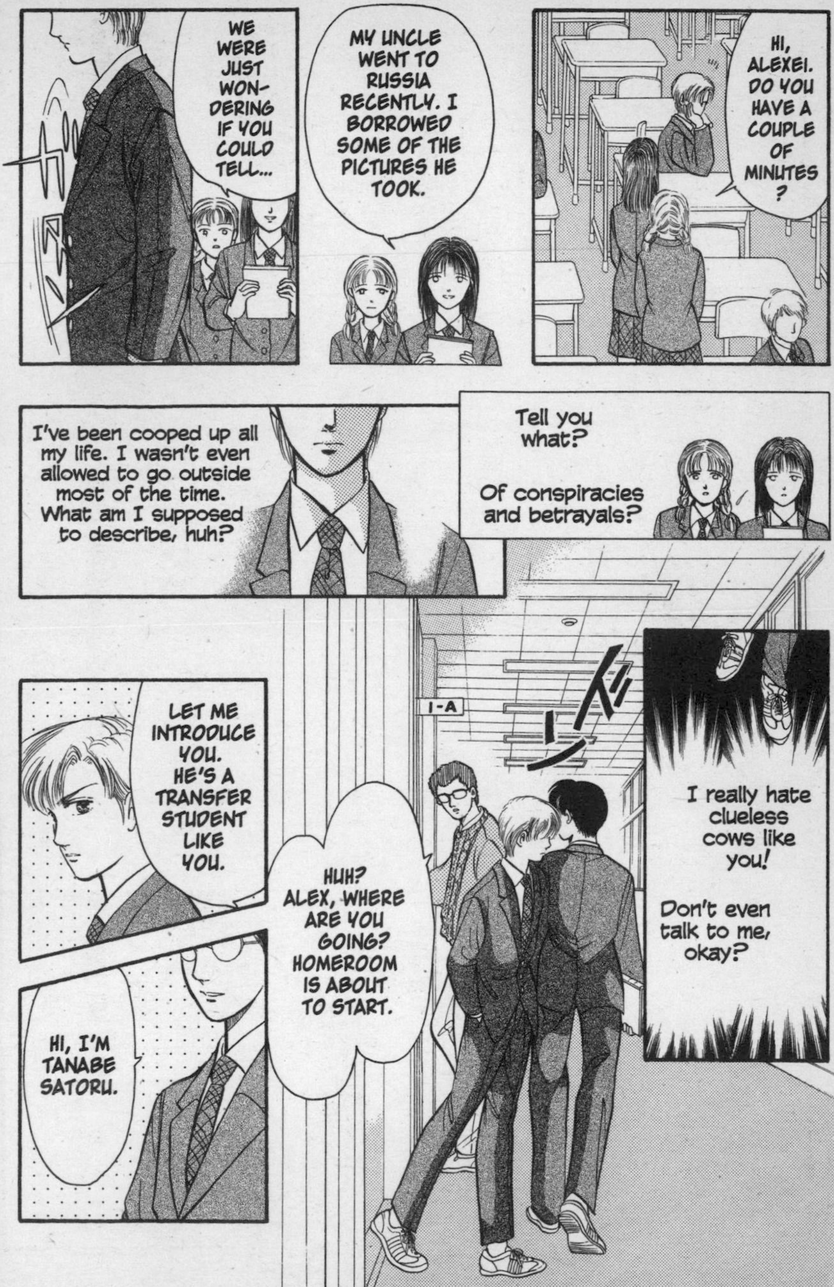
HI, ALEXEI. DO YOU HAVE A COUPLE OF MINUTES?
MY UNCLE WENT TO RUSSIA RECENTLY. I BORROWED SOME OF THE PICTURES HE TOOK.
WE WERE JUST WONDERING IF YOU COULD TELL...
Tell you what?
Of conspiracies and betrayals?
I've been cooped up all my life. I wasn't even allowed to go outside most of the time. What am I supposed to describe, huh?
I really hate clueless cows like you!
Don't even talk to me, okay?
1-A
HUH? ALEX, WHERE ARE YOU GOING? HOMEROOM IS ABOUT TO START.
LET ME INTRODUCE YOU. HE'S A TRANSFER STUDENT LIKE YOU.
HI, I'M TANABE SATORU.

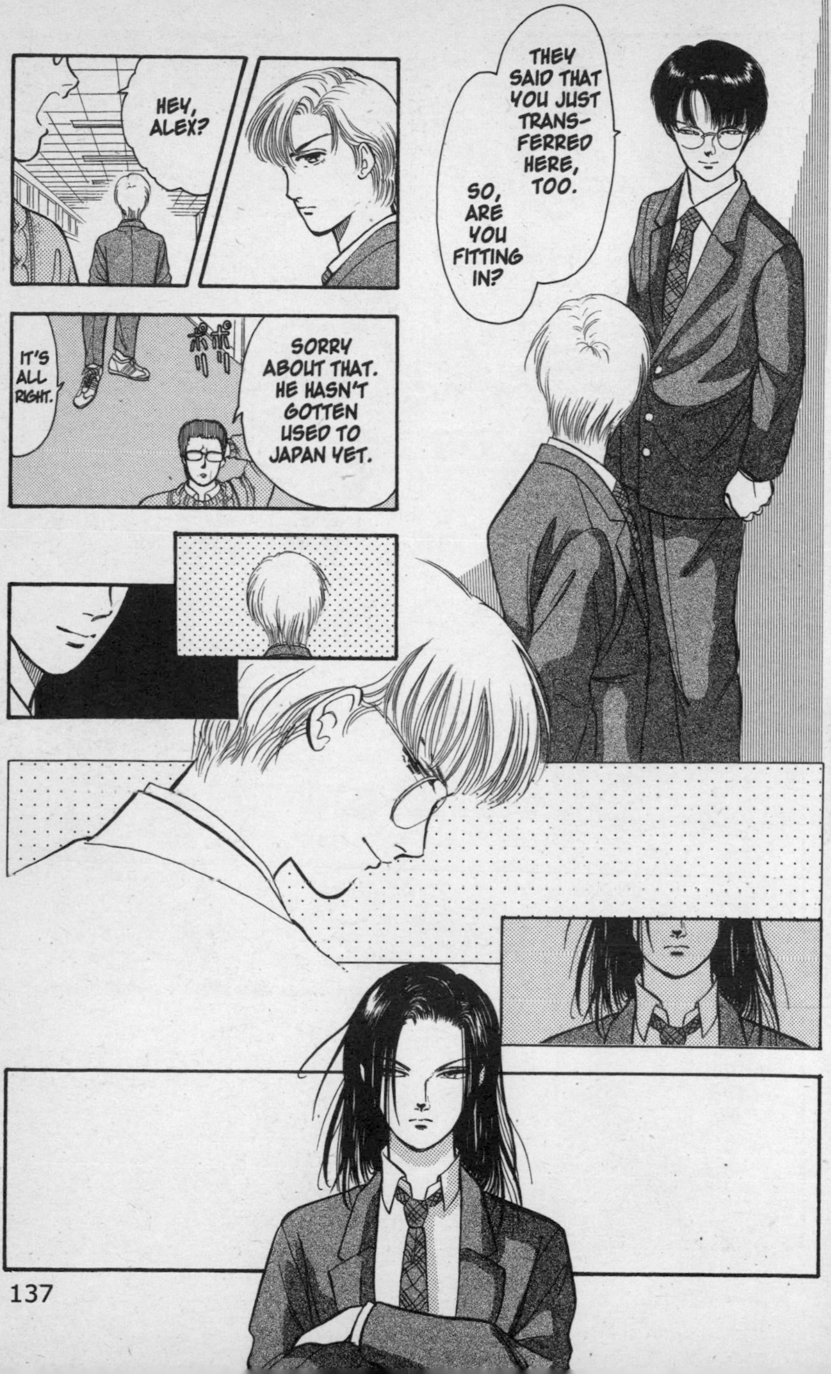
THEY SAID THAT YOU JUST TRANS-FERRED HERE, TOO.
SO, ARE YOU FITTING IN?
HEY, ALEX?
SORRY ABOUT THAT. HE HASN'T GOTTEN USED TO JAPAN YET.
ポリポリ
IT'S ALL RIGHT.

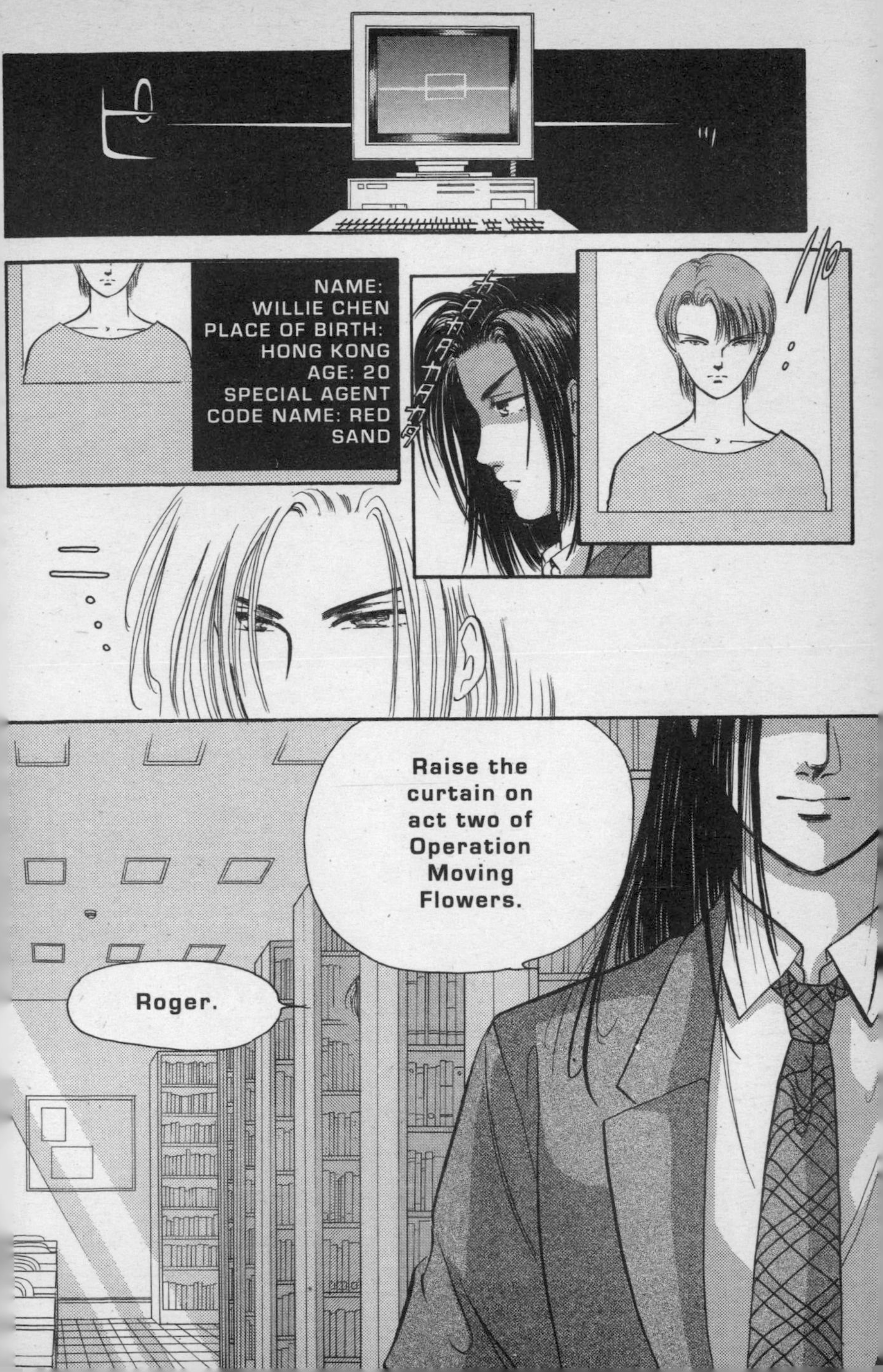
NAME: WILLIE CHEN
PLACE OF BIRTH: HONG KONG
AGE: 20
SPECIAL AGENT
CODE NAME: RED SAND
カタカタカタカタ
Raise the curtain on act two of Operation Moving Flowers.
Roger.

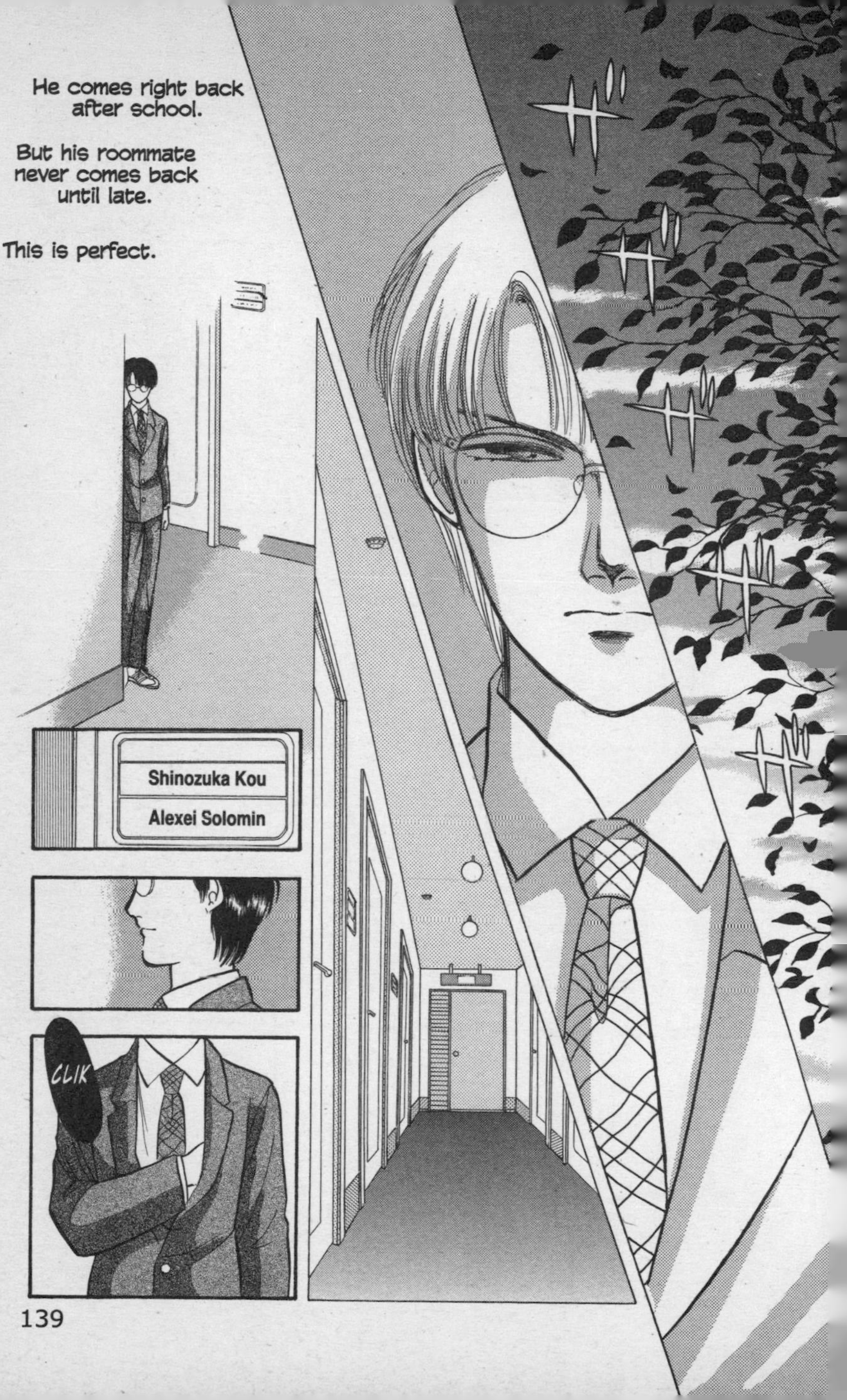
He comes right back after school.
But his roommate never comes back until late.
This is perfect.
Shinozuka Kou
Alexei Solomin
CLIK

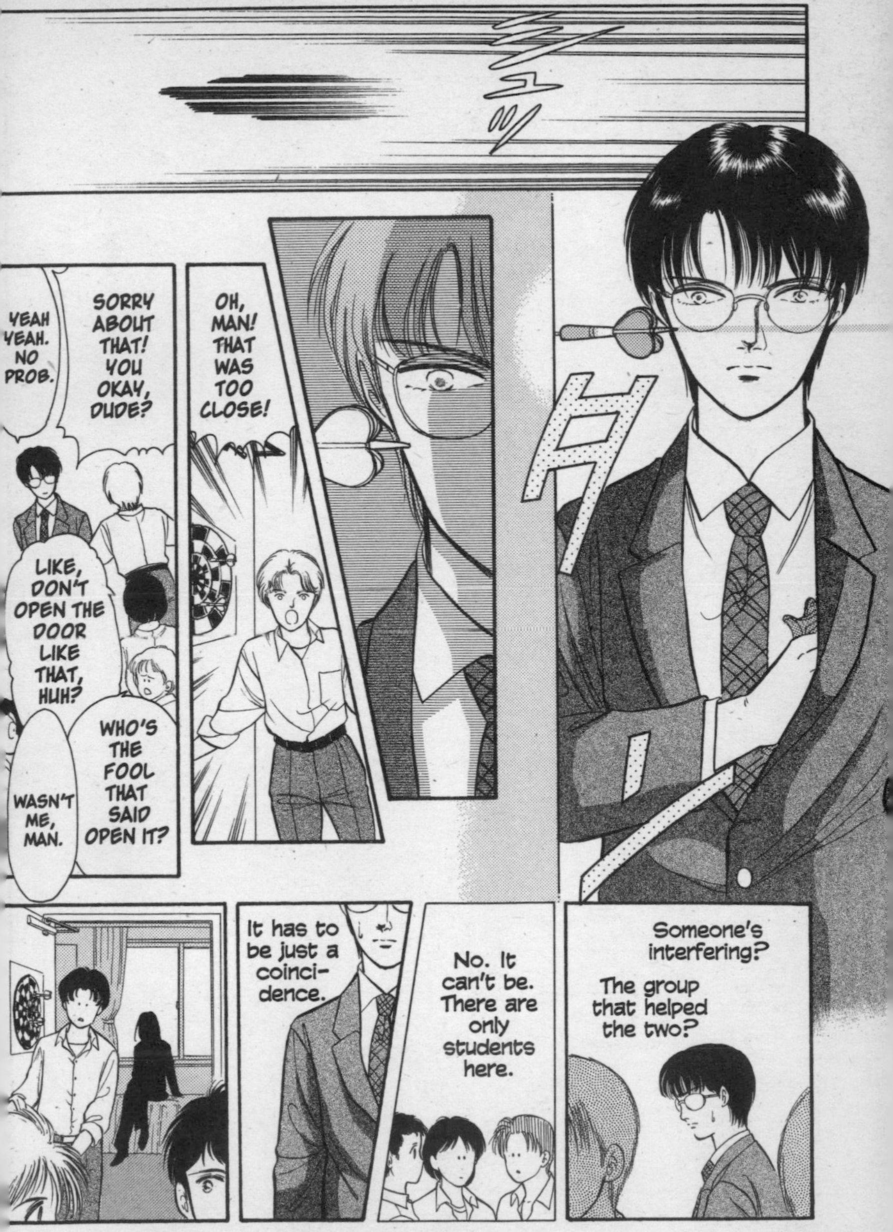
OH, MAN! THAT WAS TOO CLOSE!
SORRY ABOUT THAT! YOU OKAY, DUDE?
YEAH YEAH. NO PROB.
LIKE, DON'T OPEN THE DOOR LIKE THAT, HUH?
WHO'S THE FOOL THAT SAID OPEN IT?
WASN'T ME, MAN.
Someone's interfering?
The group that helped the two?
No. It can't be. There are only students here.
It has to be just a coincidence.

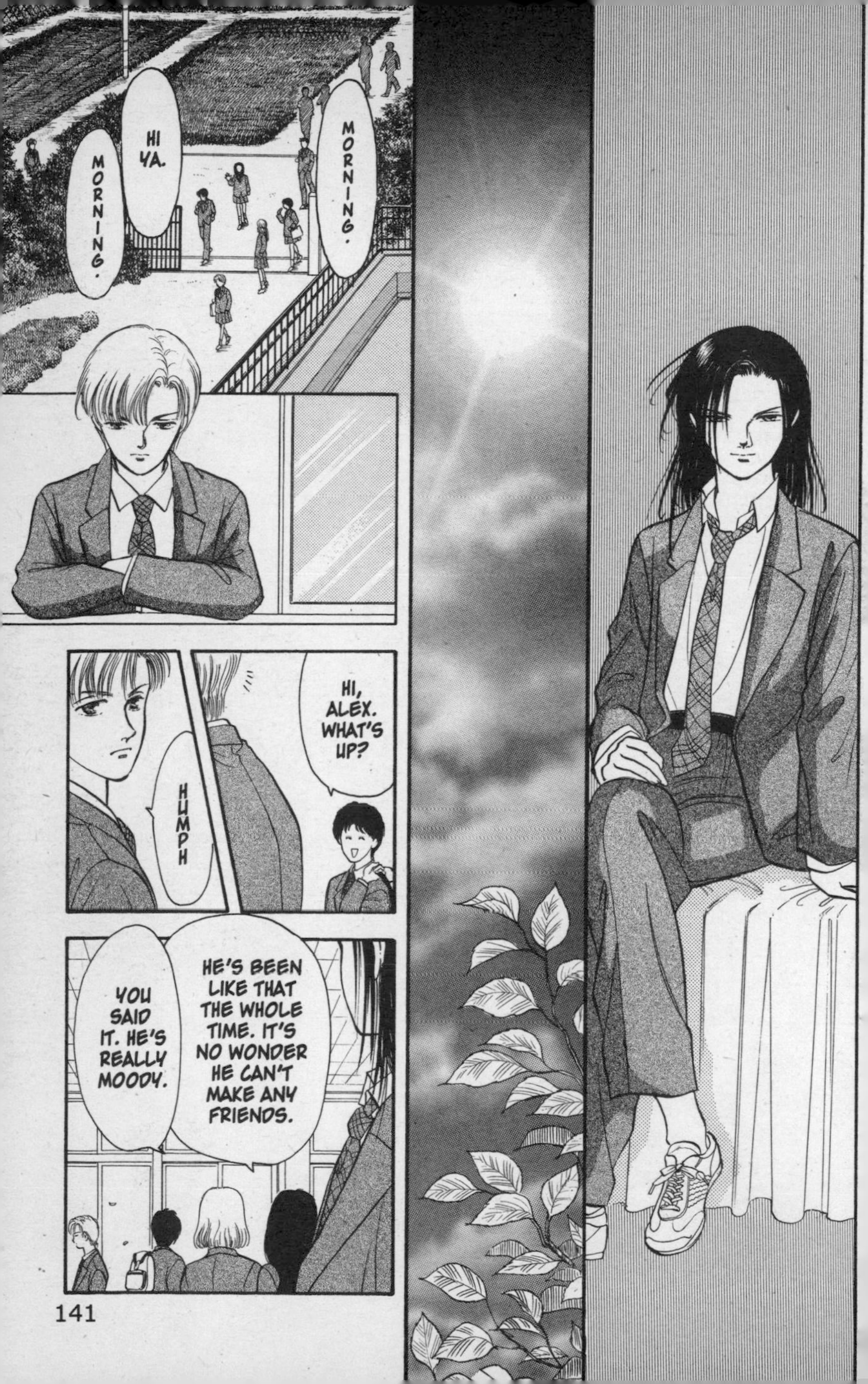
MORNING.
HI YA.
MORNING.
HI, ALEX. WHAT'S UP?
HUMPH
HE'S BEEN LIKE THAT THE WHOLE TIME. IT'S NO WONDER HE CAN'T MAKE ANY FRIENDS.
YOU SAID IT. HE'S REALLY MOODY.

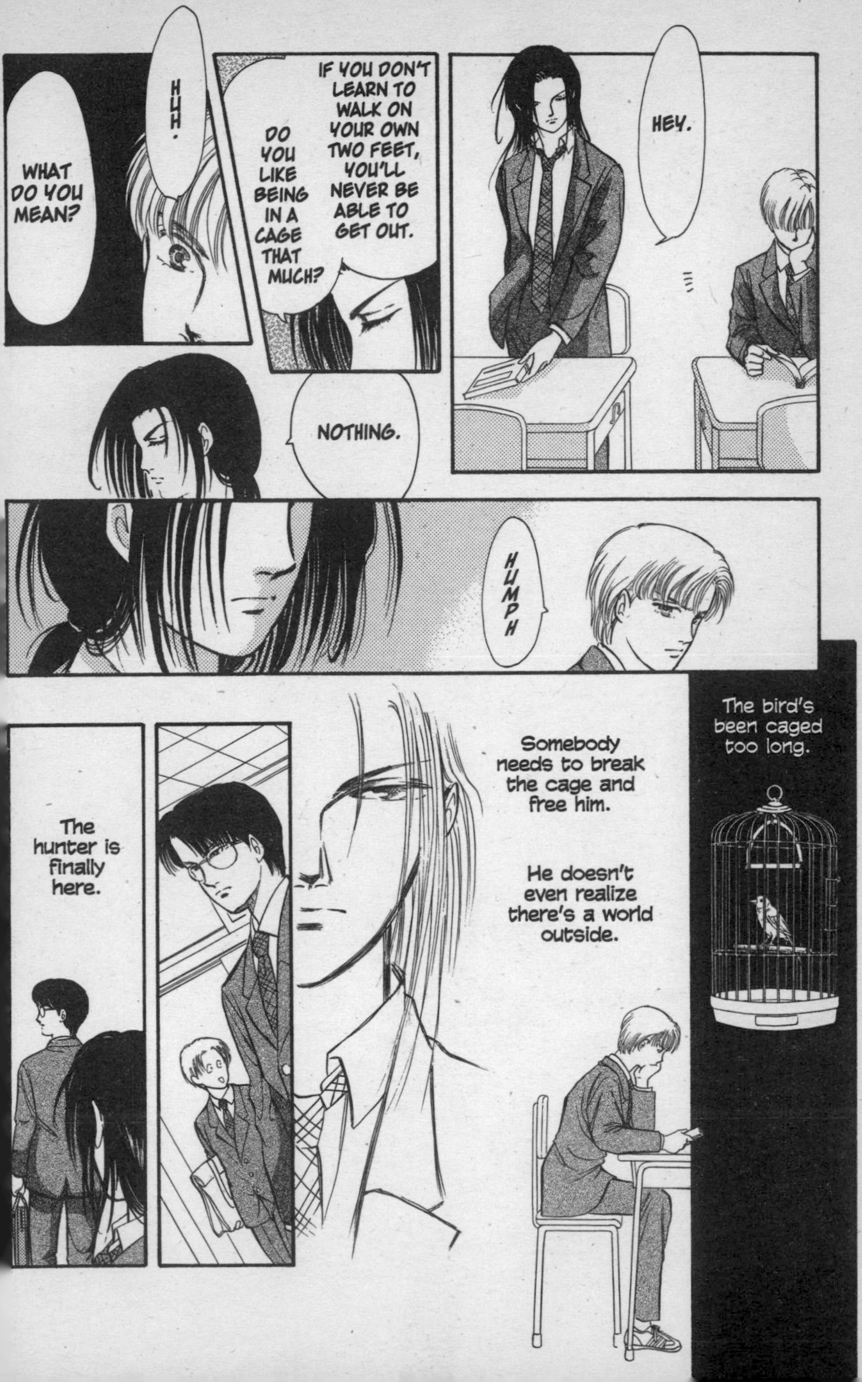
HEY.
IF YOU DON'T LEARN TO WALK ON YOUR OWN TWO FEET, YOU'LL NEVER BE ABLE TO GET OUT.
DO YOU LIKE BEING IN A CAGE THAT MUCH?
HUH.
WHAT DO YOU MEAN?
NOTHING.
HUMPH
The bird's been caged too long.
Somebody needs to break the cage and free him.
He doesn't even realize there's a world outside.
The hunter is finally here.

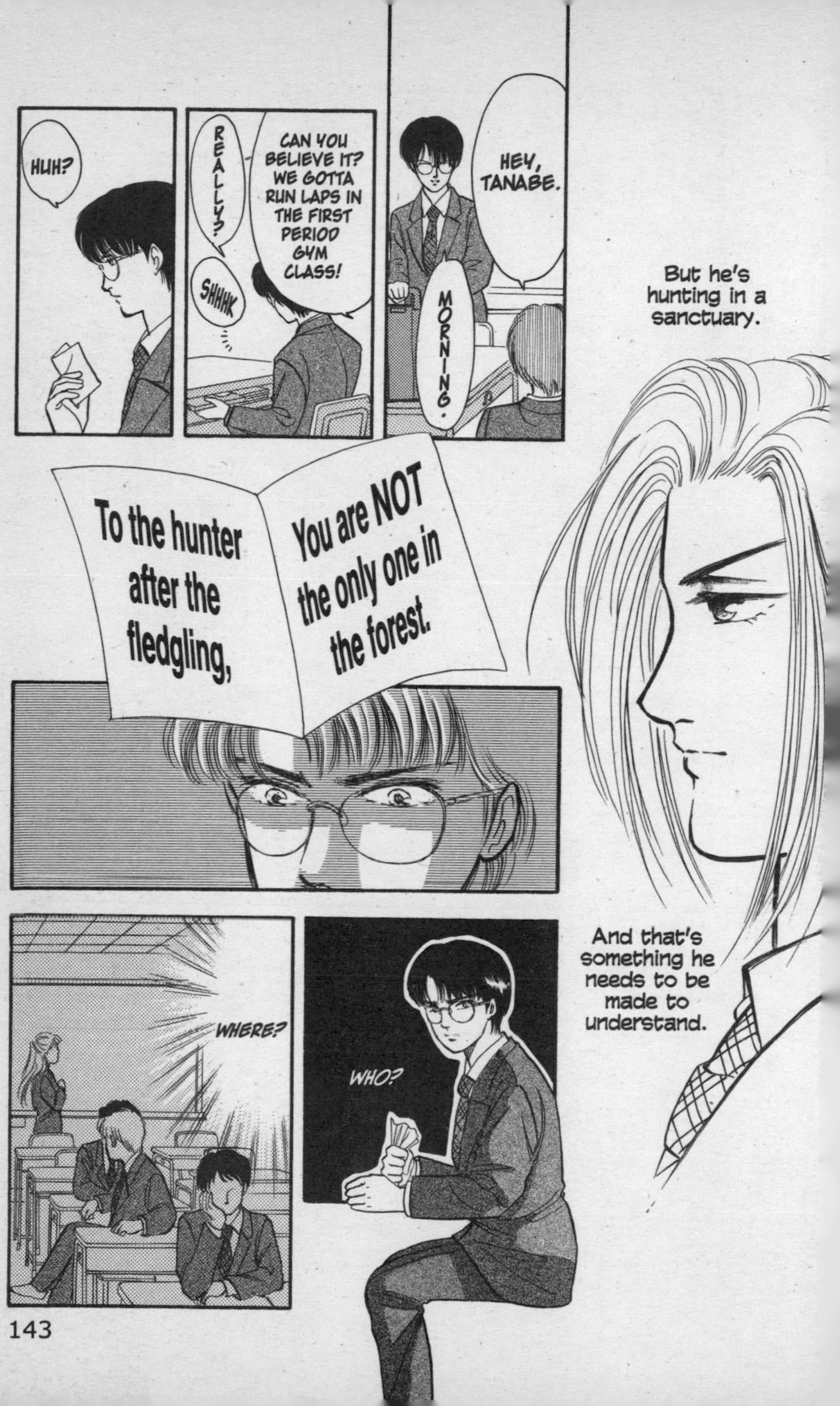

But he's hunting in a sanctuary.
And that's something he needs to be made to understand.
HEY, TANABE.
MORNING.
CAN YOU BELIEVE IT? WE GOTTA RUN LAPS IN THE FIRST PERIOD GYM CLASS!
REALLY?
SHHHK
HUH?
To the hunter after the fledgling,
You are NOT the only one in the forest.
WHO?
WHERE?

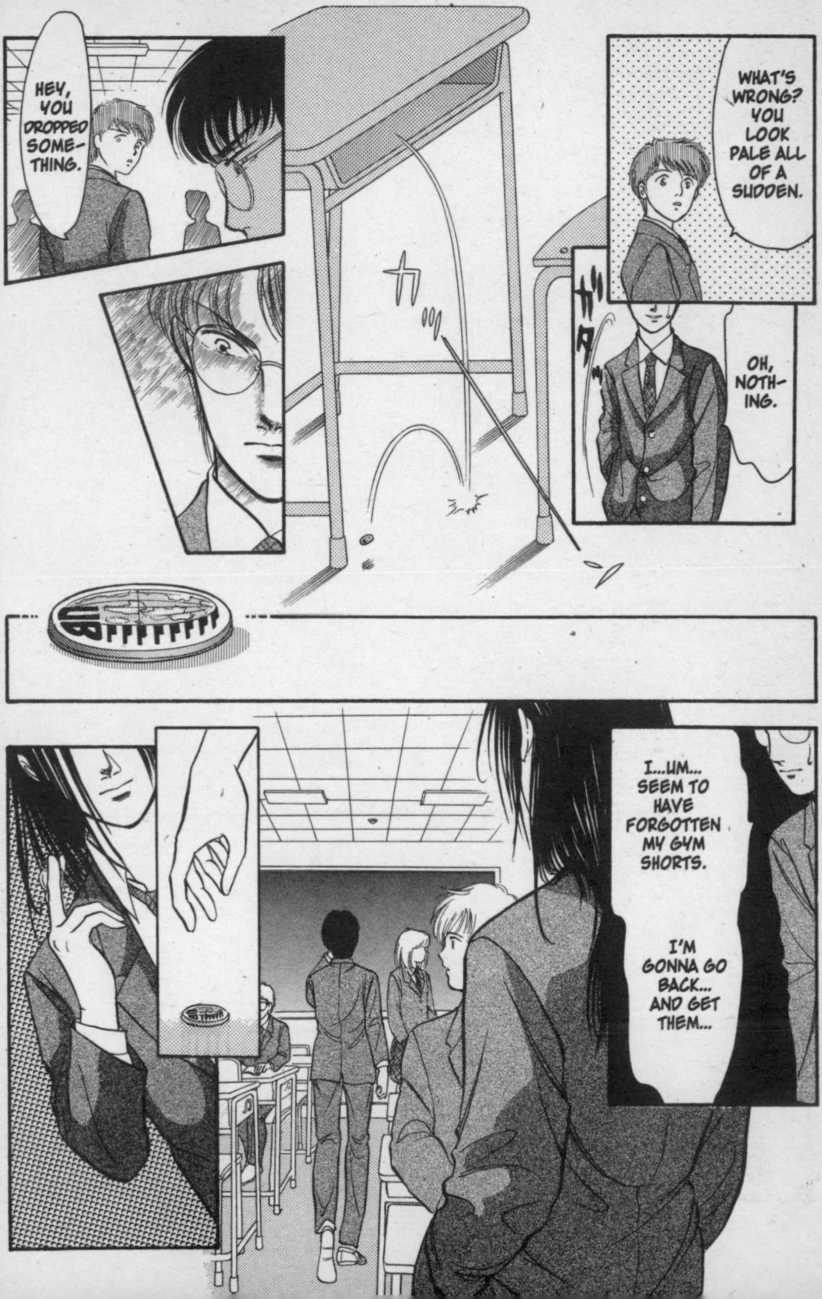
WHAT'S WRONG? YOU LOOK PALE ALL OF A SUDDEN.
OH, NOTHING.
HEY, YOU DROPPED SOMETHING.
I...UM... SEEM TO HAVE FORGOTTEN MY GYM SHORTS.
I'M GONNA GO BACK... AND GET THEM...

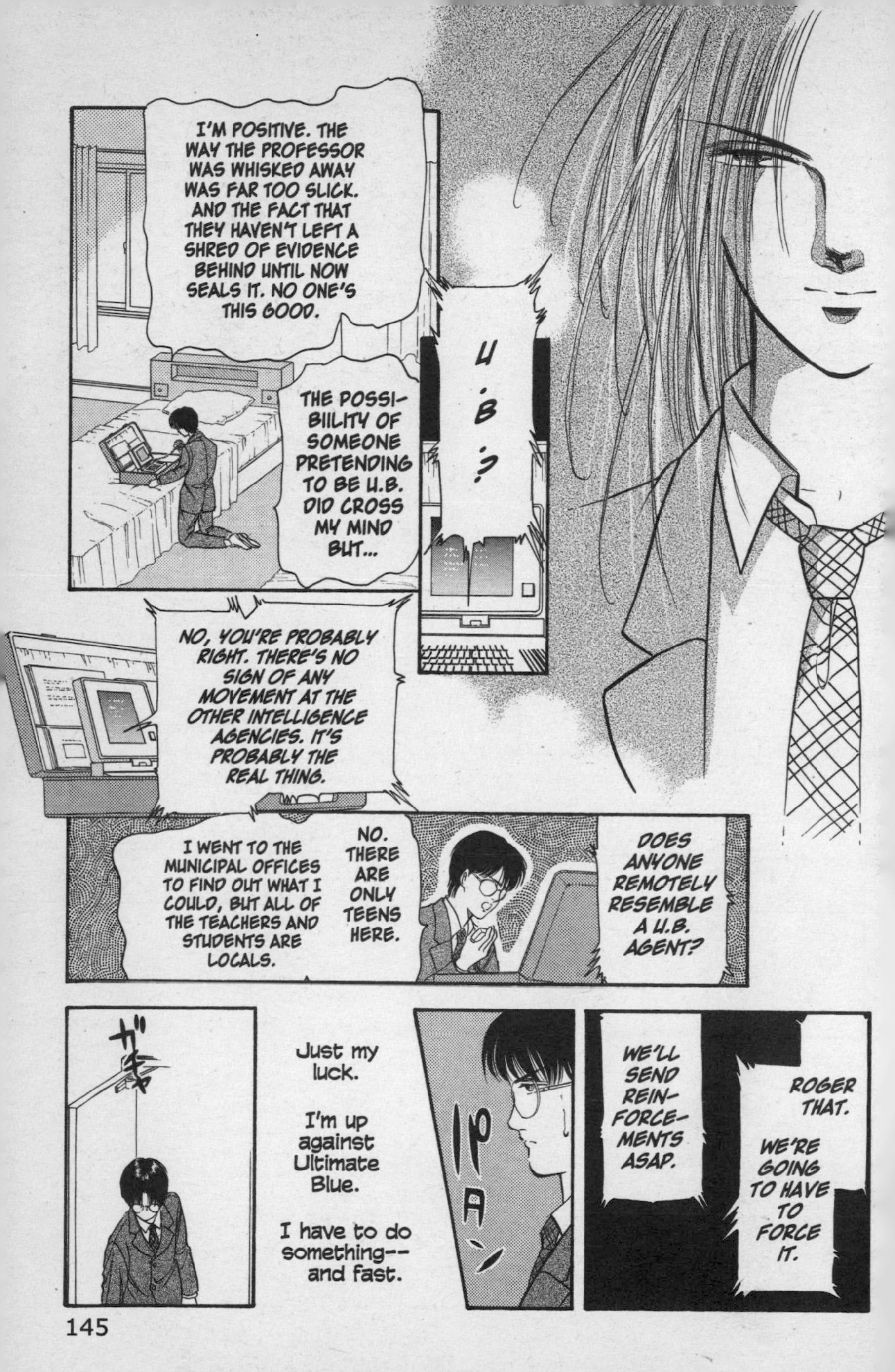
U.B.?
I'M POSITIVE. THE WAY THE PROFESSOR WAS WHISKED AWAY WAS FAR TOO SLICK. AND THE FACT THAT THEY HAVEN'T LEFT A SHRED OF EVIDENCE BEHIND UNTIL NOW SEALS IT. NO ONE'S THIS GOOD.
THE POSSI-BIILITY OF SOMEONE PRETENDING TO BE U.B. DID CROSS MY MIND BUT...
NO, YOU'RE PROBABLY RIGHT. THERE'S NO SIGN OF ANY MOVEMENT AT THE OTHER INTELLIGENCE AGENCIES. IT'S PROBABLY THE REAL THING.
DOES ANYONE REMOTELY RESEMBLE A U.B. AGENT?
NO. THERE ARE ONLY TEENS HERE.
I WENT TO THE MUNICIPAL OFFICES TO FIND OUT WHAT I COULD, BUT ALL OF THE TEACHERS AND STUDENTS ARE LOCALS.
WE'LL SEND REIN-FORCE-MENTS ASAP.
ROGER THAT.
WE'RE GOING TO HAVE TO FORCE IT.
Just my luck.
I'm up against Ultimate Blue.
I have to do something--and fast.
ガチャ

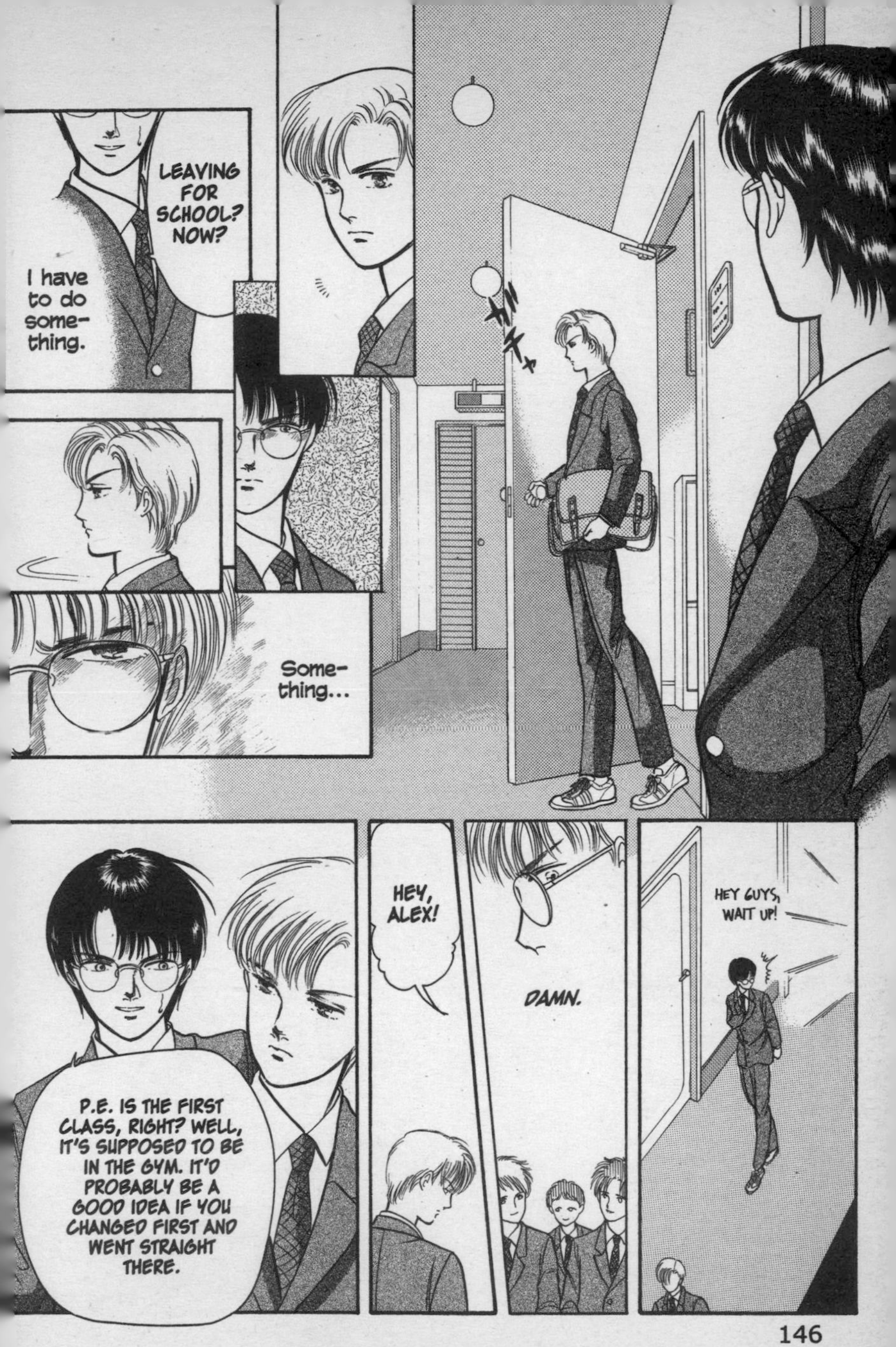
LEAVING FOR SCHOOL? NOW?
I have to do something.
Something...
HEY GUYS, WAIT UP!
DAMN.
HEY, ALEX!
P.E. IS THE FIRST CLASS, RIGHT? WELL, IT'S SUPPOSED TO BE IN THE GYM. IT'D PROBABLY BE A GOOD IDEA IF YOU CHANGED FIRST AND WENT STRAIGHT THERE.

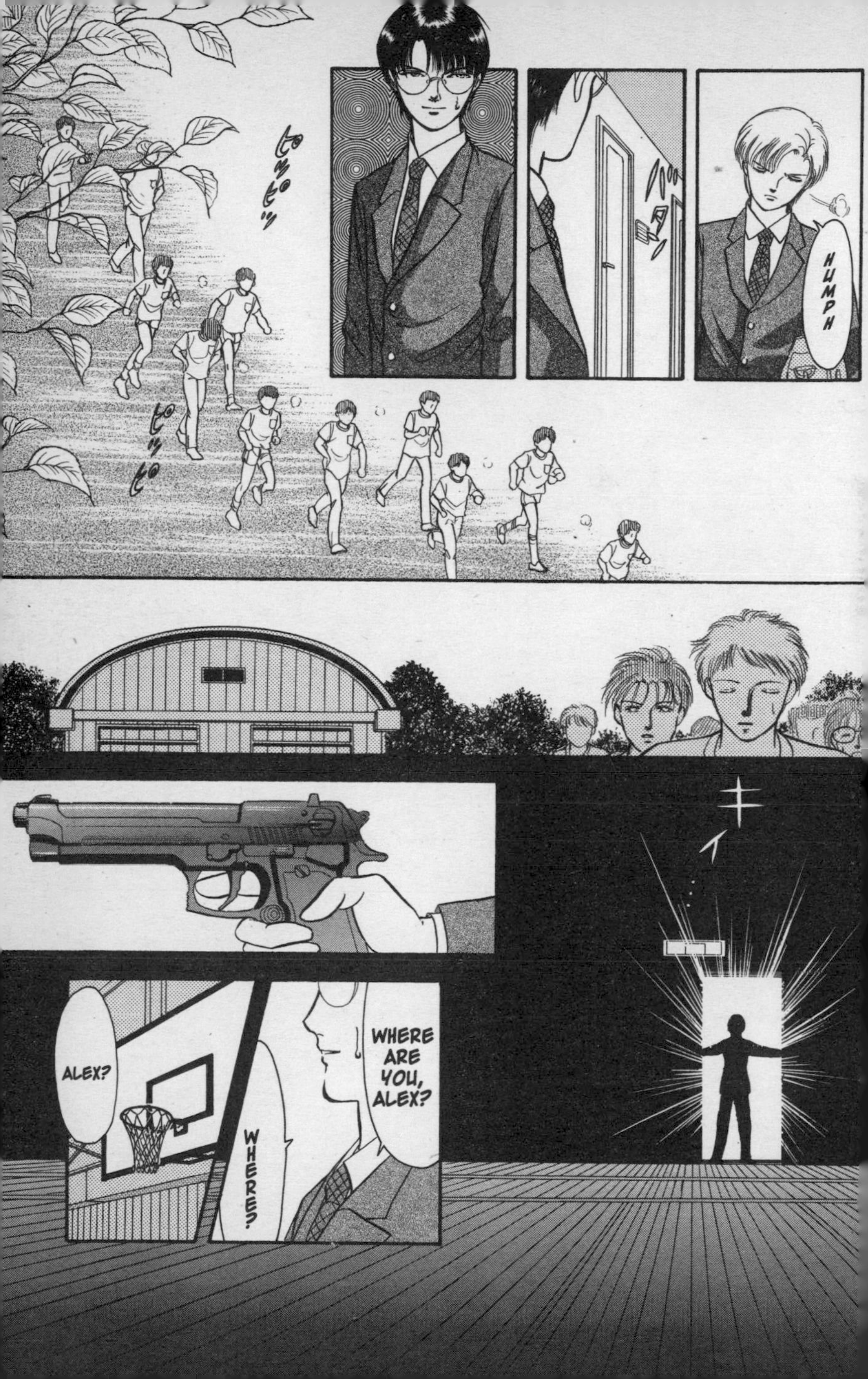
HUMPH
キイ
WHERE ARE YOU, ALEX?
WHERE?
ALEX?

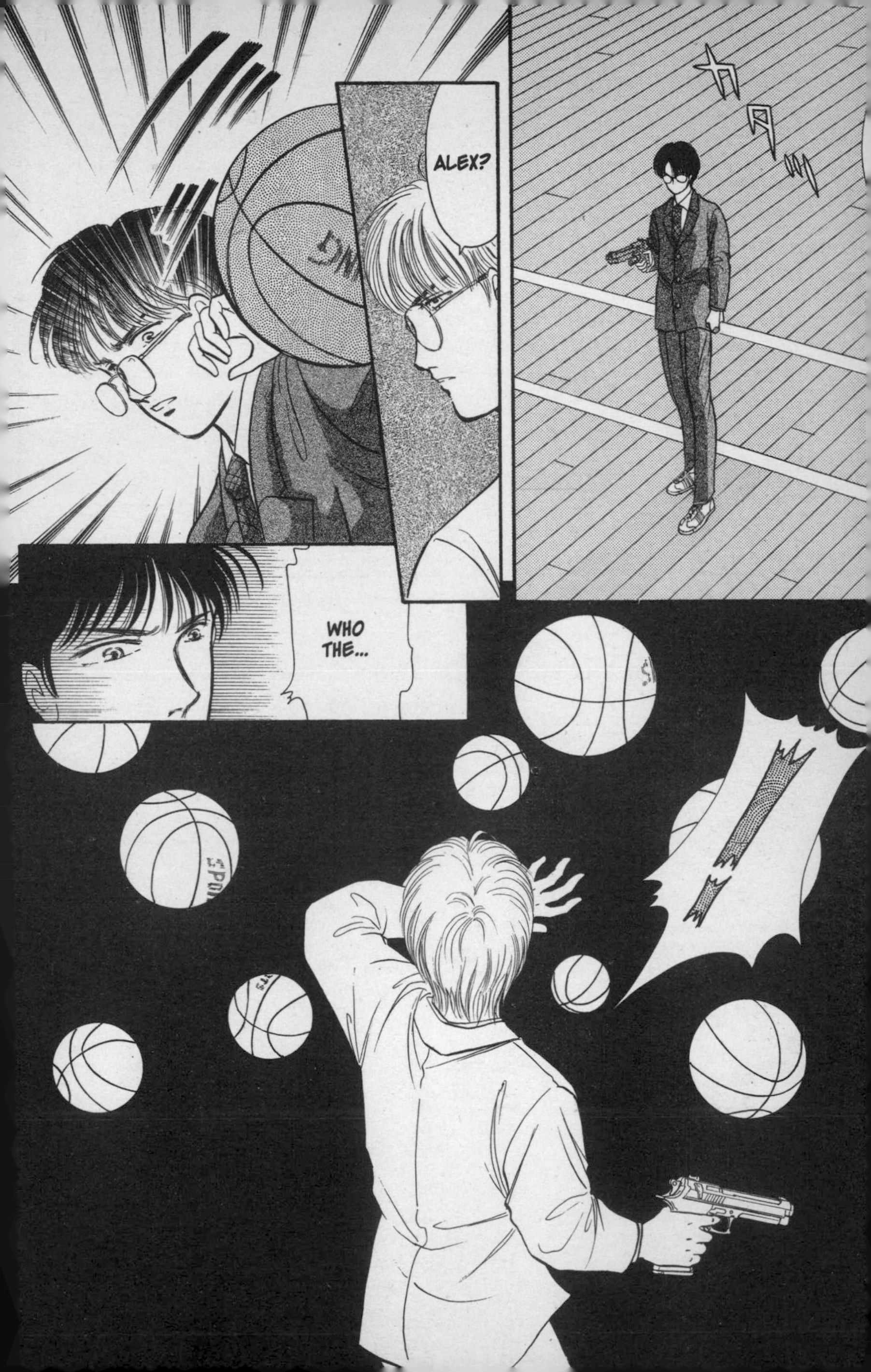
ALEX?
WHO THE...

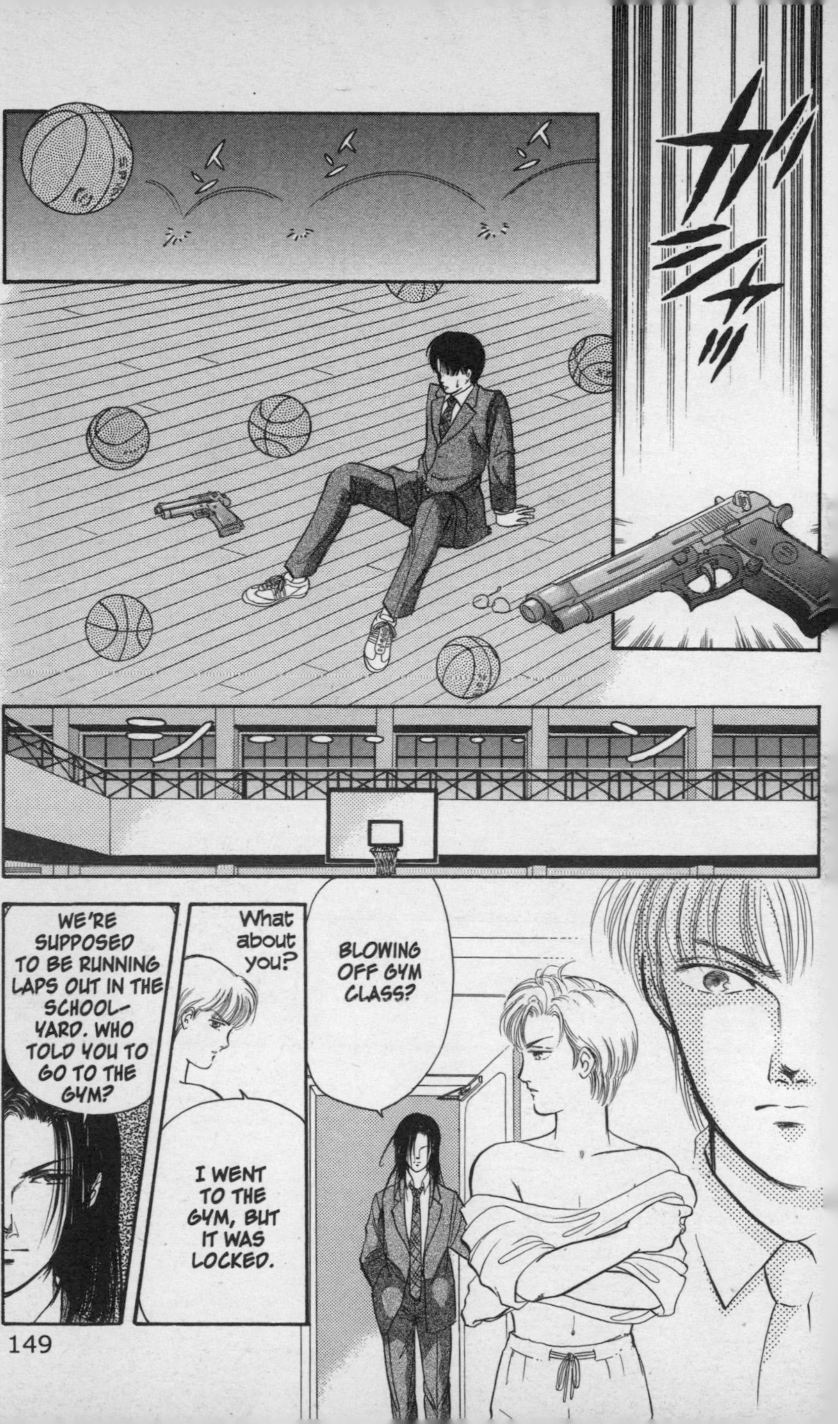
BLOWING OFF GYM CLASS?
What about you?
I WENT TO THE GYM, BUT IT WAS LOCKED.
WE'RE SUPPOSED TO BE RUNNING LAPS OUT IN THE SCHOOL-YARD. WHO TOLD YOU TO GO TO THE GYM?

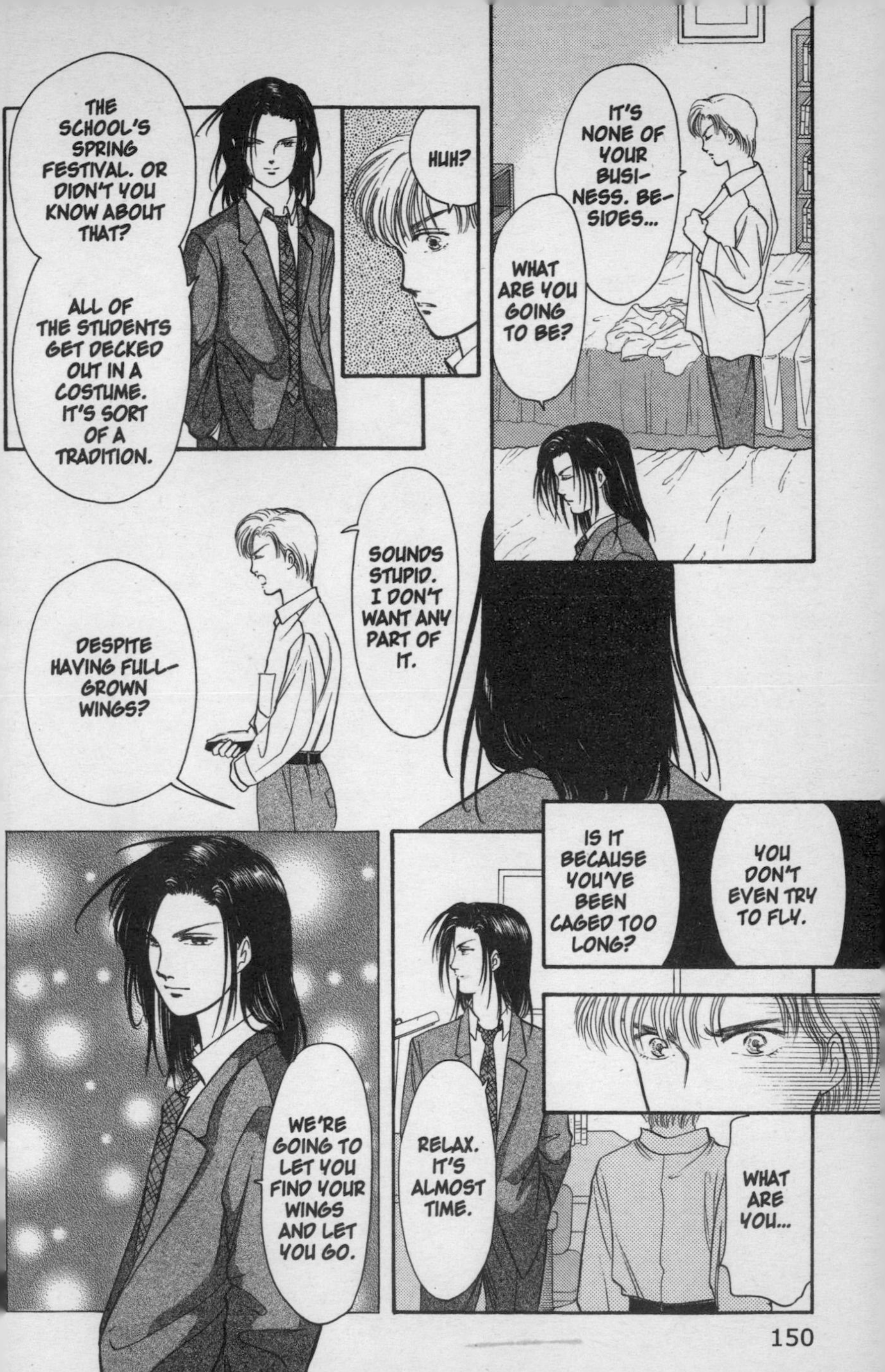
IT'S NONE OF YOUR BUSINESS. BESIDES...
WHAT ARE YOU GOING TO BE?
HUH?
THE SCHOOL'S SPRING FESTIVAL. OR DIDN'T YOU KNOW ABOUT THAT?
ALL OF THE STUDENTS GET DECKED OUT IN A COSTUME. IT'S SORT OF A TRADITION.
SOUNDS STUPID. I DON'T WANT ANY PART OF IT.
DESPITE HAVING FULL-GROWN WINGS?
YOU DON'T EVEN TRY TO FLY.
IS IT BECAUSE YOU'VE BEEN CAGED TOO LONG?
WHAT ARE YOU...
RELAX. IT'S ALMOST TIME.
WE'RE GOING TO LET YOU FIND YOUR WINGS AND LET YOU GO.

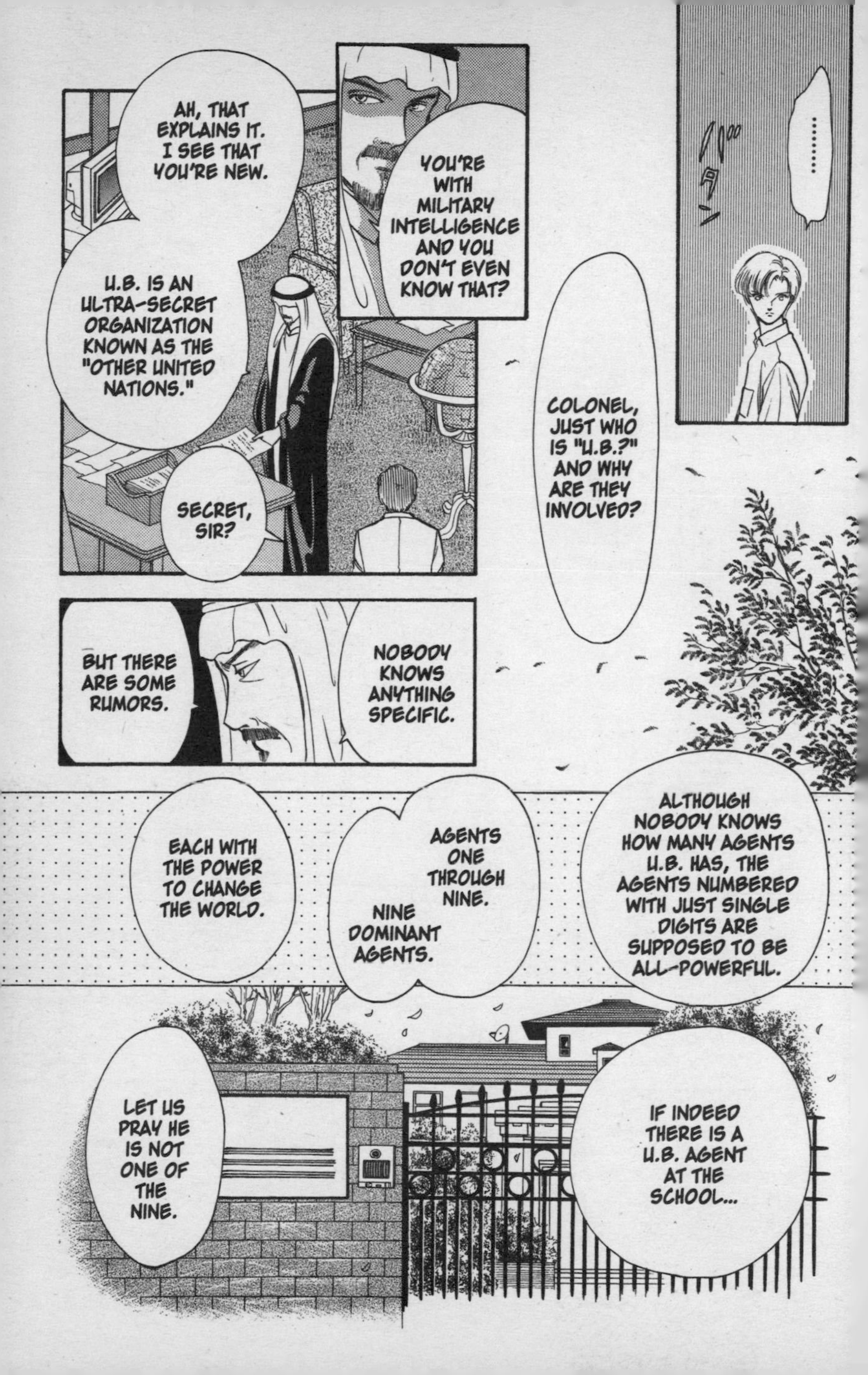
......
COLONEL, JUST WHO IS "U.B.?" AND WHY ARE THEY INVOLVED?
YOU'RE WITH MILITARY INTELLIGENCE AND YOU DON'T EVEN KNOW THAT?
AH, THAT EXPLAINS IT. I SEE THAT YOU'RE NEW.
U.B. IS AN ULTRA-SECRET ORGANIZATION KNOWN AS THE "OTHER UNITED NATIONS."
SECRET, SIR?
NOBODY KNOWS ANYTHING SPECIFIC.
BUT THERE ARE SOME RUMORS.
ALTHOUGH NOBODY KNOWS HOW MANY AGENTS U.B. HAS, THE AGENTS NUMBERED WITH JUST SINGLE DIGITS ARE SUPPOSED TO BE ALL-POWERFUL.
AGENTS ONE THROUGH NINE.
NINE DOMINANT AGENTS.
EACH WITH THE POWER TO CHANGE THE WORLD.
IF INDEED THERE IS A U.B. AGENT AT THE SCHOOL...
LET US PRAY HE IS NOT ONE OF THE NINE.

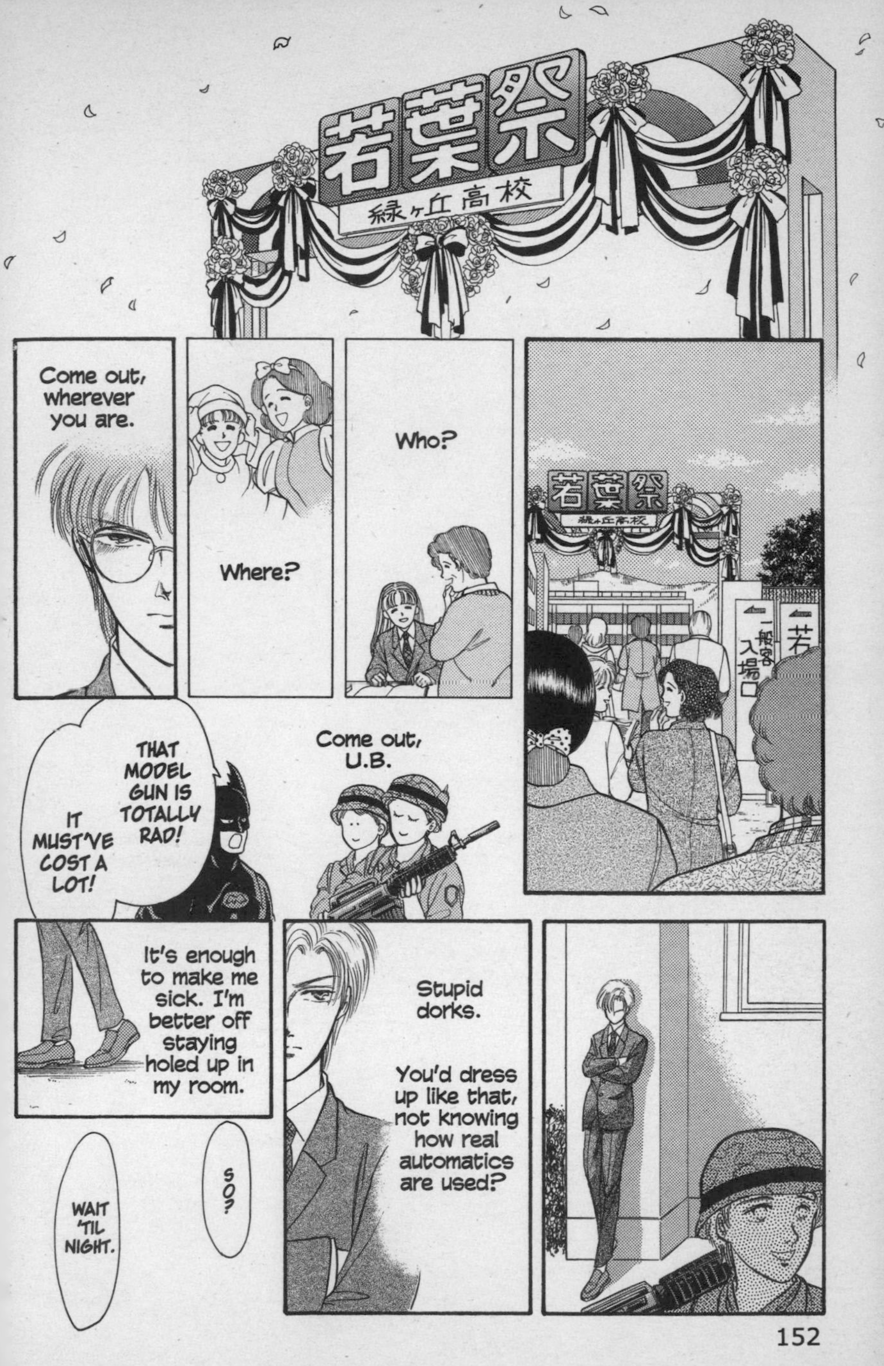
若葉祭
緑ヶ丘高校
若葉祭
緑ヶ丘高校
一般客入場
若
Who?
Where?
Come out, wherever you are.
Come out, U.B.
THAT MODEL GUN IS TOTALLY RAD!
IT MUST'VE COST A LOT!
Stupid dorks.
You'd dress up like that, not knowing how real automatics are used?
It's enough to make me sick. I'm better off staying holed up in my room.
SO?
WAIT 'TIL NIGHT.

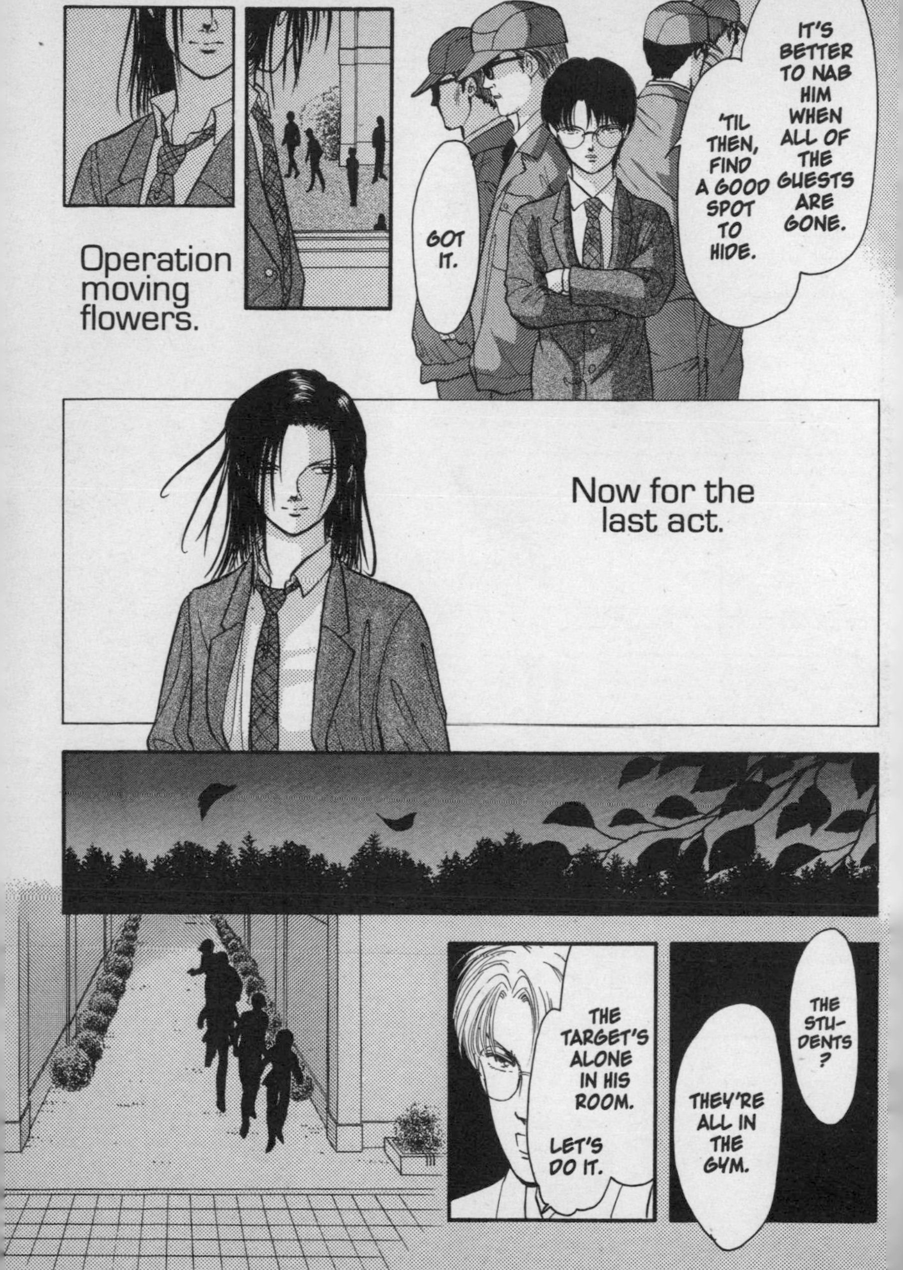
IT'S BETTER TO NAB HIM WHEN ALL OF THE GUESTS ARE GONE.
'TIL THEN, FIND A GOOD SPOT TO HIDE.
GOT IT.
Operation moving flowers.
Now for the last act.
THE STU-DENTS?
THEY'RE ALL IN THE GYM.
THE TARGET'S ALONE IN HIS ROOM.
LET'S DO IT.

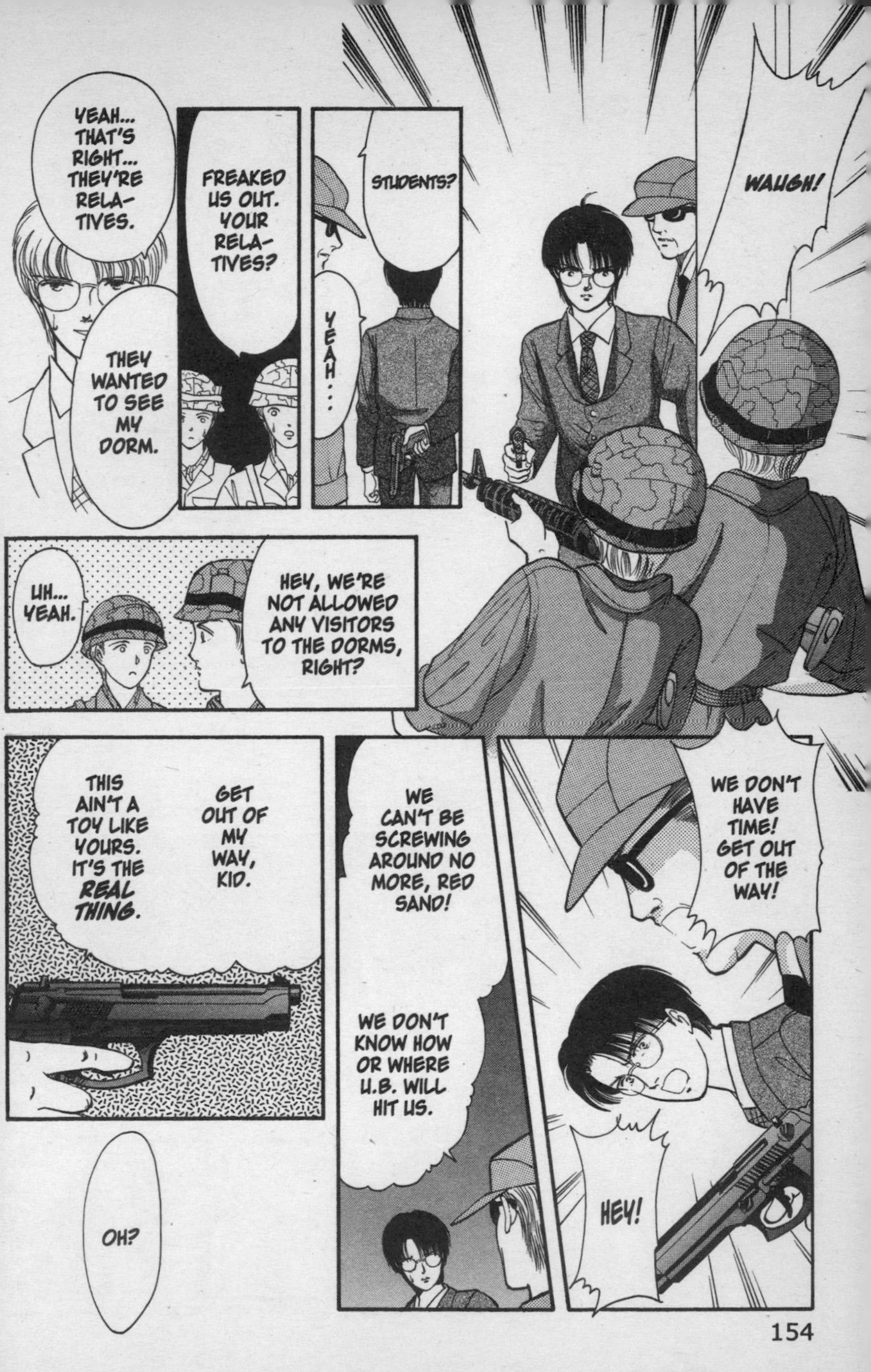
WAUGH!
STUDENTS?
YEAH...
FREAKED US OUT. YOUR RELATIVES?
YEAH... THAT'S RIGHT... THEY'RE RELA-TIVES.
THEY WANTED TO SEE MY DORM.
HEY, WE'RE NOT ALLOWED ANY VISITORS TO THE DORMS, RIGHT?
UH... YEAH.
WE DON'T HAVE TIME! GET OUT OF THE WAY!
HEY!
WE CAN'T BE SCREWING AROUND NO MORE, RED SAND!
WE DON'T KNOW HOW OR WHERE U.B. WILL HIT US.
GET OUT OF MY WAY, KID.
THIS AIN'T A TOY LIKE YOURS. IT'S THE *REAL THING*.
OH?

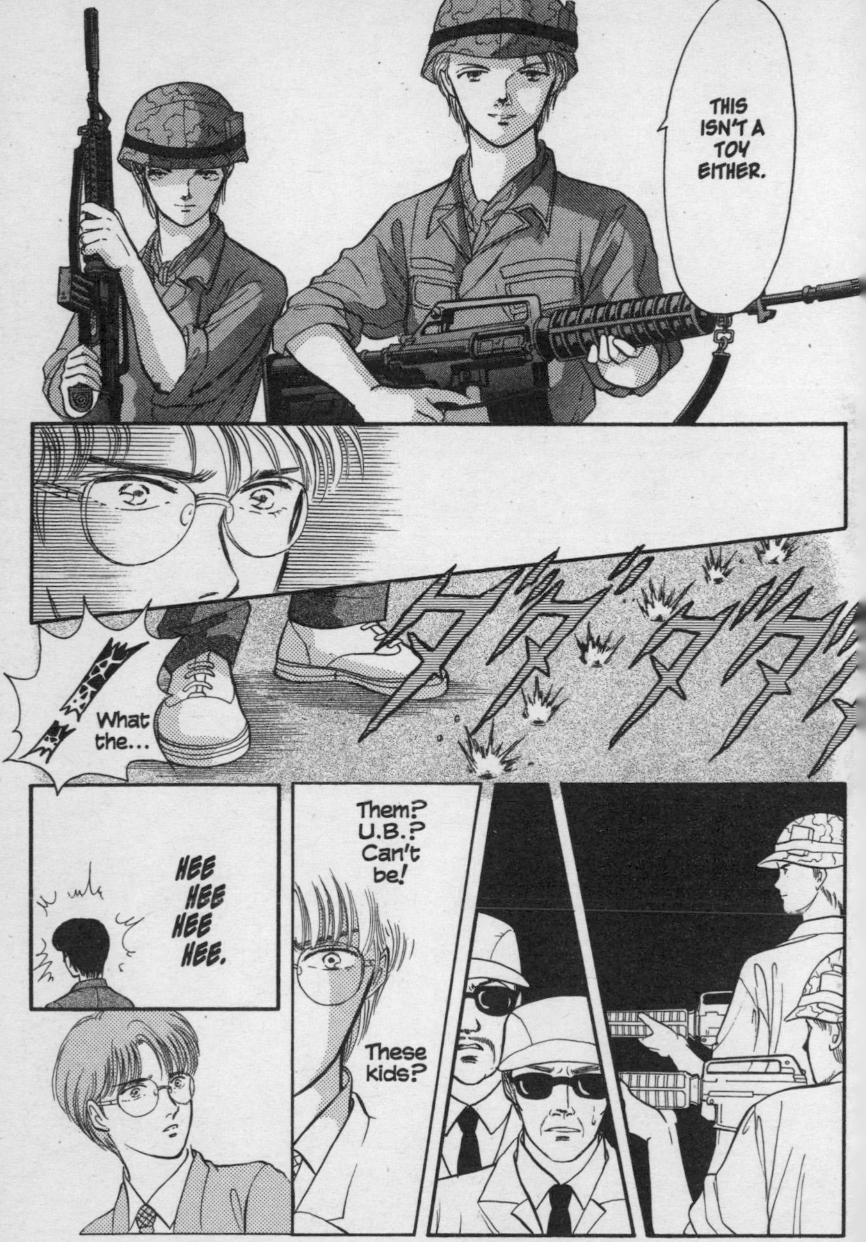
THIS ISN'T A TOY EITHER.
What the...
Them? U.B.? Can't be!
These kids?
HEE HEE HEE HEE.

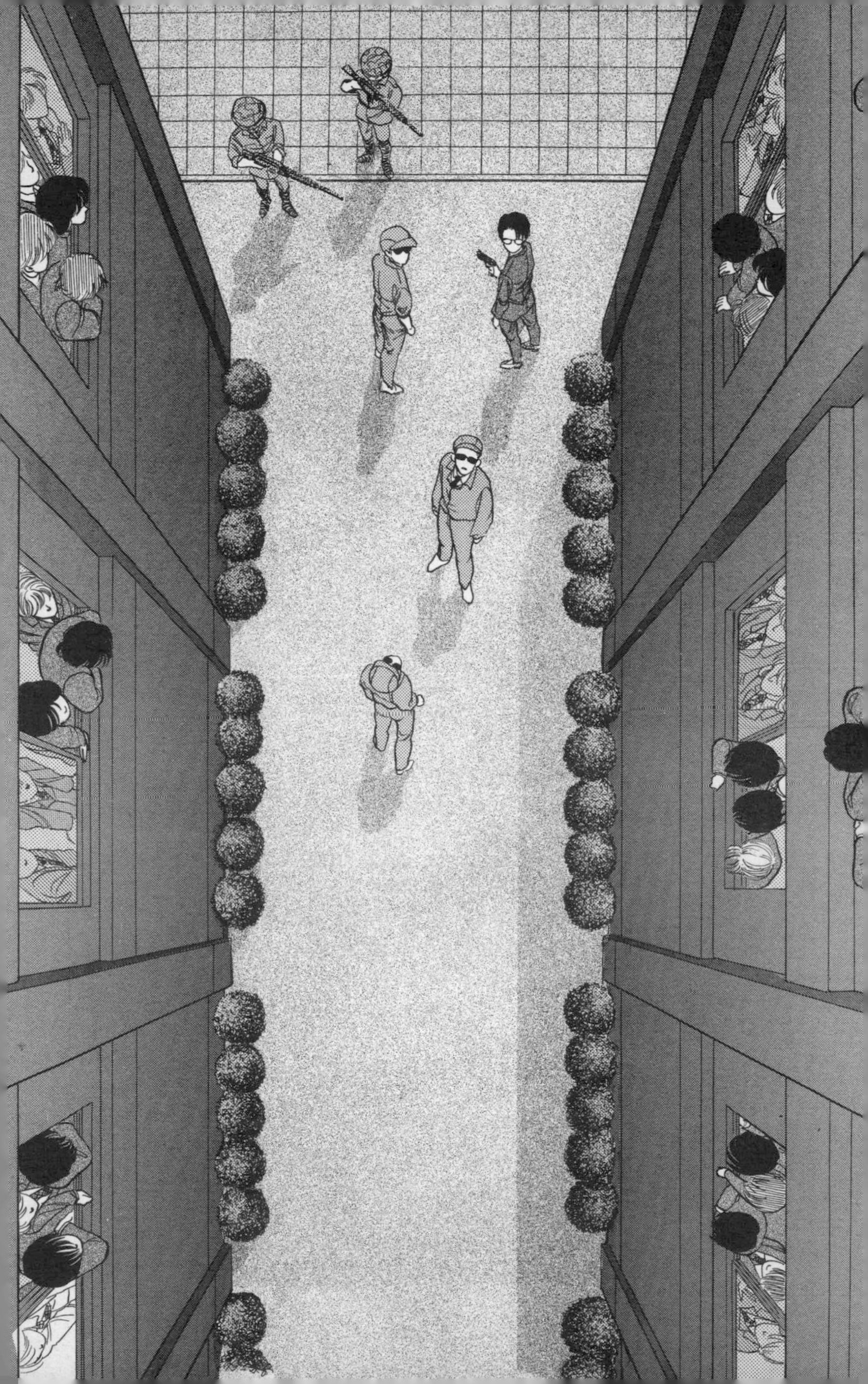

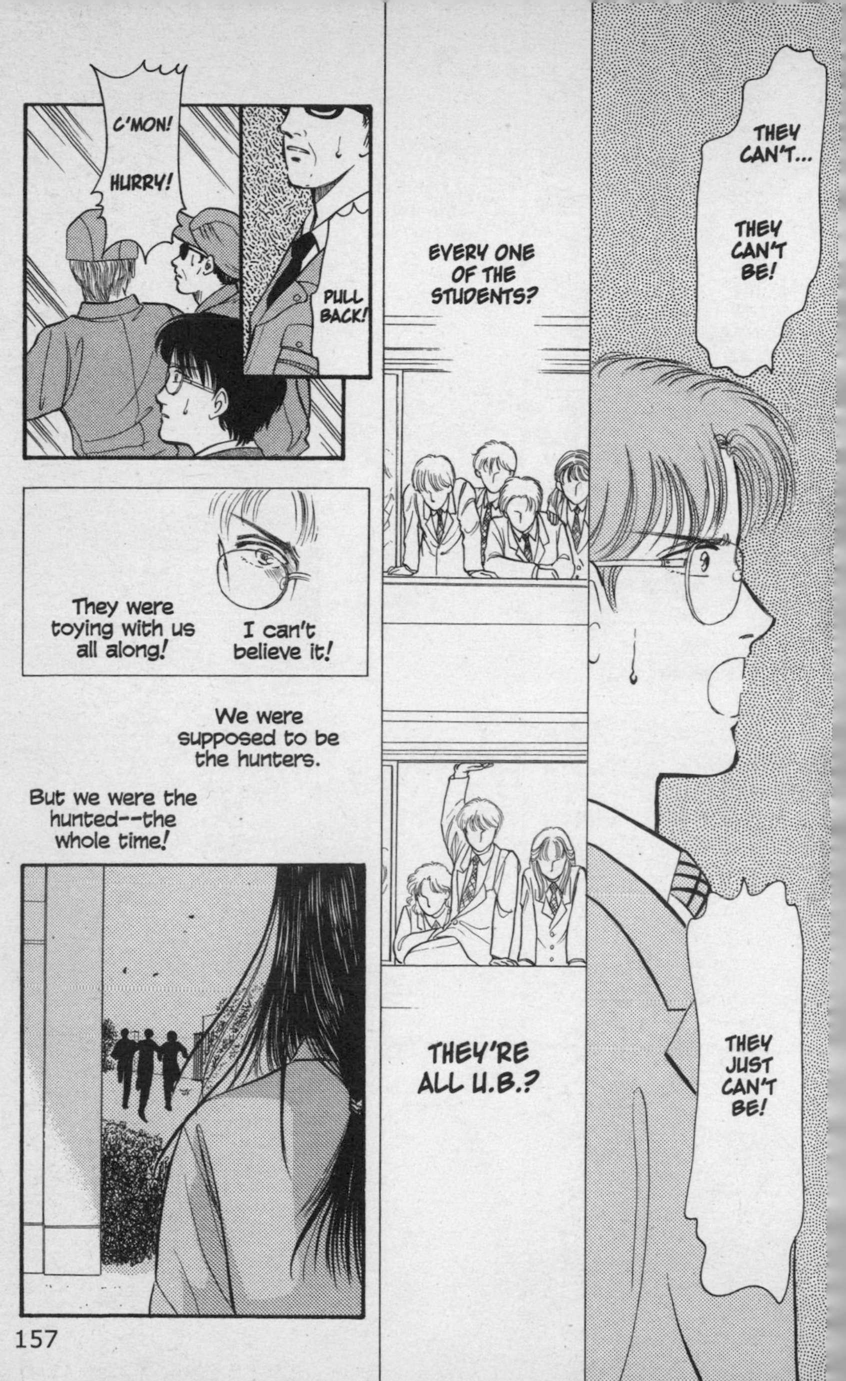
THEY CAN'T...
THEY CAN'T BE!
THEY JUST CAN'T BE!
EVERY ONE OF THE STUDENTS?
THEY'RE ALL U.B.?
PULL BACK!
C'MON!
HURRY!
I can't believe it!
They were toying with us all along!
We were supposed to be the hunters.
But we were the hunted--the whole time!

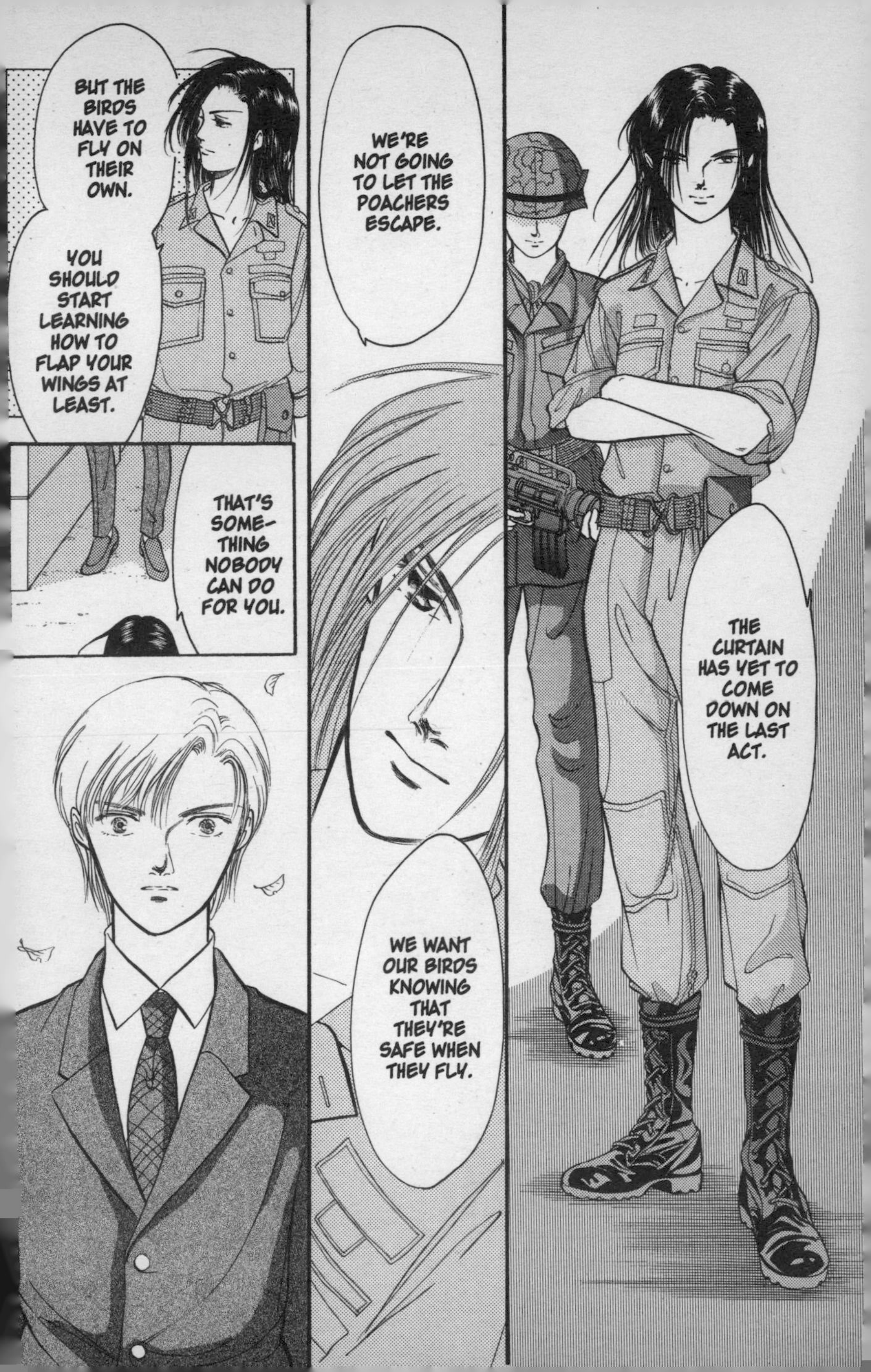
THE CURTAIN HAS YET TO COME DOWN ON THE LAST ACT.
WE'RE NOT GOING TO LET THE POACHERS ESCAPE.
WE WANT OUR BIRDS KNOWING THAT THEY'RE SAFE WHEN THEY FLY.
BUT THE BIRDS HAVE TO FLY ON THEIR OWN.
YOU SHOULD START LEARNING HOW TO FLAP YOUR WINGS AT LEAST.
THAT'S SOMETHING NOBODY CAN DO FOR YOU.

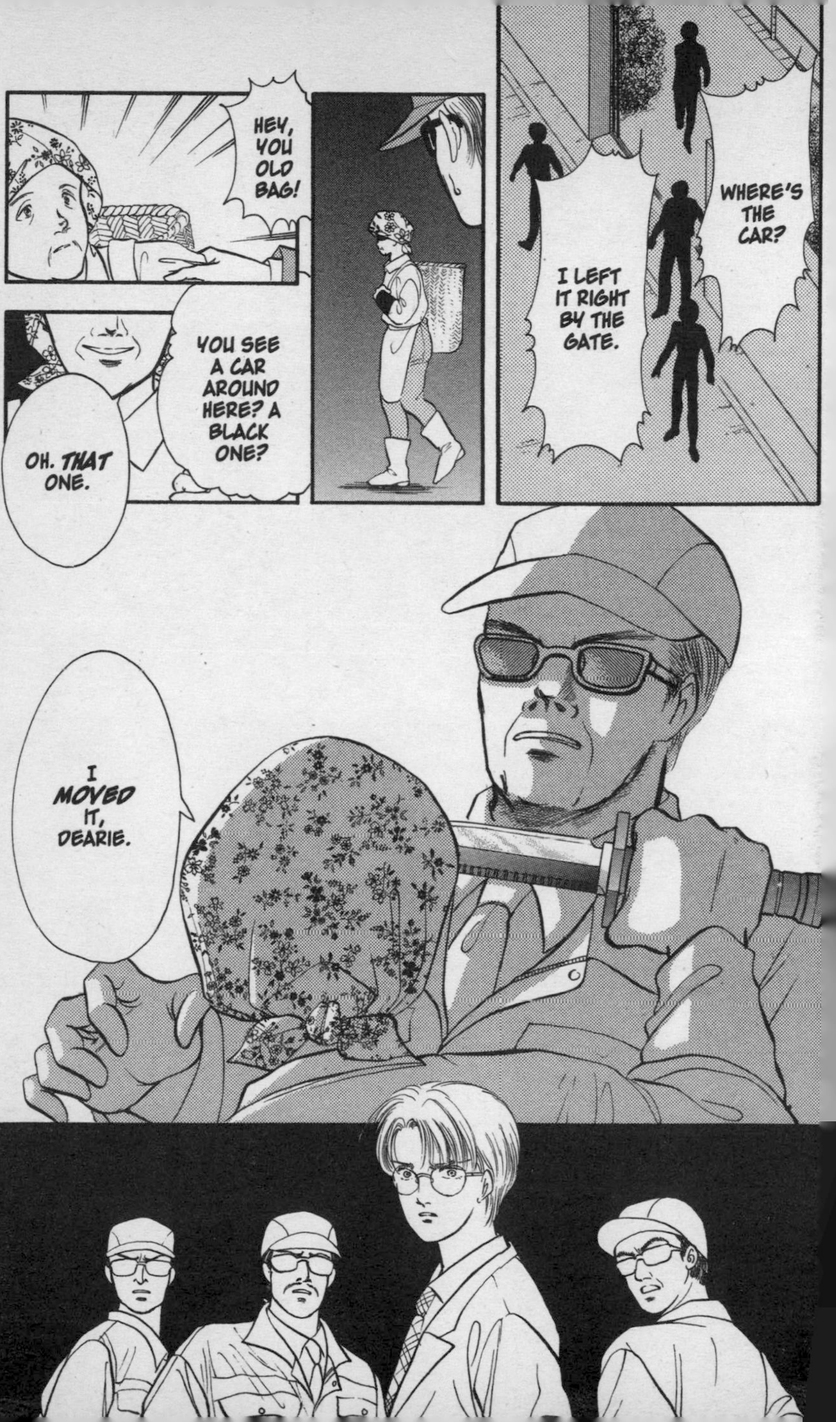
WHERE'S THE CAR?
I LEFT IT RIGHT BY THE GATE.
HEY, YOU OLD BAG!
YOU SEE A CAR AROUND HERE? A BLACK ONE?
OH. *THAT* ONE.
I *MOVED* IT, DEARIE.

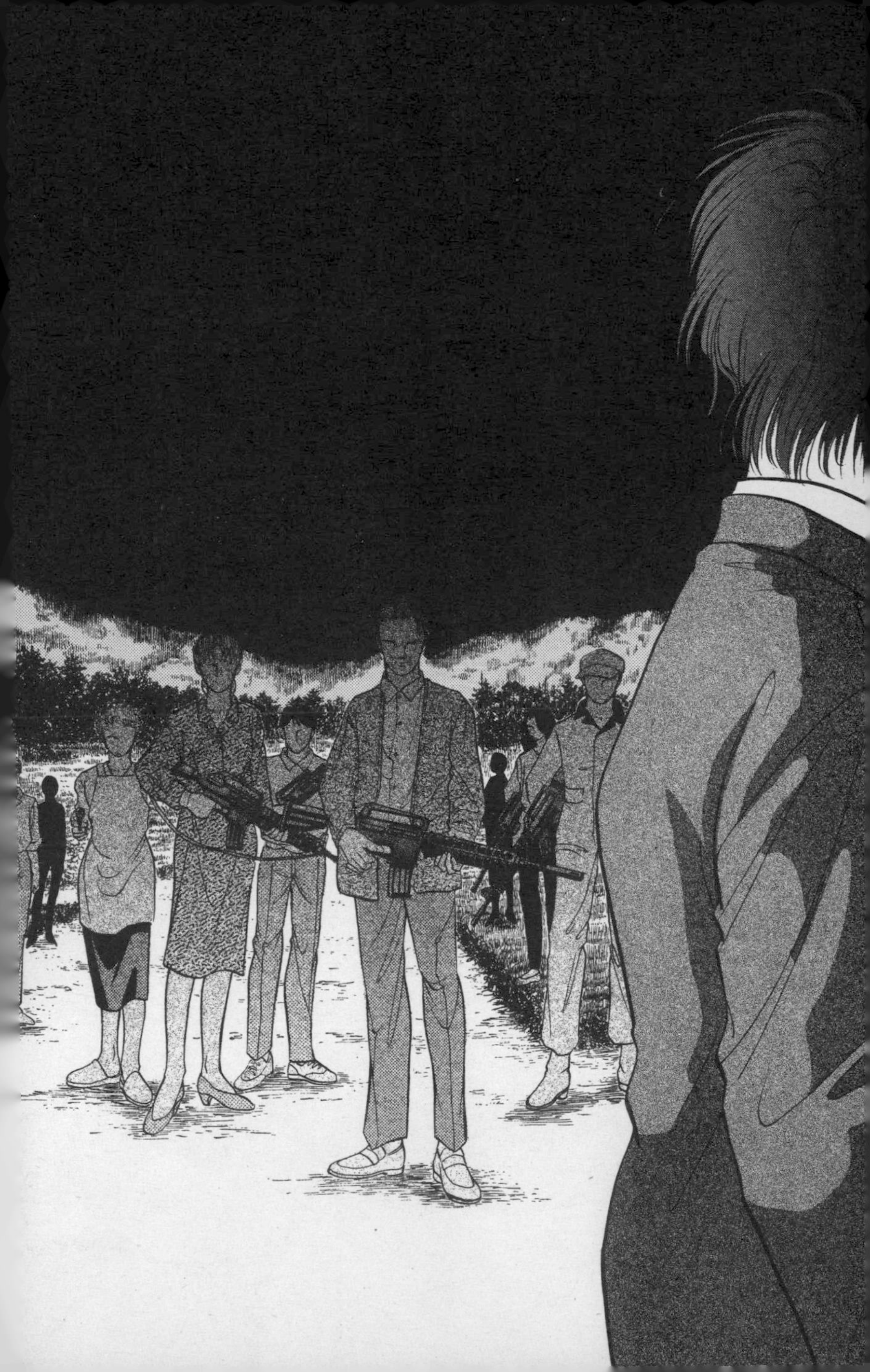

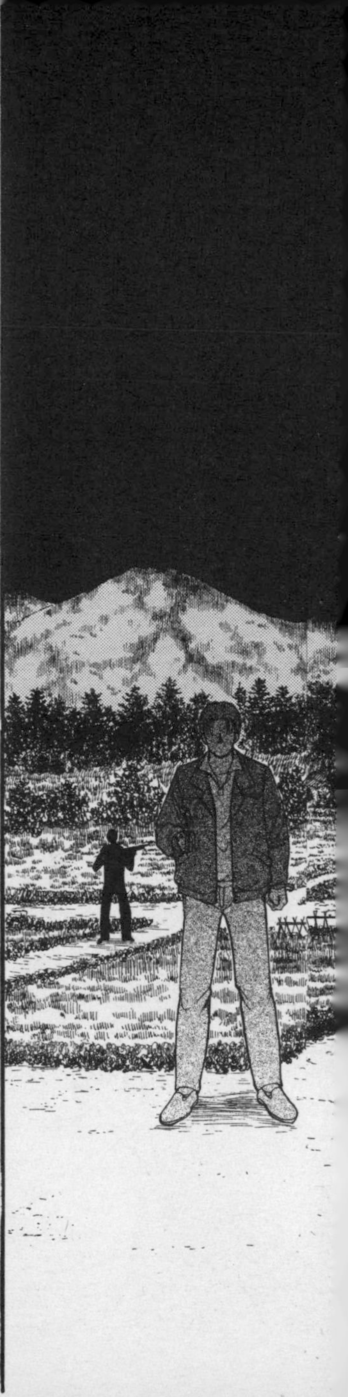

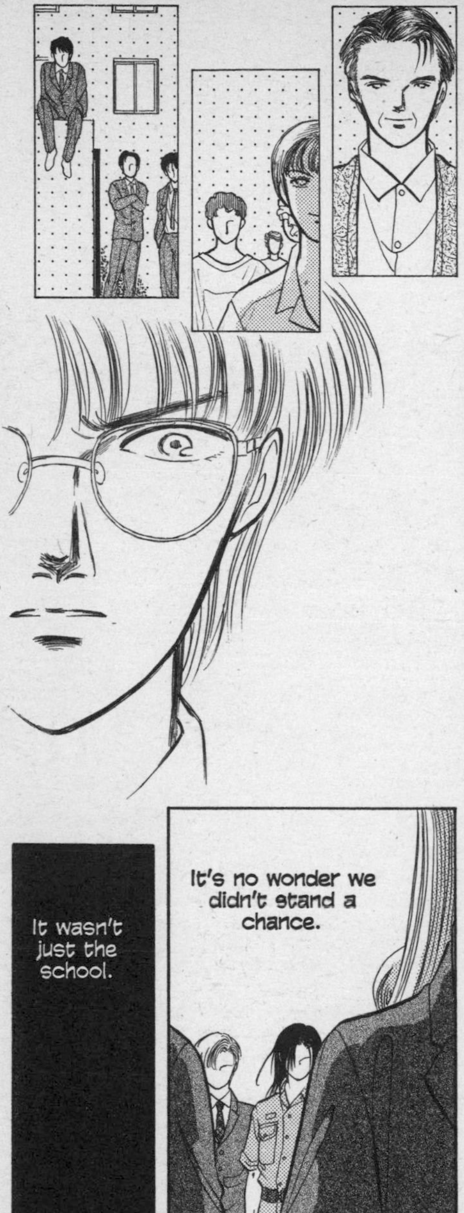
It's no wonder we didn't stand a chance.
It wasn't just the school.

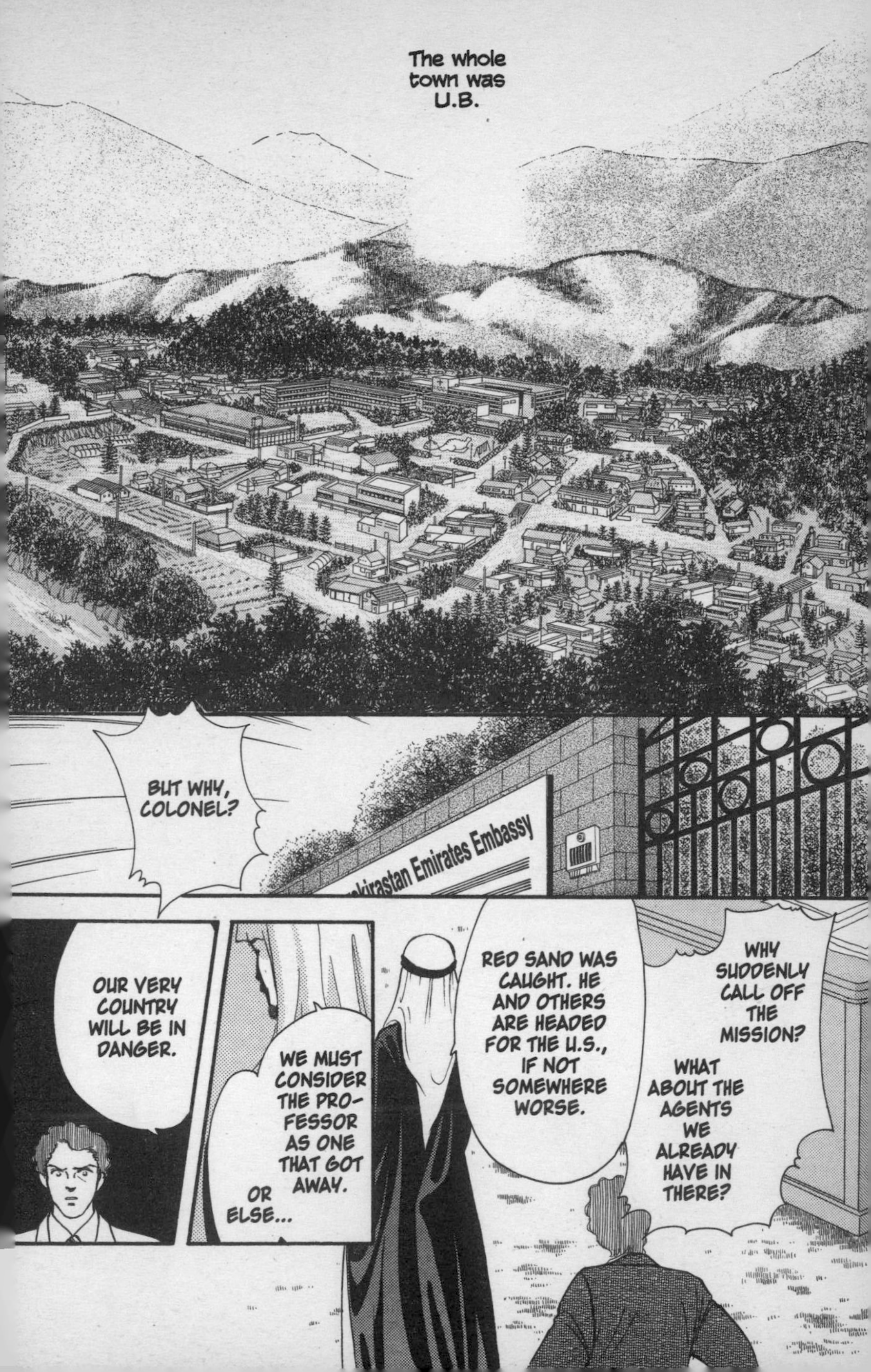
The whole town was U.B.
BUT WHY, COLONEL?
Emirates Embassy
WHY SUDDENLY CALL OFF THE MISSION?
WHAT ABOUT THE AGENTS WE ALREADY HAVE IN THERE?
RED SAND WAS CAUGHT. HE AND OTHERS ARE HEADED FOR THE U.S., IF NOT SOMEWHERE WORSE.
WE MUST CONSIDER THE PRO-FESSOR AS ONE THAT GOT AWAY.
OR ELSE...
OUR VERY COUNTRY WILL BE IN DANGER.

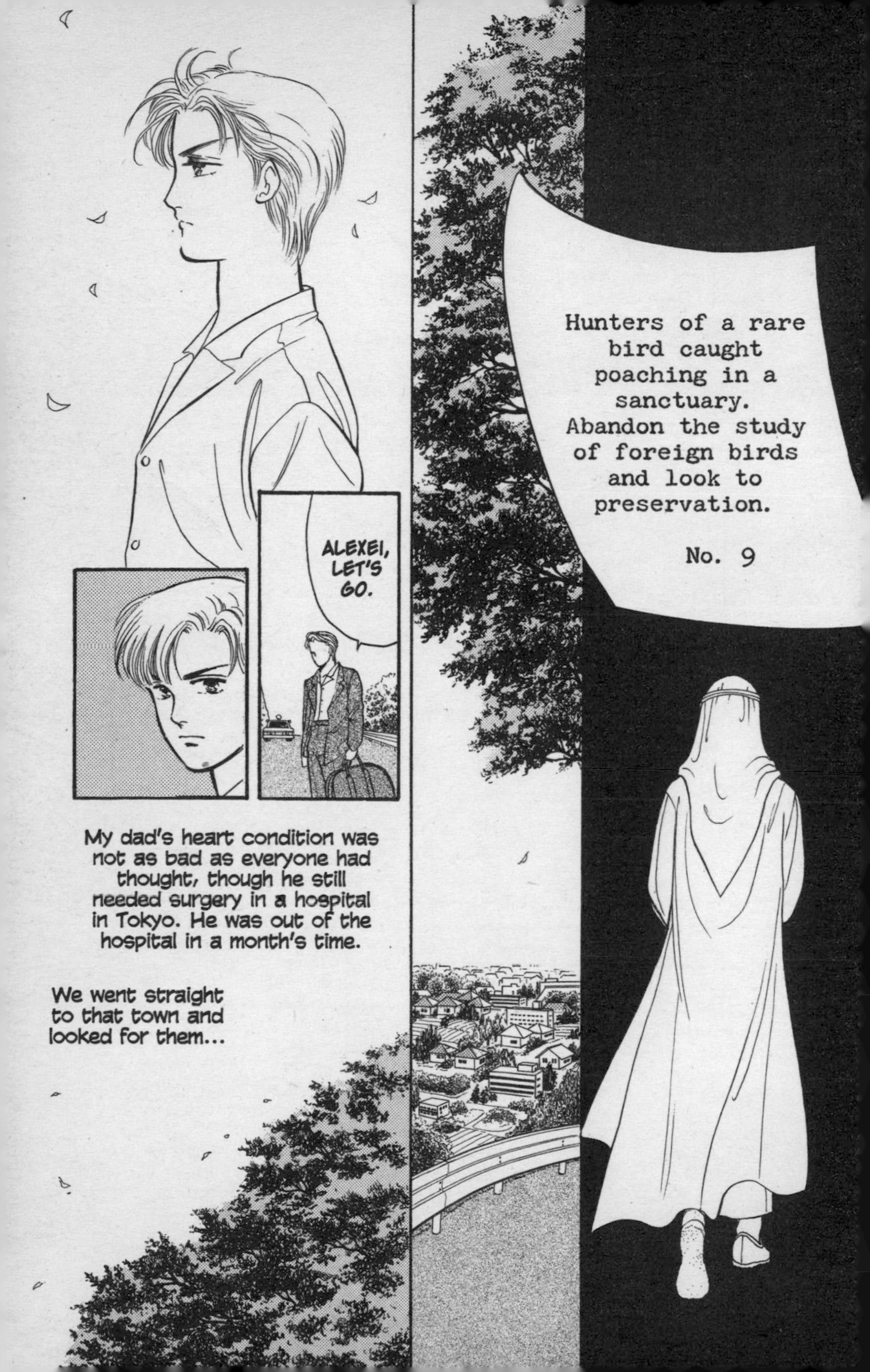
Hunters of a rare bird caught poaching in a sanctuary. Abandon the study of foreign birds and look to preservation.
No. 9
ALEXEI, LET'S GO.
My dad's heart condition was not as bad as everyone had thought, though he still needed surgery in a hospital in Tokyo. He was out of the hospital in a month's time.
We went straight to that town and looked for them...

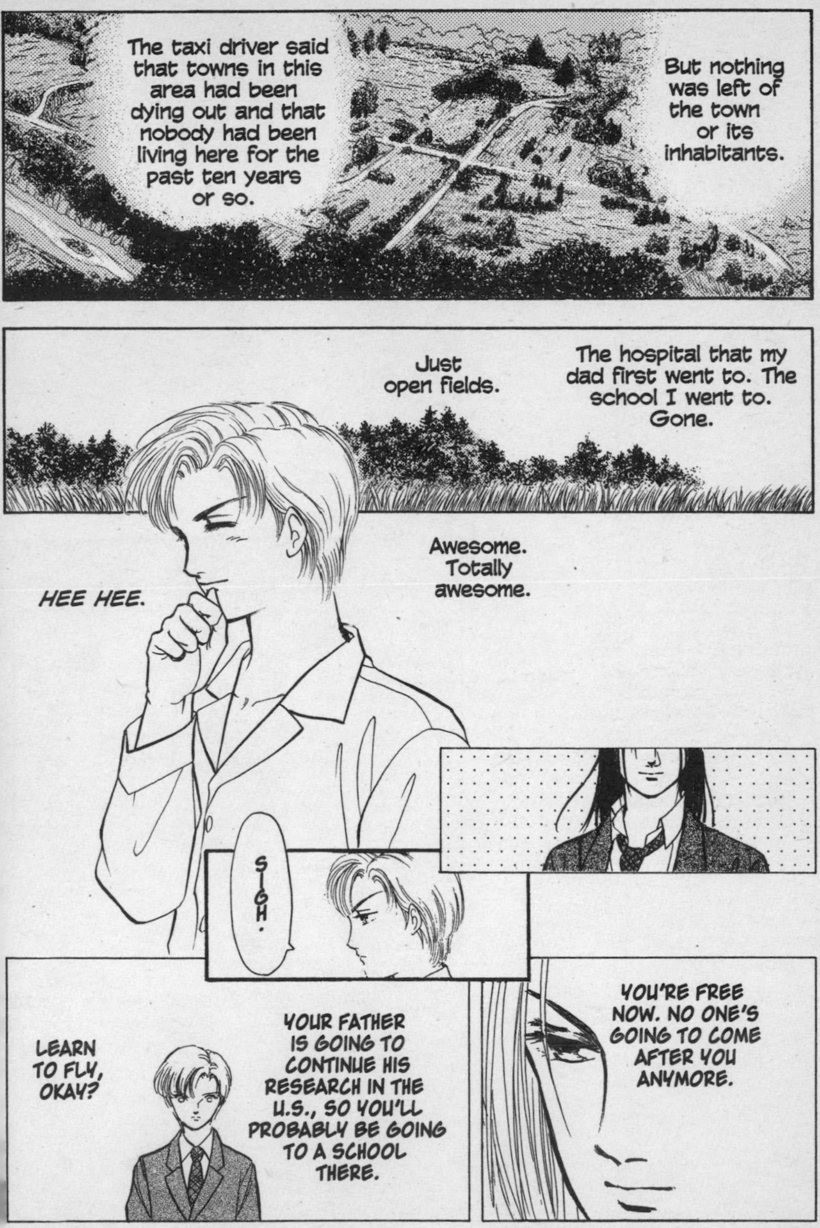
The taxi driver said that towns in this area had been dying out and that nobody had been living here for the past ten years or so.
But nothing was left of the town or its inhabitants.
The hospital that my dad first went to. The school I went to. Gone.
Just open fields.
Awesome. Totally awesome.
HEE HEE.
SIGH.
YOU'RE FREE NOW. NO ONE'S GOING TO COME AFTER YOU ANYMORE.
YOUR FATHER IS GOING TO CONTINUE HIS RESEARCH IN THE U.S., SO YOU'LL PROBABLY BE GOING TO A SCHOOL THERE.
LEARN TO FLY, OKAY?

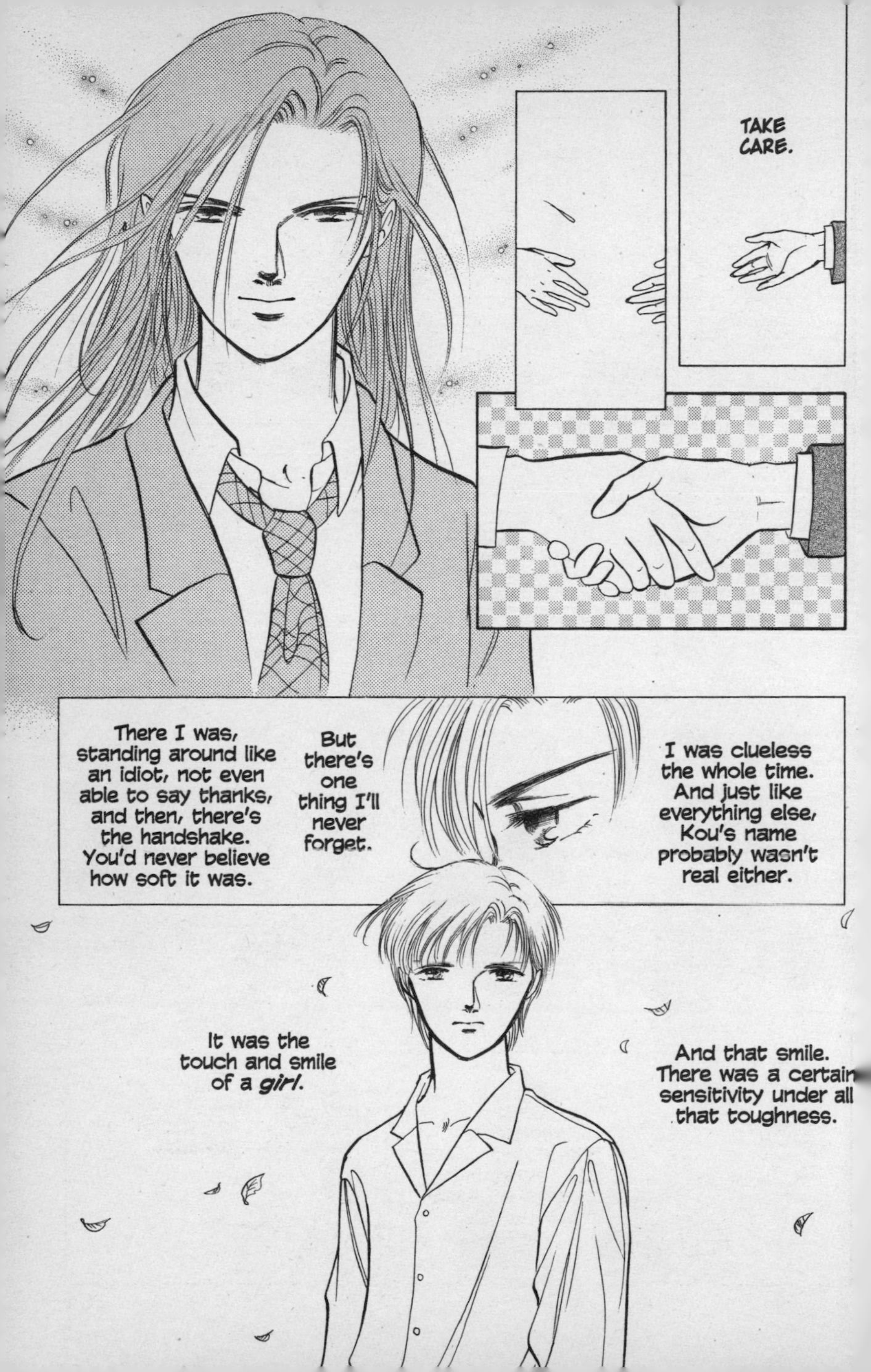
TAKE CARE.
I was clueless the whole time. And just like everything else, Kou's name probably wasn't real either.
But there's one thing I'll never forget.
There I was, standing around like an idiot, not even able to say thanks, and then, there's the handshake. You'd never believe how soft it was.
And that smile. There was a certain sensitivity under all that toughness.
It was the touch and smile of a *girl*.

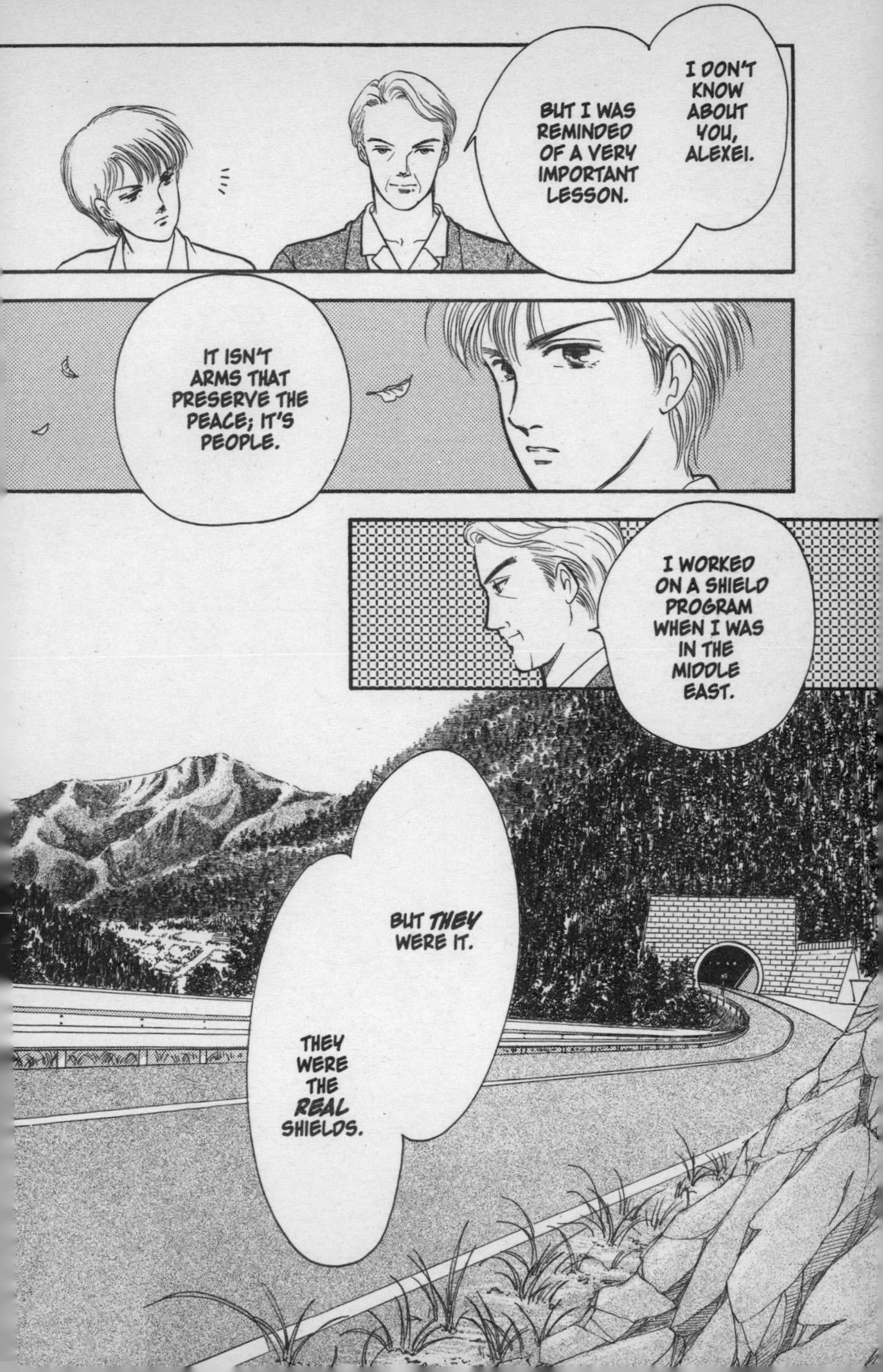
I DON'T KNOW ABOUT YOU, ALEXEI.
BUT I WAS REMINDED OF A VERY IMPORTANT LESSON.
IT ISN'T ARMS THAT PRESERVE THE PEACE; IT'S PEOPLE.
I WORKED ON A SHIELD PROGRAM WHEN I WAS IN THE MIDDLE EAST.
BUT *THEY* WERE IT.
THEY WERE THE *REAL* SHIELDS.

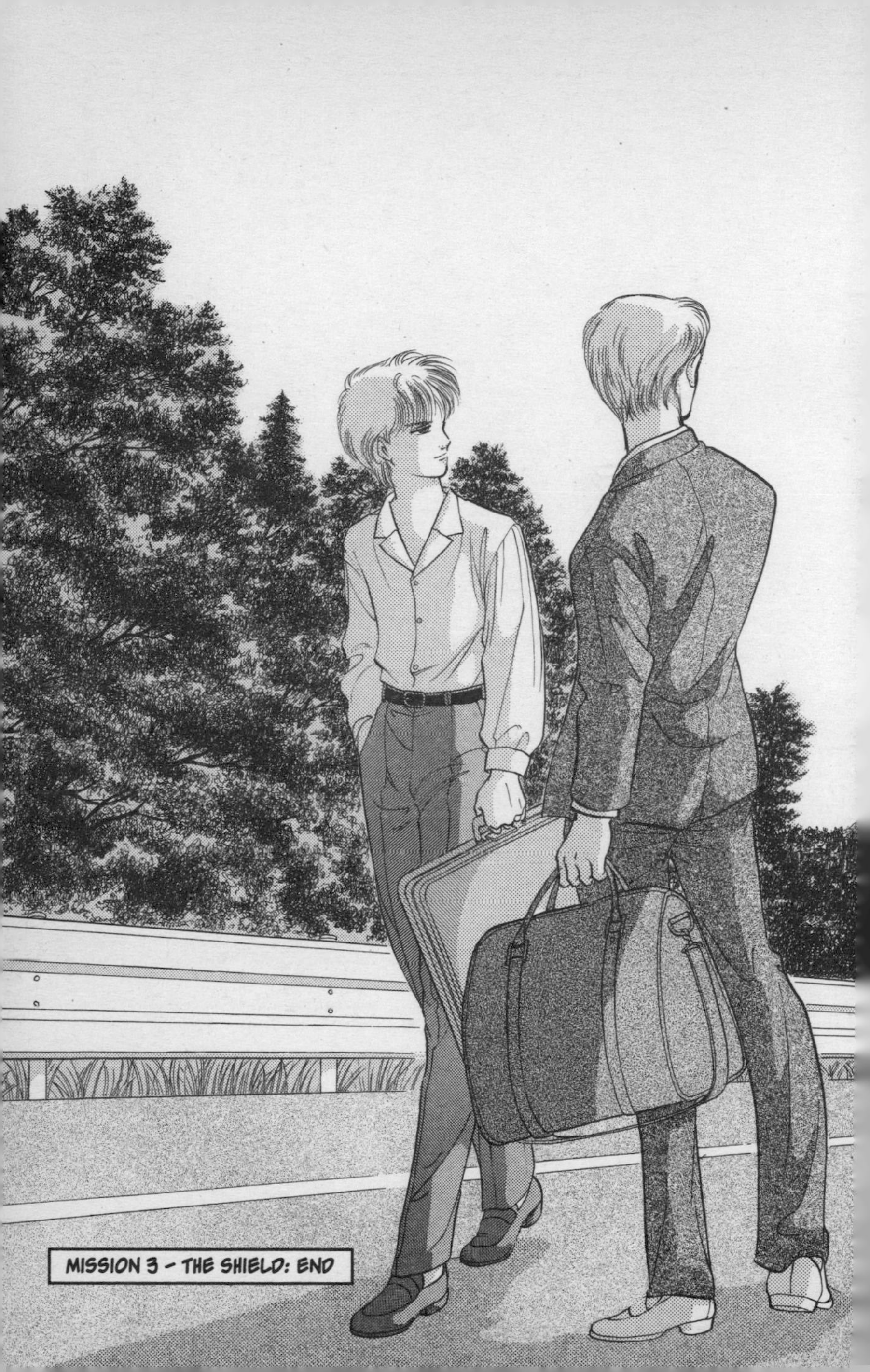
MISSION 3 - THE SHIELD: END

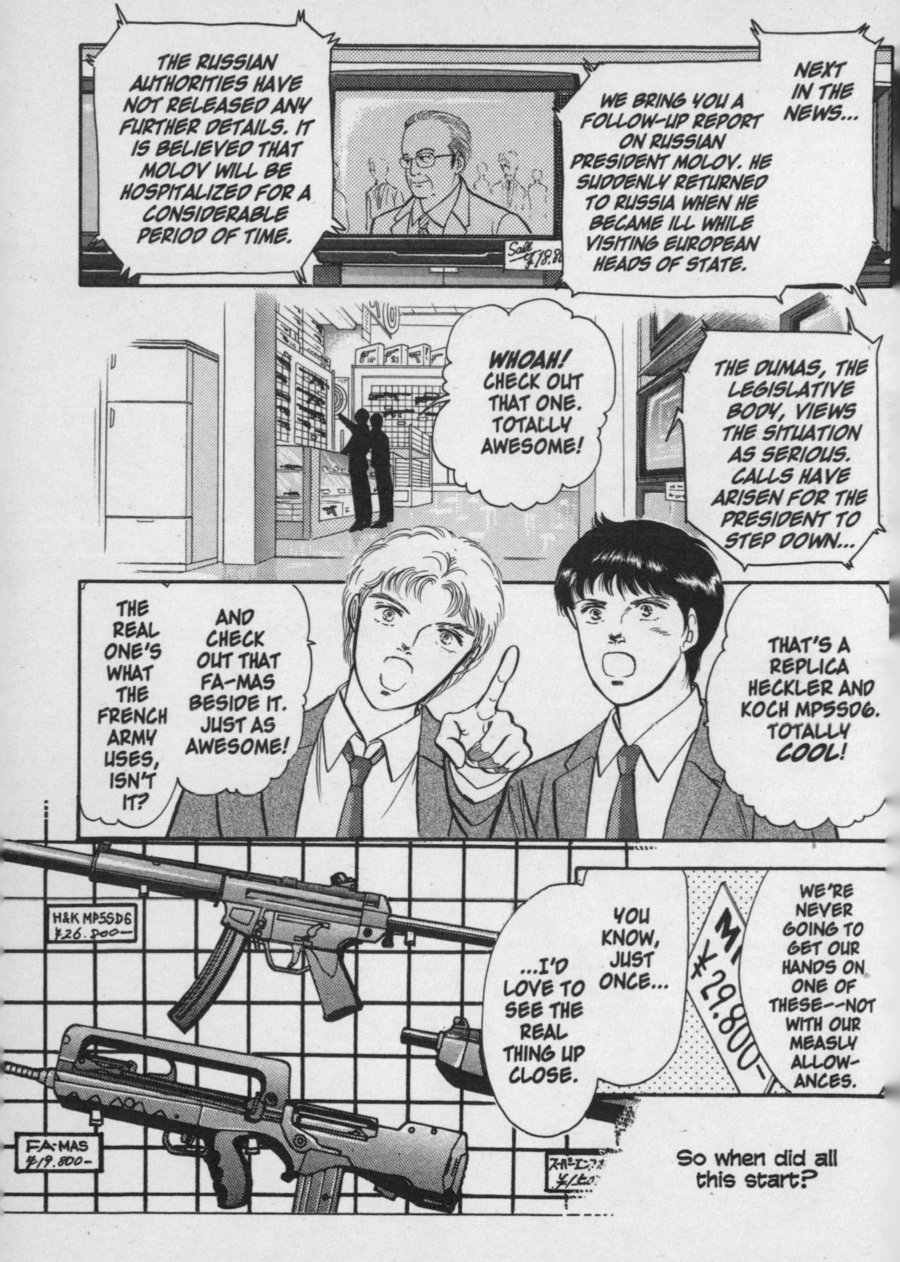
NEXT IN THE NEWS...
WE BRING YOU A FOLLOW-UP REPORT ON RUSSIAN PRESIDENT MOLOV. HE SUDDENLY RETURNED TO RUSSIA WHEN HE BECAME ILL WHILE VISITING EUROPEAN HEADS OF STATE.
THE RUSSIAN AUTHORITIES HAVE NOT RELEASED ANY FURTHER DETAILS. IT IS BELIEVED THAT MOLOV WILL BE HOSPITALIZED FOR A CONSIDERABLE PERIOD OF TIME.
THE DUMAS, THE LEGISLATIVE BODY, VIEWS THE SITUATION AS SERIOUS. CALLS HAVE ARISEN FOR THE PRESIDENT TO STEP DOWN...
WHOAH! CHECK OUT THAT ONE. TOTALLY AWESOME!
THAT'S A REPLICA HECKLER AND KOCH MP5SD6. TOTALLY COOL!
AND CHECK OUT THAT FA-MAS BESIDE IT. JUST AS AWESOME!
THE REAL ONE'S WHAT THE FRENCH ARMY USES, ISN'T IT?
WE'RE NEVER GOING TO GET OUR HANDS ON ONE OF THESE--NOT WITH OUR MEASLY ALLOW-ANCES.
¥29,800-
YOU KNOW, JUST ONCE...
...I'D LOVE TO SEE THE REAL THING UP CLOSE.
H&K MP5SD6 ¥26,800-
FA-MAS ¥19,800-
So when did all this start?

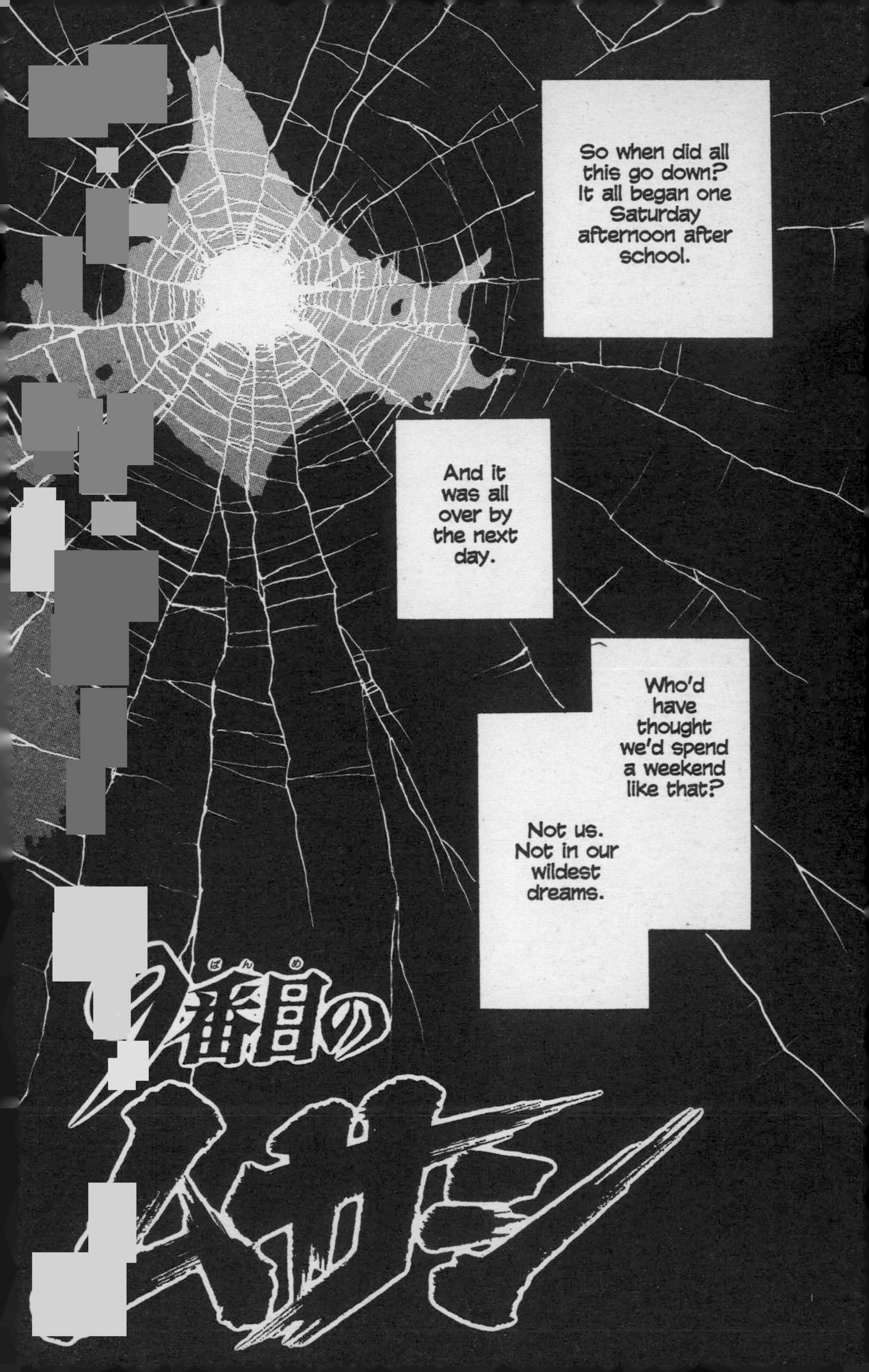
So when did all this go down? It all began one Saturday afternoon after school.
And it was all over by the next day.
Who'd have thought we'd spend a weekend like that?
Not us. Not in our wildest dreams.
番目の

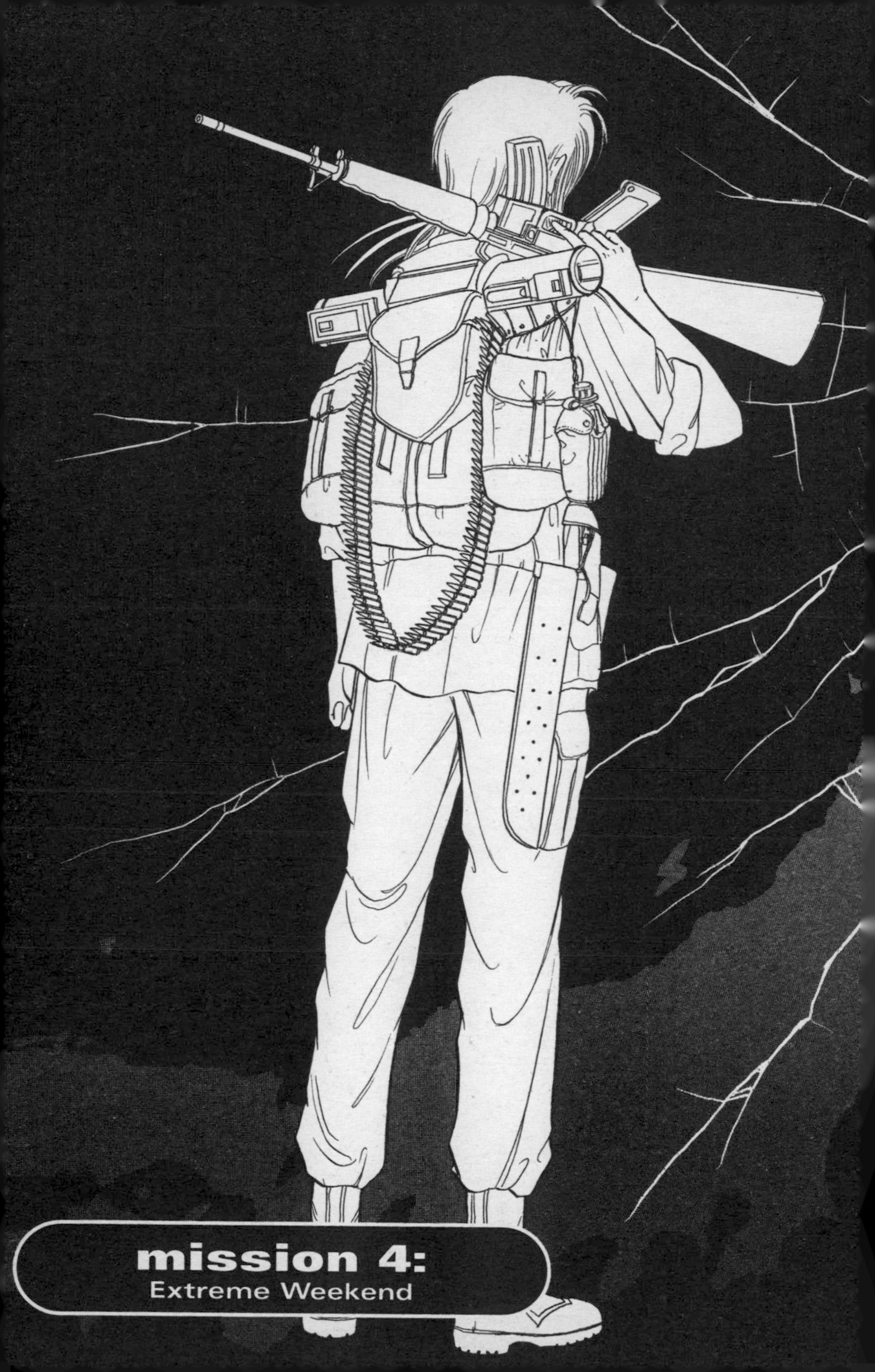

mission 4:
Extreme Weekend

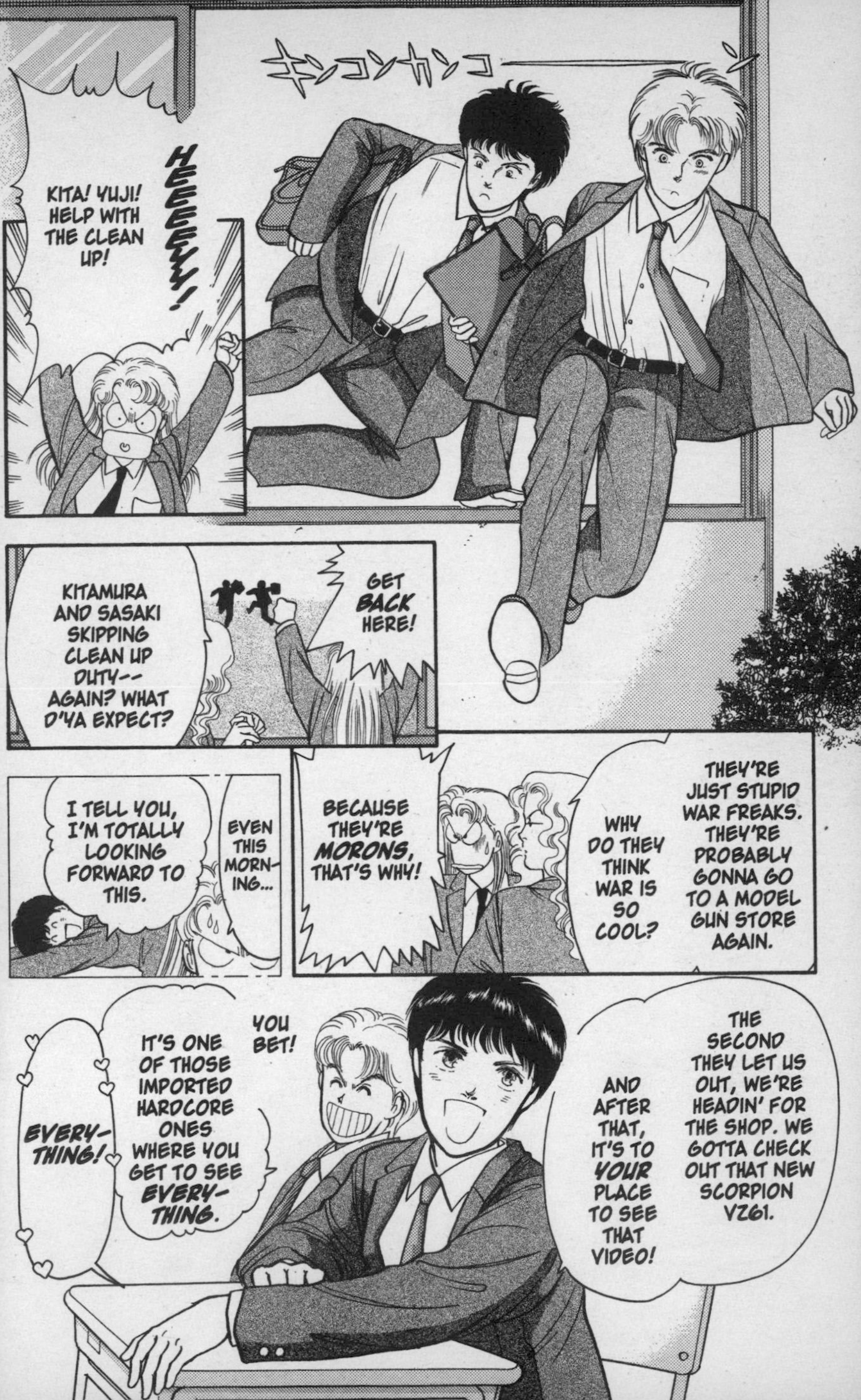
キンコンカンコ
HEEEEEY!
KITA! YUJI! HELP WITH THE CLEAN UP!
GET BACK HERE!
KITAMURA AND SASAKI SKIPPING CLEAN UP DUTY-- AGAIN? WHAT D'YA EXPECT?
THEY'RE JUST STUPID WAR FREAKS. THEY'RE PROBABLY GONNA GO TO A MODEL GUN STORE AGAIN.
WHY DO THEY THINK WAR IS SO COOL?
BECAUSE THEY'RE MORONS, THAT'S WHY!
EVEN THIS MORNING...
I TELL YOU, I'M TOTALLY LOOKING FORWARD TO THIS.
THE SECOND THEY LET US OUT, WE'RE HEADIN' FOR THE SHOP. WE GOTTA CHECK OUT THAT NEW SCORPION VZ61.
AND AFTER THAT, IT'S TO YOUR PLACE TO SEE THAT VIDEO!
YOU BET!
IT'S ONE OF THOSE IMPORTED HARDCORE ONES WHERE YOU GET TO SEE EVERY-THING.
EVERY-THING!

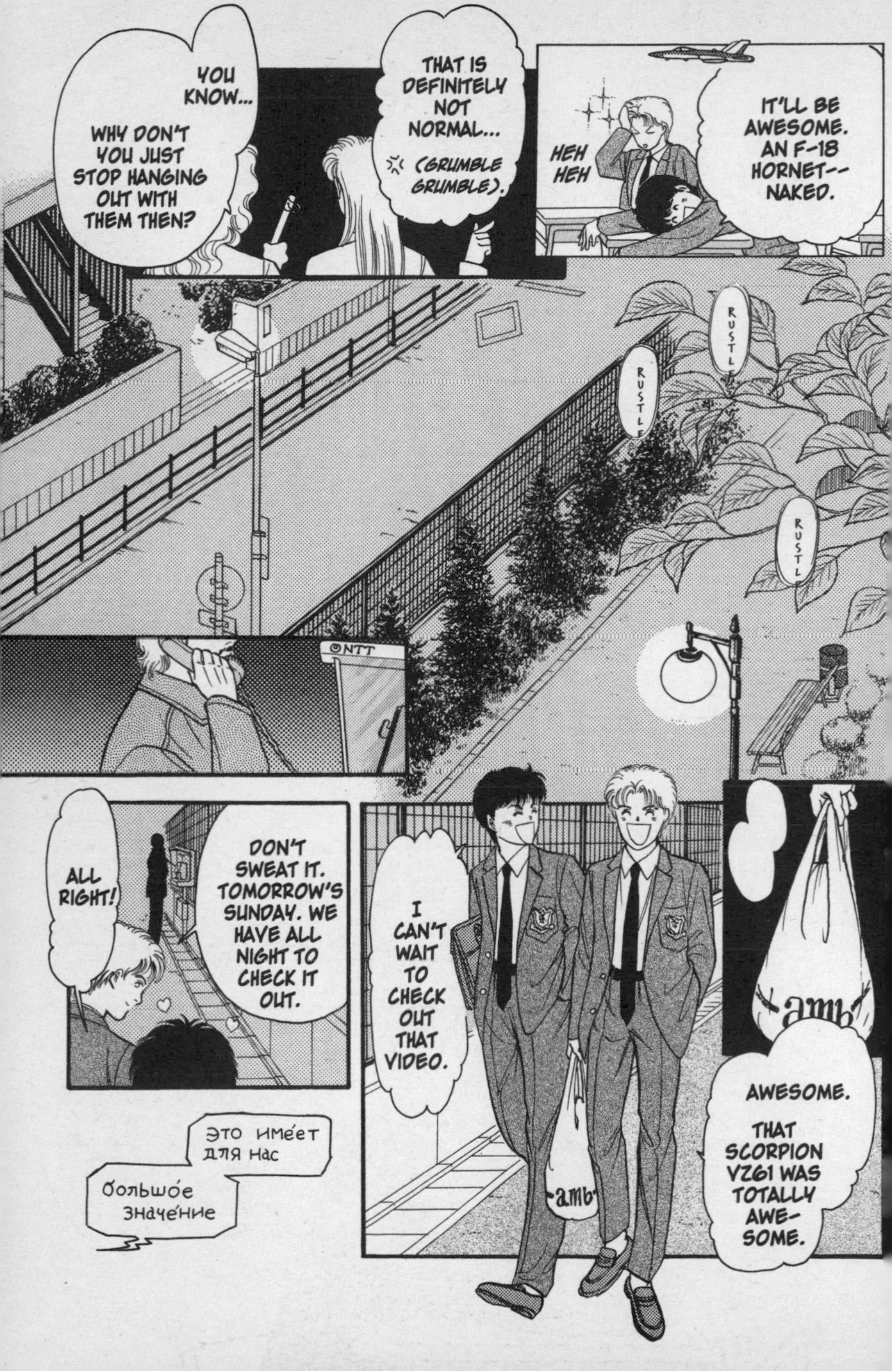
IT'LL BE AWESOME. AN F-18 HORNET--NAKED.
HEH HEH
THAT IS DEFINITELY NOT NORMAL...
(GRUMBLE GRUMBLE).
YOU KNOW...
WHY DON'T YOU JUST STOP HANGING OUT WITH THEM THEN?
RUSTL
RUSTLE
RUSTL
NTT
AWESOME.
THAT SCORPION VZ61 WAS TOTALLY AWE-SOME.
amb
I CAN'T WAIT TO CHECK OUT THAT VIDEO.
amb
DON'T SWEAT IT. TOMORROW'S SUNDAY. WE HAVE ALL NIGHT TO CHECK IT OUT.
ALL RIGHT!
Это имéет для нас
большóе значéние

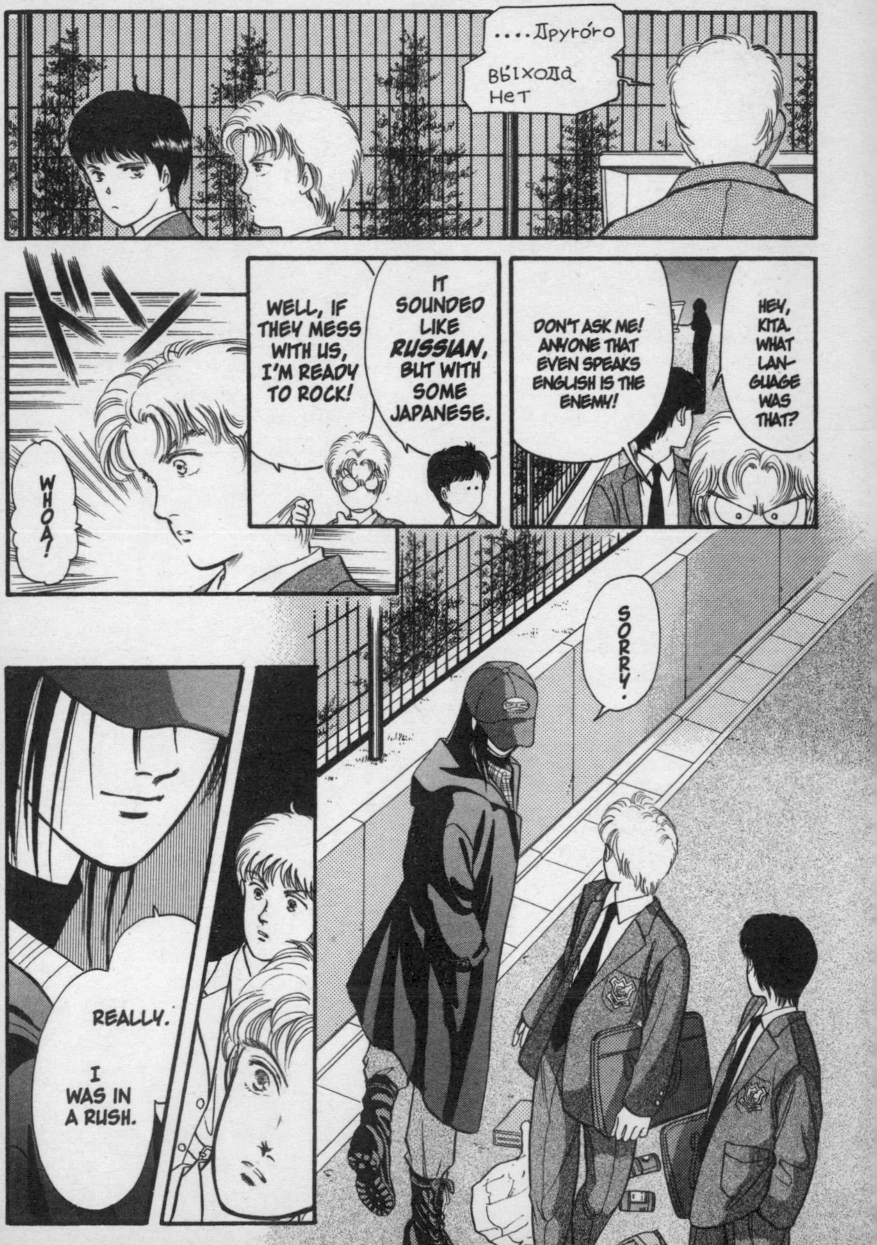
....Другóго выхода нет
HEY, KITA. WHAT LANGUAGE WAS THAT?
DON'T ASK ME! ANYONE THAT EVEN SPEAKS ENGLISH IS THE ENEMY!
IT SOUNDED LIKE *RUSSIAN*, BUT WITH SOME JAPANESE.
WELL, IF THEY MESS WITH US, I'M READY TO ROCK!
WHOA!
SORRY.
REALLY.
I WAS IN A RUSH.

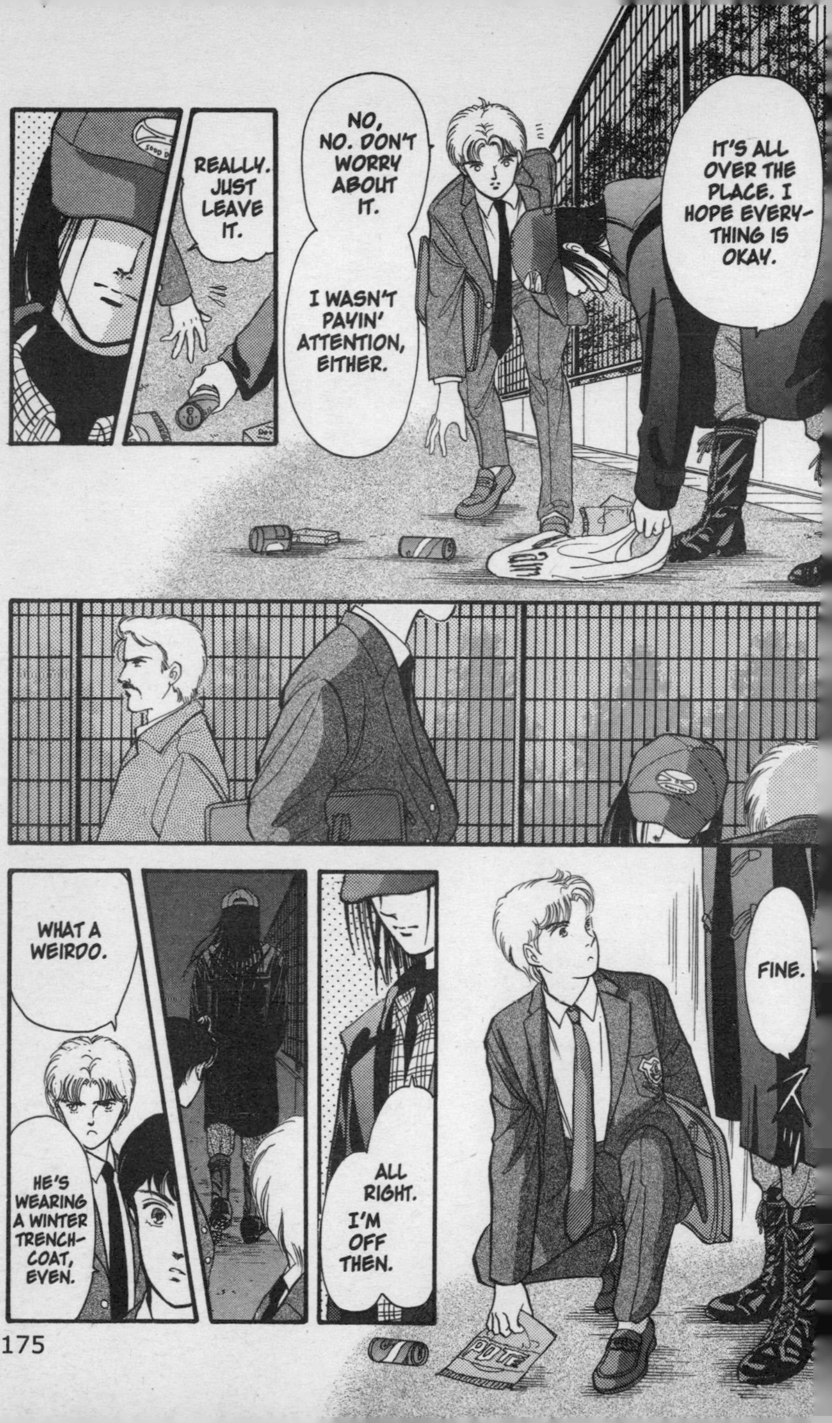
IT'S ALL OVER THE PLACE. I HOPE EVERYTHING IS OKAY.
NO, NO. DON'T WORRY ABOUT IT.
I WASN'T PAYIN' ATTENTION, EITHER.
REALLY. JUST LEAVE IT.
FINE.
ALL RIGHT. I'M OFF THEN.
WHAT A WEIRDO.
HE'S WEARING A WINTER TRENCH-COAT, EVEN.

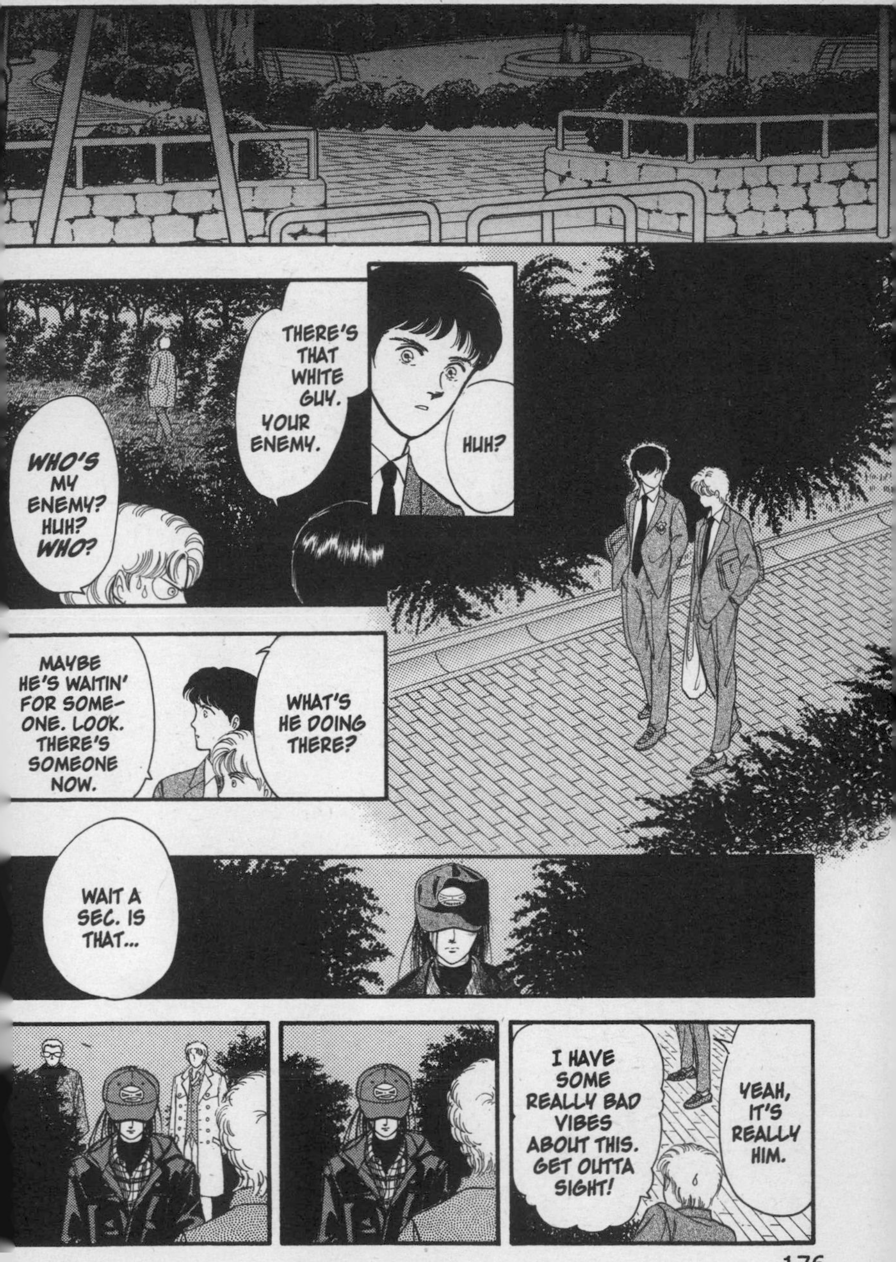
THERE'S THAT WHITE GUY. YOUR ENEMY.
HUH?
WHO'S MY ENEMY? HUH? WHO?
WHAT'S HE DOING THERE?
MAYBE HE'S WAITIN' FOR SOME-ONE. LOOK. THERE'S SOMEONE NOW.
WAIT A SEC. IS THAT...
YEAH, IT'S REALLY HIM.
I HAVE SOME REALLY BAD VIBES ABOUT THIS. GET OUTTA SIGHT!

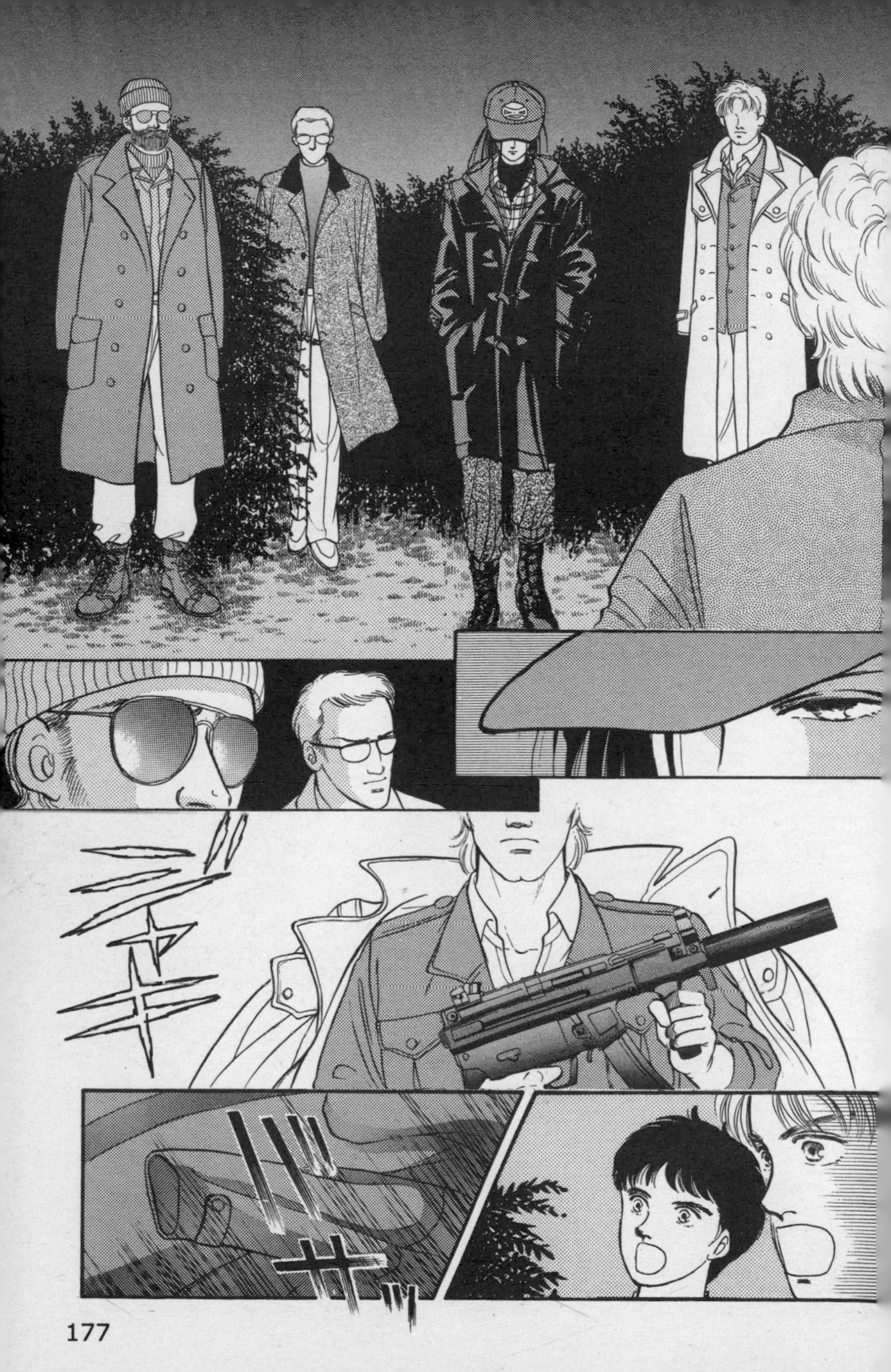

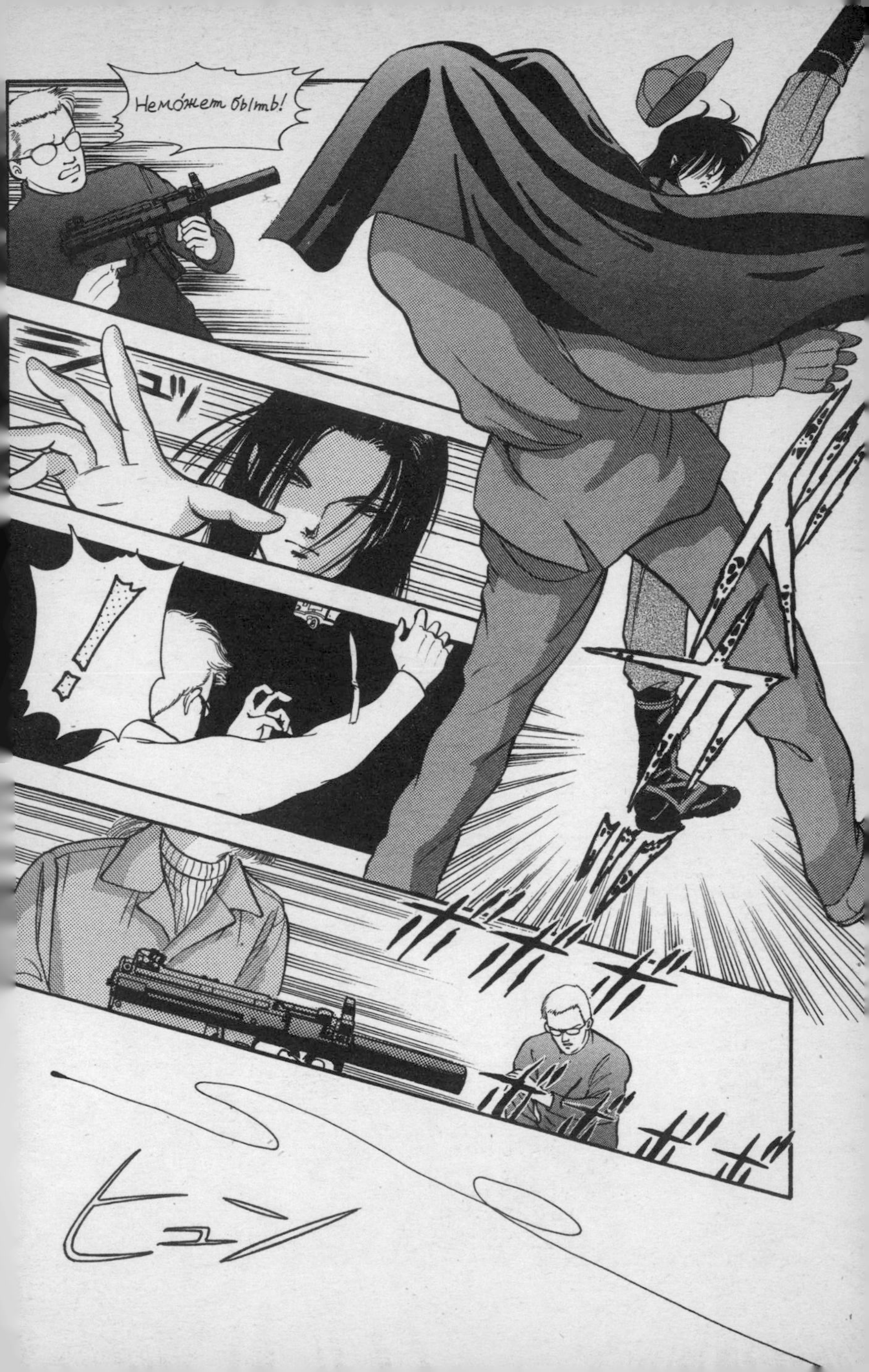
Не мо́жет быть!

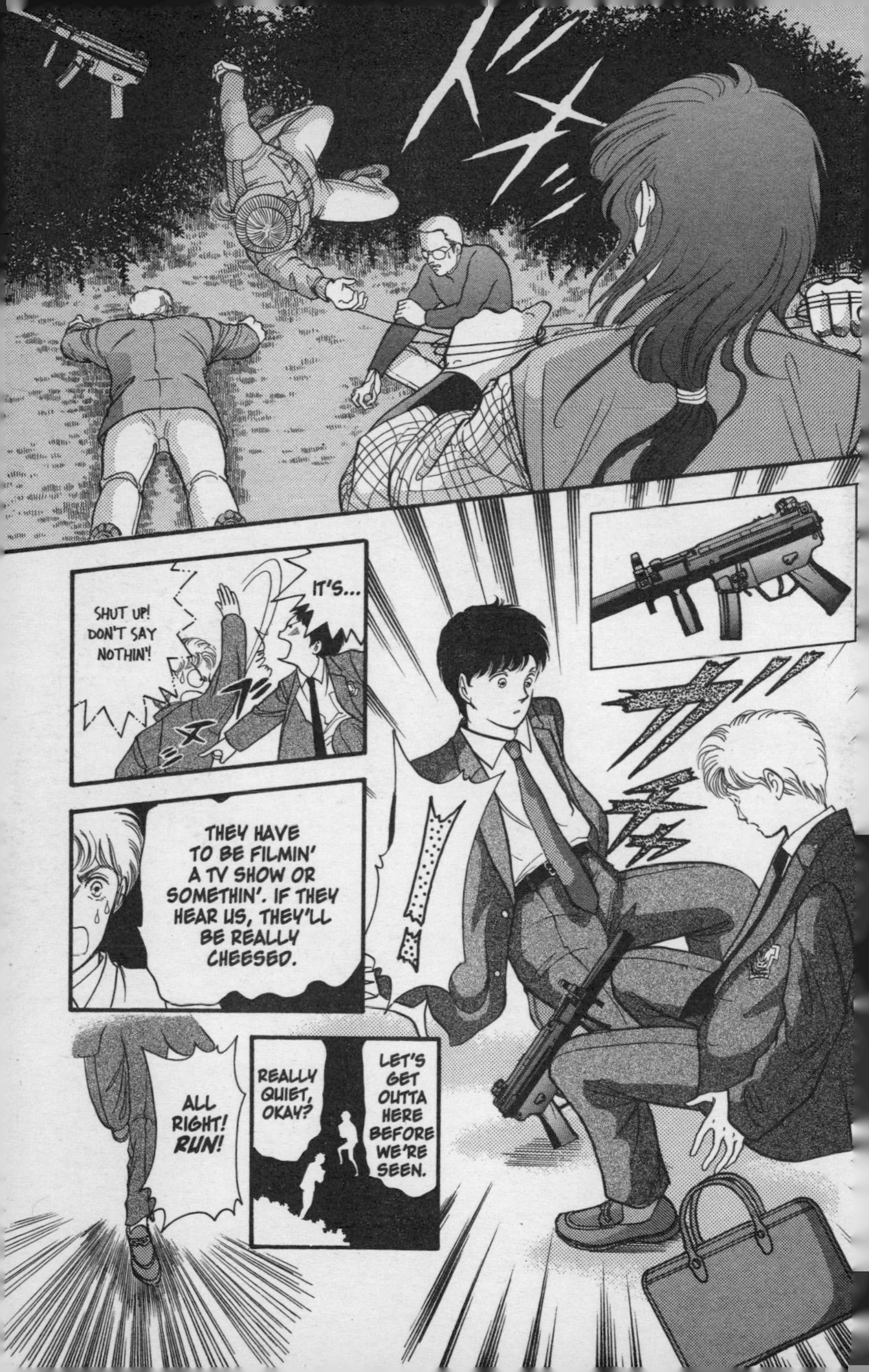
IT'S...
SHUT UP! DON'T SAY NOTHIN'!
THEY HAVE TO BE FILMIN' A TV SHOW OR SOMETHIN'. IF THEY HEAR US, THEY'LL BE REALLY CHEESED.
LET'S GET OUTTA HERE BEFORE WE'RE SEEN.
REALLY QUIET, OKAY?
ALL RIGHT! RUN!

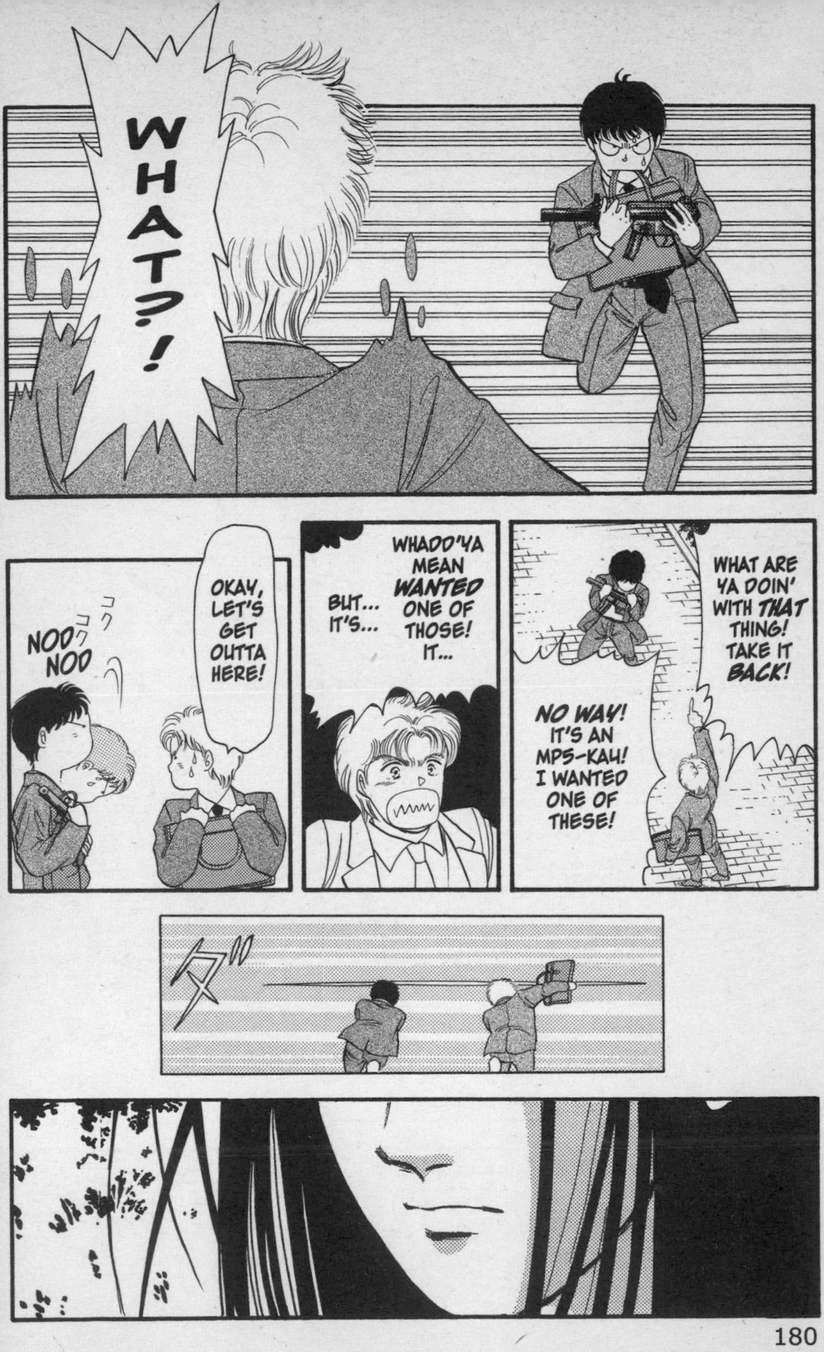
WHAT?!
WHAT ARE YA DOIN' WITH THAT THING! TAKE IT BACK!
NO WAY! IT'S AN MPS-KAU! I WANTED ONE OF THESE!
WHADD'YA MEAN WANTED ONE OF THOSE! IT...
BUT... IT'S...
OKAY, LET'S GET OUTTA HERE!
コクコク
NOD NOD
ダッ

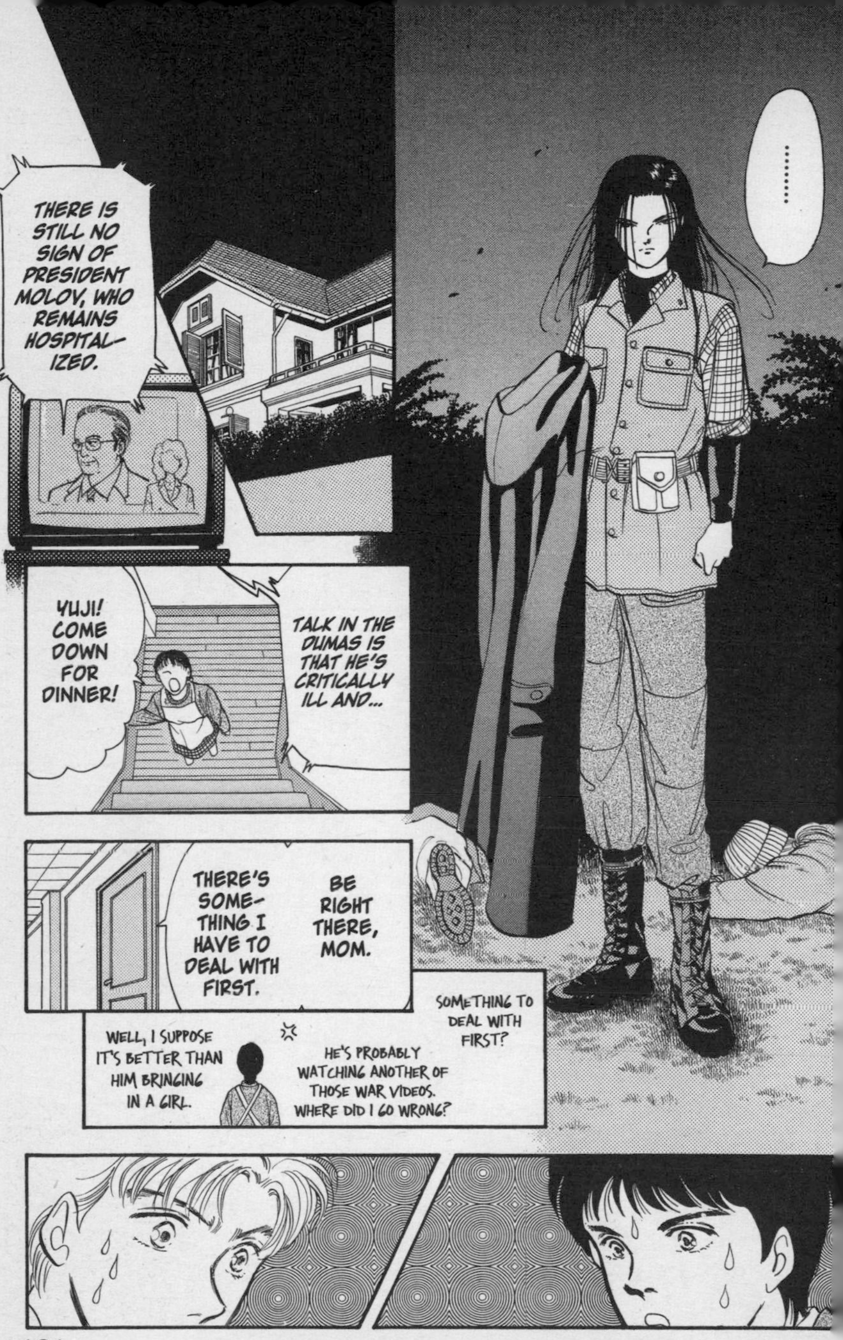
......
THERE IS STILL NO SIGN OF PRESIDENT MOLOV, WHO REMAINS HOSPITALIZED.
TALK IN THE DUMAS IS THAT HE'S CRITICALLY ILL AND...
YUJI! COME DOWN FOR DINNER!
BE RIGHT THERE, MOM.
THERE'S SOMETHING I HAVE TO DEAL WITH FIRST.
SOMETHING TO DEAL WITH FIRST?
HE'S PROBABLY WATCHING ANOTHER OF THOSE WAR VIDEOS. WHERE DID I GO WRONG?
WELL, I SUPPOSE IT'S BETTER THAN HIM BRINGING IN A GIRL.

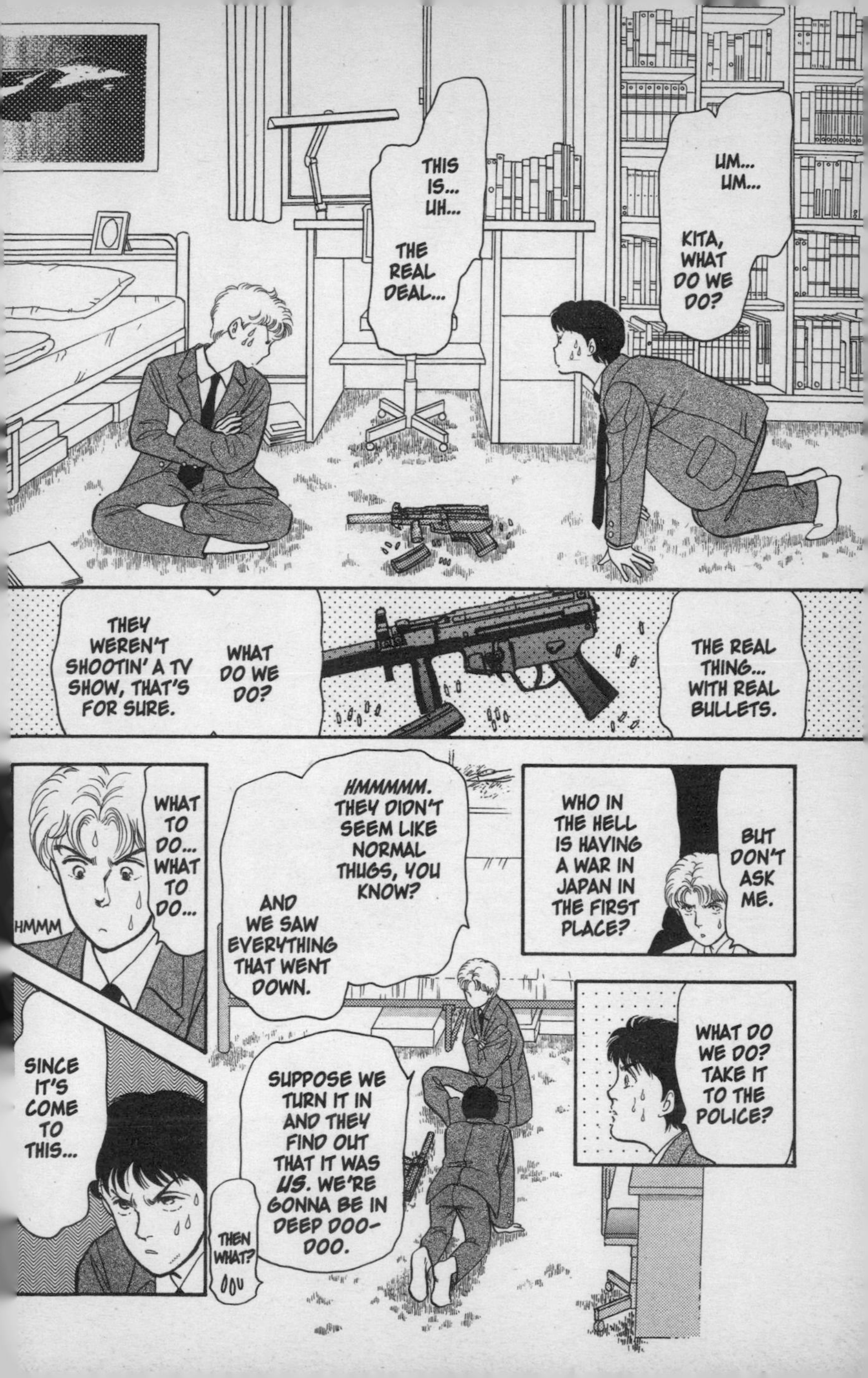
UM... UM...
KITA, WHAT DO WE DO?
THIS IS... UH...
THE REAL DEAL...
THE REAL THING... WITH REAL BULLETS.
WHAT DO WE DO?
THEY WEREN'T SHOOTIN' A TV SHOW, THAT'S FOR SURE.
WHO IN THE HELL IS HAVING A WAR IN JAPAN IN THE FIRST PLACE?
BUT DON'T ASK ME.
HMMMMM. THEY DIDN'T SEEM LIKE NORMAL THUGS, YOU KNOW?
AND WE SAW EVERYTHING THAT WENT DOWN.
WHAT TO DO... WHAT TO DO...
HMMMM
WHAT DO WE DO? TAKE IT TO THE POLICE?
SUPPOSE WE TURN IT IN AND THEY FIND OUT THAT IT WAS *US*. WE'RE GONNA BE IN DEEP DOO-DOO.
THEN WHAT?
SINCE IT'S COME TO THIS...

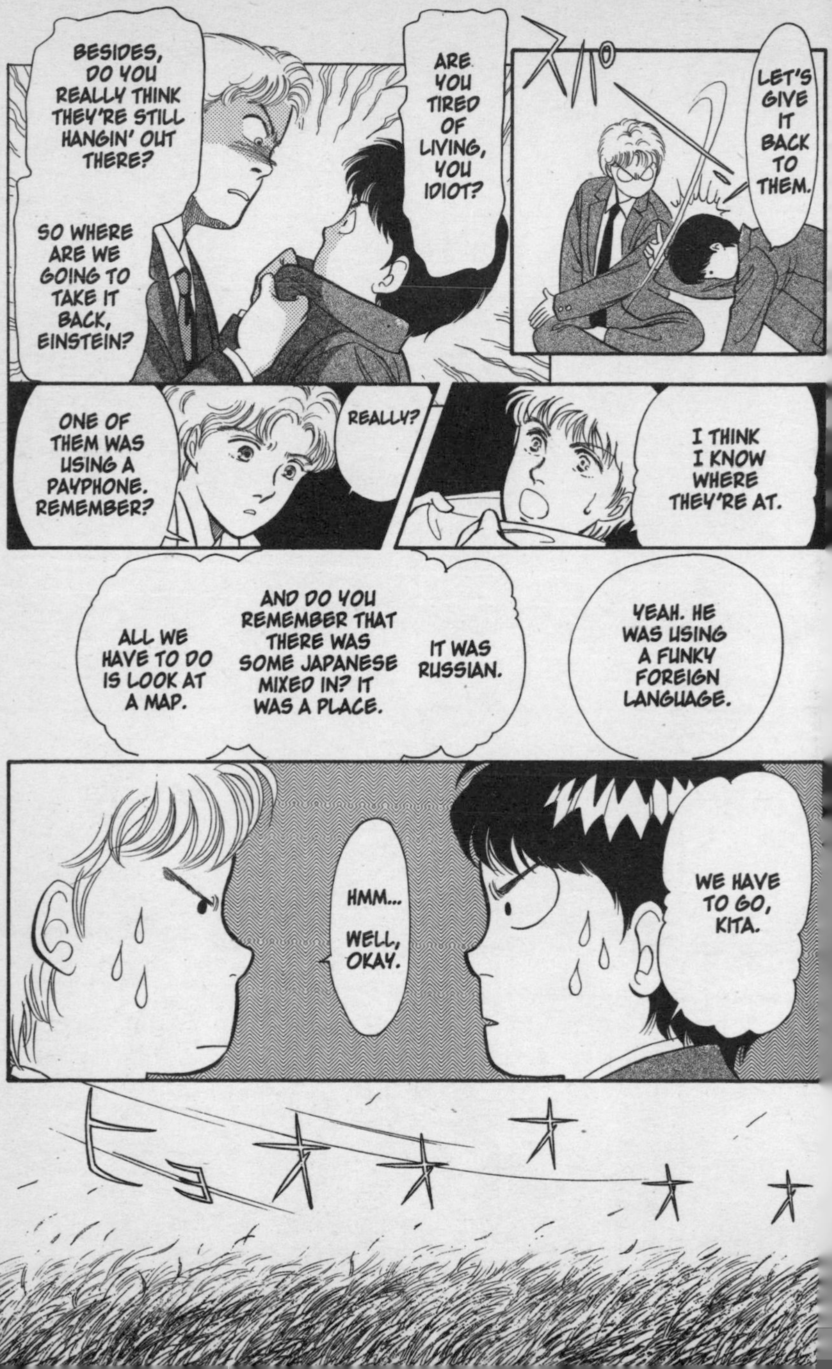
スパ
LET'S GIVE IT BACK TO THEM.
ARE YOU TIRED OF LIVING, YOU IDIOT?
BESIDES, DO YOU REALLY THINK THEY'RE STILL HANGIN' OUT THERE?
SO WHERE ARE WE GOING TO TAKE IT BACK, EINSTEIN?
I THINK I KNOW WHERE THEY'RE AT.
REALLY?
ONE OF THEM WAS USING A PAYPHONE. REMEMBER?
YEAH. HE WAS USING A FUNKY FOREIGN LANGUAGE.
IT WAS RUSSIAN.
AND DO YOU REMEMBER THAT THERE WAS SOME JAPANESE MIXED IN? IT WAS A PLACE.
ALL WE HAVE TO DO IS LOOK AT A MAP.
WE HAVE TO GO, KITA.
HMM...
WELL, OKAY.

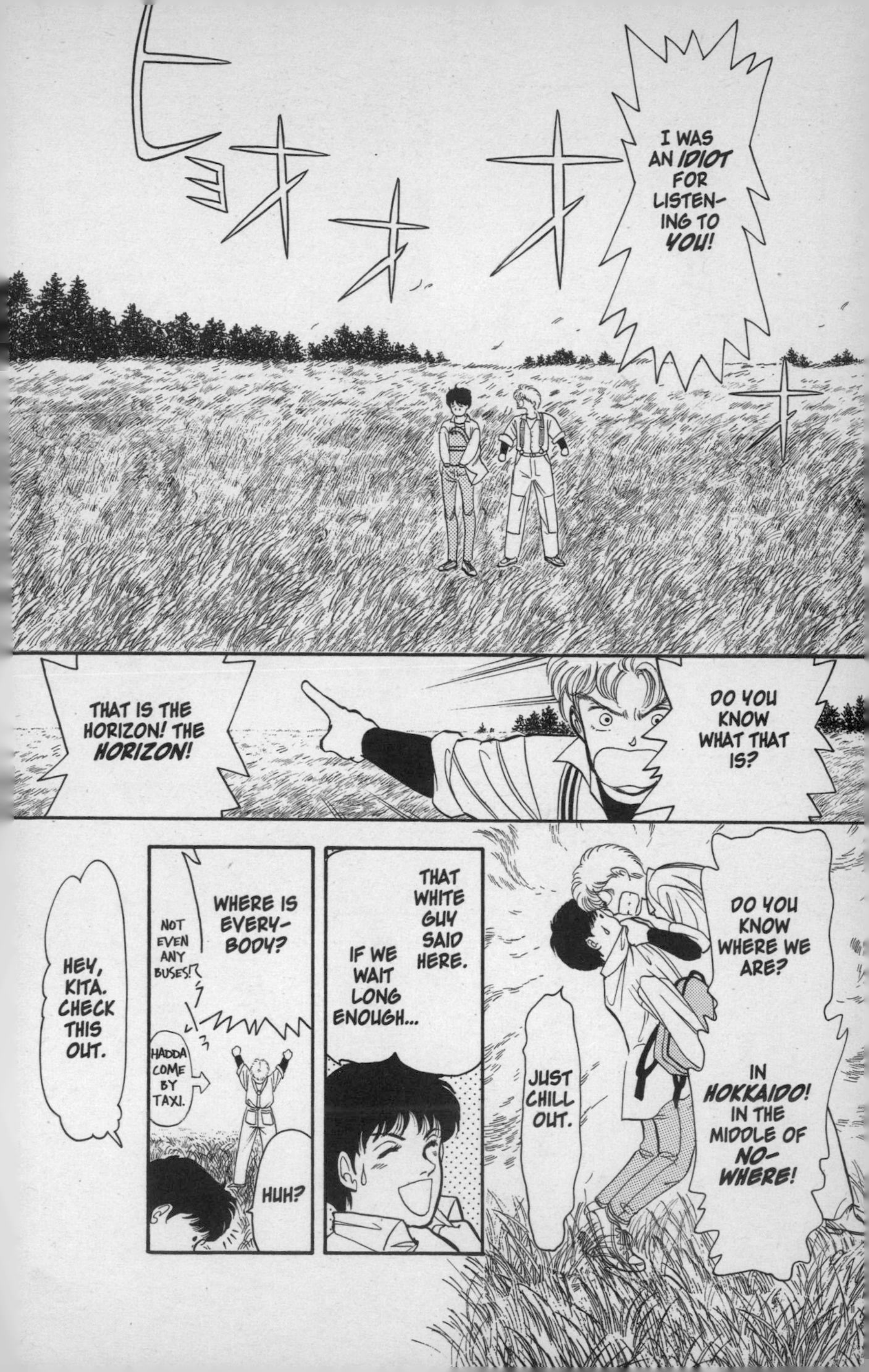
ヒョオォオォ
I WAS AN IDIOT FOR LISTENING TO YOU!
DO YOU KNOW WHAT THAT IS?
THAT IS THE HORIZON! THE HORIZON!
DO YOU KNOW WHERE WE ARE?
IN HOKKAIDO! IN THE MIDDLE OF NO-WHERE!
JUST CHILL OUT.
THAT WHITE GUY SAID HERE.
IF WE WAIT LONG ENOUGH...
WHERE IS EVERY-BODY?
NOT EVEN ANY BUSES!?
HADDA COME BY TAXI.
HUH?
HEY, KITA. CHECK THIS OUT.

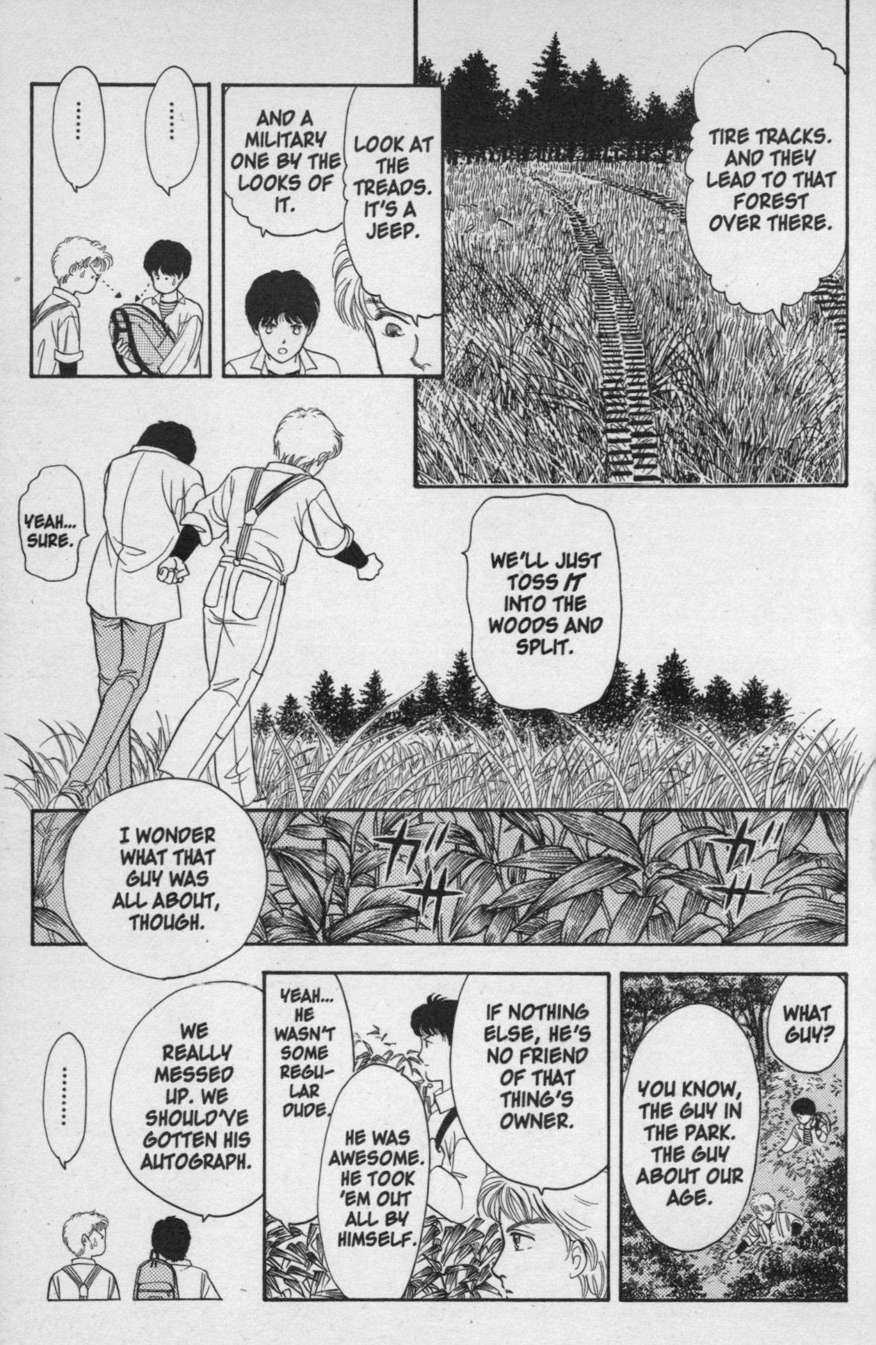
TIRE TRACKS. AND THEY LEAD TO THAT FOREST OVER THERE.
LOOK AT THE TREADS. IT'S A JEEP.
AND A MILITARY ONE BY THE LOOKS OF IT.
......
......
WE'LL JUST TOSS IT INTO THE WOODS AND SPLIT.
YEAH... SURE.
ガサ
ガサ
I WONDER WHAT THAT GUY WAS ALL ABOUT, THOUGH.
WHAT GUY?
YOU KNOW, THE GUY IN THE PARK. THE GUY ABOUT OUR AGE.
IF NOTHING ELSE, HE'S NO FRIEND OF THAT THING'S OWNER.
YEAH... HE WASN'T SOME REGU-LAR DUDE.
HE WAS AWESOME. HE TOOK 'EM OUT ALL BY HIMSELF.
WE REALLY MESSED UP. WE SHOULD'VE GOTTEN HIS AUTOGRAPH.
......

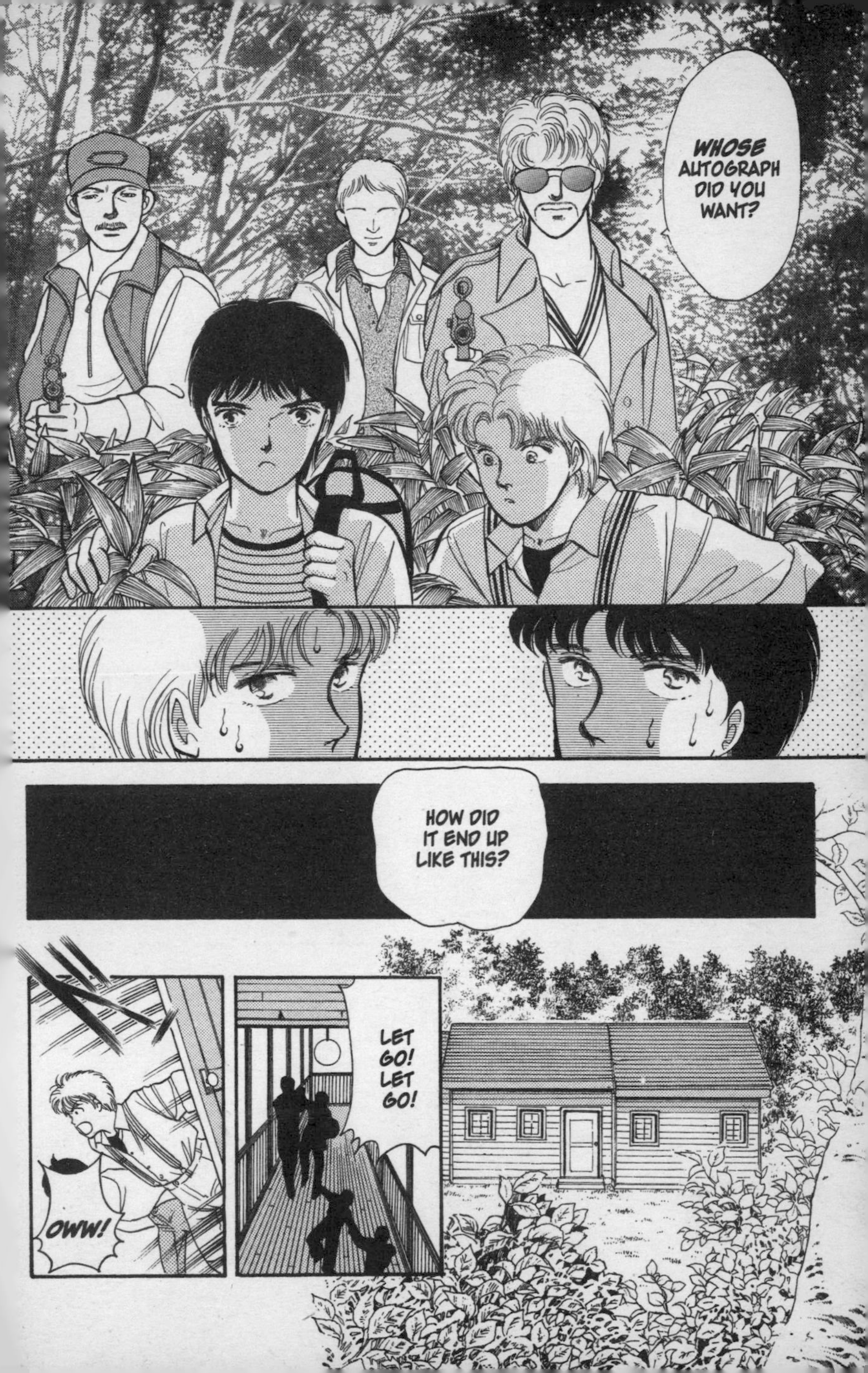
WHOSE AUTOGRAPH DID YOU WANT?
HOW DID IT END UP LIKE THIS?
LET GO! LET GO!
OWW!

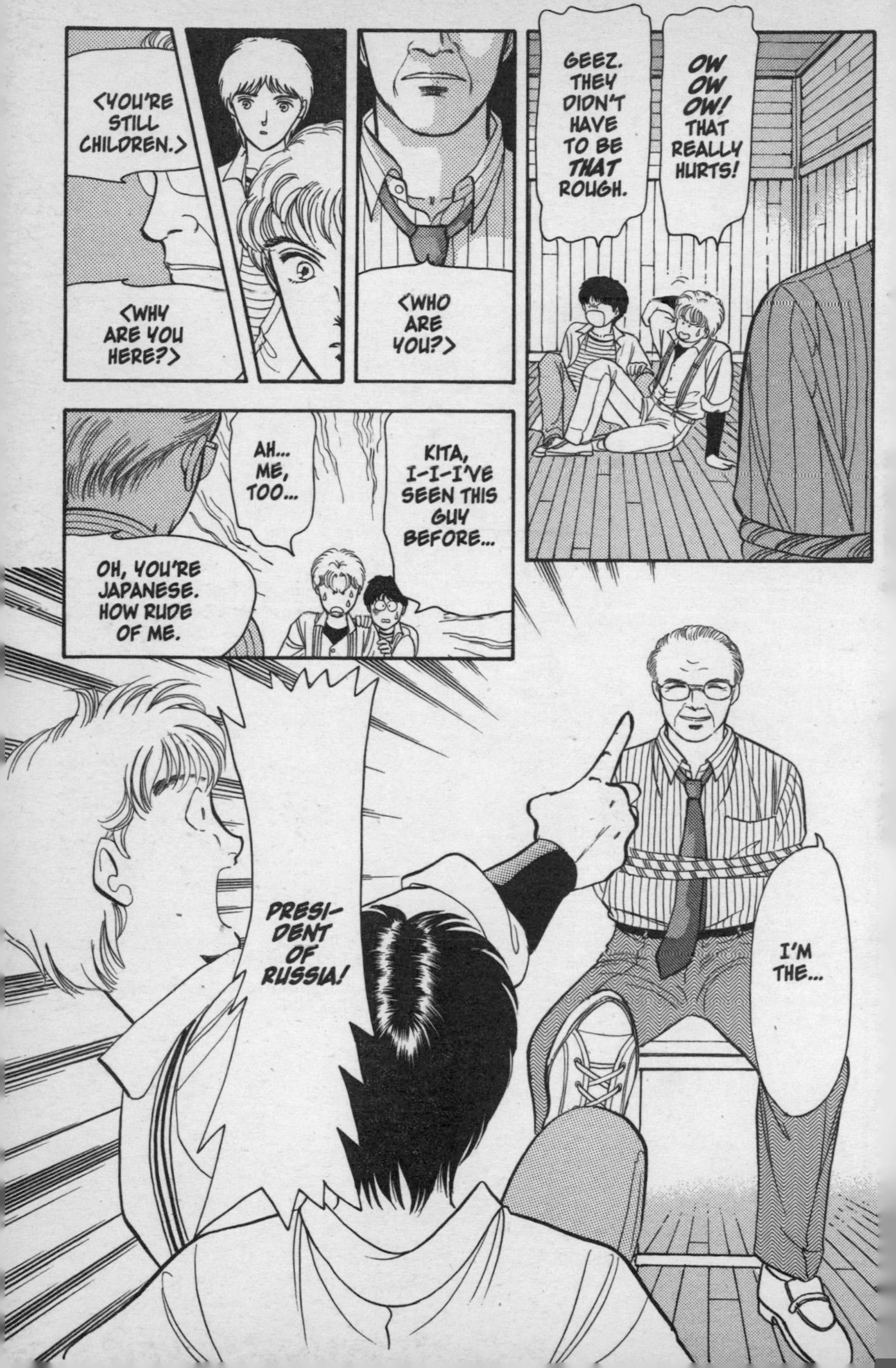
OW OW OW! THAT REALLY HURTS!
GEEZ. THEY DIDN'T HAVE TO BE THAT ROUGH.
<WHO ARE YOU?>
<YOU'RE STILL CHILDREN.>
<WHY ARE YOU HERE?>
KITA, I-I-I'VE SEEN THIS GUY BEFORE...
AH... ME, TOO...
OH, YOU'RE JAPANESE. HOW RUDE OF ME.
I'M THE...
PRESIDENT OF RUSSIA!

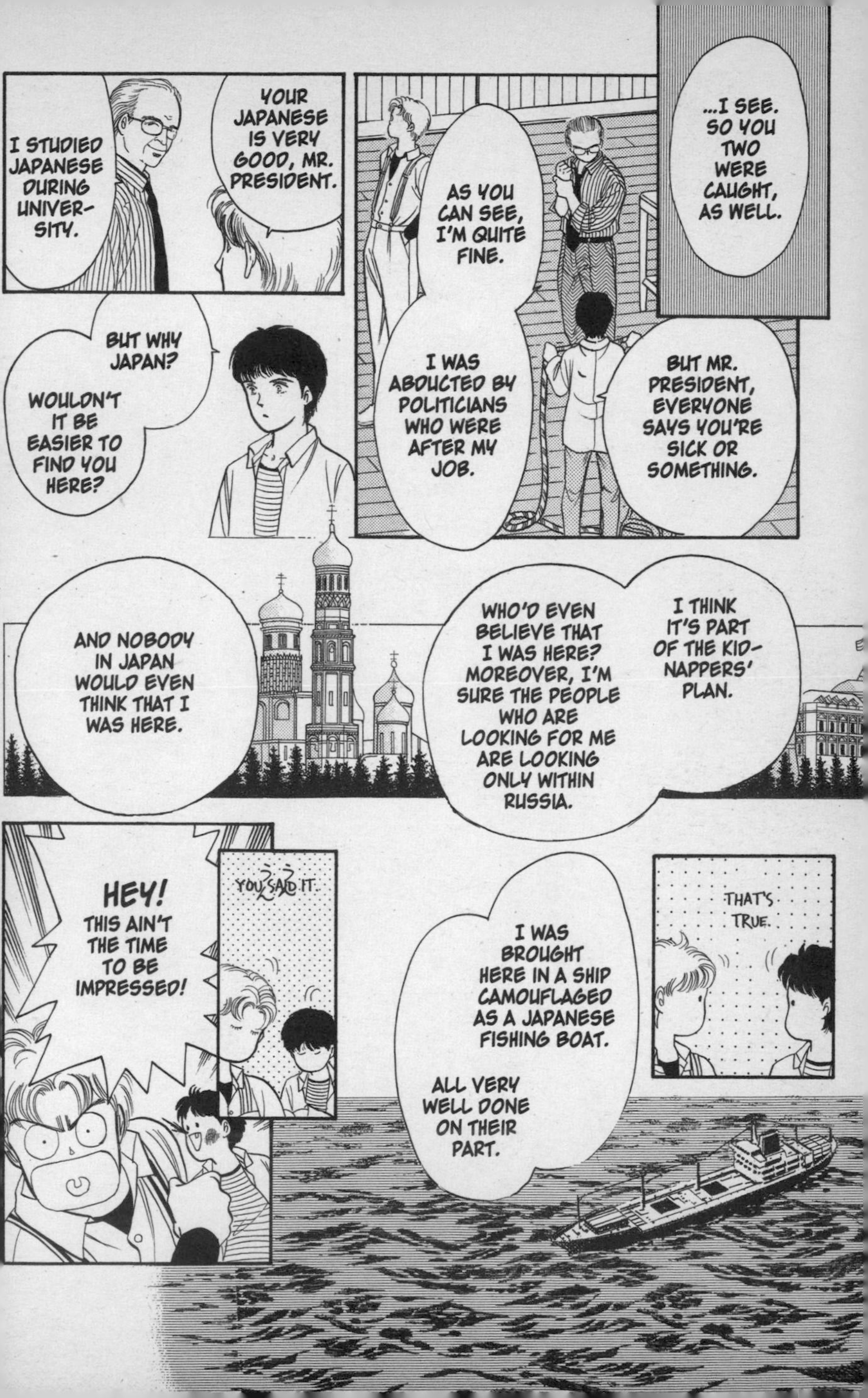
...I SEE. SO YOU TWO WERE CAUGHT, AS WELL.
AS YOU CAN SEE, I'M QUITE FINE.
YOUR JAPANESE IS VERY GOOD, MR. PRESIDENT.
I STUDIED JAPANESE DURING UNIVER-SITY.
BUT MR. PRESIDENT, EVERYONE SAYS YOU'RE SICK OR SOMETHING.
I WAS ABDUCTED BY POLITICIANS WHO WERE AFTER MY JOB.
BUT WHY JAPAN?
WOULDN'T IT BE EASIER TO FIND YOU HERE?
I THINK IT'S PART OF THE KID-NAPPERS' PLAN.
WHO'D EVEN BELIEVE THAT I WAS HERE? MOREOVER, I'M SURE THE PEOPLE WHO ARE LOOKING FOR ME ARE LOOKING ONLY WITHIN RUSSIA.
AND NOBODY IN JAPAN WOULD EVEN THINK THAT I WAS HERE.
THAT'S TRUE.
I WAS BROUGHT HERE IN A SHIP CAMOUFLAGED AS A JAPANESE FISHING BOAT.
ALL VERY WELL DONE ON THEIR PART.
YOU SAID IT.
HEY! THIS AIN'T THE TIME TO BE IMPRESSED!

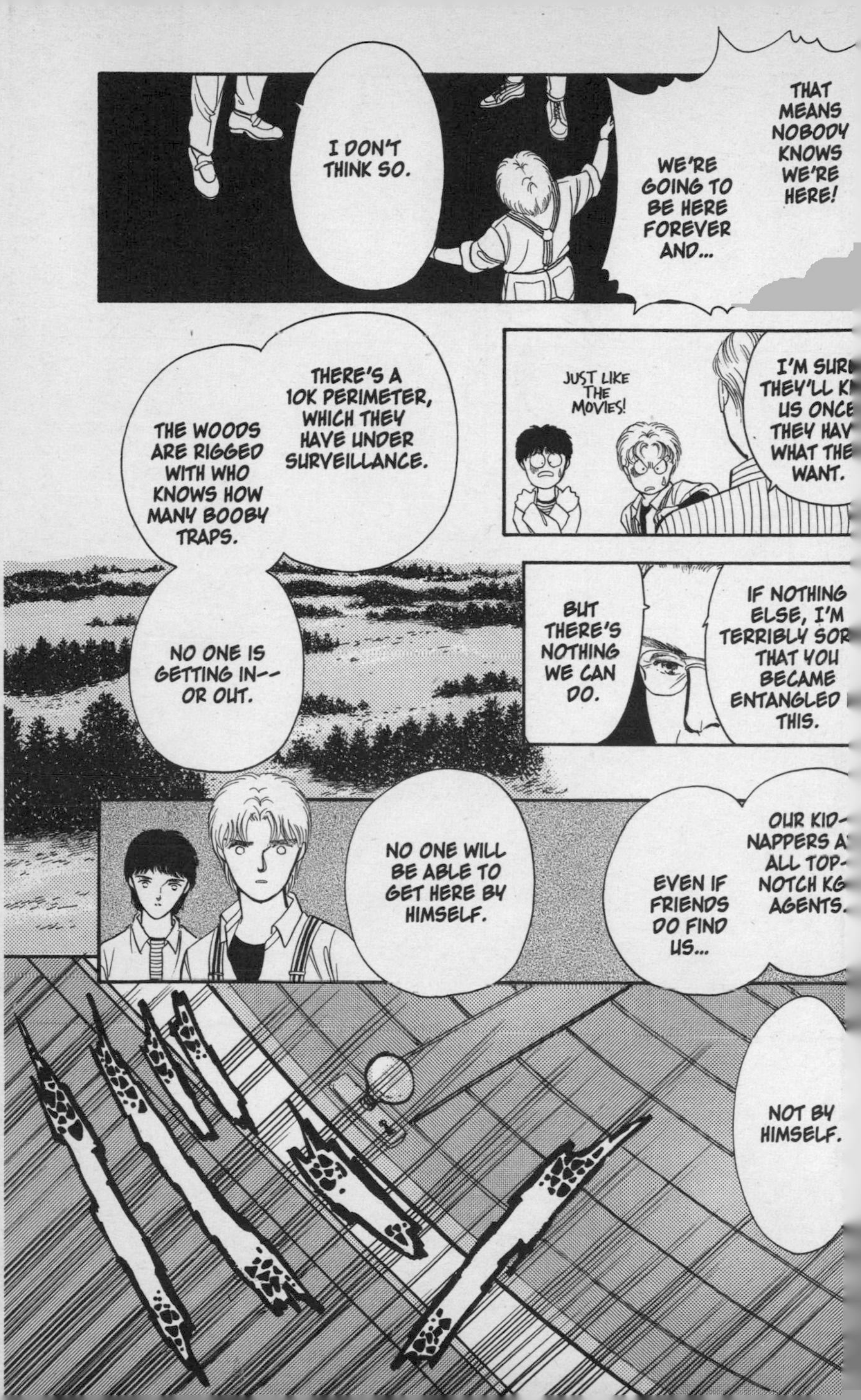
THAT MEANS NOBODY KNOWS WE'RE HERE!
WE'RE GOING TO BE HERE FOREVER AND...
I DON'T THINK SO.
I'M SUR THEY'LL K US ONCE THEY HAV WHAT THE WANT.
JUST LIKE THE MOVIES!
THERE'S A 10K PERIMETER, WHICH THEY HAVE UNDER SURVEILLANCE.
THE WOODS ARE RIGGED WITH WHO KNOWS HOW MANY BOOBY TRAPS.
IF NOTHING ELSE, I'M TERRIBLY SOR THAT YOU BECAME ENTANGLED THIS.
BUT THERE'S NOTHING WE CAN DO.
NO ONE IS GETTING IN-- OR OUT.
OUR KID- NAPPERS A ALL TOP- NOTCH KG AGENTS.
EVEN IF FRIENDS DO FIND US...
NO ONE WILL BE ABLE TO GET HERE BY HIMSELF.
NOT BY HIMSELF.

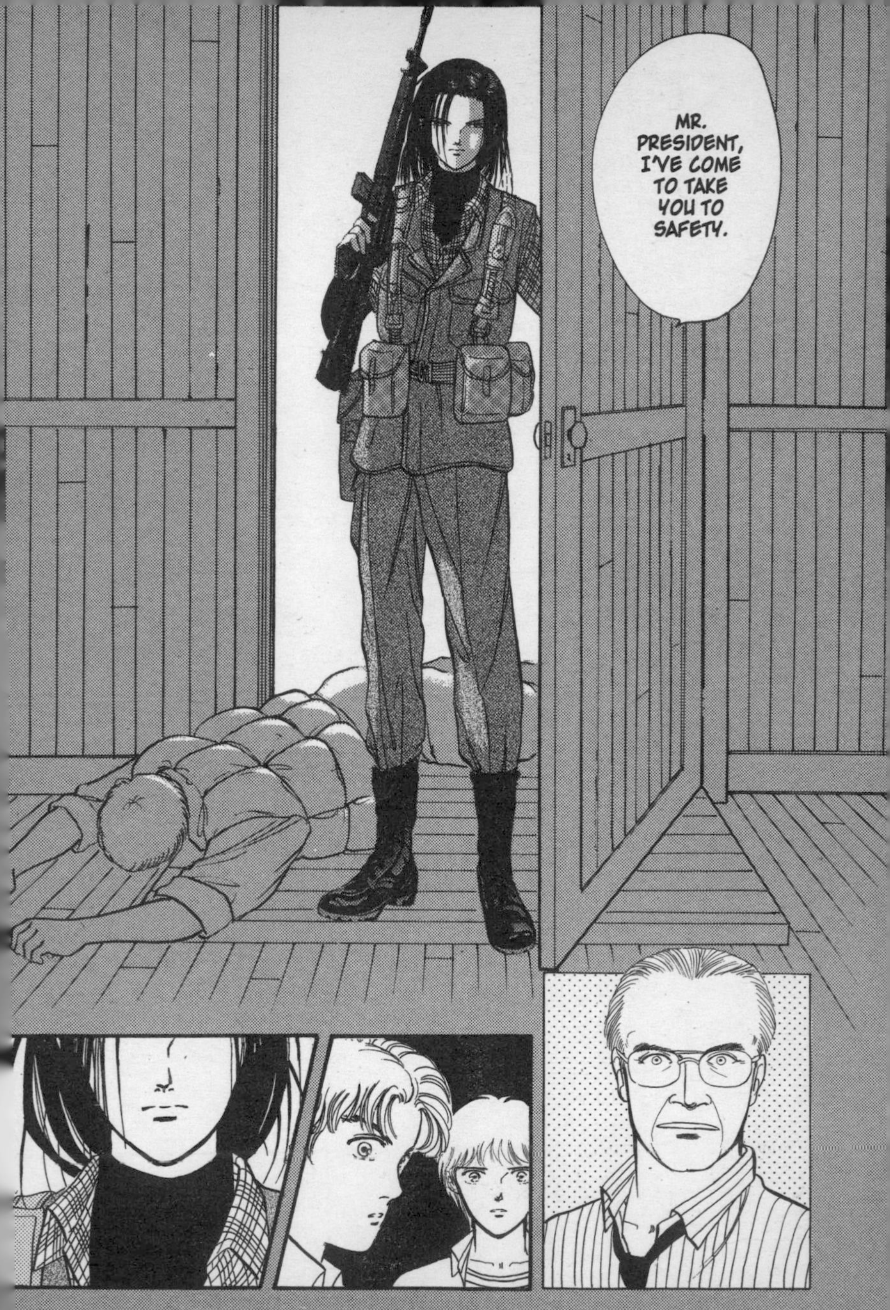
MR. PRESIDENT, I'VE COME TO TAKE YOU TO SAFETY.

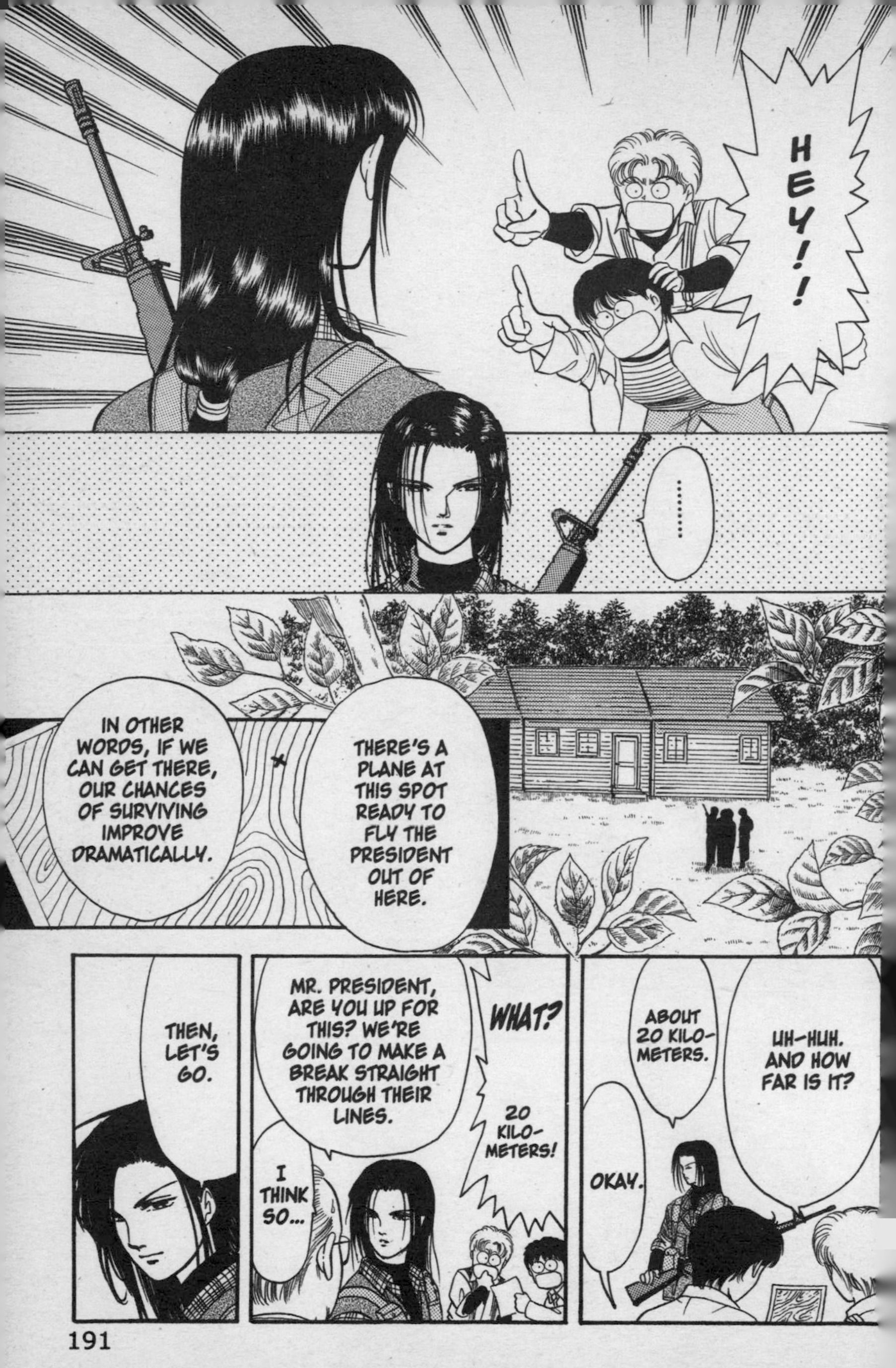
HEY!!
......
THERE'S A PLANE AT THIS SPOT READY TO FLY THE PRESIDENT OUT OF HERE.
IN OTHER WORDS, IF WE CAN GET THERE, OUR CHANCES OF SURVIVING IMPROVE DRAMATICALLY.
UH-HUH. AND HOW FAR IS IT?
ABOUT 20 KILOMETERS.
OKAY.
WHAT?
20 KILOMETERS!
MR. PRESIDENT, ARE YOU UP FOR THIS? WE'RE GOING TO MAKE A BREAK STRAIGHT THROUGH THEIR LINES.
I THINK SO...
THEN, LET'S GO.

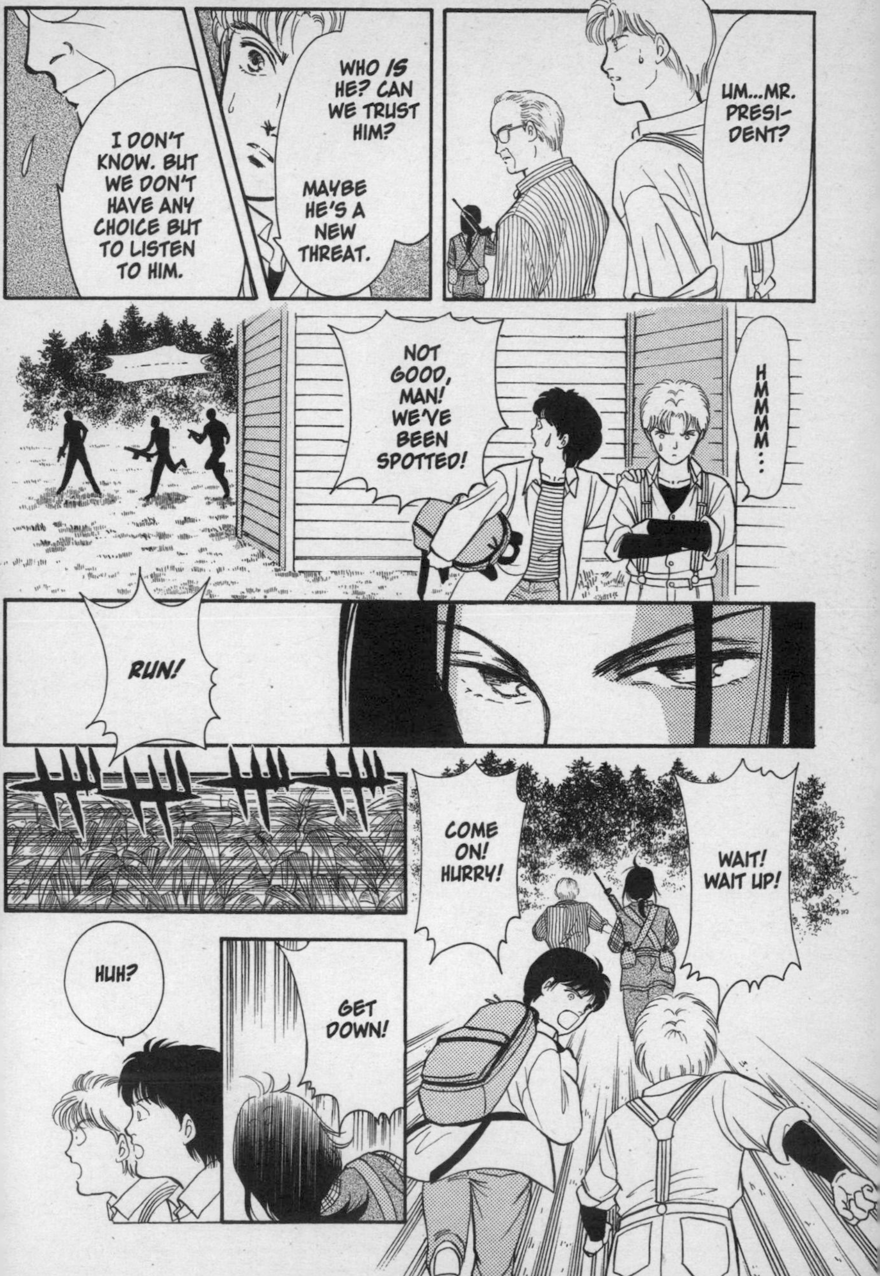
UM...MR. PRESIDENT?
WHO IS HE? CAN WE TRUST HIM?
MAYBE HE'S A NEW THREAT.
I DON'T KNOW. BUT WE DON'T HAVE ANY CHOICE BUT TO LISTEN TO HIM.
HMMMM...
NOT GOOD, MAN! WE'VE BEEN SPOTTED!
RUN!
WAIT! WAIT UP!
COME ON! HURRY!
GET DOWN!
HUH?

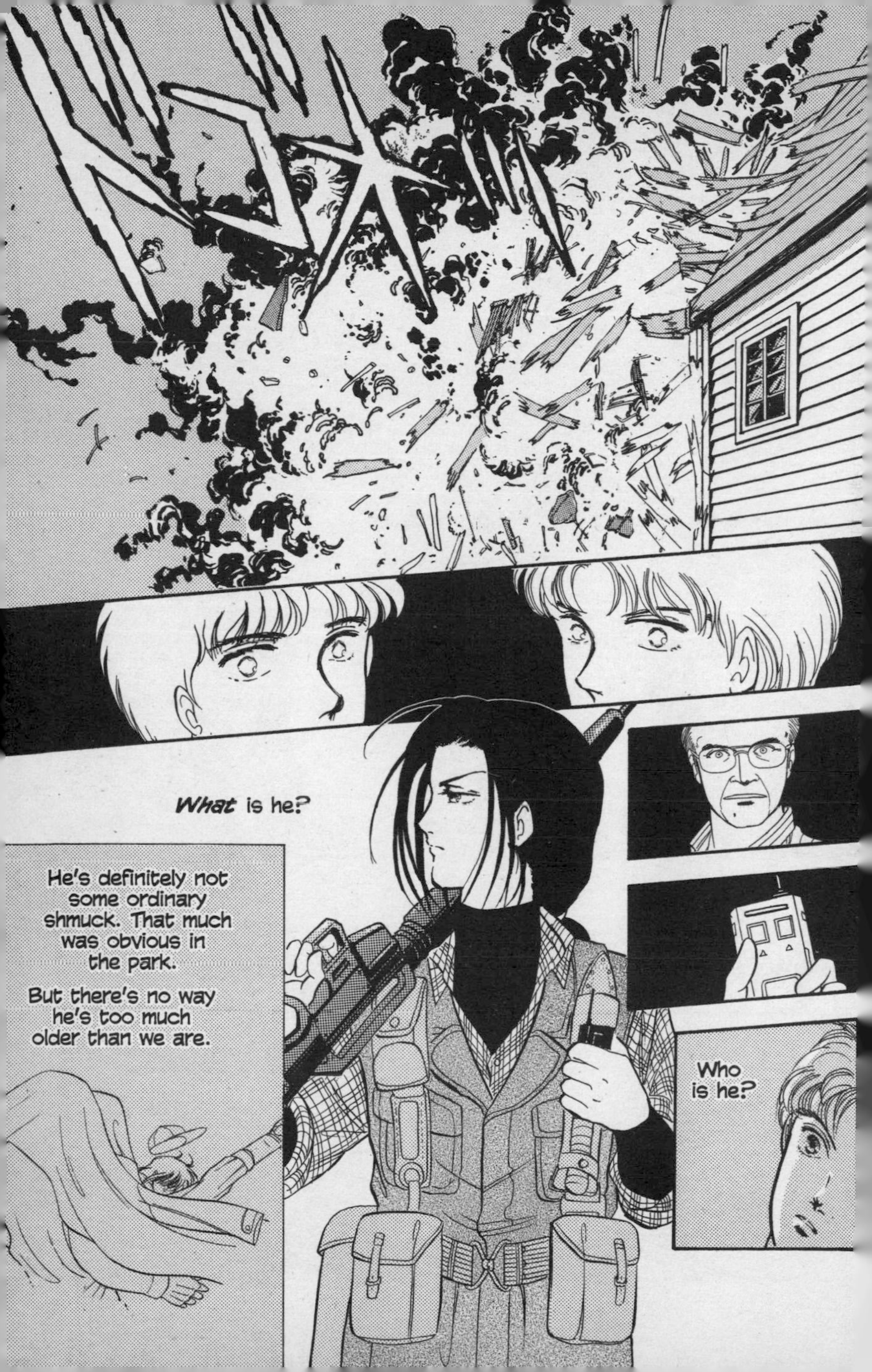
Who is he?
What is he?
He's definitely not some ordinary shmuck. That much was obvious in the park.
But there's no way he's too much older than we are.

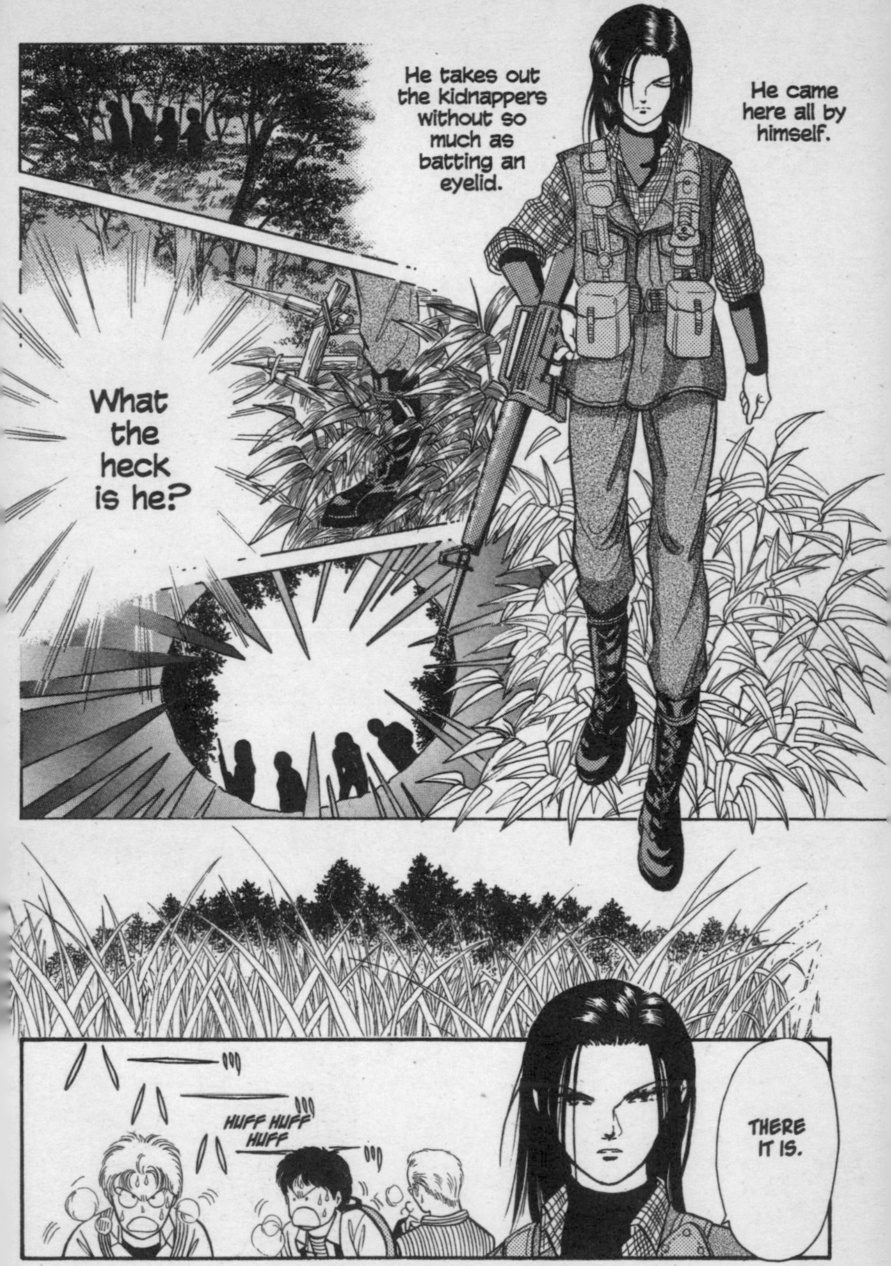
He came here all by himself.
He takes out the kidnappers without so much as batting an eyelid.
What the heck is he?
THERE IT IS.
HUFF HUFF HUFF

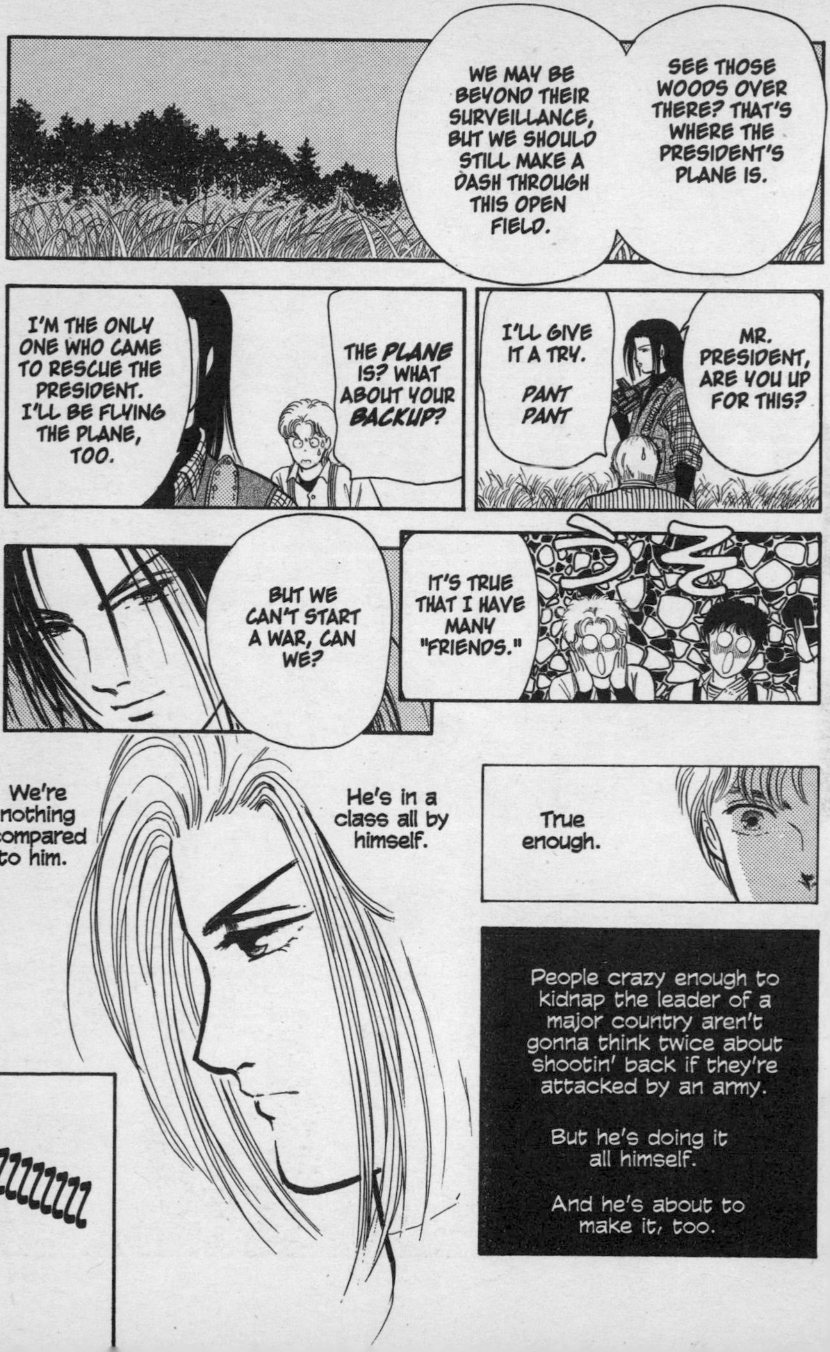
SEE THOSE WOODS OVER THERE? THAT'S WHERE THE PRESIDENT'S PLANE IS.
WE MAY BE BEYOND THEIR SURVEILLANCE, BUT WE SHOULD STILL MAKE A DASH THROUGH THIS OPEN FIELD.
MR. PRESIDENT, ARE YOU UP FOR THIS?
I'LL GIVE IT A TRY.
PANT PANT
THE PLANE IS? WHAT ABOUT YOUR BACKUP?
I'M THE ONLY ONE WHO CAME TO RESCUE THE PRESIDENT. I'LL BE FLYING THE PLANE, TOO.
IT'S TRUE THAT I HAVE MANY "FRIENDS."
BUT WE CAN'T START A WAR, CAN WE?
True enough.
He's in a class all by himself.
We're nothing compared to him.
People crazy enough to kidnap the leader of a major country aren't gonna think twice about shootin' back if they're attacked by an army.
But he's doing it all himself.
And he's about to make it, too.
BZZZZZZZZZZ

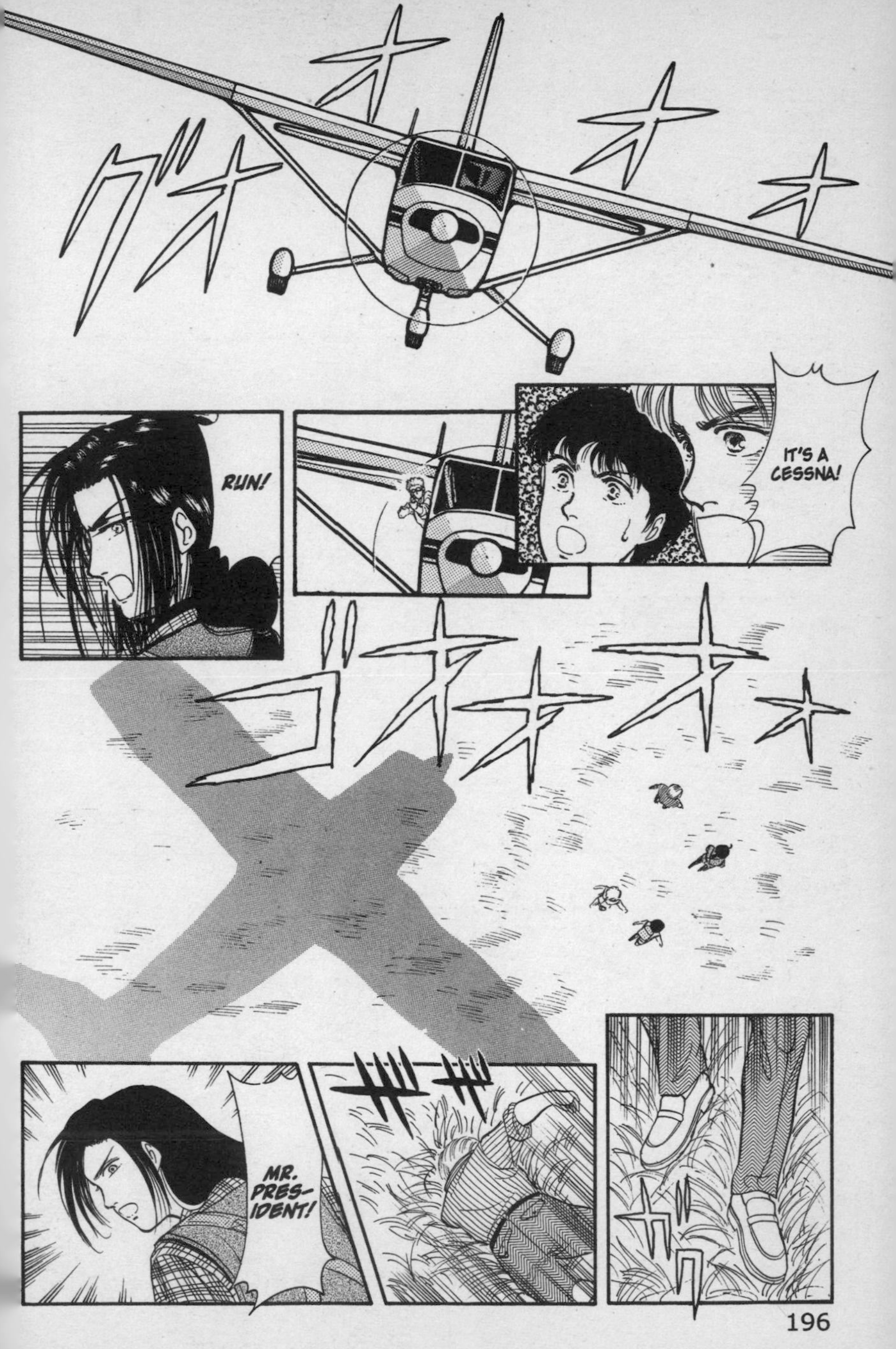
IT'S A CESSNA!
RUN!
MR. PRES-IDENT!

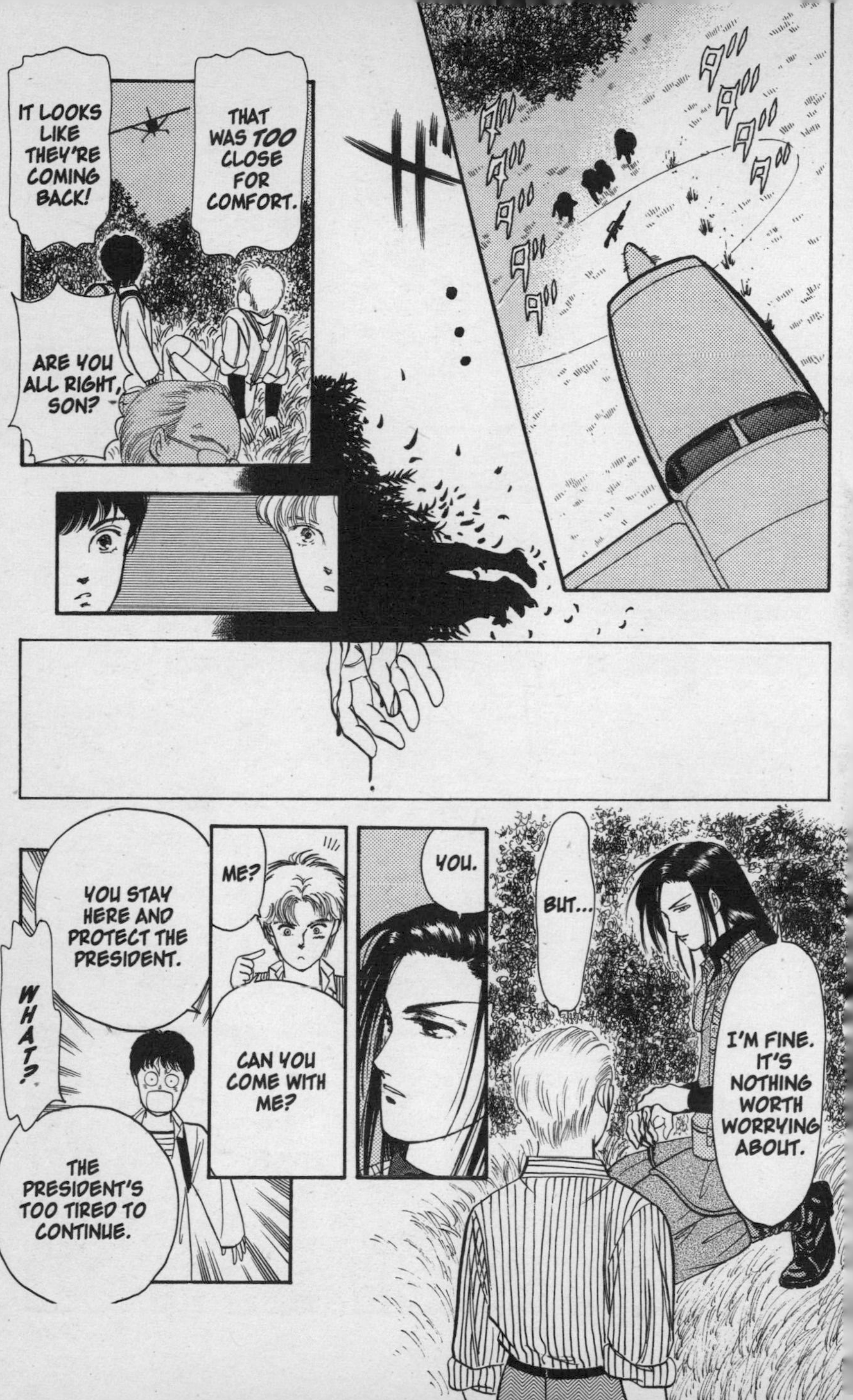
THAT WAS TOO CLOSE FOR COMFORT.
IT LOOKS LIKE THEY'RE COMING BACK!
ARE YOU ALL RIGHT, SON?
BUT...
I'M FINE. IT'S NOTHING WORTH WORRYING ABOUT.
YOU.
ME?
CAN YOU COME WITH ME?
YOU STAY HERE AND PROTECT THE PRESIDENT.
WHAT?
THE PRESIDENT'S TOO TIRED TO CONTINUE.

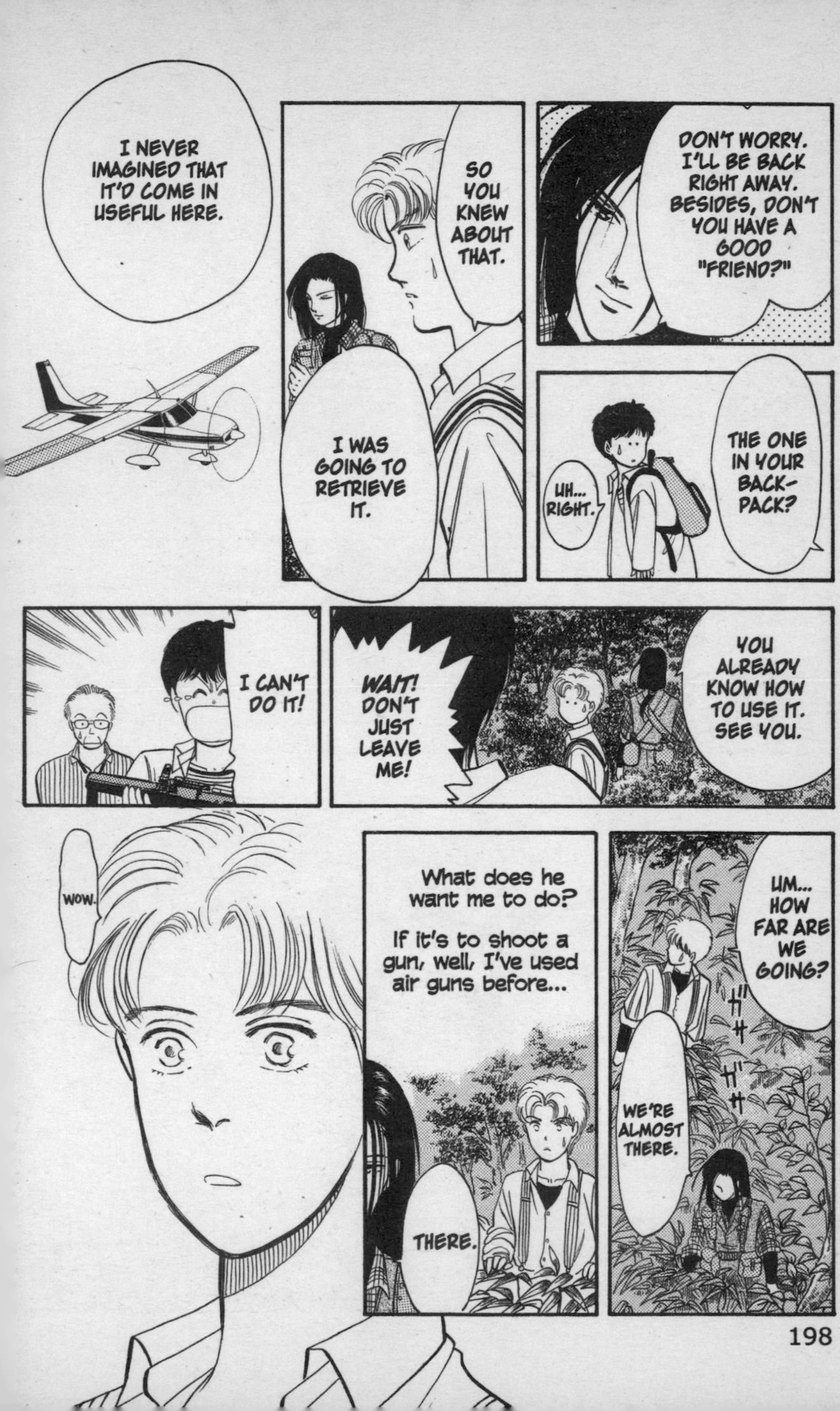
DON'T WORRY. I'LL BE BACK RIGHT AWAY. BESIDES, DON'T YOU HAVE A GOOD "FRIEND?"
THE ONE IN YOUR BACK-PACK?
UH... RIGHT.
SO YOU KNEW ABOUT THAT.
I WAS GOING TO RETRIEVE IT.
I NEVER IMAGINED THAT IT'D COME IN USEFUL HERE.
YOU ALREADY KNOW HOW TO USE IT. SEE YOU.
WAIT! DON'T JUST LEAVE ME!
I CAN'T DO IT!
UM... HOW FAR ARE WE GOING?
WE'RE ALMOST THERE.
What does he want me to do?
If it's to shoot a gun, well, I've used air guns before...
THERE.
WOW.

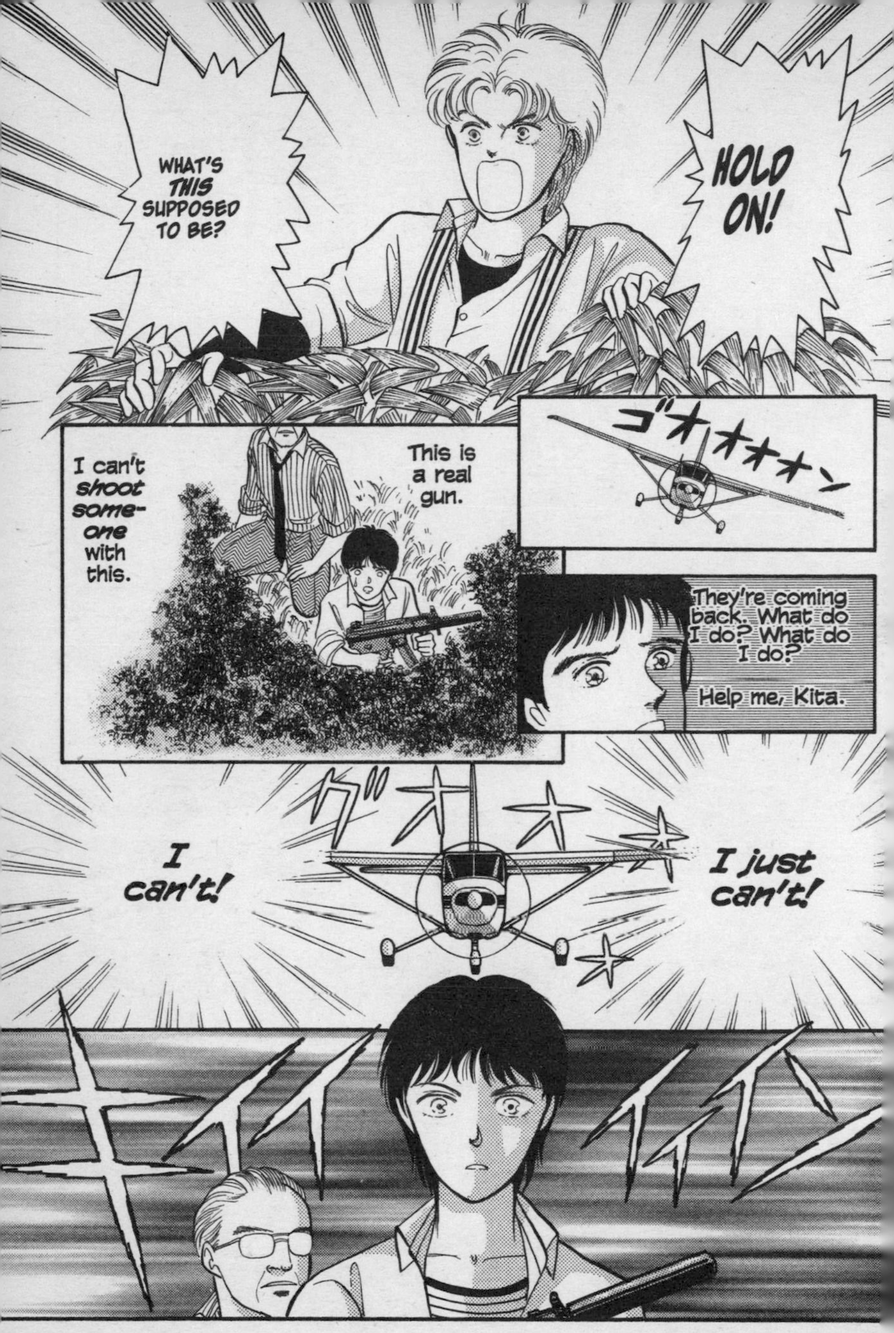
HOLD ON!
WHAT'S THIS SUPPOSED TO BE?
ゴオオオオン
They're coming back. What do I do? What do I do?
Help me, Kita.
This is a real gun.
I can't shoot someone with this.
グオオオ
I just can't!
I can't!
キイイイン

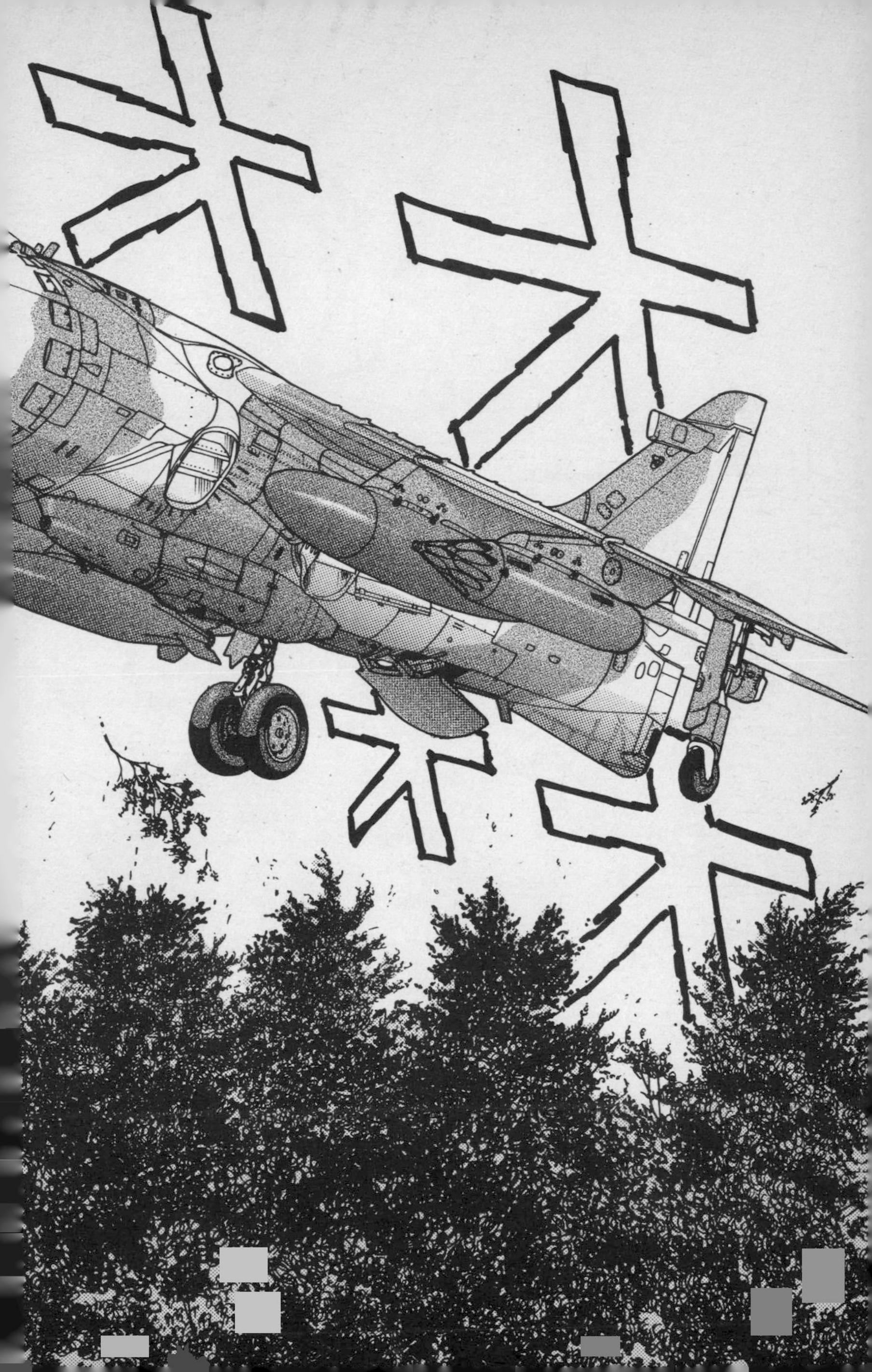
オオオオ

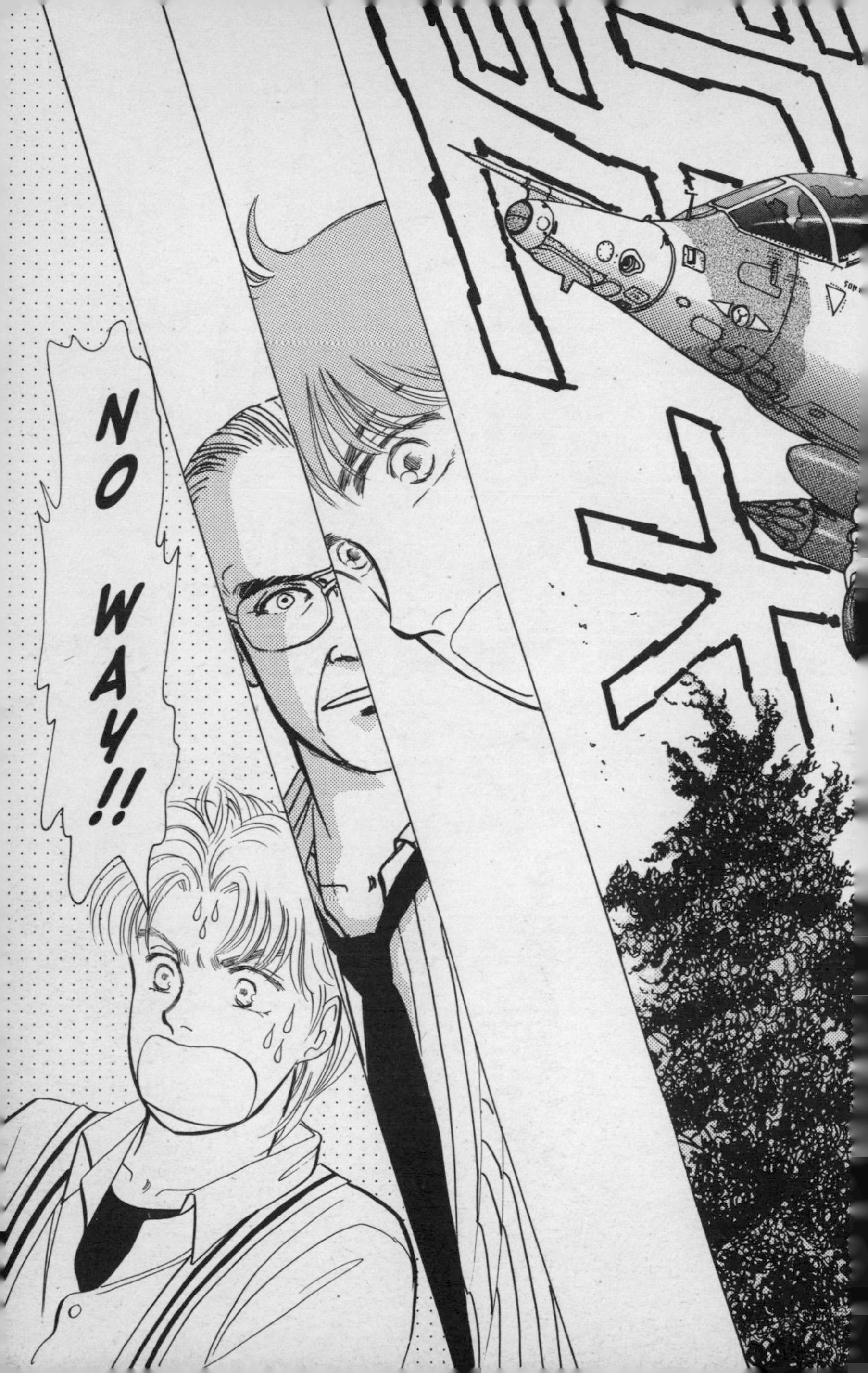
NO WAY!!

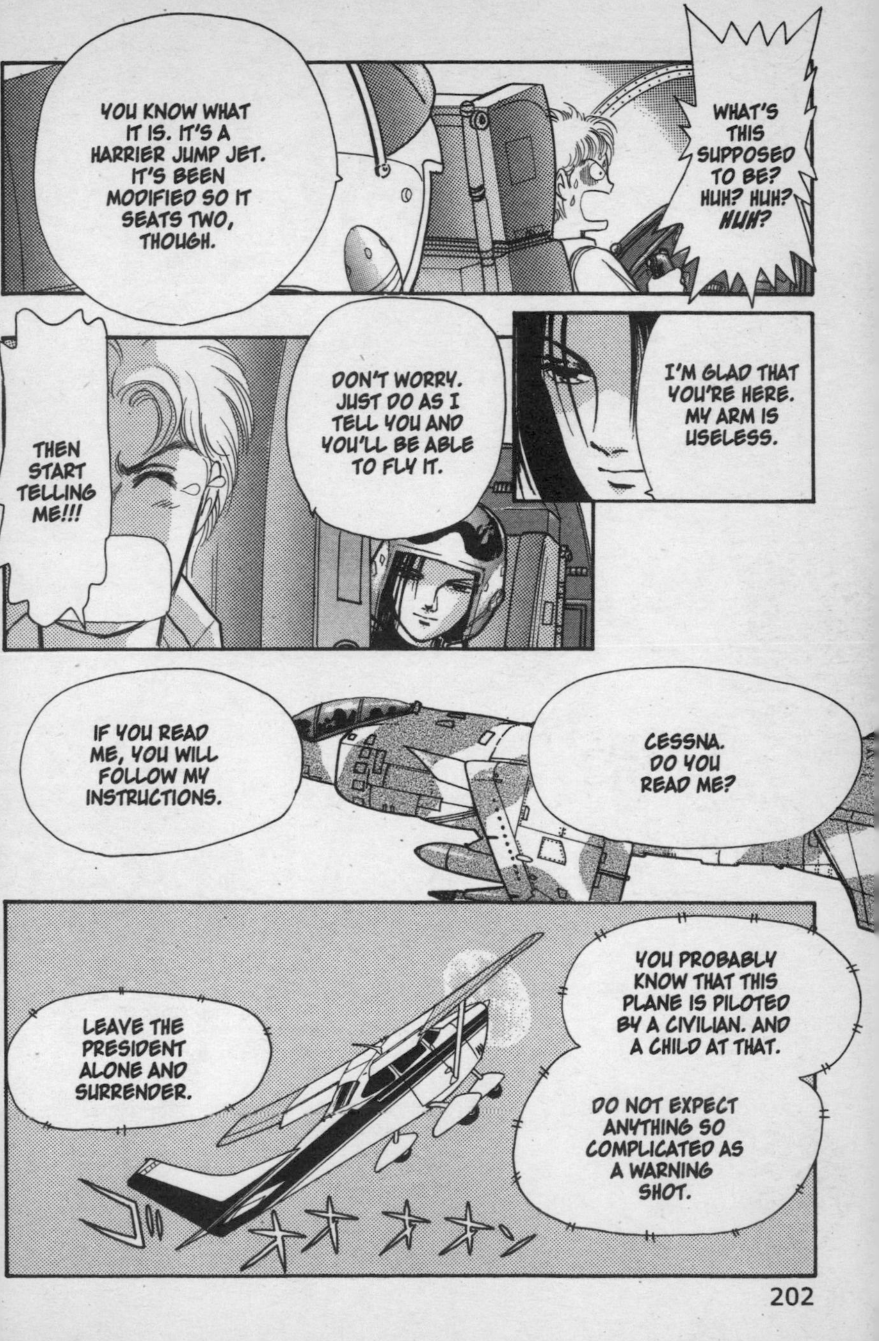
WHAT'S THIS SUPPOSED TO BE? HUH? HUH? HUH?
YOU KNOW WHAT IT IS. IT'S A HARRIER JUMP JET. IT'S BEEN MODIFIED SO IT SEATS TWO, THOUGH.
I'M GLAD THAT YOU'RE HERE. MY ARM IS USELESS.
DON'T WORRY. JUST DO AS I TELL YOU AND YOU'LL BE ABLE TO FLY IT.
THEN START TELLING ME!!!
CESSNA. DO YOU READ ME?
IF YOU READ ME, YOU WILL FOLLOW MY INSTRUCTIONS.
YOU PROBABLY KNOW THAT THIS PLANE IS PILOTED BY A CIVILIAN. AND A CHILD AT THAT.
DO NOT EXPECT ANYTHING SO COMPLICATED AS A WARNING SHOT.
LEAVE THE PRESIDENT ALONE AND SURRENDER.

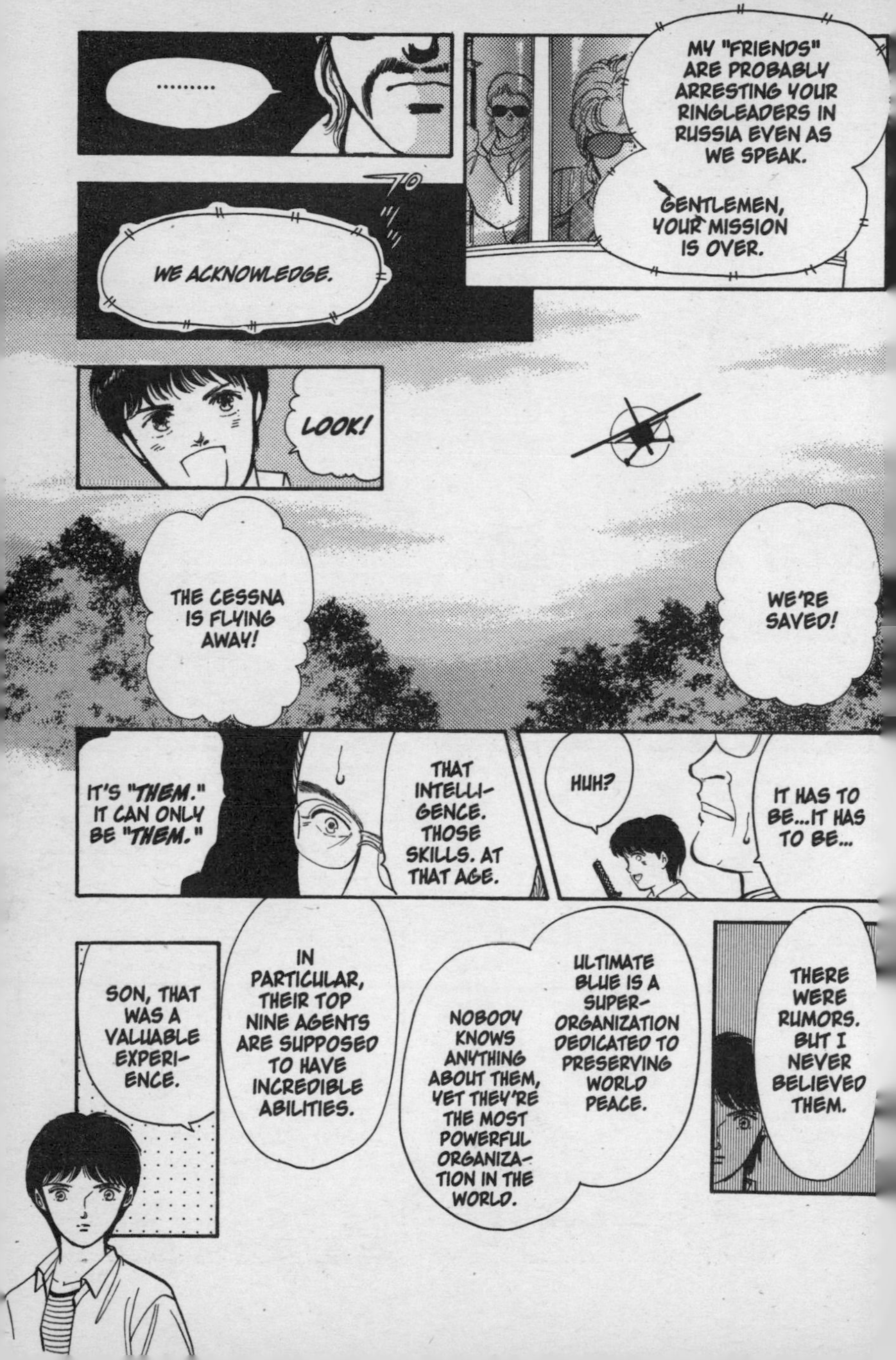
MY "FRIENDS" ARE PROBABLY ARRESTING YOUR RINGLEADERS IN RUSSIA EVEN AS WE SPEAK.
GENTLEMEN, YOUR MISSION IS OVER.
....
WE ACKNOWLEDGE.
LOOK!
WE'RE SAVED!
THE CESSNA IS FLYING AWAY!
IT HAS TO BE...IT HAS TO BE...
HUH?
THAT INTELLI-GENCE. THOSE SKILLS. AT THAT AGE.
IT'S "THEM." IT CAN ONLY BE "THEM."
THERE WERE RUMORS. BUT I NEVER BELIEVED THEM.
ULTIMATE BLUE IS A SUPER-ORGANIZATION DEDICATED TO PRESERVING WORLD PEACE.
NOBODY KNOWS ANYTHING ABOUT THEM, YET THEY'RE THE MOST POWERFUL ORGANIZA-TION IN THE WORLD.
IN PARTICULAR, THEIR TOP NINE AGENTS ARE SUPPOSED TO HAVE INCREDIBLE ABILITIES.
SON, THAT WAS A VALUABLE EXPERI-ENCE.

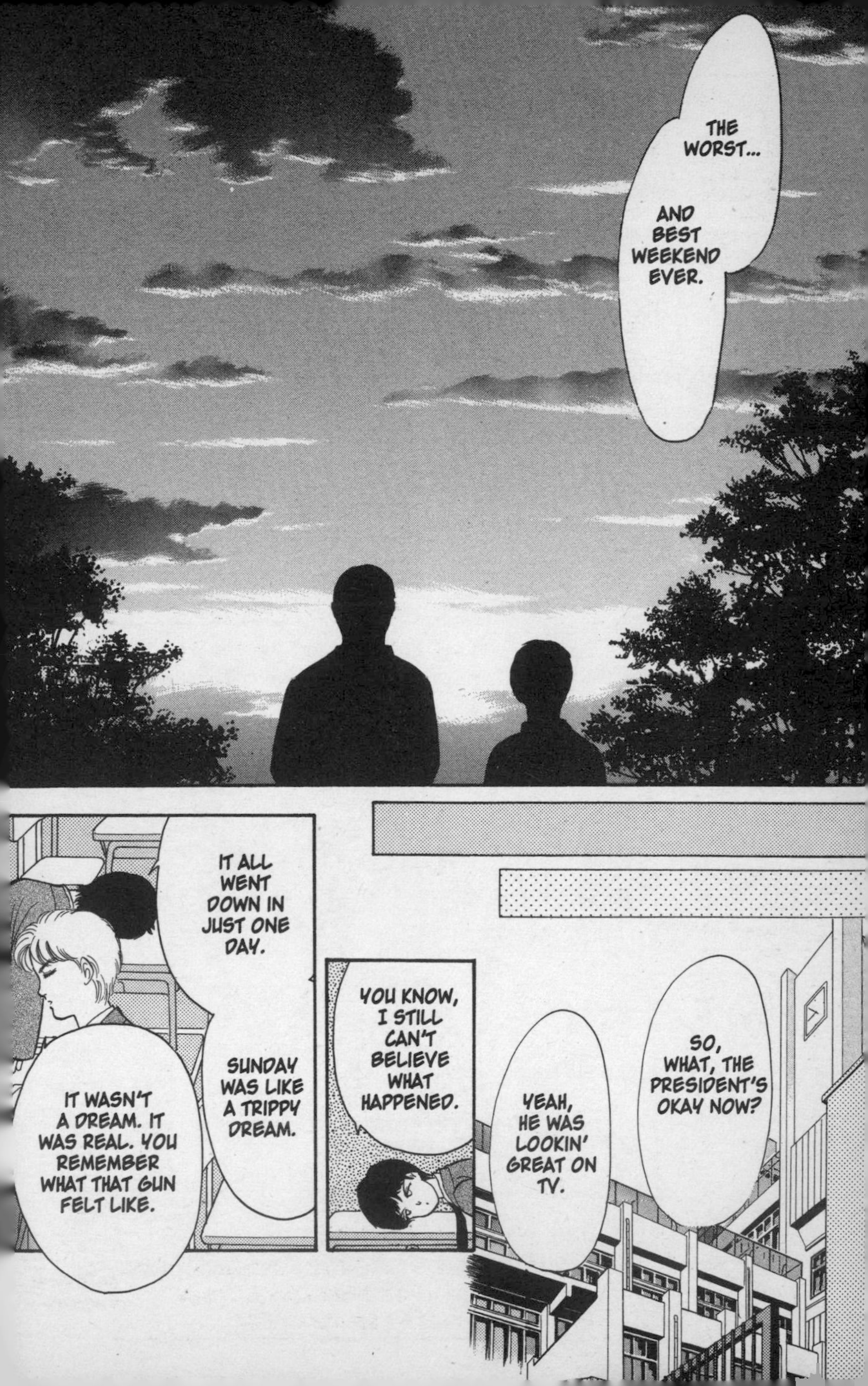
THE WORST...
AND BEST WEEKEND EVER.
SO, WHAT, THE PRESIDENT'S OKAY NOW?
YEAH, HE WAS LOOKIN' GREAT ON TV.
YOU KNOW, I STILL CAN'T BELIEVE WHAT HAPPENED.
IT ALL WENT DOWN IN JUST ONE DAY.
SUNDAY WAS LIKE A TRIPPY DREAM.
IT WASN'T A DREAM. IT WAS REAL. YOU REMEMBER WHAT THAT GUN FELT LIKE.

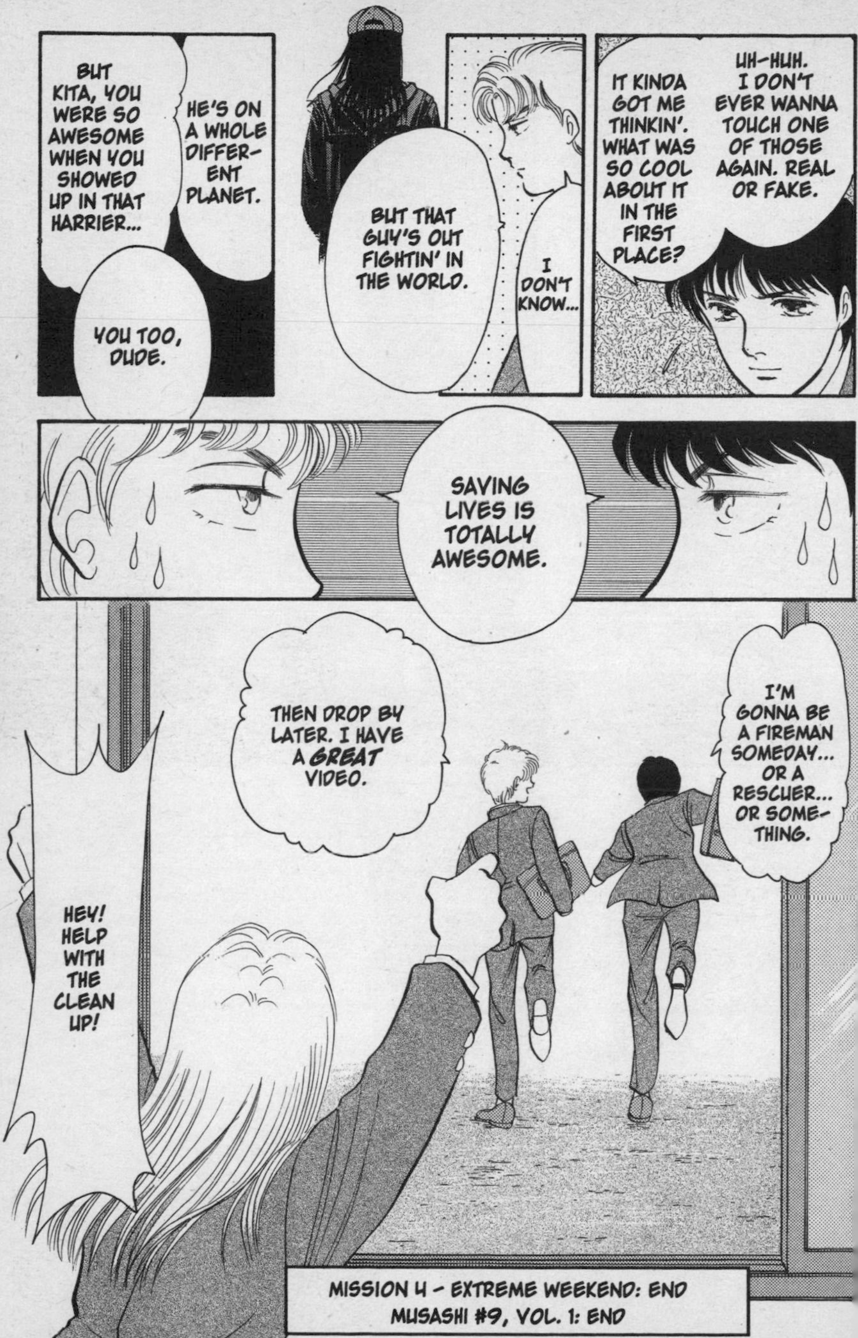
UH-HUH. I DON'T EVER WANNA TOUCH ONE OF THOSE AGAIN. REAL OR FAKE.
IT KINDA GOT ME THINKIN'. WHAT WAS SO COOL ABOUT IT IN THE FIRST PLACE?
I DON'T KNOW...
BUT THAT GUY'S OUT FIGHTIN' IN THE WORLD.
HE'S ON A WHOLE DIFFER-ENT PLANET.
BUT KITA, YOU WERE SO AWESOME WHEN YOU SHOWED UP IN THAT HARRIER...
YOU TOO, DUDE.
SAVING LIVES IS TOTALLY AWESOME.
I'M GONNA BE A FIREMAN SOMEDAY... OR A RESCUER... OR SOME-THING.
THEN DROP BY LATER. I HAVE A GREAT VIDEO.
HEY! HELP WITH THE CLEAN UP!
MISSION 4 - EXTREME WEEKEND: END
MUSASHI #9, VOL. 1: END

Jim Lee
Editorial Director
John Nee
VP—Business Development
Jonathan Tarbox
Group Editor
Paul Levitz
President & Publisher
Georg Brewer
VP—Design & Retail Product Development
Richard Bruning
Senior VP—Creative Director
Patrick Caldon
Senior VP—Finance & Operations
Chris Caramalis
VP—Finance
Terri Cunningham
VP—Managing Editor
Dan DiDio
VP—Editorial
Alison Gill
VP—Manufacturing
Rich Johnson
VP—Book Trade Sales
Hank Kanalz
VP—General Manager, WildStorm
Lillian Laserson
Senior VP & General Counsel
David McKillips
VP—Advertising & Custom Publishing
Gregory Noveck
Senior VP—Creative Affairs
Cheryl Rubin
Senior VP—Brand Management
Bob Wayne
VP—Sales & Marketing

 DC Comics, a Warner Bros.
Entertainment Company.

Translation and adaptation
by Tony Ogasawara

John Layman — Lettering
John J. Hill — CMX Logo & Publication Design
Ed Roeder — Additional design

ISBN: 1-4012-0540-2